W9-BBB-203

ANTISEMITISM IN MODERN FRANCE

ANTISEMITISM
IN
MODERN FRANCE

by

ROBERT F. BYRNES

The Prologue to the Dreyfus Affair

New York · HOWARD FERTIG · 1969

PREFACE TO THE 1969 EDITION

The storm raised in France by General de Gaulle's remark on November 6, 1967, that the Jewish people are "an elite people, sure of itself and domineering," revealed that antisemitism remains a lively force and a significant issue in France, seventy years after the Dreyfus Affair. Moreover, the general's virtual apology to the Grand Rabbi of France, Jacob Kaplan, who charged that such statements opened the way to antisemitism, shows that active, energetic resistance to even casual criticisms remains the most effective supplementary force against antisemitism which a healthy democratic society can provide.

The persistence of antisemitism through all the upsets and revolutions of modern times demonstrates that it must still be considered one of the most pervasive of our political and social issues and perhaps the most true reflection of the discontents of our age. It is clear that the popular base of antisemitism—the traditional hatred of the Jew as the killer of Christ and as the representative of a different people and a rival religion—still survives, even in countries like France, where the power of the Christian faith is clearly much weaker than it was several centuries ago. It is evident also that the hopes for a new Europe, a supranational Europe, were misplaced or exaggerated, and that the revival of nationalism, in France as elsewhere, has strengthened the traditional fear and distrust of those who are in any way different. Moreover, the resurgence of antisemitism in the countries ruled by Communists, particularly the U.S.S.R. and Poland, has shown that the tradition of antisemitism among the "revolutionary workers," which Toussenel and Marx began more than a century ago, retains some of its early force and thrives in a new kind of national socialism. Finally, the establishment, survival, and 1967 military triumph of Israel has injected a new international tone into antisemitism, one which General de Gaulle's remark reflected, for the role of Israel in international politics has created a new force behind the old antisemitic arguments in the domestic politics of many countries.

In short, antisemitism persists, in France as elsewhere. In fact, recent events show profound new areas where the hatred is strong, such as among American blacks, some of whom now see the Jew as the principal immediate bar to their rapid advance. Indeed, the appearance of antisemitism in Harlem, as well as in rural Picardy and Brittany, shows that it reflects the unsettled condition of the world in which we live. The process of modernization through which every people in the world is now rushing has created so many disturbances—economic, social, intellectual, and political—that the traditional scapegoat, the Jew as innovator and conservative, as intellectual and as successful professional man, as radical and as successful entrepreneur, has again become the target of accumulated dissatisfactions and hatreds.

This study was completed twenty years ago, just after the Third Reich and the Second World War had revealed the depths to which antisemitism could lead. I thought at that time that the light from the Nazi fires had provided such insight into this great scourge that further research could only add clarity to the main lines of history. Alas, the continued strength of the old hatred, its appearance among new groups and in new forms, and the new insight provided by the research tools of sociology and psychology all reveal that antisemitism as a lively, virulent phenomenon still deserves the most careful research if we are to understand the world in which we live.

ROBERT F. BYRNES

Indiana University
March 15, 1969

PREFACE

I PROPOSE in this volume to describe the causes and course of the antisemitic movement in France before the explosion of the Dreyfus Affair so seriously threatened the very existence of democratic government there. I have tried to discover and explain why an antisemitic, antidemocratic philosophy and an antisemitic party should develop such strength in France as to place the entire nation in the shadow of civil war for two years. This volume is, therefore, a history of France in Europe from the establishment of the Third Republic through 1894, with special emphasis upon the campaign led against the Jews in France during those years. It is a portrayal of the thread of antisemitism running through French history against the background of the society which fostered the campaign against the Jews in France and against democratic and constitutional government.

The Prologue to the Dreyfus Affair is the first of three volumes which will trace the course of antisemitism in modern France. The Dreyfus Affair, which will be the subject of the second volume, was the most serious crisis modern democratic society faced between the Civil War in the United States and the rise of Communism and Fascism throughout Europe after the First World War. It was a battle of ideas fought with books and papers and ballots. Since the Dreyfus Affair itself was a kind of war, there were victors, but they were victors only in the sense that they had not been defeated. The problems remained, many of them more serious because of the bitterness and destructiveness of the struggle, and on the edge of the stage the defeated forces regrouped themselves under other flags and other leaders. Developments in Europe and in France itself during and after the First World War ultimately led to another wave of antisemitism and allowed those forces once overcome to triumph and to rule France through Pétain and Laval. These later developments and the Vichy system will be the subject of the third volume.

The history of antisemitism in modern France is a specialized subject, but an understanding of the antidemocratic forces and of their roots in French history should be valuable to everyone interested now in the preservation and extension of constitutional and democratic government. This book was written to be read and to help abolish the barrier which now exists between the historian and his fellows. It is at the same time a book for scholars. It was written for everyone interested in the history of modern Europe, in the history of modern France, and in the history of the Jewish people and of antisemitism.

It was written most of all, however, for everyone interested in the faults, the failures, and the future of democracy. Everyone who seeks the preservation and expansion of the democratic freedoms and opportunities agrees that antisemitism is both evil and dangerous, but even scholars disagree on the reasons for the strength and virulence of antisemitism in modern times. As a case study of antisemitism, this work should suggest that antisemitism reflects the stresses and strains which new forces and ideas have placed upon democracy and that the origins of Fascism, and of all of the contemporary totalitarian systems, lie very deep indeed in contemporary society.

The question of proportion is of especial significance in the study of a phenomenon such as antisemitism, particularly since I have sought to describe the course of antisemitism against a broad European and French background. Overestimating or underestimating the importance of the ideas and the movement described against the setting provided by the political, economic, social, institutional, and intellectual history would distort and destroy the accuracy of the entire picture. The vicious and noisy aggressiveness of Drumont and his supporters has made it extremely difficult to discover and describe the true extension and depth of the power of antisemitism in France. Throughout my research and writing, I have been aware of this serious issue. I believe that the analysis presented here portrays accurately and correctly the real significance of this historical phenomenon during these years.

The word "antisemitic" today lacks a specific meaning, for most antisemitic movements are not directed against all Semites, but only against the Jews, and in some cases, the preponderant force is not antisemitic but anti-Judaic. Throughout this essay, the word "antisemitism" will refer to social and political agitation, feeling, and action directed against the Jews, or against the Jews and their religion.

The bibliographical essay for the first two volumes will be included in the second volume, on which much of the work has already been completed. This decision was a reluctant one, even though the footnotes in both volumes are full. However, the full critical bibliography in the second volume will provide in one place a complete account of all of the voluminous antisemitic literature in modern France before 1914 and of the other important primary and secondary sources. It will at the same time eliminate much of the repetition which would have resulted from bibliographies in both volumes.

I should like here to express my warm gratitude to Professor Laurence B. Packard of Amherst College, who first stimulated my interest in history, and to Professors William L. Langer and Donald C. McKay of Harvard University, under whose direction this study was begun. My initial research was made possible by fellowships granted me by Amherst College and Harvard University, and the completion of this study was encouraged by financial aid provided by the Rutgers Research Council. The Social Science Research Council very generously enabled me to spend a summer in Paris to obtain materials not available in this country. A large number of rare books, pamphlets, and papers were made available by Mr. Lee Max Friedman of Boston, whose private collection of antisemitica is unrivaled and who demonstrated extraordinary kindness and solicitude in opening his library to me.

This book could never have been written but for the constant encouragement and aid of my wife, and the happy inspiration provided by our children.

ROBERT F. BYRNES

CONTENTS

ANTISEMITISM IN MODERN FRANCE

I

EUROPE AND FRANCE IN MODERN HISTORY

THE MAIN FORCES

1. The European Setting

ANTISEMITISM in France, of course, reflects more than French history. The position of the Jews in earlier European history, the contemporary riots and pogroms directed against the Jews in central and eastern Europe, the anti-intellectualism becoming more and more common throughout Europe, the rise of nationalisms throughout all of Europe, all demonstrate that the history of French antisemitism cannot be described properly without its European background.

Three developments in European history between 1850 and 1880 are particularly important to an understanding of European history from 1880 to 1914: the change from what the late Professor Robert C. Binkley called the "federative polity" which prevailed in 1850 to the system of military alliances made by increasingly nationalistic states which was being formed by 1880; the tremendous development of the industrial system, throughout western Europe in particular, upsetting Europe in much the same way the barbarians had centuries earlier; and, thirdly, the thriving attack upon the bases of European civilization, the idea of law, the belief in the brotherhood of man, the high opinion of the impor-

3

tance of the individual, and the value of reason as an approach to all problems on all levels. This campaign prospered in part because of the conditions established by the international anarchy and the revolutionary economic and social changes provided by the other two principal forces.

THE COLLAPSE OF FEDERALISM

Because of the emphasis placed in modern politics upon the state and upon the idea of sovereignty, there is no really precise definition for what Professor Binkley called federalism or federative polity. In 1850, however, there was a concert of Europe. Moreover, the principle of arbitration between states, which involved the assumption that all states had equal rights, and the rule of law between nations and within groups, such as the German Bund, were generally accepted. The idea of balance of power in 1852 meant that "no state could obtain aggrandizement without the consent of the others."

By 1880, all of these systems and assumptions had been shaken and destroyed. The rule of force had replaced the rule of law. Between 1815 and 1850 there had been no wars involving two of the major powers, but between 1850 and 1870 there had been four: England and France against Russia in the Crimean War, 1854–1856; France against Austria in the Italian War in 1859; Prussia against Austria in the Seven Weeks' War in 1866; and Prussia against France in the Franco-Prussian War in 1870. Not only were the new Italy and the new Germany created by the force of arms against the will of their neighbors, but Russia in 1870 tore up the Black Sea clauses of the 1856 Peace of Paris without any regard for the wishes of the other signatories, who afterwards weakly acquiesced.

By 1880, the concert of Europe had ceased in fact to exist. This had been "the instrument by which the five powers gave their assent to the acts of a state." It had been "a legislative authority and a conference procedure," but it had failed to prevent all of these four wars. These failures and the dissatisfaction which the defeated power felt in each instance destroyed not only the concept of the concert of Europe but also the practice of what might be called "a government of Europe by the European powers." With the collapse of the concert as a supervisory agent and with the arrival of rule by force, there also came an end, of course, to arbitration.

By 1880, the definition of the idea of the balance of power had changed sharply. Balance of power was no longer a system whereby peaceful territorial change could be managed to the satisfaction of all of the five great powers, or at least without causing great dissatisfaction to any of the powers, but it was becoming a system which balanced two hostile groups of states against each other. This was considered a method of preserving peace, but it was really at that time a way by which both groups could prepare for the ultimate war which broke out in 1914.

The consequences of these developments in international relations are enormous and have much to do with explaining developments in all fields in Europe after 1880. There was after 1870 no form of government for Europe, and, as a consequence, Europe slipped into the international anarchy of the alliance system. In addition to that, the old conservative monarchical states which had supported the status quo and peace in the first third of the century were no longer so conservative nor so inclined to peace. Both Austria and Russia lost so heavily in these decades that they became dissatisfied or "revisionist" powers. Many Frenchmen, because of the defeat France suffered in 1870 at the hands of Prussia, were also revisionist, or wanted revenge.

The wars of the 1850's and 1860's also helped stimulate the growth of nationalism, one of the most powerful and dangerous forces of modern history. The conquering Germans, for example, not only rewarded their political system and their military and civilian leadership with an increased confidence, but they also exalted the virtues of the German race. This was particularly unfortunate because in doing this they adopted some of the racial theories current at that time, establishing solid foundations upon which Hitler was to build later. The spirit of revenge and the growth of racial nationalism not only helped to breed the war of

1914, but they also encouraged militancy and the use of force in domestic relations inside each of the European nations, including even democratic France.

A third important consequence of this development was the conclusion drawn by many statesmen and by the common people from the history of the 1850–1870 period that "war pays." The great Napoleon had been finally defeated and overthrown a half century earlier, so that the glamour which he had given war by his enormous successes had lost a little of its brilliance. Bismarck, however, unified Germany with a ruthless, anti-Parliamentarian domestic policy and three quick successful foreign wars, so that both he and the idea of force were elevated to positions of great respect. Moreover, here again the conversion of some of the current theories in biology proved a disaster, for Darwin's ideas concerning the triumph of the most fit were translated into social Darwinism, or "the survival of the fittest" in international politics.

A final result was that not only did the federative principle fail to unite Germany, Italy, and Austria, but Germany and Italy acquired governments led by the militarists and conservatives. Thus, men such as Bismarck and Cavour, who had accomplished the unification of those two countries, gave them centralized state systems, conservative and militaristic institutions, and a direction and temper which was in effect to determine the policy of those governments until the end of the First World War. Similarly, the Austrian Empire did not develop, as it might have, as a peaceful federal system, but became a Dual Monarchy. The Austrian advice to the Hungarians provides a fitting symbol and, in a sense, an epitaph for this development: "You control your barbarians, and we will control ours." [1]

THE INDUSTRIALIZATION OF EUROPE

The coming of the industrial system to Europe cannot be so sharply defined as those changes in international organization and attitude which occurred in the two or three decades after 1850,

---

[1] Much of the interpretation in this section was taken from Professor Robert C. Binkley's very stimulating *Realism and Nationalism, 1852–1871* (New York, 1935), especially 157–63, 299–306.

but it is probable that the establishment and expansion of industrialism is the most important single factor in the history of the past two centuries. The so-called Industrial Revolution is not a revolution in many senses, for it was not a quick, sharp, violent change. It was and is still a revolution, however, in that it was "the fundamental change or series of changes in the ways of working, travelling, and living" which have been occurring over the past two hundred years.

This series of changes began in England in the second half of the eighteenth century, spread to Belgium, France, and Germany on the continent during the first third of the nineteenth century, and has spread through eastern Europe and the rest of the world during the last one hundred years. There have been at least four separate waves in this change: the initial one provided by the steam engine and the railroad; the second one in the last third of the nineteenth century provided by steel and electricity; the third stimulated by the automobile and airplane, electronic developments, and the movies; and the fourth, which is just now beginning, by atomic energy. The impact of some of these waves has just within the last half century reached Russia and India, and areas such as China and the Near East are just now beginning to feel the shock of this enormous revision.

Europe has been driven together by this development into a natural economic unity which has been resisted and obstructed by nationalistic politicians and peoples, driven by other forces earlier described. The consequence has been friction and war, so that western Europe and England, which might have been immeasurably enriched by this development, are now so weak that only American aid and a renewed effort towards political and economic unity can save them.

In a very real sense, the history of Europe and the world during the past one hundred and fifty years is the story of the consequences of the industrial system's development. Any textbook on modern European history summarizes these results effectively, but for the clarification of the theme of this book, emphasis will be placed on those which are particularly pertinent.

The nineteenth century has been very properly called "The Growing World." It was an era of tremendous change, of belief in the value and permanence of change. It was the age in which the railroad redefined Europe in the same way that Columbus and Magellan changed the meaning of the word "world" in the sixteenth century. The economy of every European country has been altered by this development, changing Essen and Coventry and Lodz from sleepy peasant villages to tremendous, busy, and bombed industrial centers. New classes as well as new areas have risen to importance, challenging, uprooting, and on occasion overthrowing the old. Versailles, for example, today has little more importance than the wonderful decadent aristocracy of P. G. Wodehouse.

Millions of people have been driven by the force of this revolution from their ancestral farms to the new industrial cities, while other millions have been driven from the Old to the New World. In spite of this enormous emigration, the population of Europe continued to increase as it never had before, rising from one hundred eighty-seven million in 1850 to four hundred sixty-three million in 1914. In other words, the face as well as the character of Europe in 1914 were very different from what they had been in 1850 and vastly different from what they had been in 1815.

The impact of the wave after wave of the Industrial Revolution upon European, and then world society, has produced and will continue to produce millions of "displaced persons." The constant change, the continuous uncertainty, and the economic failures and depressions have created a great sense of insecurity for millions of "displaced persons," beliefs and loyalties have been shaken or destroyed, and means of livelihood have been smothered by new processes and new centers of production. These people are looking and will continue to look in this disturbed world for rest and comfort in the arms of some guarantor, and they have assaulted and will continue to assault some minority group as the cause of their misfortunes. The traditional scapegoat has been the Jew, but peoples have on occasion selected and magnified others: Catholics, carpetbaggers, Negroes, cattlemen, Wall Street. French history has shown that an area can be antisemitic even though it has no Jews, just as a powerful country can be wildly frightened by a Communist scare when it has only a handful of ineffectual, discredited Communists.

Another consequence of the industrialization of western Europe was a contribution to the revival of conservatism, which the successes of Bismarck had already stimulated. The height of liberalism in Europe in the nineteenth century was from 1850 through 1880. It began earlier in England, and there were flashes of power temporarily after 1880. The natural heirs to the power and leadership the liberals had given were the democrats and the social democrats. One of the strange problems of modern European history is why democratic socialism failed to develop greater support and to acquire political power in western Europe before 1914. Europe in many respects tried to stand still after 1880 as liberalism died out, for the democrats and social democrats failed to acquire political power and the conservatives were allowed to govern. Perhaps the best way to indicate that this did happen is to compare the social reforms of the New Deal in the United States in the 1930's with the "state socialism" of Bismarck in Germany in the 1880's. President Roosevelt in a depression crisis pushed through legislation much of which Bismarck, the great conservative, had given Germany fifty years earlier!

One of the great reasons for this decline of liberalism and revival of conservatism was the impact of the industrial change upon the industrial leaders. Most businessmen in the early nineteenth century were liberals, and the various liberal parties derived their strength from the business community. Liberals sought freedom for the individual and his enterprise from government controls, they opposed the dominant role of the churches and of the churches' ideas in politics, economics, and education, they supported various nationalisms so long as nationalism represented a revolt of the oppressed and a revolt which did not cost the liberals any money, and they wished a weak, "passive policeman" state which would ensure order, provide the minimum services, and require few funds from its citizens.

However, when the growth of the industrial system transformed businesses into Big Businesses, with monopolies dominating some fields, the interests and views of the businessman began to change. Governments can protect established concerns, particularly monopolies, not only against possible domestic rivals, but also against foreign competition. The old liberal thus began to demand a protective tariff from his government as new sources of supply appeared, some of them created by the businessmen themselves through the export of machinery. Moreover, when the supply of labor became short in the final two-thirds of the nineteenth century, as the farm and the factory began to compete for the worker and as the worker began to use the vote, the trade union, and the threat of socialism, again the businessman began to show alarm and to turn towards conservatism.

The interests of the big businessman, of his state, and of his old rival, the conservative agriculturalist, began to combine in the 1860's and 1870's. The depression of 1873, which increased all of the pressures on business, and the almost simultaneous flooding of the European food market by American, South American, and Russian wheat and cattle, which drove the landed class to demand protection for European agriculture, drove business, or the old liberals, and agriculture into a new and stronger conservative grouping. The successes of Bismarck and Cavour and the Paris Commune's horrors stimulated this development at the same time, and the rise of socialism throughout western Europe after 1870 provided a constant threat from that time forward. In effect, the industrial system's developments uprooted liberalism in western Europe and gave the conservatives—now conservative nationalists—another opportunity to rule.

THE INTELLECTUAL ASSAULT UPON THE FOUNDATIONS

The third great factor or force which developed in Europe from 1850 through 1880 and which became one of the important characteristics of the subsequent years, as well as one of the factors leading to the rise of movements such as antisemitism, was the

general attack delivered by a growing number of important intellectuals upon the very bases of western European civilization.
These elements basic to European civilization have, of course,
been assailed throughout European history, but never were conditions so favorable to the assault and never has the attack been
so powerful, thorough, and brilliantly executed as it has been
during the past century.

The primary targets in this campaign were the ideals and attitudes which had been firmly implanted in the "climate of opinion" of western Europe through a long struggle which became
most vigorous with the opening of the Renaissance. The attempt
to interpret the universe in terms of thought, to provide rational
principles for individual and social life, and to overrule everything
irrational has been carried out in a variety of ways throughout
European history. Seventeenth-century France, for example, believed that reason could best be expressed through the rational
will of a ruler such as Louis XIV. The mercantilist policy of
Colbert, who was trying to impose a rational organization upon
the economy of France, is as typical of the outlook of that era
as the philosophies of Descartes and Leibniz.

The eighteenth century, which shared with the seventeenth the
assumption that there were eternal truths, emphasized the rational
approach to an even greater degree. Professor Paul Hazard has
termed the period from 1685 to 1715 "the crisis of the European
conscience." In his celebrated book, he has demonstrated how the
most decisive characteristic of the Enlightenment, "the critical
spirit," conquered during those years, making the eighteenth-
century advances possible. The Enlightenment emphasized the
connection between the rational approach and individual freedom.
It declared that the eternal truths could best be discovered by
"the cooperation of all free individuals," where the seventeenth
century had believed that the rational will descended from above,
from a Louis XIV. The eighteenth century also believed that
economic progress could be made most effectively with greater
freedom, so it has Adam Smith to compare with Colbert. It is
from this great century and the American and French Revolutions,

which tried to put into effect the political philosophy of that century, that most of our liberal and democratic beliefs derive.

The nineteenth century seems pre-eminently the age of rationalism. Never before in the history of man had science made such tremendous progress. The conception of the eighteenth-century philosophers that the universe was governed by certain immutable laws seemed to be correct. The nineteenth century appeared to be discovering "the laws of nature and nature's law," and the world of the unknown was fast diminishing. It has been said that science in the middle of the nineteenth century was "comprehensive and comprehensible." Hegel developed a deterministic philosophy, and Marx produced "scientific socialism." The age of positivism and of materialism seemed to have all of the tools and all of the answers.

However, as Mr. Toynbee has pointed out, "nothing fails like success." As the scientific discoveries increased in number, the scientists began to note that some of the newly discovered facts did not fit into any of the old patterns and, as a matter of fact, conflicted with many of the current theories. When the physicists developed new tools and new definitions, a very different concept of matter, "the ultimate reality of nineteenth-century science," was born. Many of the new verities were questioned by these developments. At the same time, the nineteenth-century liberal economic theories were undermined as there rose an increasing doubt as to the natural harmony of uncontrolled economic interest in free enterprise.

One of the wisest American historians, the late Carl Becker, once wrote that the eighteenth century was an age of faith as well as of reason, while the thirteenth century was an age of reason as well as of faith. Man is pulled between these two polar points of faith and reason, rarely going very far in either direction. Various ages have had illusions that they were wiser than other ages have been, but the differences have always been quite small and the greatest distinctions have been in learning, not in understanding or wisdom.[2]

[2] Carl Becker, *The Heavenly City of the Eighteenth Century Philosophers* (New Haven, 1932), 8.

Today reason is still a recognized, useful tool, but in the perpetual, unremitting struggle for domination over man's mind between reason and unreason, the final quarter of the nineteenth century witnessed unreason's gripping some of the best minds in Europe and turning the twentieth century towards a balance of antirationalism. This dominant attitude helps differentiate the "climate of opinion" of the eighteenth century from that of the twentieth, and it has proved to be one of the basic causes for movements such as antisemitism.

Moreover, this assault on the critical spirit or rational attitude is only a part of the general campaign against those very bases of western civilization which the preceding centuries had strengthened. The idea of government by law, which was defined so well in the American Declaration of Independence and the American Constitution, is one of the foundations under attack. Another is the conception of the brotherhood of man, which has of course been riddled both by Nationalism and by Marxian Socialism. A third is the high opinion of the importance of the individual and of the individual's rights, particularly against the corporations, the church, and, above all, the state.

All of these principles and attitudes are essential to the preservation and expansion of democracy. All have been under heavy attack from leading philosophers and intellectuals from every country in Europe. Pobedonostsev and Dostoyevsky, Wagner and Nietzsche, Carducci and d'Annunzio, Taine and Maurras, all have assailed these foundations, strengthened the counterattack against democracy, and created conditions in which antisemitism and other related movements could flourish.

In *Crime and Punishment*, which was published in 1866, Dostoyevsky has the "hero," Rodion Romanich Raskolnikov, murder a miserly old-clothes dealer and her sister because he wanted money for his education and so he might help others, but, more important, to demonstrate how different from and superior to the great mass he was. Raskolnikov declared that he "wanted to be a Napoleon." Tolstoy in *War and Peace*, which he wrote from 1865 to 1869 and which was already by 1870 a tremendously influential book in Russia, made of Napoleon the symbol of Reason.

To Tolstoy, Napoleon represented the consequences of the eighteenth century and to Dostoyevsky, imitating Napoleon or attempting to organize society rationally led to willful murder. To both of them, reason was a destructive monstrosity. Raskolnikov confessed his crime and realized happiness in submission and suffering, while Russia in *War and Peace* fought off the invasion of reason and rediscovered herself in her traditional ways and customs.

These novels are significant in Russian history and significant in the general change which was beginning in Russia and in Europe at that time. Dostoyevsky had been interested in socialism in 1847 and in 1848 and had even spread illegal literature in Russia in 1848. Tolstoy had never been a revolutionary, but he promoted education for his serfs in the 1850's; he tried to free his serfs even before Emancipation in 1861, and after 1861 he proposed a much more equitable distribution of property for the serfs than his fellow landlords were willing to give.

Dostoyevsky and Tolstoy, of course, were Russian, and the strength of the critical approach to problems was much weaker in Russia than in western Europe. However, they were Europeans, sensitive to European events and currents, and significant nineteenth-century European intellectuals. Moreover, their attitudes and attitudes similar to these were to become almost representative among intellectuals in western Europe during the next four or five decades. None of the great French novelists of the same generation were afflicted in the same way, but the succeeding generation produced novelists like Huysmans, who was a spiritualist, and Maurice Barrès, who had many of the attitudes towards blood, the state, and the individual which Hitler developed and then put into practice.

If one defines the bases of western European civilization as the critical spirit or the emphasis on rationalism, the belief in government by law, the emphasis upon the rights and freedoms of the individual, and the belief in the brotherhood of man, it can clearly be seen how these elements were attacked in varying ways by many of the most prominent Europeans. A brief study of a few of the leading intellectuals prominent in this assault, omitting for the moment the French, should demonstrate the character of the climate in which movements such as antisemitism developed in Europe after 1880.

Heinrich von Treitschke was the most influential German historian and political scientist during the first twenty-five years' existence of the German Empire. Throughout his professorial career at Freiburg, Heidelburg, and Berlin, in his historical works, particularly his five-volume *Deutsche Geschichte im 19. Jahrhundert*, as the editor of the *Preussische Jahrbücher*, and, above all, by his lectures during the final two decades of his life, he drove into eclipse the scientific and objective history of Leopold von Ranke and led the German nationalist historians to an exaltation of Germany and the Germans. The son of an army officer but, like Bismarck, prevented by physical reasons from fulfilling his ambition to become an army officer himself, Treitschke reflects to a very great degree the Germany molded by Bismarck. As a youth in 1848, he supported the aspirations of the national and liberal German revolution in that year. As a young man he became a liberal, but after 1866 and 1870 he adopted the tragic policy of most of the members of the German Liberal Party in considering the tremendous successes of Bismarck more important than their own liberal principles. After accepting Bismarck's extra-constitutional processes, Treitschke and the National Liberals became the Iron Chancellor's most fervent supporters.

The German National Liberals resemble in a way the French Radical Socialists, "who were neither Radical nor Socialists." The National Liberals were simply nationalists, and nationalists to a very high degree. Treitschke attacked all of the foundations basic to a constitutional and democratic Europe. His glorification of Germany and the Germans and his attacks upon minorities such as the Jews riddled the idea of the brotherhood of man. His declarations that individuals were not important, that even small states did not have a right to exist, and that powerful, nationalistic, well-organized large states should alone rule, weakened another prop of the old ideas and attitudes. These large states should, of course, be administered and directed by the strongest and most able individuals, and Treitschke had a distinct contempt for democratic governments and for the average man.

The emphases in Treitschke on the great man, on the strong state, on the ruthless use of power, on the belief that it was "the highest moral duty" of the state to increase its power, and on the pre-eminence of foreign policy not only destroyed the rights of the individual and led to an increased emphasis upon organization and control of all from the center, but also abandoned the belief in a government of Europe by Europe, in the rights of all nations, and in the rule of law. One can hardly laud force, deny natural law and all universal values, denounce Catholics, Jews, Socialists, pacifists, and democrats, and at the same time believe in the critical spirit, or rationalism. Treitschke therefore constitutes one of the most open and influential sources of dictatorship in modern times, and both openly and indirectly he helped bring antisemitism into the modern world.

The emphases in the music and in the philosophy of one of Treitschke's outstanding contemporaries, Richard Wagner, were somewhat different from those of the nationalist historian, but led to many of the same consequences. It is striking to note that Wagner took part in the German revolution in 1848–1849 as a liberal, even though it is clear that his liberalism was not then on very secure foundations. Driven to despise France, the French, and the French heritage because of three dreary and unsuccessful years he spent in Paris in the 1840's, Wagner became an extreme nationalist and a racialist after the failure of the Revolution of 1848–1849. An open exponent of antisemitism, Wagner preached the formation of an organic German state with a Führer at the head. He developed a vague socialism, just as many of the French antisemites did later, and his ideas on Germany's role in Europe prepared the way for Hitler. His attacks upon modern culture have led some to term him a *Kulturbolshevist*, and his belief in dynamism, his emphasis on becoming rather than being, and his rejection of reason and intellectualism indicate that Wagner too had a responsible role in establishing a temper and climate in Europe in which antidemocratic movements could begin and thrive.

There are a great number of other German intellectuals of the period from 1850 through 1914 who supported and strengthened the assault and the positive program of Wagner and Treitschke. Friedrich Nietzsche, Paul de Lagarde, and Adolf Wagner are among these influences. Italy produced a number of men who made the way ready for Fascism, but D'Annunzio, Carducci, Papini, and Corradini appeared later and had effects very similar to those of the two Teutons described. Perhaps Thomas Carlyle and Karl Marx will serve best to indicate that this drive was not confined to Germany and Italy and that it had further overtones as well.

Thomas Carlyle has perhaps unjustly been described as a "forerunner of fascism," but there were elements in the sensitive and dyspeptic Scotchman's criticism of the Victorian Age which were ultimately more than criticism of "the condition of England" and did help lead to sympathy for authoritarian government. Carlyle, whose chief gift was "a capacity for moral indignation," had harsh contempt for constitutional and democratic government. He had a deep scorn for the abilities and intelligence of the great mass of mankind, and in his *History of Frederick the Great*, completed just the year Tolstoy began *War and Peace* and the year before Dostoyevsky published *Crime and Punishment*, he elaborated the thesis that the great man was and should be the determining factor in history. In his admiration for the enlightened despots, it is important to note that he turned to the great Prussian king. He considered the Teutons to be a particularly superior people because they were Protestant, morally more virtuous, and not afflicted by the cult of reason.

Karl Marx was without a doubt one of the greatest thinkers and one of the most important men produced in the nineteenth century. In spite of the fact that he was an extreme rationalist himself and that he hoped to help establish a socialist state with complete equality, there are many elements in his philosophy and in the methods he suggested and used which weaken the bases and foundations described earlier and which helped prepare for totalitarian governments in the twentieth century.

To begin with, the materialistic or economic interpretation of history developed by Marx by implication gives man little or no power over his own future, which means that man is a pawn of developments over which he has no control. The idea that the forms of production determine the nature of the social structure and that these forms have a logic all their own leaves little influence for man. This can be seen clearly on the reverse side, for Marx ridiculed the Utopian Socialists because they believed a socialist society could be attained when man had been persuaded to change through appeals to justice, humanitarianism, and reason. Marx's theory on the relentless inevitability of the collapse of capitalism and the coming of socialism was, of course, one of his greatest attractions to those who wanted to be on the victorious side.

Marx was really more an evolutionist than a revolutionist, as the preceding paragraph has demonstrated. However, Marx certainly described the change he foresaw as a revolutionary one, took part, with Engels, in the uprisings in 1848–1849 in Germany, and glorified the Commune of 1871 after it had been crushed. He pointed out that although the changes within society are brought about by changes in the means of production, which cannot be controlled by man, those changes can and should be hastened by man. Moreover, the very popular phrase, "dictatorship of the proletariat," in itself a meaningless phrase, appeared first in Marx's *Critique of the Gotha Program*, which was written in 1875. Although the meaning of the celebrated phrase is unclear, there can be no doubt that Marx spoke for a strong government, even a dictatorial government, and the states interpreting Marxism today, which show no evidence of withering away, are a reasonable extension of Marx's theories.

One other manner in which Marx contributed to the undermining of the foundations of a democratic system was in his definition of classes and of the inevitability of perpetual class war.

Treitschke, Wagner, Carlyle, and Rhodes divided mankind into
groups on racial, or at least national lines. Marx's division was
along different lines, but it was division, and the tension and friction between the groups was perpetual, ending any "illusions" of a
belief in the brotherhood of man, at least until the complete
triumph of Communism.

As just demonstrated, the history of Europe during the second
third of the nineteenth century was marked by decisive developments in the political and diplomatic, economic, and intellectual
fields. The domestic history of France during the same period was
not quite so sharply affected by some of these forces, economic in
particular, as the remainder of Europe, but, even so, one must
comprehend this section of French history to understand the
forces and factors influential after 1880.

2. The French Setting

THE POLITICAL BACKGROUND

ALL of French history since the French Revolution has in a sense
been a reaction to the Revolution, which is even today one of
the principal touchstones by which one separates or distinguishes
French political parties. Many conservatives, particularly the
monarchists, throughout the nineteenth century fought the ideas
and ideals of the Revolution and sought to return to the principles and practices of the Old Regime. Other conservatives
sought to perfect some effective blend between the established
traditions of France and the aims of the Revolution, which was,
of course, gradually becoming a part of French tradition. Others,
who might be called the radical Republicans, sought for France
the establishment of the aims of the great revolutionaries: a constitutional and democratic Republic, a state freed from church influence, and a unified and strong country. Still others wished to
surpass these old aims by giving them a nineteenth-century
translation, applying them to the new economic order which began to appear late in the century.

The French Revolution, in other words, has divided France

more than it has united her. Moreover, the very nature of the revolutionary aims and the brief successes they enjoyed during the height of the revolutionary period have in effect helped delay the acquisition by France of the democratic republic she sought in 1792. It seems a perfectly fair statement, for example, to say that England, although not Great Britain, had gone further towards the acquisition of "Liberty, Equality, and Fraternity" at almost every point in the nineteenth century than the French had. The French Revolution began an era for France and provided new problems and new solutions for those problems which have kept the French people busy, and divided, for the past century and a half.

The most challenging and stimulating period in nineteenth-century French history is the reign of Louis Napoleon, 1848–1870. A nephew of the great Napoleon, Louis Napoleon was elected President of the Second Republic in December, 1848. He overthrew this Republic with a military coup d'état on December 2, 1851, and a year later he established the Second Empire with himself as the Emperor Napoleon III. During the next eighteen years, he tried to solve the problem of Liberty and Order and to give France a new unity. At the same time, he also tried to control and even to direct the new force which Clio had released from her bottle, the industrial change, a wave of which struck France during the Second Empire. He was more than a Frenchman, for he wanted to remake the entire map of Europe, giving each national grouping the right to govern itself and thereby eliminating some of the nationalist tensions which were already leading to the outbreak of wars.

Napoleon III was quite clearly a failure, although the soundness of many of his visions and aims has been more fully realized as history has progressed. He was "the first of the modern dictators," but gradually throughout the 1860's he surrendered his complete powers until, shortly before the outbreak of the Franco-Prussian War, France had a popular constitutional monarchy. He was remarkably successful in promoting the industrialization of France, and he did attempt to eliminate some of the most gross evils common to early industrialism everywhere. He failed miserably, however, in his foreign policy. France by 1871 had rival powers on her northeastern and southeastern frontiers where in 1851 she had had disorganized and weak confederacies. Both of these new states, Germany and Italy, owed their unification in part at least to the efforts of Napoleon III, but their presence, their power, and their aggressive nationalism drove many Frenchmen into hostility towards their Emperor. Moreover, although his policy had accumulated a considerable amount of glory in the Crimea, Egypt, and the Far East, it had been an expensive policy. In addition, the Mexican expedition had not only been costly but had been a complete and disastrous rout for France and for French interests.

It was the failure in foreign policy which in 1870 brought the Second Empire down. Bismarck's new Prussia, aggressive, tough, prepared at home and on the diplomatic front, trapped the unwary, overeager, and poorly prepared French into war. The French army was badly organized, poorly led, and quickly overwhelmed. The dreams of the sick Emperor of alliances with Italy and Austria against Prussia proved to be only dreams. The Emperor and the Empire crashed, and on September 4, 1870, the Third Republic was proclaimed in a galvanized and revolutionary Paris.

The Franco-Prussian War of 1870, the resounding French defeat in that war, and the disappearance of the Second Empire were in many ways the turning points of all modern European history. They sealed the fate of the "federative polity," against which Napoleon III's forceful seizure of power had been one of the first blows. They substituted for that system one of international anarchy in which two systems of alliances and races for allies, arms, and the initiative prevailed. They elevated Bismarck's newly united Germany, a conservative, nationalistic, militaristic Germany, to the position of dominance in Europe and ensured that "blood and iron" should receive more respect and admiration from all Europeans than had ever been the case before.

This war also eliminated Napoleon III, who with all his faults and failures might have provided France and Europe with more peaceful and durable solutions to their pressing problems than they have yet found. Napoleon III had one quality or ability which very few French statesmen or leaders since his time have displayed and another quality which has been pre-eminently lacking among all French leadership since 1870. Like Gambetta, Boulanger, and de Gaulle, he was able briefly to unite a majority of Frenchmen around him and to provide an antidote to that shocking lack of unity which is such a characteristic of modern France. It might be noted here that both Boulanger and de Gaulle were generals and that Gambetta was in effect a war lord in 1870 and 1871. Moreover, each of these three men united France only for very brief periods, and each was successful even then largely because he stood for revenge against a Germany which had just crushed or was threatening France.

The other quality which Napoleon III had and which has been so completely lacking since is imagination. Almost a half century before the change struck with full force he had a more effective appreciation of the impact of the industrial system on France than most politicians, including the Socialists and Communists, who have lived through the great transformation. He was a better European and had a sounder comprehension of the necessity of providing for the drives of nationalism, liberalism, and socialism than all but a very few of the French leaders who have followed him.

The Franco-Prussian War was a disaster also because it saddled France with a war which was not over, though it had already been lost, and with a new government for which there had been even less preparation than for the Second Republic in 1848. The Third Republic, it should never be forgotten, was born of a defeat, a defeat administered by an enemy whom the French have hated for centuries and whom in 1870 they considered a brash upstart. France fought that war through to its dreary conclusion in what were probably the most unusual circumstances in which any modern war has ever been contested. The peace treaty in 1871 provided for military occupation by the Germans of twenty-one French departments until a crushing indemnity had been paid, as well as for the loss of one department and a good part of a second. Both of these lost areas were bright jewels for France. They were particularly serious losses because they had been pawns in the struggle between France and Germany for generations. They forced the French to revise completely their defensive strategic arrangements; they included areas which had developed most industrially in the 1860's; and they included large sources of supply of iron, one of the ores which is vital today to any nation which dreams of great power.

The Third Republic was born not only from the ashes of defeat in foreign war but also in the conflict of the most bitterly fought civil war in nineteenth-century European history. The interpretation of the Commune as an attempt at a socialist revolution has been discredited everywhere in the world where scholarship is free. Marx and Engels, who saw their inevitable revolution breaking out at every industrial crisis during the 1850's and 1860's, were completely mistaken in seeing the Paris rising in 1871 as the first blow struck by the embattled workers. Certainly a revolutionary movement which failed to molest the *Banque de France* and whose only social legislation was the prohibition of night work in bakeries can hardly be called socialist. The Commune was prompted by Paris resentment over the grueling difficulties of the successful German siege of Paris, the belief of thousands of patriotic Paris workers that the government which was signing the Treaty of Versailles with Bismarck was betraying France, and the radical republican Paris feeling of alarm and contempt for the very conservative, even monarchical legislature of "cow fanciers" which France had just elected.

The interpretation of the Commune then held by Marx and Engels, although incorrect, was shared by Thiers and the French conservatives. Their fright, added to the rage they felt at the spectacle of France's degrading herself before Germany and Europe, made the bloody week of May 21–28, 1871, one of the most ferocious of modern history. Approximately twenty thousand of those who fought for the Commune against the army of the Thiers government in Versailles were killed, some in the battle and some in reprisal, and fifty thousand more were arrested. The fear and hatred and bitterness engendered by this desperate struggle affected all of the history of the Third Republic.

The Franco-Prussian War not only destroyed the Second Empire, but it also weakened the grip of the Republicans on their newly established Republic. The Republicans' desire to carry on the struggle against Germany after the collapse of the Empire led to an overwhelming electoral victory in 1871 for the monarchists, who had been left out of the struggle during the late Empire between the imperial administration and the rising young liberals and radicals and who might have disappeared entirely, just as the Stewart party did in England, if only given sufficient time. The war and the politics of the war thus revived the monarchists, allowed them to dominate French politics until 1879, and, most important of all, allowed them to determine the issues on which politics most of the time from 1871 until 1914 should be fought. The struggle over the French Revolution's issues was never so bitter in the nineteenth century as it was in the years after 1871. French politicians were forever fighting old issues, forever looking backwards, forever struggling over terrain familiar to the conservatives and upon which they could best rally their forces.

The great hope of the monarchist forces was, of course, to reestablish the monarchy. They had the political power in France to do this, and to do it easily, but there were two problems. One was that they had two contenders to the throne, the Bourbon Count of Chambord, whose grandfather, Charles X, had been driven from the throne in 1830, and the Count of Paris, whose grandfather, Louis Philippe, had succeeded Charles X in 1830 and had been driven into exile by the Revolution of 1848. This particular difficulty was finally solved in August, 1873, when the younger Count of Paris yielded to his childless elder with the agreement that he should succeed to the throne on the death of the Count of Chambord.

The other obstacle, however, could not be overcome. The Count of Chambord suffered from the education given him by his grandfather, his mother, the Duchess of Angoulême, and long residence in Frohsdorf, an Austrian castle located well back in the eighteenth century. He refused to rule France without the Bourbon white flag, while the great majority of Frenchmen, including many of his own supporters and almost all of those of the Count of Paris, insisted upon the tricolor, the blue, white, and red flag under which the great victories of the Revolution and Napoleon had been won. The white flag was politically impossible, the Count of Chambord was adamantine, and so on November 20, 1873, the monarchists had to compromise for time. They did this by electing Marshal MacMahon president for seven years to hold the throne ready for the Count of Chambord, or, if he should die, the Count of Paris.

Although the monarchists had failed in their major constitutional aim by 1873, they still held the upper hand in French politics and in the government. A monarchist was president, the monarchists had a majority in the National Assembly elected in February, 1871, and the conversion of that Assembly into a constituent body gave them the determining voice in drawing up the Constitution of 1875. The revolutionaries of September 4, 1870, had proclaimed France a republic, and Thiers had been named President of the Republic in August, 1871. The Third Republic, tolerated from 1871 through 1875 as "the government which divides us least," was really established, however, only in January and February, 1875, when the monarchist National Assembly passed a number of laws which provided France with a constitution. The crucial decision, on the famous Wallon amendment, endorsed the Republic by only one vote, 353 to 352.

The Constitution of 1875 lasted until July, 1940, so that it provided the most stable system of government France has had since the end of the Old Regime. It was, however, very weak, as might have been expected of a constitution drawn up under such circumstances. It was "a thing of shreds and patches." It lacked a Declaration of the Rights of Man, it was unplanned and uncoordinated, and it contained no reference to the administrative system or its connection with the legislative and executive bodies. Most important of all, however, this constitution failed to define the division of functions between the legislature and the executive. France had cabinet government in form after 1875, but the real power always lay in the hands of the legislature. Never could the executive, the cabinet or the ministry, appeal to the country by dissolving the legislature and staging a general election.

There was one exception to this, and it was this exception which established the rule. When the first elections under the new constitution were held in the winter of 1876, the Senate remained under the control of the conservatives while the Republicans won control of the Chamber of Deputies. When Jules Simon, the premier, failed to repress or to denounce outbursts of anticlericalism in the Chamber, President MacMahon, elected in 1873 to make a monarchical restoration still possible, on May 16, 1877, or *seize mai*, forced Simon to resign. This action on the part of the President brought on the *seize mai* crisis of 1877, in which the President ultimately yielded to the Chamber of Deputies and the country. MacMahon's defeat represented not only a permanent blow to the prestige and power of the French presidency, but it was also the last time in which either the president or the premier in France dissolved the Chamber and appealed to the country on an issue.

The major consequence of the nature of the French constitution and of the development and the outcome of the 1877 crisis extends far beyond the constitutional sphere. Except in times of very great crisis, such as 1902, 1917, and 1926, France has had extremely feeble governments. On other occasions, even during some great crises, the government has been very weak, as in 1889, 1898–1900, 1916, 1934, and 1940. This weakness has allowed issues to drift and has given the enemies and the hangers-on of democracy very free play. Probably even more important than that, it has made French politics more than ever a game or a profession, carried on with little or no concern for the needs of the country. Since the ministry could not dissolve the Chamber, the deputy in France did not need to fear his electorate. This led to numerous "deals" and constantly shifting governments. The club spirit which prevailed in the Chamber was very aptly described in 1914 in a book by Robert de Jouvenel, entitled *La République des camarades*, or the *The Republic of Pals*. Government by friendly cliques is not effective government, whether it be in the French Chamber or the American Senate, which in the twentieth century has developed the same spirit and approach.

The governing bodies in France, in other words, isolated themselves more and more from the problems of the day. This was particularly unfortunate because of the emphasis on the past and on old issues which conservative dominance had already given them. All of this might have been avoided if the Constitution of 1875 had provided for effective ministerial government, had drawn a distinction between the legislature and the executive, and had given the ministry the right to dissolve the Chamber and appeal to the country.

In the elections held on the fifth of January, 1879, the Republicans gained control of the Senate, giving them power in both houses of the legislature for the first time. Three weeks later, when the Minister of War refused to cease transferring President MacMahon's conservative and monarchical friends from their high army commands, the president resigned. This allowed the Senate and Chamber of Deputies to elect a Republican, Jules Grévy, to the presidency, so that now for the first time the Republic was in the hands of the Republicans.

The experience of the Republicans from 1870 through January, 1879, had been so much disturbed by the great power of the monarchists over the Republic that the moderate Republicans, or Opportunists, who were to rule France from 1879 until 1885, set out immediately to destroy the roots of the conservatives' power. These lay in the Catholic Church and in the control which the Church had over the French educational system and, therefore, the mind of France, through its congregations and teaching orders. One of the basic drives behind the French Revolution had been to cripple the power of the Church, and it is one of the tragedies of French history that this entire issue had to be fought over again from 1879 through 1906.

Napoleon, who had made the same discovery as Lunacharsky on

attacking a religious organization, "the harder you hit a nail on the head, the deeper it goes into the wood," had made the Concordat with Pope Pius VII in 1801. The Emperor and the Pope settled the issue concerning the Church property confiscated during the Revolution, provided that the French government should pay the salaries of the clergy, placed the entire system of higher education in the control of the French government, and provided that the higher clergy in France should be appointed by the French government and confirmed by the Pope. The influence of the Church in France grew again throughout the first half of the nineteenth century as the faith of the French in their Revolution and in Napoleon was shaken, as romanticism revived the reverence for the Middle Ages and its most important surviving institution, and as the Restoration, the July Monarchy, and the Second Empire showed an appreciation for the contribution the Catholic Church could make to ensuring their stability. It was one of the liberal leaders, Guizot, who in 1833 had a law passed which gave the Catholic Church effective control of primary school education in France. Louis Napoleon, as president of the Second Republic, not only crushed the Roman Revolution in 1849 and restored Pius IX to power there, but in 1850 he greatly increased the Church's power in French secondary education. During the 1850's, as Emperor, he allowed more congregations of women and cleansed the educational system of anticlericals.

The Catholic Church for the fifty or sixty years following 1850 suffered from the precipitate decline which affected all organized religion in Europe from 1850 through 1900 or 1910. The Papacy ceased to exist as an important state power as the new Italy seized the Papal States in the 1860's and made Pius IX "the prisoner in the Vatican" in 1870. The one-time liberal Pope acquired compensation in the spiritual realm for these worldly defeats, but defining the dogmas of the Immaculate Conception in 1854 and that of Papal Infallibility in 1870 had little temporal influence. Moreover, the encyclical *Quanta cura*, with the *Syllabus errorum* appended in 1864, was such a forthright attack on everything which the nineteenth century took for granted that the Papacy and the Church lost credit among even their supporters. Through-out the 1870's, Bismarck waged the *Kulturkampf* against the Church in Germany, weakening its powers with every device he had at hand, although he was not able to gain victory over the Church.

More serious for Catholicism than its unsuccessful duels with the new national states were the beliefs and assumptions of the century which were undermining the Catholic faith of millions. There were numerous reasons for the general religious decline. The state, the new national state with its ceremonies and symbols, its army and navy, its schools and social services, was a rival of the religious groups for the loyalties and faith of their members. The new nationalism became a sort of religion for millions as the century wore on, and socialism had the same effect for many workers. Moreover, the scientific discoveries and the philosophies which derived from the new science seemed to leave little room for established religious beliefs, if not to abolish or eliminate them. An age which put its belief in realism, or in materialism and posi-tivism, was not only irreligious but also antireligious.

The French Republicans, bred in the Revolutionary tradition and, as Thibaudet has pointed out, "educated by Michelet," could not be expected to realize how weak their opponent was, or seemed to be. The walls of Jericho, after all, had not fallen without at least a trumpet blast and a great shout. Moreover, the French Republicans were more impressed by the apparent revival of the Catholic Church and its influence in France in the 1870's than they were with its seeming decease elsewhere. The Archbishop of Paris in 1873 led the French Catholics to adopt the idea of constructing a basilica on the heights of Montmartre, overlooking the great, flat city of Paris. The Assembly gave its permission, and the Republicans watched the erection of a daz-zling white eclectic structure which they felt was a concrete evidence of Catholic power in France and of French admission that the country's sins against the Church had been responsible for the catastrophe of 1870. Increased power for the Church in the French educational system in 1873 stimulated this fear also.

while the Social Catholic movement, begun by two Catholic aristocrats, Count Albert de Mun and the Marquis de La Tour du Pin, made possible an alliance between the Catholic aristocracy and the gullible workers.

As a consequence, the first plank in the Opportunist program was an anticlerical one. Jules Ferry, who was to become one of the most hated men in France for this and his imperial policy, led both the Opportunists and Radicals in this assault. After the Senate had blocked a law which would have given the government the right to close all schools operated by the unauthorized religious orders, Ferry by decree dissolved the Jesuits and forced all the remaining unauthorized orders to petition for authorization, which they refused to do. All teachers were required to obtain a teacher's certificate through graduation from a state normal school, which closed off the flow of monks and nuns into the state schools. In 1882, religious instruction in the state schools was forbidden, and primary school education was made free and compulsory. It appeared that the grip of the Church on the minds of the future had been broken.

The Opportunist educational program, followed in 1884 by a law which allowed divorce, naturally infuriated many Catholics. Many Catholics who had not previously been monarchists now supported the enemies of the Republic in their attacks on "the slut" because they considered these "infamous laws" a direct attack upon the Church, as indeed they were. Moreover, they were quick to notice that a high proportion of the leaders promoting the anticlerical legislation were Protestants and Jews. Thus, the angry monarchist, Bishop Freppel, in 1882 denounced July 14, the great national holiday, as "only the anniversary of the most odious massacre in our history." In a speech attacking the divorce law in the Chamber of Deputies in 1884, he asserted that the entire anticlerical campaign was "a Semitic movement."

The consequences of this development are very apparent in the political history of France during the next twenty-five years. Much of the antisemitic campaign's strength and policy derived from the disasters which befell the monarchists in the 1870's and the Catholic Church from 1879 through 1884. Boulangism, the crisis caused by the Panama scandal, and, above all, the Dreyfus Affair have their roots in the bitterness of the monarchists and in the dissatisfaction of the Catholic leaders at the Church's being deprived of the privileges it had enjoyed throughout most of the century. In other words, the Republicans were forced in some degree to fight a defensive battle after 1884, on ground well chosen by their adversaries and over issues which should have been solved a century earlier. This was, of course, not the first time that a small but well-placed and well-organized minority has forced a government to change its very direction and to ignore more pressing realities. It was, however, a tragedy that the French government should have had to turn back to defend itself against these foes. As any Irishman knows, however, there is no grievance like an old grievance and no foe like an old one. The sharpness of the political struggle in France and the unscrupulousness in the use of weapons derive in great part from the nature of these political issues.

ECONOMIC DEVELOPMENTS

As has been demonstrated, the development of the industrial system throughout the world has been the most decisive fact in the history of the past two centuries. The impact of the transition from a rural, agricultural economy to an urban, industrial, and commercial economy has changed the face of the world and the lives and attitudes of all of its inhabitants. One of the unusual and most decisive aspects of modern French history is the manner in which French institutions and ideas have been affected by this revolutionary development, for France has resisted this change more successfully than any other country in the world.

There are a number of reasons why France has been less influenced by industrialism than other western European countries and is, in a sense, therefore less "modern" than her neighbors. The tremendous pre-eminence of France on the continent, particularly from the Age of Louis XIV through the French Revolution and Napoleon, rather naturally led the French to be less willing to modify their institutions, or less willing to have them modified, than other nations and peoples who did not have that glorious recent past and the established approaches and loyalties. In other words, France began "to idolize ephemeral institutions."

It might be objected here that the history of England from the middle of the seventeenth century through 1815 was even more significant for England and for Europe, although not so glamorous or so glorious, than the same period for France. England at the same time, however, was almost completely transformed by the tremendous industrial revolution. There are a number of reasons for this difference. For instance, in spite of the fact that the armies of the Duke of Marlborough defeated those of the generals of Louis XIV, Blenheim Palace will never rival Versailles, even as a symbol. It is not now, and was not then, the Age of Marlborough, or Newton, or Addison and Steele, or Peter the Great, but the Age of Louis XIV. The French king put a stamp or an impression upon his country and his age which the French have never successfully overcome.

A second major point here is that the French Revolution represents in many ways not the overthrow of the system of Louis XIV, but its culmination. The monarchy strove with Richelieu, as with Colbert, to centralize all political and economic power in the hands of the Paris or Versailles government, and it was the Revolution and Napoleon which completed that centralization. Moreover, the Revolution promoted the expansion of and sanctified the concepts of extreme individualism and private property which had grown under the Old Regime and which have helped to delay France's making a satisfactory compromise with the industrial system and with its healthiest offshoot, social democracy.

In addition to the glorified past and the sanctified economic system which the Third Republic inherited, modern France has inherited customs solidified into law which have strengthened the traditional individualism of the French peasant and helped him ward off the overwhelming conformism of industrialism. The emphasis on primogeniture, on total inheritance of the land by the oldest son, has frozen the old system and delayed the coming of the new economy. The division of the land of the Church and the nobility during the Revolution has strengthened this attitude, and the defensive attitude of the peasant towards his land might well be called the great political reality of France in the nineteenth century. No visitor to France even after the Second World War can fail to note the tremendous sense of private property there. Probably nowhere in the world are there so many walls, fences, and hedges, and nowhere do these barriers guarantee so well not only private ownership but also privacy.

There are other important factors, of course, in addition to these which derive from the great French traditions. There were in the seventeenth and eighteenth centuries so many people who felt, like Voltaire, that "France can be happy without Quebec," that French people did not leave "the fair land of France" in sufficient numbers to win the wars of commerce and empire from England. Great Britain, as a consequence, not only won the treasure, the raw materials, and the markets of empire, but also received a tremendous stimulus from the empire which jolted and challenged her peoples and her institutions to greater and higher efforts. France did not receive those material benefits and that stimulation, although subsequently in the late nineteenth century she acquired an empire which in 1914 was twenty times as large as it had been in 1870 and which contained a population greater than that of France herself.

The French Revolutionary Wars from 1792 through 1815 hampered France in becoming an industrial nation. These wars gave the great rival, England, a quarter of a century of island peace and prosperity to benefit from the industrial leadership she seized late in the eighteenth century. They forced the French government and French industry to concentrate upon the immediate war needs, with the same devastating effect on industrial progress that the Nazi strain imposed on German economy and science after 1933. Moreover, the enormous drain on energy, manpower, and resources which these wars entailed seriously weakened France, while the political divisions which spring from the Revolution have really never been healed.

However, even if these other factors had not been effective, the extremely able and intelligent population of France lacks large deposits of coal, one of the ores most important to any country during the first three waves of the industrial revolution. The coal deposits of France are only one-eighth as large as those of Germany, and during the first half of the nineteenth century even Belgium was producing more coal than France. Not only are the French supplies inadequate, but about one-half of them are produced in Pas-de-Calais in the extreme northern corner of the country. France has therefore not only had to purchase large quantities of this decisive industrial element from England, Belgium, and Germany, but she has had to pay transportation costs and high prices to her industrial rivals. This situation could have been alleviated somewhat if France had shown more foresight in developing her water-power facilities, but both the French government and private industry showed little imagination and initiative in this field until after the end of the Second World War.

As a consequence, as the late great authority on French economic history, J. H. Clapham, pointed out, France never went through an industrial revolution in the first half of the nineteenth century. In 1848, true factory conditions were exceptional in France, where the workshop and the small establishment were still typical. The rural population in 1776 was 67.6 percent of the total French population, and even as late as 1911 still more than half of the French people, 55.9 percent, lived in the countryside. Germany's relative industrialization can be seen clearly in her population transfer, for 65 percent of her population in 1870 was rural and in 1910 only 40 percent. As late as 1902, the French government's subsidies for sailing vessels in the French maritime service exceeded those for steamships; in 1914 only 55 percent of the total tonnage of the French mercantile marine was steam tonnage.[3]

As Professor Clapham demonstrated, the industrial revolution

[3] J. H. Clapham, *The Economic Development of France and Germany, 1815–1914* (Cambridge, 1928), 53–58, 70, 160–66, 235–43; Carlton J. H. Hayes, *A Political and Cultural History of Europe* (New York, 1939), II, 218–19; Shephard B. Clough, *France. A History of National Economics, 1789–1939* (New York, 1939), 242–43.

in France really began only about 1895, more than a century after it is generally agreed to have begun in England and more than a half century later than the dates usually assigned to Belgium and Germany. Using the iron and steel industry as an index, he indicated that as late as 1850 more than half of the French iron ore was smelted in little charcoal furnaces. There was great progress made under the Second Empire, but this was nullified by the loss of Alsace and Lorraine in 1871 and the depression of 1873, which cast a pall over most French industry for approximately two decades. With the discovery and exploitation of the enormous Briey iron supplies in 1894 and the simultaneous great expansion of electric power, France began to move more rapidly along the industrial path most of her neighbors had followed earlier. Even in 1914, however, France still had to import steel ships and locomotives, even though she was then the world's largest exporter of iron ore.

The concomitant of the industrial development and the scientific progress in Europe in the nineteenth century was the tremendous growth in population. The total population of Europe rose from one hundred eighty-seven million in 1850 to four hundred sixty-three million in 1914. In England, Wales, and Scotland, the population increased from ten and one-half million in 1801 to almost forty-one million in 1911. Prussia in 1815 had about eleven million people, while united Germany in 1871 had forty-one million and in 1914 almost sixty-five million.

While the population of Europe as a whole and of her rivals in particular was rising very greatly, the increase in France was relatively small. France in 1815 had more than twenty-seven million people, but this figure had risen by 1871 to only thirty-six million and by 1914 to only forty million. The consequence of this was that population pressure was added to industrial pressure, forcing the French after 1870 to consider every issue, domestic or foreign, against the background of a Germany growing ever more populous and powerful. Since a nation today must be a heavily populated industrial power to be a military power, France has been forced not only to yield the dominant position she held on the continent from Richelieu through Napoleon III, but she has also been placed in a weak defensive position towards any enemy, particularly Germany. That was recognized even by the generation of Gambetta, Déroulède, and Foch.

Gambetta was, after all, unsuccessful in 1870–1871, and France voted very heavily for peace in February, 1871. Déroulède's *Ligue des Patriotes*, founded in 1882 to promote the strengthening of France for revenge against Germany, was never a very large movement. Déroulède by 1886 had already led the League astray into a program for constitutional revision, but the collapse of Boulangism in 1889, the disgrace of Déroulède and his retirement from politics after the Norton affair in 1893, and then the complete fiasco of his attempted revolt in 1899 indicate that Déroulède was colorful and widely known, but not really very influential. The influence of the French nationalists before 1914 has been overrated by historians because their leaders were such able and striking men and because the historians have concentrated their studies upon the forces which led to war in 1914.

The magnificent achievements of the French army during the First World War, especially in the first three years, also tended to give greater prominence to French preparation and eagerness for war than was really due. There was tremendous enthusiasm in 1914, almost as great as in 1870. There was a tremendous amount of vigor and confidence in the ranks of the army as well as in the staff. Plan No. 17, for example, manifests the extreme overconfidence of the French General Staff, which believed a small holding force could halt the tremendous German drive on the German right while the French, in parade uniform, were to pour through Lorraine to the Rhine. This confidence, the general French *élan*, even Bergson's *élan vital*, and the incredible blissful ignorance of Nivelle and his staff in 1916 demonstrate French optimism and assurance, but do not reflect a spirit of French aggressiveness before the war.

Most Frenchmen were certain as early as 1875 that war against Germany would be folly, unless the Republic should have powerful and resolute allies. Fear of Germany was stronger than the desire for revenge, and it was generally agreed that everyone should think always of Alsace and Lorraine, but never speak of them. The French people were more interested in maintaining peace and enjoying the fair land of France than in regaining the lost provinces. In other words, in international relations on the continent from 1871 through 1914 France had primarily a conservative role.

France was conservative, or at least not dynamic, in foreign relations on the continent of Europe from 1871 through 1914 in large part because she did not become an industrial power until fairly late in that period and even then was not very sharply transformed by the industrial revolution. If one compares the Germany of William II, the England of Palmerston and Disraeli, and the United States of Theodore Roosevelt with the France of Grévy and Loubet, one can see that that vital disruptive and energizing factor was absent from France, although the Third Republic demonstrated a great deal of vigor in other fields.

The consequences of this are quite considerable. Primarily, it indirectly strengthened the general conservative tendency in France, already very strong after the Commune. In addition, during the first two decades of the Third Republic it directly strengthened the conservatives, who were the peace party in 1871 and who were not transformed until Boulanger appeared. Then, when the Third Republic acquired reactionary Russia as an ally early in 1894, the credit, and the political reward, for strengthening the country's position went to the conservatives. When the Dreyfus Affair drove France sharply into two camps, the conservative forces were behind the army, a strong France, and a vigorous foreign policy, while the Radicals and Socialists were driven into an antimilitaristic and even an antipatriotic policy. With the international crises in Morocco and the Balkans developing after the turn of the century and with the revival of nationalism about 1908, French conservatism received another injection. In other words, France's relatively weak internal position operated almost always throughout this whole period to the advantage of the conservatives. This was particularly unfortunate, as will be shown in some detail, because it was among these conservatives, given renewed power, that antidemocratic movements such as antisemitism grew.

France was affected but not transformed by the industrial system. France has rather successfully resisted industrialism, and she has remained to a rather high degree a middle-class country, a country of the small, free farmer, the artisan, and the small businessman. Those groups in other countries of Europe were to a great degree overwhelmed by the economic forces of the nineteenth and twentieth centuries, but France until today has remained the country of small business. Many of the qualities and the products which charm the Frenchman and the foreigner alike, the flowers, perfumes, gloves, wines, mushrooms, splendid fruits, dresses, and journals, are after all largely products of the small farmer and artisan in France.

The artisan and craftsman were so well entrenched in France before the economic changes struck, especially in what might be called the luxury industries, that it proved impossible to dislodge them. This middle-class craftsman and specialist has not only resisted economic change effectively, but he has used such products of the new system as the gasoline engine and the electric motor to improve his position. The small farmer has taken advantage of the migration from country to town to enlarge and round out his property, and he has used his legislative influence to obtain tariffs protecting his markets. Moreover, many peasants, artisans, and small businessmen not only resisted industrial change, but became such conservatives that they began to resist everything new, such as the appearance of new ideas, new taxes, new racial groups, including the Jews, and even the Republic when they believed the Republic struck their special interests.

This great group with its vehement opposition to economic change has helped maintain France as a very conservative country. It is a glory of France, and yet a halter for France. It has frozen France into its old economic institutions; it has collaborated with big business to make France one of the most conservative and yet, politically, least stable countries in the world. One of the anomalies of modern history is that the country where almost all of the Socialist thinkers before Marx lived and wrote has made little progress towards democratic socialism and has today the weakest Socialist party in free Europe. The Socialist party was stronger in 1914, but the situation even then led a great authority to write, "In the France of 1914 there was probably less 'practical socialism,' less socialist achievement in the broadest sense, than in any other country of western Europe." [4]

The corollary of the industrialization of western Europe has been the rise to power first of the bourgeoisie, and then of the working class. Radical democratic parties and socialist parties have appeared in every country changed by the industrial system. Even in the United States of America in 1950, the word "labor" is commonly used by all politicians, newspapers, and commentators to refer not just to the industrial workers, but to all workers. Labor and industry are the only two poles to which these makers of opinion would have American domestic policy gravitate.

The rise of parties seeking first political democracy and then, its natural sequel, social democracy, has been an inevitable result of the coming of industrialism. The appearance of socialism and socialist parties has been another stimulant to conservatism, particularly in France, where the horrors of the Commune in 1871, the vogue of anarchism in the early 1890's, and the internationalism of socialism alarmed a country which was conservative and where patriotism was a great civic virtue.

A final consequence of the economic change in France and of the manner in which it has been directed is the increasing importance of the city of Paris. "The city of light" has been the heart of France since the first Capetian kings, and the intellectual, political, and social predominance it acquired in the seventeenth century has never been lost. The Revolution concentrated French political power in the capital city, and throughout the nineteenth century the city strengthened its empire over all French culture.

The concentration of population in France demonstrates how Paris maintained and even improved its position during the nine-

[4] Clapham, *op. cit.*, 272.

teenth century. Between 1801 and 1850 the percentage of the
population in France living in towns of more than twenty thousand inhabitants rose from 6.75 percent to only 10.6 percent. Just
before the First World War, this percentage figure was only 26
percent. During the first half of the century, very few French
towns and cities increased their populations, while that of Paris
rose from 548,000 in 1801 to about one million in 1850. On the
other hand, in the single decade 1821–1831, six British cities—
Sheffield, Birmingham, Manchester, Liverpool, Leeds, and Brad-
ford—all grew more than 40 percent. In 1801, England and Wales
possessed only fifteen towns with more than twenty thousand inhabitants; ninety years later there were one hundred eighty-five.
The final proof of the tremendous predominance of Paris lies in
the statistics for the three decades after 1870. From 1870 through
1900, the population of France increased by one and four-fifths
millions. Almost half of that total increment (eight hundred thousand) was added by the city of Paris alone.[5]

There are several significant consequences of this development.
First of all, as the political revolutions most concretely show, he
who controls Paris controls France. Paris is the capital and center
and heart of France to a degree to which no other city in any other
country can aspire. London has Birmingham, Manchester, and
Edinburgh; Berlin has Bremen, Hamburg, Dresden, and Cologne;
New York has Boston, Washington, Chicago, Detroit, San Fran-
cisco, and New Orleans, as rival regional centers. Paris really has
no rivals. The consequence is that Paris has acquired the lead, the
dominance in almost all fields over other urban concentrations.

This position becomes particularly important when it is related
to other developments after 1870. Rapid population increases in
concentrated areas have always brought the evils of inadequate
housing and congestion, low wages, child labor, unemployment,
and insecurity. The concentration of the population increase in
Paris meant a concentration of that kind of discontent there. Paris,
moreover, attracted as a magnet great crowds of men who were

[5] Clapham, *op. cit.*, 53–54, 158–59; Carlton J. H. Hayes, *A Generation of*
Materialism, 1871–1900 (New York, 1941), 103.

able to express that discontent, because it was the intellectual center of France and even, at that time, of Europe.

Hundreds of young French intellectuals thus poured into the capital of the Third Republic, eager for fame as teachers, doctors, lawyers, musicians, composers, authors, critics, artists. The general slump of the French economy from 1873 through 1895 seriously affected these ambitious young people. More than 125,000 people were employed in Paris by the newspaper industry alone in 1900.[6] There was such a surplus of men for the newspaper industry that wages for the news staff and the administration in particular were very low. These men were especially dissatisfied because most of them had had high hopes of distinguished careers as authors, not as journalists. In other words, Paris manufactured or attracted an "over-production of intellectuals," and these intellectuals became critics of society and of the Republic. It is they who became the spokesmen for all the discontented in Paris and in France, and it is they who assigned responsibility for their failure or dissatisfaction, not to themselves or the historical forces just described, but to the democratic system and to groups such as the French Jews who seemed to profit from their degradation and failure.

THE INTELLECTUAL SCENE

No one with a knowledge of the history of the Third Republic before the First World War can demonstrate that the reaction in France against the fundamentals of European civilization was overwhelming, or even stronger than the forces and ideas which maintained and expanded those bases. France by 1905 had very clearly destroyed the attack on the Republic led by those who wanted unquestioned reliance upon the army, a restoration of Church control over French life, and the complete destruction of reason and of the rights — and even the life — of an individual if the needs of the state should require it. Historians from other lands frequently declare that the Dreyfus Affair is a blot on the history

[6] Eugène Tavernier, *Du journalisme, son histoire, son rôle politique et religieuse* (Paris, 1902), 270–300.

of France and distinguishes French history from other histories. In a very real sense, the Dreyfus Affair was a national disgrace. The fact that a very vocal minority in France should almost drive the country to civil war to prevent the revision of an unjust trial of a Jewish army officer indicates that reason, law, and respect for the rights of the individual were in perilous straits.

The Dreyfus Affair, however, should also be interpreted as one of the glories of France. One has only to recall the desertion by the Liberals in Germany to Bismarck, the antisemitic outrages in Russia in the 1880's and 1890's, which called forth significant protest only outside of Russia, and the unrivaled power and popularity of the House Un-American Affairs Committee in the United States in 1948 to recognize that there are Dreyfus Affairs, Matteotti murders, Petkov trials, and Sacco and Vanzetti trials in the history of every nation. The Dreyfus Affair is a glory of France because the French made it their *affaire*. In France, from 1897 through 1900, hundreds and thousands of Frenchmen of every religion, profession, and class rose to denounce iniquity, to demand the rule of law, to defy the powerful corporate bodies, and to put their positions and even their personal safety in peril before enraged mobs. Not only did these thousands stand up and fight, but they won. Both struggles and victories like that are rare in human history, and it is to the honor and credit of that generation of Frenchmen that the issue was raised, that it was fought in the open, and that those who wanted the illegal and unjust punishment of an innocent individual were thwarted.

The predominant intellectual temper in France before the First World War was shaped by a solid faith in the Third Republic and in the democratic processes. Most French men and women sought the liberty and equality of the French Revolution. They had quite abandoned the Jacobin traditions and were generally rather moderate. It was a realistic generation. It was a confident generation, but one which did not expect a great deal or wish for too much. It was a part of the nineteenth century and reflected the faith of that century in progress, spiritual as well as material. It has been described as a generation that sought individualism, but not rugged individualism. It preferred weak governments and had an instinctive fear of able and ambitious politicians. It was representative of a country of small business, and it wanted a world designed for the little man, with the government intervening when necessary to protect the small man, the individual.

There were hundreds and thousands of representatives of that temper in France, all rendering distinguished service during the Dreyfus Affair. Zola in literature, Clemenceau in journalism and politics, Gabriel Monod in the University, Father Frémont of the Catholic Church, all fought for the supremacy of reason and law and the rights of the individual. Perhaps the best selection of defenders of the democratic cause then was made by Professor Roger Soltau: Alain, Anatole France, Charles Péguy, and Jean Jaurès. The qualities and lives of these men reflect the attitudes and ideas dominant then in the Third Republic.

Emile Chartier, widely known as a very popular and influential *lycée* professor and newspaper philosopher, wrote under the pseudonym *Alain*. Thirty years old when the Dreyfus Affair began to stir violence in 1898, he became the "philosopher" of the Radical party. There was much of the Jeffersonian democrat in Alain, and he was a radical in the early nineteenth-century meaning of the word. He feared all government, because he felt governments by nature tended to expand their powers and to become authoritative. He preferred democratic government as the weakest kind of government and because the ruled can exercise control over the rulers most easily under the democratic system. He was a consistent opponent of conformity, from whatever direction it might be imposed. Where Jefferson believed in the necessity of a revolution every twenty years, the alert and suspicious Chartier could easily have adopted as perpetual slogans, "Eternal vigilance is the price of liberty" and "Throw the rascals out." His philosophy was not only influential but in many ways admirable. It is one of the tragedies of France that neither Alain nor the Radical party was able to advance from this essentially negative and defensive program to one which would not only offer a more imaginative appeal to the French, but would also face more effectively the economic realities of modern times.

The philosophy of Anatole France at the time of the Dreyfus Affair was similar to that of Alain, although both before and after the great crisis his political and social views differed from those of the Radicals. Anatole France was a novelty in modern French history. Most Frenchmen in politics and literature began life on the Left and gradually moved to the Right, obscuring their positions by giving the Rightist parties what appeared to be Leftist names. France was the son of a royalist, had a Catholic education at the *Collège Stanislas*, was a Boulangist, after the Dreyfus Affair became a Socialist, and died a Communist in 1924. Very bookish, a Parnassian poet, a critic, then a novelist and an historian, France was essentially reserved, timid, and even lazy. He was fifty years old when Captain Dreyfus was arrested in 1894, and he was at that time by no means of the stature of Zola or Alphonse Daudet, to say nothing of Bourget and Huysmans.

The Dreyfus Affair not only made a man of Anatole France, but it also brought him to the fore as one of the leading Dreyfusard intellectual lights. After the sudden death of Zola in 1902, he replaced the great naturalist fighter as the voice of the human conscience. The years from 1898 or 1902 to 1914 were those in which he rose to eminence as the "senior statesman" of French letters and the spokesman of the intellectuals.

Probably the most important quality in the work of Anatole France is the emphasis placed on reason. Familiar with the Greek and French classics, particularly the French of the eighteenth century and the French Revolution, France denounced all arbitrary authority and all institutions and traditions which bound man and man's thought. As a Dreyfusard, he fought for rule by law and the rights of the individual. "He flayed superstition, intolerance, injustice, demagogy, and dictatorship, eloquently defended freedom of thought, liberal education, and science, and advocated mass education, the separation of Church and state, social reform, labor organization, and the rights of minorities."

Like Alain, he considered democracy the least objectionable political system. However, he broke from Alain and the Radicals because he saw that "splendid individualism" was not enough in the twentieth century. Led by his feeling for social justice, his knowledge of the principles behind the French Revolution, and his admiration for the great Socialist leader, Jean Jaurès, Anatole France became a Socialist and pointed out that the logical consequence of political democracy was social democracy. His irony and social satire ultimately became more destructive than his socialism was constructive, as he became disillusioned at the political consequences of the Affair, but his rational approach and his ideas are typical of much of the best of France.

Anatole France, as both his writings and photographs of him show, was suave and urbane. Charles Péguy was a born rebel, "a bundle of contradictions," a free-lance who was "a heretic to every cause to which he belonged." Péguy left the *Ecole normale supérieure* before completing his course, established a socialist publishing company and bookstore, fought as a Dreyfusard, broke with his Socialist financial supporters because they insisted his concern follow the Socialist policy, and in 1900 established his own journal, the *Cahiers de la quinzaine*. He used this journal as a fountain for his ideas and for the ideas of many of the other young writers of that period, with some of whom he disagreed.

Péguy represents rampant individualism. He fought his way free from every authority which tried to repress or control or even direct him in any way. He fought that man might be free, but he was primarily a moralist who always struggled for truth and justice and refused to compromise with falsehood and politics. Péguy was a Catholic but an anticlerical Catholic who did not go to mass or to communion. He was a Socialist, but he rejected discipline and remained a nationalist. He attacked militarism in the Dreyfus Affair, but he loved service in the French army and completed his military service even before he went to the *Ecole normale supérieure*. Péguy was interested in universals and believed he was dying in 1914 for France as a defender of reason, law, and the belief in the perfectibility of man.

One of the greatest men the Third Republic produced before
the First World War and one of the finest defenders and promoters of democracy and the democratic process was Jean Jaurès.
This enlightened social democrat brought the best of French tradition together. By training and predilection an heir to the Jacobin
tradition, Jaurès at the *Ecole normale supérieure* led the protest
against the government's removing a distinguished Catholic professor from his post. This stand for academic freedom in a sense
is typical of the attitude of Jaurès towards rule by law. His
philosophy was rooted in the Republic and in France, for Jaurès
inherited nationalism with the rest of his Jacobin faith. He believed that the Republic and the democratic process could be used
to weaken those forces which still emphasized tradition rather
than reason and to advance the French and the rest of the world
towards fraternity.

Alarmed by the viciousness of the revival of the Right which
Boulangism had indicated, Jaurès after 1889 began to see that
reaction could best be crippled if its economic powers were removed. By 1892, he was a convert to socialism, to a democratic,
humanitarian, generally un-Marxian socialism. The role of Jaurès
in the history of French socialism and in the history of France
from 1892 through his assassination in 1914 is an enormous one
which cannot be told here. That career, however, and the temper
and reasonableness of this Socialist make him representative of
the mature, humanist French tradition. He remained a French
nationalist, supporting tariff laws, urging the peaceful and cultural
expansion of the French empire, and supporting the thesis that
France should be strong, although he disagreed with many Frenchmen on just how military strength might be most easily acquired.

He was a constant influence in the Socialist party — and throughout France — for conquest of political power through the ballot.
He defended and reinforced the democratic process throughout its
greatest crisis in France. He saw more clearly than most Socialists
that the future of socialism was irretrievably bound to that of the
democratic Republic. In other words, he was the greatest single
force in keeping the Socialist party in the democratic path, influencing other parties through that policy too.

Jaurès should also be noted as a Socialist who believed in the cooperation of classes, not in class war. He assumed that the logic of history would not only bring socialism peacefully but would even earlier lead all of the democratic parties into socialism. One of the main tenets of his political program, his belief that the Radical party would become socialist once it had conquered the Church, was foiled. That was a sensible assumption, however, and the failure of the Radicals to follow that path has not only weakened both the Radical and the Socialist parties but has also contributed seriously to placing France in the crisis in which she has been struggling now for several decades.

Jaurès was a rationalist, a humanitarian, a defender of political liberty and of democratic government, and a genuine believer in the brotherhood of man. Alain, Anatole France, Charles Péguy, and millions of French men and women shared many of those beliefs with him. Even when their political and economic programs differed or clashed, these men shared the free, rational approach and the general regard for the rights and beliefs of others which are fundamental to the maintenance and development of democratic society. Unhappily, as in every society in every age, there were many people who did not share those beliefs, and most important of all, that rational, tolerant, and peaceful attitude. It is difficult to measure the number and the significance of this undermining group, but it seems certain that in France after 1880 or 1890 there was a rather large number of able, vocal, and even eloquent individuals and organizations diametrically opposed to the democratic process and to the belief in the value of reason. It is in the atmosphere provided by such forces that movements like antisemitism grew.

Albert Thibaudet has pointed out that "during the last thirty years of the nineteenth century the combination of words, Taine-et-Renan, made in the world of letters a sound as indivisible as Tarn-et-Garonne." [7] These two men together dominated French historical writing and criticism during the years from 1860 through 1890 to such a degree that even Zola's significance in

[7] Albert Thibaudet, *Histoire de la littérature française de 1789 à nos jours* (Paris, 1936), 343.

French cultural history does not exceed theirs. Born only five years apart, becoming influential at approximately the same time, and dying within a year of each other, they are generally considered inseparable twins, both radiating and reflecting the same ideas. As Professor McKay has demonstrated, however, a comparison of the qualities of these two men and their basic assumptions demonstrates that one of them, Taine, represents the seeds of the antirational, anti-intellectual romanticism which was to prepare France for antisemitism and the various violent anti-Republican movements which have appeared since.

Ernest Renan, from Catholic and conservative Brittany, came to Saint-Sulpice in Paris to study for the priesthood. He withdrew from this famous seminary, but it might still be said that he became a priest, a priest of science and of the unreligious state, if not of the Catholic Church. He offended Catholics very deeply by his *Vie de Jésus*, published in 1863, which portrayed Jesus as an extraordinary but, on the whole, simple-minded man. Sixty thousand copies of this were sold in less than six months, and more than three hundred pamphlets in reply were provoked within three months. This controversial book helped make his *Histoire des origines du christianisme* a great success and to make Renan one of the most influential, and detested, men of his generation.

For a Catholic and for a fundamentalist Protestant, Renan's attitude towards religion and towards Christianity in particular is at least blasphemous. However, that should not obscure the fact that Renan represents the scientific, positivistic, materialistic second half of the nineteenth century at its very best. He was always rational, critical, tolerant. He sought always to demonstrate scientifically any view he had, and he was not moved by sentiment or prejudice. It is particularly important to note that Renan was one of the great Semitic scholars in France and that his five-volume *Histoire du peuple d'Israël*, which was published between 1887 and 1893, when antisemitism was rising in France, could not be used by the antisemites, even indirectly, against their chosen enemies.

Taine in ability and distinction was certainly the equal of Renan, but he, on the contrary, has had a generally disastrous influence on

French letters and French life. One of the outstanding students at the *Ecole normale supérieure* in the nineteenth century, Taine was so learned and his knowledge was considered so prodigious that he was called "The Scholar." A great literary critic, the handpicked successor to Sainte-Beuve, and a celebrated historian of art, Taine was led by the French debacle in 1870 and the Commune of 1871 to explain, as a doctor, why these disasters had befallen France. The six volumes of *Les Origines de la France contemporaine*, which were published between 1871 and 1893, have been termed "probably the most eloquent historical work in French literature." [8]

Taine ascribed the defeat of 1870 and the "disgrace" of 1871 to the French Revolution and to the individualism and democracy which it had tried to give France. Taine used rationalism to demonstrate what he described as the natural evils of the reliance upon reason. He demonstrated great scorn for the capacities of man and urged that France recognize that the average man is an irrational brute who must be ruled by his aristocratic superiors. "The great book of the French reaction" implied that France should return to the monarchy, the aristocracy, and the Catholic Church if it hoped to survive and to recover from the crushing military and social disasters of 1870–1871.

Les Origines de la France contemporaine, a rather natural reaction of an aloof, cold conservative to the fall of the Second Empire, was important for other reasons as well. It "furnished a conscience, an ideology, and images to all the parties of the Right. Barrès and Maurras derive in part from it." Moreover, it emphasized that race, environment, and *Zeitgeist*, or the spirit of the times, are the determining factors in history. Man has little or no control over his own destiny, which is manipulated and driven by Taine's trinity, "the internal mainspring, the external pressure, and the acquired momentum." Under this deterministic philosophy of history, man is just a "rudderless rabbit," with no real understanding of the forces present and, in any case, no ability to control them.[9]

[8] *Ibid.*, 350.
[9] *Ibid.*, 345–49; Hayes, *A Generation of Materialism*, 12–13, 245.

An analysis of the history of French literature during the last
two-thirds of the nineteenth century should demonstrate even
more clearly than the sharp comparison of Renan and Taine some
of the salient characteristics of French intellectual developments
which helped to undermine the appreciation of reason and law in
France. This is both a difficult and a dangerous process, for the
history of literary techniques and practices is one in which the
essential can easily be obscured by the frivolous, the significant
hidden by the blatant and colorful. Moreover, this is not an attempt
to evaluate literature as art, but to demonstrate some of the under-
lying assumptions fundamental to some of the threads running
through the literary history of this period. The contributions of
the symbolists to the deepening and enriching of French poetry,
for example, are tremendous, but that is not the issue which is to
be illuminated here.

The most important poetic group or school in the last decade
of the Second Empire was called the Parnassians. These poets, the
most prominent of whom included Leconte de Lisle, Coppée, and
Sully-Prudhomme, were very precise and technically perfect.
They excelled in the sonnet, the form of verse in which the
mechanics of poetry demonstrate their properties best. Cold, un-
sentimental, logical, rather sterile, proud of their scientific ob-
jectivity and detachment, the Parnassians were a natural reaction
to romantic excesses, although they wrote under the guardianship
of one of the greatest of the romantics, Victor Hugo.

The naturalist novel dominated French prose from late in the
Second Empire until about 1890 to a far greater degree than the
Parnassians ever even pretended to lead French poetry. Moreover,
through the tremendous sales of the novels of the leading naturalists, Zola, Alphonse Daudet, and the Goncourts, and because
these naturalists took part in the important controversies in art,
politics, political theory, science, and philosophy, the naturalists
were a very significant force throughout that entire period of
French history. The naturalists hardly constituted a school, although Zola coined the word "naturalist" and gave them more
actual as well as titular leadership than any of the Parnassians was
able to give that group.

To Zola, naturalism in the novel meant applied science, and the very latest science at that. He was perhaps more deeply impressed than he should have been by some of the theories prominent in the 1860's. However, just as Taine considered that he should as a doctor analyze and cure the ills of France, so Zola reflected the optimism of the century and thought he could determine the social ills in the body politic by the application of scientific methods. He considered himself a kind of sociologist recommending remedies to France in the coating of his novels, particularly his twenty-volume study of the life of the Rougon-Macquart family under the Second Empire.

This belief in science was not shared to the same degree by his most eminent naturalist contemporaries, Daudet and the Goncourts, but it is still there. The last of the naturalists, Huysmans, who wrote as the school was dying out and who soon veered off into mysticism, lacked completely this Zola quality.

A second quality of Zola, the emphasis on the senses, was also not shared so deeply by his fellows. As anyone knows who has ever read Zola, especially *Germinal*, Zola leaves no room for philosophy, for psychology, or for any of the subtle sciences. He is a realist, and even a brutal realist, omitting nothing and even elevating the sordid, the diseased, the filthy. Someone once called Zola and Guy de Maupassant "intellectual garbage collectors," and the phrase has a certain exactness.

In spite of his seeming eagerness to describe the seamy side of life, Zola was without question a humanitarian. His purpose was to uplift, to reveal the plagues and scourges so that they might be wiped out. Daudet was emphatic on this quality also, and his romantic, sentimental, and benevolent pictures of Paris workers in particular demonstrate why his naturalist novels should also be considered novels of social criticism. The criticism of the bourgeoisie and of the conservative, conventional, hypocritical, middle-class society obvious among the naturalists is not a distinguishing feature, because that society was under attack from all angles. It should be noted, though, that this was criticism of bourgeois society by bourgeois.

A reaction in literature and in life to the Second Empire, Parnassian poetry, bourgeois Paris, and the smug confidence in science and in man, so evident among the naturalists, was rather inevitable. There were many ways in which this criticism was expressed — in politics by the Republicans, Socialists, monarchists, and by a new nationalism; in art and music by the impressionists; in science in the tremendous interest in the still great unknown, astronomy; in literature by the great vogue of mystery stories and of romantic travel tales, such as those of Jules Verne, and also, by symbolism in French poetry. This symbolist movement or school was, thus, one of the protests against conditions considered stupid or intolerable. It was one of the most important protests, however, because of the intellectual, or, rather, anti-intellectual qualities it manifested and because of the continuing influence it has had in literature and, of course, in life, including politics, since then.

Symbolism is difficult to define both in meaning and in time because there was really no symbolist school or master. By nature a highly individualistic and even anarchic movement, it was more certain of what it fought than what it proposed. It was a development in French poetry which enjoyed its most significant flowering in the years from 1870 through 1890, although its roots lie even earlier than Baudelaire's *Les Fleurs du mal* in 1857 and its influence in poetry and in art is by no means extinct even now. It was a poetic revolt against the French world of the last part of the nineteenth century, particularly against the emphases on reason, reality, and standards, forms, and values. It sought to weaken and replace reason and reality through the use of intuition, magic and the occult, the subconscious and even the unconscious, insanity, and hysteria. It substituted hazard or chance in its attacks on the reasoned order, and it deliberately attacked memory because it considered that any mnemonic devices assumed there was reality, that there were facts. It replaced order and fact with the unreal and prophecy.

Symbolism sought to abolish all limitations, to free the poet's fancy, and to reach beyond the old barriers to the mysterious unknown. The science and the positivism of the nineteenth century had, in appearance at least, extended the limits of knowledge to such a degree that the unknown, the romantic unknown, seemed to be dissolving, and the symbolists, disgusted with the real world of naturalist and realist prose, escaped to seek "the unknowable and the infinite."

Since the symbolists considered it ridiculous to describe an elusive reality or to explain an unknowable world, they believed literature should cultivate strangeness, mystery, and obscurity. "It should express the poet's inner visions through suggestive metaphors and fluid melody. Against the bourgeois worship of activity and success, it should celebrate the rarest and most complex forms of beauty. . . . In a world where every appearance has a hidden meaning, symbols are the only possible vehicle of eternal mysteries." [10]

The history of the symbolists, their forerunners, and their successors in French poetry will demonstrate the sources and the significance of their qualities and beliefs.[11] The roots lie in the romantic movement, and tradition ascribes Rousseau a vital role in the creation and expansion of the romantic doctrines. Rousseau raised sentiment and intuition to unprecedented heights as literary attitudes, and he also foreshadowed the tools of the symbolists in his use of a kind of superhuman trance and in his development of mysticism.

It was von Arnim and Gérard de Nerval, however, who early in the nineteenth century began the search for what lay beyond the barriers of the real world. They were not trying to escape or deny this world, for their aim was simply to increase or heighten their enjoyment of this world. Gérard de Nerval is a particularly good illustration of the tendencies, for he dabbled extensively in illuminism and in the occult traditions and wrote some of his finest poetry while in "exile" from this world in a dream world

[10] Henri Peyre, "French Symbolism," *Columbia Dictionary of Modern European Literature* (New York, 1947), 292.

[11] Much of the material in this section is derived from Enid Starkie, *Arthur Rimbaud* (New York, 1947); Anna Balakian, *Literary Origins of Surrealism* (New York, 1947); Georges Lemaître, *From Cubism to Surrealism in French Literature* (Cambridge, 1941); Jean Pommier, *La Mystique de Baudelaire* (Paris, 1932); Marcel Raymond, *De Baudelaire au surréalisme* (Paris, 1933).

of his own. He was insane during a great deal of his life and committed suicide while out of his mind. He and von Arnim not only sought another world, but they also confused the world of fantasy with the real world, scrambling the meanings of time and space and thus leading to the distortion and disorder of the symbolists.

The search for the infinite rather clearly connects the symbolists with the romantic movement. However, there are so many meanings common for romanticism and the word itself has become such an overworked epithet that the use of it now is generally unwise. It should be easier, however, to understand symbolism and to place it in general literary history as well as in the history of literature in the second half of the nineteenth century if one notes that symbolism has three of the four characteristics Professor Lovejoy has located in romanticism: these are the search for the infinite, "dynamism" or "the assumption of the primacy, in reality and in value, of process, striving, cumulative becoming, over any static consummation," and diversitarianism, or an exaggerated emphasis upon the belief that there is a natural and necessary diversity of men and ages and people. These characteristics distinguish both the romanticists and the symbolists from the Enlightenment and from the qualities characteristic of the eighteenth century.[12]

The impressionist school in French painting rose to its great productive period, although the appreciation of its work was not simultaneous, at almost the same time as symbolism in French poetry. The men who became the impressionists began to gather in Paris around 1855 and 1860, staged their first group exhibition in 1874, and had rather openly disbanded by 1886. The symbolists and the impressionists have a number of characteristics in common, the most significant of which is the aim at expression through the evocative power of music or of light. Renoir declared, "Treating a subject in terms of the tone and not of the subject itself is what distinguishes the impressionists from other painters." [13] The

[12] Arthur O. Lovejoy, "The Meaning of Romanticism for the Historian of Ideas," *Journal of the History of Ideas*, II (1941), 257–78.

[13] Quoted by John Rewald in *The History of Impressionism* (New York, 1946), 271–72.

impressionists, like the symbolists, did not seek to re-create reality. They, too, were subjective, not objective, and they used light gloriously in their interpretations of nature. The symbolists sought to use the musical quality of their poetry just as the impressionists used light. The most obvious instance of that is the poetry of Baudelaire, who, it is interesting to note, was a defender of Wagner's music in France.

The revolt against reason exemplified by the cult of illuminism grew slowly throughout the nineteenth century. Balzac wrote two novels in the early 1830's on insanity, implying that it was superior to reason in that it was a manifestation of human contact with the infinite. Interest in the occult and in spiritualism was very strong in Victor Hugo, who was a convert to the mystical and irrational devices even before he left France for exile in opposition to the rule of Napoleon III. During the 1850's at his home on the Isle of Jersey, the unhappy and lonely romantic devoted a great deal of his time and even of his writing to table-turning séances where he conversed with his dead daughter, with some of the most distinguished men the world has produced, and with God Himself. It was primarily Hugo's fears concerning his own sanity (his brother died insane and his other daughter was insane) which led him to cease these practices.

Baudelaire in this was far more significant than Hugo, whose spiritualist writings were not widely known until long after his death. This great and gifted poet established a bridge from the romantics to the symbolists and also inaugurated the use of symbols to "break down the barriers of logical and intellectual control" so that he might make of his poetry "a sensitive instrument to receive impressions from beyond." The author of excellent translations of the works of Poe and an admirer of De Quincey, Baudelaire lived a life as strange as those exotic creatures, used opium to help him reach his dream world, and died a paralytic aphasiac.

Baudelaire is particularly important and illustrative because the theory of art found in his sonnet, "Les Correspondances," is the basis of symbolism. He believed there were "correspondances," or hidden and secret meanings, between objects in the material world and in the spiritual world. The artist's symbols reveal these connections and fuse the two worlds. He hoped to combine all the arts in his search for these obscured meanings, and he believed that music, the music of poetry, for example, had the evocative power of freeing man and revealing the secrets. *Lohengrin* one day released him from time and space, and he hoped his poetry would perform the same function for himself and his readers. It was to make this more possible that he became an alcoholic and a drug addict.

Baudelaire not only sought to break down the logical barriers of this world and "to flee from reason and reality," but he also attempted to penetrate the new unknown, the Absolute, the Abyss, no matter what the risk. His predecessors, from Rousseau and Nerval through Hugo, had only dabbled in the occult and in the search for the infinite. Baudelaire abandoned himself, surrendered to the defiance of nature's forms and laws. He sought ultimately to ridicule and destroy all human values, and he influenced his successors not only by his techniques but also by this nihilism.

The techniques and ideas of Arthur Rimbaud, who ceased writing poetry in 1873 at the age of nineteen, illustrate also the destructiveness of the symbolists' attack on the world they saw and the contribution their attack on the bases of civilization had upon the intellectual, social, and political history of France. A precocious young boy with a very severe mother, Rimbaud grew up in the dull middle-class town of Charleroi near the Belgian frontier. Shaken by the Franco-Prussian War and by the German invasion and then occupation of Charleroi, Rimbaud was upset further by his experiences in Paris just after the siege. At that time he began to read the standard illuminist, occult, and magic books, as well as those of Balzac and Baudelaire. He was one of the many Frenchmen of those years seriously influenced by the Cabala, the collection of Hebrew traditions concerning the interpretation of the Old Testament, which is the source of most occult philosophy. This revealed to Rimbaud that "he who could harmonize completely with the laws of eternal power and strength would become a creator like God." This fiery doctrine overwhelmed Rimbaud's young mind, particularly when it was supported by the anticlerical Michelet's denunciation of the Middle Ages and Michelet's glorification of the medieval sorcerers, alchemists, and magicians for reviving science.

Rimbaud became a combination of Lévi and Merlin trying to follow Baudelaire in his flights into the Absolute. He failed as miserably as Baudelaire had already done, chronicled the disaster and his disillusion in 1873 in *Une Saison en Enfer*, and abandoned poetry ultimately for adventure in Egypt and Abyssinia.

Rimbaud fought reality and reason with his poetry and with his life. He ruined his health in orgies with Verlaine, he used opium in his attempt to break down the barriers, and he rejected reason and law by choosing the life of empire, of action, when he abandoned his writing. He improved upon Baudelaire, for he stressed the unconscious element in writing, as the surrealists did much later. As his most able biographer has pointed out, "Literary youth, the world over, finds today in Rimbaud the expression of its impatience with the past, with tradition, its disgust with accepted standards, and with what so-called civilization has made of the world in which we live today."

The qualities of the poetry of Baudelaire and Rimbaud, their general aims, and the strange and unusual devices they used in their personal lives and in their poetic techniques are perhaps extreme and not representative of symbolism. Lautréamont, who died in 1870, however, had the same approach and similar desires. His scorn for science was demonstrated when he left the great engineering school, the *Ecole polytechnique*, and in his poetry he sought to denounce and renounce reason and to seek the Absolute through mysticism. With the rise to significance about 1885 of Mallarmé, the schoolteacher who provided whatever leadership symbolism was to have, the techniques, although not the objectives of symbolism, were revised.

Mallarmé, in his teachings and in his poetry, sought to annihilate time and space and to break down the limits or barriers keeping reason and unreason, the finite and the infinite, apart. He sought to make poetry suggestive, and it was he who stressed its evocative power. He also had a great interest in the fusion of the arts, and was influenced by Wagner's music to formulate clearly his views on the music of poetry. It is interesting and important to note that one of the symbolist journals to appear in the 1880's was called *La Reine wagnérienne*.

Symbolism with Mallarmé in a sense became respectable. There was less emphasis on spiritualism, the use of dope to achieve the dream state was generally abandoned, and the magic of words began to replace the media of occultism and simulated or real insanity. Where Rimbaud had used free verse without conscious effort, with and after Mallarmé the symbolists created a calculated free verse. Alliteration, phonetics, the poem in prose, and other technical devices began to replace the intuition and unrestrained imagination of writers such as Rimbaud and Baudelaire.

The symbolist movement, which might well be called the poetic revolution of the second half of the nineteenth century, is an extremely significant development, not only in French history, but also in European history, for it had great influence outside of France, particularly in England and Germany. Aside from generating a glorious era in French poetry, which is not the subject here, it also represents a part of the pattern or climate of opinion out of which continued and more serious assaults upon reason and law have developed.

Symbolism was not only a dangerously antirational and nihilistic movement in the manner already described, but it has had a second serious consequence in later literature. Its thrust for the absolute has led to a general disdain for all limits or standards. Moreover, it has accustomed literature to the idea of "indefinite revolution and to an artistic Blanquism," to a literary anarchism. The search for the infinite by definition cannot be successful, but the symbolist quest has led each succeeding generation to attempt to overthrow its predecessor and to abolish its techniques while the youth sail off again "into the wild blue yonder." [14]

[14] Albert Thibaudet, *Histoire de la littérature française de 1789 à nos jours* (Paris, 1936), 487.

The significance of this literary movement in its own time will be seen more clearly as it is demonstrated that Drumont's anti-semitism and the general attack on the democratic process from the Right developed in the same period. It can also be suggested, however, by surveying briefly one strand of its influence in later art history. It is quite clear now, for example, that movements such as cubism, futurism, dadaism, and surrealism have roots in this poetic source. Moreover, the influence of this literary school, even such an esoteric one, upon the plastic arts, painting, and even politics has been considerable. The Paris cultural world was so tightly interwoven with the political and social world that a ripple anywhere had repercussions everywhere. Perhaps a few examples of this interconnection will demonstrate how intellectuals and their ideas have had concrete influence in political history in modern times.

The French government from 1840 to 1848, led by an historian, Guizot, was overthrown by a movement led by another historian, Thiers, and was replaced by the Second Republic, whose leading figure during its first few months of existence was a poet and historian, Lamartine. In that same generation, it is worth noting that Marx found additional proof of his theories in Balzac's novels, and that Daumier's caricatures were more influential in France than King Louis Philippe's pious platitudes.

Another example of this can be selected from the career of Emile Zola. The great naturalist novelist in 1866 defended the early impressionist painters so vigorously in the Paris newspaper, *Evénement,* that the readers' protests forced the editor to cease publishing Zola's articles. In 1898, Zola rose to his greatest moral height to assault the established corporate bodies in a ringing denunciation of the injustice done to Captain Dreyfus. During the tremendous tension of the next two months, he braved the courts and the mobs in his struggle for truth, just as he had defended the painters in 1866 when they were being ridiculed for their conceptions.

Perhaps the finest example is the life of Marinetti, the celebrated Italian poet, who was educated in Paris during the 1890's and became a convert to symbolism. From this poetic movement, Marinetti adopted its scorn for reason and standards as well as its revolutionary urge. He was the first to translate Mallarmé into Italian, and he wrote much of his poetry in French, although he was a vehement Italian nationalist. On February 20, 1909, Marinetti published in *Figaro* in Paris the manifesto of a new school, the futurists. This denounced the past, all of the past, and described the goal of the futurists in these words:

> "We futurists uphold the ideal of a great and strong scientific literature, which, free from all and every classicism and pedantic purism, will magnify the most recent discoveries, the new intoxication of speed, and the celestial life of aviators. Our poetry is poetry essentially and totally rebelling against all used forms. The tracks of verse must be torn up and the bridges of things already said must be blasted and the locomotives of our inspiration must be started toward the coming, toward the boundless fields of the New and the Future! Better a splendid disaster than a monotonous daily re-run! We have put up too long with the station masters of prosody." [15]

This statement is a catalogue of the ideas and beliefs which have placed the free world in jeopardy: the denial of law; the search for the Absolute or infinite; dehumanization, particularly in the worship of the machine; the superiority of action, and rapid action at that, over reason; the careless nihilism; and the glorification of force and violence. Marinetti fought in the streets of Italy for his doctrines and exerted a decisive effect upon Gabriele d'Annunzio, who gave Italy the black shirts and the precedent for Fascism in 1919. Moreover, he was a personal friend of Mussolini and one of the founders of Fascism, for which he had already provided much of the platform.[16]

One of the unusual literary and art groups to thrive in Paris during the decade before the outbreak of the First World War was the cubist movement. Picasso was the outstanding painter of this school, but the poet Apollinaire was its spokesman and in a

[15] Quoted in Carlton J. H. Hayes, *A Political and Cultural History of Europe* (New York, 1939), II, 836.

[16] Ruth S. Morand, "Filippo Tomasso Marinetti," *Columbia Dictionary of Modern European Literature* (New York, 1947), 512–13.

sense its philosopher. Apollinare came to Paris from Rome in 1898, just in time to become an heir of the symbolists. To their search for a "new full order of reality," their mystical approach, their attempt to express the evocative power of music in poetry, and their attack upon the established criteria of taste, the literary cubists added a few additional qualities.

One of these new characteristics was strong admiration for the primitive, as distinct from the cultured or traditional, which they derived from the primitive painting of the "douanier" Rousseau and from the currently popular African carving. Another was an increased emphasis upon writing unconsciously, and a third was the use of surprise, novelty, and mystification to bewilder and confuse the reader.

The cubist painters demonstrated the same objectives, although naturally their techniques differed somewhat from those of their associates in literature. Their primary aim was to eliminate from art any connection with a reasonable or sensible reality. To do this, they used the usual escapist means, plus cubist techniques. Borrowing from the African carving, they tried to reduce all form to a geometric design, breaking up the old reality, in other words, and substituting one which they considered both new and superior.

Apollinare was a supporter of the futurists in Italy and really the founder of surrealism. Although cubism itself was crushed and overwhelmed by the First World War, it passed the symbolist influence on to the dadaists and surrealists. The dadaists sprang more from the war itself than from the earlier groupings, but their utterly meaningless writings, paintings, and festivals destroyed the movement in 1921. The suicide in 1918 of one of the leading dadaists, Jacques Vaché, is representative. He killed himself to give supreme proof of his scorn for life, and he "took a friend with him" by giving him an overdose of dope as a kind of joke. The world had certainly slipped backward a long way from the time when Kirilov killed himself in *Crime and Punishment* to destroy the idea of God through destroying the fear of death.

Surrealism represents a kind of peak — or nadir — for those forces unleashed in protest against the positivist, realist, and prose world more than fifty years earlier. The manifesto issued in October, 1924, by André Breton, the surrealist leader, is as informative in its own way as Marinetti's declaration for futurism:

Surrealism is the psychic automatism by means of which the artist intends to express either verbally, or in writing, or in any other way, the real working of his thought. It is dictated by his thought with complete absence of any control of his vision, and without any aesthetic or moral preoccupation. Surrealism is based on the belief in a superior reality of certain forms of association which have been hitherto neglected, in the omnipotence of dreams, and in the free and disinterested play of thought.[17]

This indicates the characteristics of surrealism, many of which should be recognized as derived through history from Baudelaire: the rejection of this dreary world and the search for the unknown; the contempt for intelligence and thought; the use of dreams, instincts, and the subconscious to reach that superior, surreal world beyond the reach of the shackles of reason; and the elevation of chance, hazard, and disorder over order and reality. The surrealists believed that man should free his mind from reason. Their "psychic automatism" or stream of consciousness writing was a device which they thought would enable man to reach the surreal truth, just as Rimbaud had thought the Cabala, drugs, and dreams would stimulate his imagination so he might reach the infinite. On occasion, they have even tried to simulate insanity in their attempt to destroy reason and to explore the superior world beyond the barriers. Surrealism thus constituted in the 1920's and 1930's at least one of the most colorful assaults upon the rational process that modern times has seen.

Salvador Dali represents surrealism for most Americans, and George Orwell's analysis of Dali in his essay on Dali's autobiography illuminates particularly well the qualities of surrealism. Orwell summarized it as "a direct, unmistakable assault on sanity and decency . . . and even on life itself." Dali's book, "a strip-tease act conducted in pink limelight," emphasizes the char-

---

[17] André Breton, *Manifeste du surréalisme. Poisson soluble* (Paris, 1924), 46, quoted in Enid Starkie, *Arthur Rimbaud* (New York, 1947), 421.

acteristics now so familiar throughout this entire record: thought-
lessness and the rejection of reason, the emphasis on force and
violence, sexual liberty and perversity, and, to emphasize the
interest in disease, destruction, and death, a very obvious necro-
philia.[18]

The forces and factors present in the intellectual and social
atmosphere of the Third Republic before the First World War
included other elements as dangerous to the rule of reason and
law and the belief in the rights of the individual and in the brotherhood of man as the philosophy of history of Taine and the objectives and techniques of the poetic revolution. These forces attacked the foundations of democratic society from a different
angle, but the assault was at least as serious. Some of the dangers
inherent in these factors were recognized at the time, for the
movements for political and social revolution were more obvious
than the revolution in poetry, but some of the implications fundamental to these forces became evident only later.

The revolutionary forces which assaulted the rule of reason
and law, both from the Left and the Right, had two common characteristics. One was the appeal to action and violence, which is
at once a repudiation of reason and a denial of law, and the other
was the belief in a utopia. This vision of the perfect human society is a clear indication that these revolutionaries were seeking
"the little blue flower," that they were romantics in politics. It is
one of the paradoxes and ironies of history that Marx, the self-
styled "scientific socialist" who scornfully labeled his predecessors "Utopian Socialists," was himself a Utopian Socialist, as
much misled by his confidence in his deterministic system as they
had been by their confidence in man and in the idea of Progress.
It is important to note here that there is a more than casual resemblance between the utopian schemes of these believers in
violence and the quest for the infinite and the Absolute of the
symbolist poets and their successors.

Marx's criticism of the Utopian Socialists is very helpful in
understanding some of the assumptions basic to Marx's methods

[18] George Orwell, *Dickens, Dali and Others* (New York, 1946), 170–84.

and philosophy. He ridiculed his predecessors in socialist thought because they believed that people could be convinced of the truths of socialism simply by reading about them. He denounced them for their childlike belief in progress, "the Renaissance bed-time story," and for their assumption that natural law and man's inherent desire for justice would lead humanity to them. He demonstrated clearly that their methods were based on emotion and that there was no analysis in any of their works of the mechanics of the capitalistic system.

Marx was correct in his criticism. Saint-Simon, Fourier, Cabet, and Robert Owen in particular had demonstrated a lack of knowledge of the economic system as well as an overconfidence in man's ability to recognize their truths and to follow them. It is tragic to think now of Saint-Simon's conviction that his "new Christianity" would be universally accepted once his books appeared, and it is equally touching to remember Fourier's confidence in the universal spread of the phalansteries once a few were established. It should be illuminating to note that their qualities and attitudes are lacking in Marx, that Marx wrote of an iron determinism instead of "the providential facts" of the Utopians and de Tocqueville, that Marx believed in class warfare and not in man's humanity to man, that Marx was convinced that the bourgeoisie out of economic self-interest would not only refuse to see the light of socialism but would try to destroy it. Marx meant social war, where the Utopians meant peace, and his combination of the quest for a utopia and the use of violence are distinctive of an important thread running through the history of the past century.

The Marxists and the Marxian Socialist parties in France talked of violent revolution and of scientific socialism, but Jules Guesde, the most rigidly orthodox of Marx's followers in France, had to fight a battle from 1879 until 1914 against the French tendency to develop "splinter" socialist parties and against the general drift towards reformism, or cooperation with the enemy class and state for social reform. The struggle had a variegated history, but although Guesde won a formal victory in 1905 with the formation of a united "French Section of the Workers' International,"

Jaurès ultimately conquered and led all the Socialists to support the Republic in 1914.

The anarchists serve as an even more apt illustration of the revolutionary blend of a utopian dream with violent methods. Anarchism in France derives in part from the French Revolutionary tradition and in part from the influence upon French thought of Proudhon and two outstanding Russians, Bakunin and Kropotkin. Bakunin, who was a kind of born rebel, was a generation earlier than Kropotkin. A great romantic and the participant in several ridiculously unsuccessful comic-opera revolutions in central and eastern Europe and in France, the personable but child-like and unlearned Bakunin was the antithesis of Marx. He never really assumed that there was any other manner of effecting political or social change than through force, and his dream was that there be a socialist Europe formed by the free federation of communes.

Kropotkin was a dissident from the Russian aristocracy also, but his anarchist vision has a grandeur lacking in his unruly predecessor. A man of great nobility of character and very similar to Eugene V. Debs, his contemporary, in his moral fervor, Kropotkin became an anarchist as a consequence of his conflict with the Russian state system in the 1860's and 1870's and his admiration for the practical anarchism of the Jura watchmakers. A resident in western Europe from 1876 until 1917, when he returned to new disillusion in Russia, Kropotkin influenced the French exiles in Switzerland and helped spread anarchism in France. Kropotkin sought to destroy all of society's control over man in the same way that the symbolists attempted to smash all the limits of reason and reality. It was one of his disciples, Jean Grave, who said: "Our propaganda among the people ought to show them that in a revolution, instead of going stupidly to the *Hôtel de Ville* to proclaim a government, we ought to go there to shoot whoever tries to set one up." [19]

After some riots in the Haute Loire and a bomb explosion in

[19] Quoted in Denis W. Brogan, *The Development of Modern France* (London, 1940), 300.

Lyon in 1882, anarchism became a cause of great concern to all Frenchmen. The dream of complete individualism or of a system where all should agree in a communion of interests — surely a utopia — and the attraction of bomb-throwing drew some of the oppressed and probably more of the restless and bored young men and women into the movement. A series of anarchist outrages so alarmed and frightened France that in 1894 the government rather effectively crushed the movement by applying ruthless legislation. This revolt, however, with its blend of a vision and violence, represents a part of the pattern in French social life of which symbolism and antisemitism are also elements.

Perhaps the most fascinating blend of the utopia and the use of violence was in the revolutionary syndicalist, or trade union movement, particularly in the philosophy instilled into those militants by French law until 1884, when the government finally allowed trade unions under rather strict controls. As the trade unions and *bourses du travail*, or labor exchanges, developed, the various Socialist parties attempted to bring them under their control. The syndicate leaders were so insistent upon their decision to stay out of politics that in 1894 even the Guesdist party, the most strictly Marxian, relinquished its quest. The trade unions, which were organized nationally as American unions are, formed the *Confédération Générale du Travail* or C.G.T. in 1895. In 1893, the *bourses du travail*, which were local organizations of all the trades in the area, formed a national federation. This federation in 1902 joined the C.G.T., which retained both forms of organization, giving the militants in control of that organization the largest single group in the organized labor field. At no time before the First World War, however, did the C.G.T. include much more than a third of organized French labor, and probably the militant views of the leaders did not reflect the more reformist views of the great majority of the membership. The fact that the syndicalist move in France did not accept proportional representation gave real control to the small unions, which could be more easily seized by the more radical.[20]

[20] James A. Estey, *Revolutionary Syndicalism* (London, 1913).

The French labor movement was much influenced by Marx. It was his influence which led the syndicalists to consider the state the instrument of the bourgeoisie, or an "extension of the capitalist factory," and therefore to remain aloof from the politics of the bourgeoisie. There was a great Proudhon influence in the move also, particularly in the emphasis upon revolution or direct action and, more especially, in the vague vision of the future utopia. The syndicalists never wrote a great deal about what they should do once their enemies had been conquered, but apparently they wished each syndicate to be a kind of producers' cooperative. The bourgeois state was to be replaced by a federal republic of these associations. This was, in other words, federalism, or Proudhon's "anarchism of groups." As students of this force have pointed out, their vision lacked elements necessary for a stable state and a productive economy, but their objective was less important, even to them, than the means by which they proposed to attain it.

The year before the formation of the C.G.T. the trade union congress adopted the principle of the general strike. Rejecting the ballot, the syndicalists proposed to seize economic power and then to abolish the political power of the state through "direct action." The strike of all the workers would secure economic control for them. Until it was successful in that venture, the general strike was to galvanize the workers, train them in the value of cooperation, educate them on the class struggle, and serve as a kind of challenge or gymnastic exercise to keep them fit. The other direct methods of the syndicalists were sabotage, such as slow work, poor quality, damage to the machinery, and antimilitaristic propaganda and action, to remove from the bourgeois state its most formidable weapon against the workers, the army.

The syndicalist movement grew slowly in the 1880's and 1890's in rivalry with the various Socialist parties. The Dreyfus Affair gave it a tremendous stimulation, however. Socialist participation in the Left cabinets did not bring the social reforms which many had expected. The effectiveness of actual pressure in the streets, by anti-Dreyfusard and Dreyfusard mobs alike, demonstrated the value of a kind of direct action. Moreover, the wave of disillusion which swept over many Dreyfusards when they felt that many politicians had used Dreyfusism to increase their political capital led to a revulsion against political methods.

As a consequence, the revolutionary syndicalist move both reached its peak from 1902 to about 1910 and acquired its philosopher and seer, Georges Sorel. This retired engineer influenced the syndicalists and was influenced by them. His ideas are important in illuminating the trade union aims and techniques, as well as for demonstrating a new thread in the pattern of violence and anti-intellectualism which forms a background for the anti-semitic movement.

Sorel was a retired highway engineer who devoted his life after 1892 to a study of social problems. A pessimistic member of the middle class, which he thought had lost the vigor which had driven it to its dominant economic and political position, he had lost confidence also in the political system of the bourgeoisie. Sorel's interest was in life, action, vigor, even violence, and he had a deep scorn for intellectuals. He had a deep admiration for the working class because he believed it had the vitality and lust for action and power which he sought. He declared that "force is the midwife of progress," and like many intellectuals—and many un-intellectual members of the quiet and sedentary middle class—he worshiped men of action and erected them into heroes.

Sorel was influenced by Proudhon more than by Marx. He was more disturbed by finance capitalism and the big banks (or the Wall Street myth) than he was by industrial capitalism. Moreover, he desired more to drive the workers on to violence than to erect a new economic system, socialist or otherwise. In other words, Sorel attached more significance to means than to ends. As a matter of fact, he exalted the methods of the syndicalists to the height of myths. He emphasized the virtues of the general strike in eliminating foolish and timid beliefs in parliamentarianism, negotiation, and humanitarian reform. He believed violence was a virtue in itself, and he would have agreed with "it ain't what you do, it's the way that you do it." He went further and indicated that man does not know what he wants or why he wants it and that it is only in generating action that he puts himself in tune with the blind forces driving him.

Sorel's ideas, emphasizing action and unreason, obviously provide no solid foundation for a political objective. He approved of action and violence wherever he found it. The proletariat were his first love, but it was clear after 1910 that militant syndicalism was a failure. He hoped then that the bourgeoisie, stimulated by the challenge from the various thunderheads on the left, would lash out at their enemies. As a consequence, during the last few years before the outbreak of the First World War, he cooperated with the extreme Right nationalists, the *Action Française.* After the war, he distributed words of approval upon both Lenin and Mussolini, who at that time epitomized the extreme and forceful Left and Right. Mussolini in particular was influenced by him, and Sorel's reversal of the importance ordinarily ascribed to ends and means, his antirationalism, and his emphasis on "becoming, not being," have had a generally disastrous influence in French and European history.[21]

[21] Sigmund Neumann, "Georges Sorel," *Encyclopedia of the Social Sciences,* XIV, 262–63.

II

ANTISEMITISM IN FRANCE

BEFORE 1886

1. The Great Hatred in History

THE HISTORY of the Jewish people since before the time of Christ has been scarred by agitation and action directed by their neighbors against them. The Jewish people had seized their chosen land for themselves from its original inhabitants, but that was, and is still, not an unusual incident. Riveted together both by their historic past and by their common destiny, the Jewish people unfortunately chose for their Promised Land an area which was destined to be the crossroads of the world. With civilization concentrated before the time of Christ in the Near East, Palestine became the door through which every imperial people had to go, whether they came from Egypt or Anatolia, from Arabia or Macedonia, from Mesopotamia or Rome. A small people but a tightly unified people, the Jews fought desperately, and usually successfully, to retain their territory. The more overwhelming the pressure, the more firmly did they cling to each other and to their religion. However, with the crushing of Judah in the sixth century before Christ and then the exile or dispersion from Palestine in the centuries immediately after the life of Christ, the Jewish state ceased to exist.

The state was destroyed and the people were scattered, but the religion and the heritage, cultural and national, remained.

> *The hammer shivers glass*
> *But iron by its blows is forged.*

The Jews proved to be unique people, however, for they were convinced they were the Chosen People and that their God was the God of all. The natural feeling of superiority and, therefore, of aloofness, and the magnificent stubbornness of the Jews constitute some of the principal causes for the resentment directed against them. Driven into areas where their belief in themselves and in their religious mission was not only derided but also considered criminal, they refused in general to abandon themselves and their souls to another religious faith. With the Christian Roman Empire and its successor states as fully convinced of their religious mission as the Jews were of theirs, a conflict was inevitable. The minority, as intolerant in this case as the majority, was hounded, herded into ghettos, deprived of opportunity to live on the land, and even thrashed with arguments taken from their own finest critics in their own religious writings.

There is really nothing unusual in this treatment of the Jews, either by the empires which broke the hard shell of the community or by the rival religions. That kind of policy has frequently been adopted towards other minorities by other conquerors. The history of Ireland from the sixteenth century down to less than three decades ago is evidence, for the English in modern times have treated this other European people as severely as the Jews have been handled on many occasions in the past. The history of Poland, during the past two centuries in particular, provides another record of noble devotion by a people to its religious and cultural traditions and the brutal reaction which that consistency and resolve produced among its conquerors, in this case German and Russian. No one familiar with German policy towards the Poles under Hitler or with the Russian policy towards them from 1831 until 1917 could fail to note that the conquerors have been even more ferocious in our "enlightened" age than they were two cen-

turies ago and that the ferocity has been greatest when the Poles
have been most defenseless.

THE RELIGIOUS ISSUE

There are elements in the history of the Jews, however, which
have made their history far more tragic than even that of the Irish
and Polish people in the modern era. To begin with, it has been
commonly believed now for almost two thousand years by bil-
lions of people that "the Jews," corrupted by their own vices and
the perversities of their religion, are responsible for the death
of their own Messiah and the Christian God. Moreover, Christians throughout the Christian era have been particularly horrified because "the Jews" have forever refused to recognize the
divinity of their victim. Freud once asserted that there is a corollary from this: every Christian is turned against the Jews because
"the Jews" will not admit they killed God and are therefore not
cleansed, which makes them even more objects of revulsion.[1]

The interpretation of this tragic incident has had appalling
consequences. This interpretation has been a real basis for some
antisemitism, not in the esoteric definitions given by the psychologists on the various complexes which have derived from this
incident, but in the sheer fact that there have often been clear
antisemitic overtones in the drama of Calvary as it has been presented in Christian religious instructions and services. The ascribing of this act, which must remain incredible to every Christian, to a whole people, "the Jews," has provided a fertile soil for
antisemitism for those Christians who have been little influenced
by the true Christian values and Christian spirit but who have
been affected by the tone of some of their literature concerning
Christ's life and death.

There is a second element in the history of the Jews and of
western Christendom in particular which requires illumination so
that modern antisemitism can be understood. No sensible person
today can view the Jewish people or Judaism as a threat to our
civilization or its foundations. As a matter of fact, it is now finally

[1] Sigmund Freud, *Moses and Monotheism* (New York, 1939), 215–16.

being generally recognized that the Jewish people have made contributions of every variety, particularly ethical, to western civilization, and that much which we consider most fundamental and most precious has come through Judaism and the Jewish people. However, the unmerciful massacres of the Jews in the past two decades have strengthened the opinion that, regardless of their history and their significance, the Jewish people are a weak people and Judaism not dynamic.

The belief common today was not that of the leaders of church and state in western and southern Europe during the first twelve centuries of the Christian era. There was during those years a definite "clash of religions," each competing in a sense for the soul of the world. The Jews, who numbered nearly four and a half million at the time of Christ, with their prophetic religion, their sense of mission, and their community spirit, were considered strong and dangerous, particularly by the Christian Church. In 398 A.D., the Christian Roman Emperors outlawed conversions to the Jewish faith and the holding of Christian slaves by Jews. Throughout the early Middle Ages, the Church thundered constantly on the danger of conversions to Judaism. This fear, and the fear that Judaism would become an even more serious rival should many Jews acquire land and, thereby, rank in the feudal system, led to laws forbidding land ownership, public office, ownership of slaves, and intermarriage to the Jews. The pressures of varied kinds upon the Jews were so severe that during the first twelve centuries after Christ their population fell to approximately one and a quarter million.[2]

GEOGRAPHIC AND ECONOMIC DISLOCATION

The third element in the history of the Jewish people derives from the second, as the second is a logical development of the first. Deprived of equal opportunity in medieval society and as reluctant as all other peoples then to work the land as serfs, the Jews were

[2] Karl W. Deutsch, "Anti-Semitic Ideas in the Middle Ages: International Civilizations in Expansion and Conflict," *Journal of the History of Ideas*, VI (1945), 239–51; Uriah Engelman, *The Rise of the Jew in the Western World* (New York, 1944), 9–16.

driven into a number of desperate positions. When the crusades intensified feeling against all non-Christians, there was a large migration of Jews to eastern Europe, where ultimately the great mass of the Jewish people were to live. This was to have generally unfortunate consequences, for eastern Europe trailed western Europe in the commercial and industrial revolutions, in the Enlightenment, in emancipation, and in the liberalism and democracy of the nineteenth century. Those millions of Jews in eastern Europe — and in modern times they have constituted more than half of the Jews in the world — as a consequence were not affected greatly by these tremendous changes. Since they lived in the most backward part of Europe, they felt the reaction to the liberating forces from the hands of their conservative and reactionary rulers and neighbors. Moreover, when antisemitism became official in Russia after 1881 and millions of these Jews were driven to leave that "concentration camp area," they arrived in western Europe and the United States without even the veneer of western customs and culture. This flood stimulated antisemitism in those areas, even, on occasion, among the Jews who had been living there securely.

More serious than that particular geographical dislocation, however, was the fact that the Jews in both eastern and western Europe were driven by the land laws into concentrating in trade and finance. Their position was particularly tragic because, generally, the Jews had no rights. They were forced to live in ghettos, and their lives and their fortunes were at the mercy of the ruler's caprice. The consequences of these developments were almost uniformly unfortunate. Living in restricted quarters strengthened the family and community feeling, which is one of the glories of Jewish history. However, this concentration also stimulated isolationism and religious narrowness. Moreover, the delicate and fragile position of the Jews encouraged a fear psychology among them, and they were forced on many occasions to resort to flattery, servility, and bribery to acquire even temporary security. As a consequence, the traditional attitudes adopted by the Jew to the gentile and the gentile to the Jew were shaped to a great degree under circumstances not at all favorable to the Jew.

Even more baneful than this was the linking by the popular mind of the Jew with usury and unpopular government policies. Driven into commerce and banking when Christian law closed those trades rather successfully to most Christians, the Jews became the scapegoat for the practices common to all bankers and merchants then, whether they were Syrians, Lombards, Italians, or Jews. This was a natural development, since the Jews were already considered distinct and depraved, since many Jews were in those trades, and since they were concentrated in the towns, where their position was most obvious. Moreover, when the Mediterranean was reopened and when the crusades provided a commercial and intellectual stimulation and challenge to western Europe, the weakening of the feudal system and of the Church's grip led to competition for the Jews even in those fields of activity where they had been driven. Their rivals, naturally but unfortunately, used the old charges as a club against the Jewish merchants. As a result, these merchants in the thirteenth and fourteenth centuries suffered from the popular wrath for the policies of their royal masters and were driven from their professions, often into exile.[3]

THE EMANCIPATION OF THE JEWS

The breakdown of the medieval system, the spread of the Renaissance from Italy north, the revolution in commerce and the expansion of Europe, and the Reformation all made possible a change in the status of the Jews. The Church and the feudal landowners lost some of the controls which they had held, and the rise of the commercial middle class, of new ideas and interests, and of cities and industries gave the Jews in Europe more freedom and greater opportunity. The religious wars of the sixteenth century made their position again extremely difficult, for many of the various reform leaders were antisemitic and the Catholic Church, particularly when the Counter Reformation gained stride, showed little

[3] James Parkes, *The Jewish Problem in the Modern World* (New York, 1946), 4–20.

tolerance towards them. However, once the passions of those wars had burned themselves out, new economic, social, and intellectual forces developed which provided the most salubrious climate for the Jews which Europe has ever seen.

From the middle of the seventeenth century until 1880, there was only one major pogrom, and that in 1768 in the Ukraine, torn then by war between Russia, Poland, and Turkey. Those two centuries are the era of the rise of capitalism and of the Enlightenment. Capitalism smashed the bonds of the feudal system in much of Europe and proved to be a liberating force throughout most of the world. It was not "a Jewish invention," as Professor Sombart and others have tried at great length to prove, but it did allow the Jewish people to prosper and to break free from many of the shackles of the older systems. Under the new economy, the emphasis was placed upon production, expansion, and commerce, and not on land and agriculture. Whether the state had a mercantilist policy, like that of Colbert, or whether the state was devoted to economic liberalism, like the England of Gladstone, the Jews were valuable and therefore allowed more freedom and greater opportunity. Under the new cosmopolitan, secular, and individualistic system, the Jewish people, by almost every index, benefited.

To begin with, the population increase is very significant. In the middle of the seventeenth century, there were approximately 650,000 Jews in Europe. Two centuries later, there were about four million. In 1900, there were almost nine million, and in 1936 almost ten million Jews in Europe. To be sure, the population of all of Europe during those same years increased enormously, rising from about one hundred million in the middle of the seventeenth century to more than five hundred million in 1936. The growth of the Jewish population, however, reflects their increased opportunities to work, the abolition of the ghetto, and the weakening of antisemitism, which applied to the Jews alone.[4]

---

[4] Salo W. Baron, "The Jewish Question in the Nineteenth Century," *Journal of Modern History*, X (1938), 51; Baron, *A Social and Religious History of the Jews* (New York, 1937), II, 165–205.

More important than the growth in numbers and rise of many individuals to positions of eminence in every field of human endeavor was the trend towards emancipation of the Jews. After being "internal proletariat" for generations, the Jews during the nineteenth century were finally made equal citizens in most countries of western Europe and the Anglo-Saxon part of the world. The first publication urging emancipation and equality for the Jews appeared in London in 1714. The general principles of the eighteenth century forwarded the movement, although some of the most prominent intellectuals of the century, including Voltaire, were unable to eliminate their prejudices towards the Jews. French Jews were made equal citizens in 1791, the same year in which the first amendment to the American Constitution guaranteed general equality. The restrictions were gradually removed in England between 1829 and 1871, and before that time the Jews had acquired equality throughout the British colonies. The movement slowly spread eastward to Austria-Hungary in 1867, Sweden in 1870, Germany in 1871, Switzerland in 1874, Norway in 1891, and Turkey in 1908.[5]

The very success of the tremendous revolution which has been going on in Europe since the middle of the seventeenth century and which led, among other things, to the trend towards emancipation of the Jews everywhere, was also the cause of a reaction and the consequent renewed pressure upon the Jews. The history of the political revolutions attempted during the nineteenth century in Europe demonstrates quite clearly that it is much easier to overthrow a system, political, social, or even intellectual, than it is to replace it. Lenin and Trotsky in Russia in 1917 saw clearly that their most difficult work would come after the "revolution" had taken place, and it was the genius of the Bolsheviks in recognizing and overwhelming the danger inherent in this natural counterrevolution which ultimately assured them of control of Russia. Mr. Toynbee has demonstrated that the successful response to a challenge automatically creates a new stimulation and challenge which may be far more difficult than the problem just resolved.

[5] *Ibid.*, II, 224–44.

Just as the rise of the middle class and liberalism bred challenge, so the simultaneous emancipation and growth of the Jewish people provided problems. One of the most serious was the widening rift which appeared within Jewish society. The Jew who was freed from the old shackles sought in many cases to be completely assimilated within the society of the nation in which he lived. This led many to leave or to deny their people and their faith, or to attempt to revise or reform that faith in such a way as to make it conform to contemporary ideas and fashions. This caused difficulties in Judaism, as simultaneous "modernist" movements did also in Catholicism and Protestantism.

Another serious problem was the lack of balance in geographical and industrial location. Not only were the Jews very heavily concentrated in eastern Europe, but also, in western as well as in eastern Europe, they were led by the old urban concentration forced upon them and by the fascination of the economic forces which had freed them to concentrate their population in cities. By 1936, almost half of the Jews in the world lived in cities with more than a hundred thousand inhabitants, and more than one quarter lived in cities with more than a million inhabitants.

The Jewish people not only lived very generally in large cities, but there was a high convergence of their efforts in those industries and professions which offered the greatest stimulus to them or which were most open to them. Thus, in the middle of the nineteenth century the majority of all salesmen in Germany were Jews. Even as late as 1895, 22 percent of the salesmen in that country were Jews. In the 1880's, when the Jews formed less than 1 percent of the German population, they constituted 20 percent of the people engaged in banking. In the same country, after the First World War, 4 percent of the Jews were in the liberal professions, about twice the average in the total population. In 1900, only about 2 percent of the Jewish people in the world lived on the land. By 1936, that percentage had at least doubled. However, in that same year, only about 30 percent of the Jewish people derived their livelihood from industrial labor, and the great majority of these were skilled craftsmen.[6]

[6] *Ibid.*, II, 266-82.

The proportion of Jews in the professions and in skilled trades dwindled very sharply after the middle of the nineteenth century as industrialism progressed in each country. However, due largely to historical causes beyond the control of the Jews, they were highly concentrated in industries which were to lose their importance in the industrial system and, therefore, their defensive value, just at the time when antisemitism was to break out again.[7]

THE REVIVAL OF ANTISEMITISM

The rise of antisemitism in the Third Republic was almost simultaneous with the reappearance of the doctrine and of organized movements in Germany, the Austrian Empire, Roumania, and Russia. French antisemitism is a part of the contemporary European antisemitism as well as of the general history of feeling and agitation against the Jews. It was more influenced by the other antisemitisms than it influenced them, really an indication not only that the French movement developed a trifle later, but also that Drumont and his followers were more influenced by political, social, and intellectual developments in France than they were by theories.

There has been relatively little critical historical study made of the phenomenon of antisemitism, in spite of its significance. Sociologists and psychologists, Marxian economists and theologians have elaborated theories in their attempts to find and explain the basic and universal causes for antisemitism everywhere. Since so little thorough historical research upon the development of antisemitism was available as data for them, these theories have little practical application, although they do stimulate reflection and may help the educational system remove some of the more obvious manifestations.[8]

[7] *Ibid.*, II, 282–85; Engelman, *op. cit.*, 92–93.

[8] There was a tremendous flood of literature analyzing antisemitism in France after 1880, but it was almost entirely devoted to the particular problem as it developed then in that one country. Some of the more interesting and important general analyses, on the theoretical level, are: F. Bernstein, *Der Antisemitismus als Gruppenerscheinung. Versuch einer Soziologie des Judenhasses* (Berlin, 1926); Julien Benda, *Mon Premier Testament* (Paris, 1910); Cesare Lombroso, *L'Antisémitisme* (Paris, 1899); Isacque Graeber and Stuart H. Britt

Modern European antisemitism begins, fittingly, in Germany. Here the Catholics had imbibed the history of "the Jews' " betrayal of Christ, and the Lutheran Protestants had an additional heritage of extremely violent antisemitic charges from their extravagant leader. There was, too, the traditional feeling against Jewish middle-men, particularly among the Bavarian peasants. Nevertheless, the various German states during the eighteenth century seemed to be groping and lurching their way towards emancipation. The French influence during the years of Napoleon's conquest was great, but that was wiped out after 1814 because it was foreign and because of the romantic and nationalist reaction throughout the German states after the Napoleonic wars.

As the liberal movement spread through the Germanies in the nineteenth century, complete emancipation of the Jews followed, until with the formation of the Empire in 1871 they had obtained complete equality. This achievement was, of course, one of the principal reasons for the attack against the Jews which began almost immediately. However, there were other occasions and stimulants in the political and economic scene in Germany, many of them very similar to those we shall encounter in France.

One factor which led to the revival of "the great hatred" was the conservative reaction to the successes of Bismarck. Strange as it may appear, many Prussian conservatives who had earnestly supported Bismarck before 1870 wished to remain Prussian and not "become German" in the Empire. Their dissatisfaction at his success was increased as they witnessed the beginnings of the tremendous industrialization of Germany, which they knew could not fail to undermine their economic and political power. Their bitterness was accentuated when the Iron Chancellor built the foundations of his political position in the new Empire largely upon the National Liberals, with the help of whatever conservatives could be/persuaded to cooperate. The agricultural crisis

---

(editors), *Jews in a Gentile World* (New York, 1942); James Parkes, *The Jew and His Neighbour. A Study of the Causes of Anti-Semitism* (London, 1931); Jean-Paul Sartre, *Réflexions sur la question juive* (Paris, 1946); Ernest Simmel (editor), *Anti-Semitism. A Social Disease* (New York, 1946).

which developed in the 1870's was a mighty blow at those German elements based on the land, and the depression of 1873 and the attendant financial scandals in Germany proved to these conservatives that the new Germany was on the rapid road to perdition. This 1873 depression gave the conservatives a concrete example of "the new morality" in business and banking and allowed them to harness the good old German middle-class morality to their discontents.

German antisemitism developed from this situation. Wilhelm Marr, who is generally credited with coining the word "antisemitism" in 1879, wrote popular vitriolic pamphlets against the Jews. The leading newspaper of the Prussian conservatives used antisemitism as a political bludgeon against Bismarck and the National Liberal party, which included several prominent Jews among its leaders. Some of the newspapers and legislators of the Center party, the new and powerful Catholic party founded by Windhorst, made the Jews responsible for the *Kulturkampf*, which was raging bitterly at that time. Wagner returned to Bayreuth in 1872, and his music and his antisemitic writings both carried a message to the German people, particularly after the entire *Ring* was first performed at Bayreuth in 1876. Wagner helped also to introduce the ideas of Gobineau into Germany, and the racial antisemitism of this French aristocrat provided a pseudoscientific foundation. To cap this development, the famous nationalist historian, Helmuth von Treitschke, in his lectures and, in particular, in a series of newspaper articles which appeared in 1879 and 1880, gave antisemitism the halo of scholarship and respectability. Other scholars, such as Adolf Wagner and Paul de Lagarde, supported Treitschke in this conservative nationalist attack upon the Jews.[9]

Political expression to this reaction was given by a Lutheran pastor, Adolf Stoecker, who founded the Christian Socialist Workers' Party in 1878 in the time he had free from his duties as

[9] Waldemar Gurian, "Antisemitism in Modern Germany," in Koppel Pinson, (editor), *Essays on Antisemitism* (New York, 1946), 218–30; Peter Viereck, *Metapolitics. From the Romantics to Hitler* (New York, 1941), 90–125; Jean Finot, *Le Préjugé des races* (Paris, 1906), 354.

court chaplain. Stoecker was a vehement conservative, and he started this party to help fight Marxian Socialism, which Bismarck proposed to crush that same year through the passage of the antisocialist law, which forbade publications, meetings, and the collection of funds by parties which aimed to overthrow the state or the social order. Stoecker's original desire was to establish a workers' party on a moderate reform program, but the party became a more conservative middle-class party when the Berlin workers refused the lure and supported instead the outlawed Social Democrats. He alarmed both Bismarck and the Emperor, but Crown Prince Frederick was a resolute defender of him.

Stoecker's party preached a crusade against the Jews and was particularly strong, especially in the capital, from 1881 through 1884. It collected three hundred thousand names on a petition to the German government asking that Jews be excluded from all national schools, universities, and public offices. The party fell apart because many of the antisemites had economic reform ideas far more radical than Stoecker could endure. With the disgrace of Stoecker, the Christian Socialist Workers' Party collapsed, but it passed antisemitism on into the German conservative party and to Ahlwardt, who led the campaign in the 1890's. A series of disgraces struck the German antisemites in the 1890's, when Ahlwardt was imprisoned for libel in 1892 and when Baron von Hammerstein, the antisemitic conservative leader, was convicted of forgery and fraud. Nevertheless, the antisemitic vote in the *Reichstag* elections rose from 47,500 in 1890 to 285,000 in 1898 and 461,000 in 1901.[10]

Antisemitism revived in Austria at substantially the same time it reappeared in Germany, Russia, and France. The promoter of the movement when it first appeared was Georg von Schoenerer. The son of a great Austrian railroad-maker but an agronomist and landed squire himself, von Schoenerer began his political career in

[10] Walter Frank, *Hofprediger Adolf Stoecker und die Christlichsoziale Bewegung* (Berlin, 1928), 39–375; Carlton J. H. Hayes, *A Generation of Materialism, 1871–1900* (New York, 1941), 262; Gurian, *loc. cit.*, 239 (footnote); Parkes, *The Jewish Problem in the Modern World*, 44.

the early 1870's as a Liberal. He became an enthusiastic admirer of Bismarck and Bismarck's Germany, and antisemitism became the tool of the Pan-German movement in Austria. Described as "the founder of political antisemitism," von Schoenerer saw that an attack upon the Jews would force all other political parties in Austria into impossible positions, disrupt the whole fabric of the state, and thus constitute the destruction of Austria and the consummation of his dream of absorption of German Austria by the German Empire.[11]

Von Schoenerer founded the *Deutsche Volkspartei* in 1880 to promote the dissolution of his own state. The party originally grouped together all German nationalists, Jews as well as gentiles, and it had a tinge of the sectarian liberalism of the period. The "Linz Program," which was issued in the fall of 1882, thus sought, among other things, to prevent the candidacy of priests and members of corporations for parliament, to promote progressive lay education, and to pass a group of anticapitalist taxes. Von Schoenerer was particularly vehement in his struggle against the Catholic Church, a mainstay of the monarchy, and he was very influential in the wave of recession from the Catholic Church that was the greatest Austria had known since the Reformation. In 1878, he declared that "Protestantism was desirable because it corresponds to Germanism," and in 1900 he himself became a Protestant.

Antisemitism first appeared in von Schoenerer's speeches in 1879, but it was not until 1885, after a slow but definite growth, that he added a new point to the Linz Program by declaring that Jewish influence had to be removed from Austria before any reforms could be accomplished. From that time forward, antisemitism remained the foundation of his political platform. Von Schoenerer had political genius in using antisemitism as a cohesive force, as Hitler did, but he blundered very badly in 1888 and ruined his political career in Austria by staging a Hohenzollern demonstration in Vienna on the death of William I of Ger-

[11] Oscar Karbach, "The Founder of Political Antisemitism: Georg von Schoenerer," *Jewish Social Studies*, VII (1945), 3–30.

many. The disgraceful character of the outburst resulted in a four
months' jail sentence, which automatically stripped him of his
patent of nobility, disenfranchised him, and prohibited him from
running for election for five years.

Von Schoenerer was far more significant than his brief and
stormy career might indicate. The Jews of Austria-Hungary had
been emancipated in 1867, and throughout the 1870's there was
no social discrimination against the Jews in Vienna, where they
were most highly concentrated. However, by 1882, the German
Club in Vienna had established regulations excluding Jews, including baptized Jews, from membership. In 1882, some Christian
tradesmen in the capital of Austria urged abrogation of emancipation and a return to the old restrictions. In the same year, the
legislature was besieged by petitions demanding that Jewish
refugees from the current Russian pogroms not be allowed to
enter the country. The von Schoenerer program, which was very
effectively promoted by modern propaganda techniques, spread
hatred against the Jews with particular effect among the merchants, students, and farmers. Like Hitler, von Schoenerer used
the beer hall as an assembly room, and it was from a "Brown Hall"
that he led his fateful demonstration in 1888. He was a great influence upon Hitler, and *Mein Kampf* reveals Hitler's thorough
appreciation of von Schoenerer's racial concepts and Pan-Ger-
manism.[12]

The real successor to the Protestant and Pan-German antisemitism of von Schoenerer was the extremely effective and
powerful Christian Socialist party of Dr. Karl Lueger. Hitler
described Lueger as "the greatest German mayor of all time,"
and there can be no question as to Lueger's abilities. He was,
with Joseph Chamberlain, one of the pioneers of "municipal
socialism." As mayor of Vienna from 1896 until 1910, he made
it "the most 'socialized' and best administered city" of the era.
Vienna municipalized its gas, water, and streetcar systems and
closed the zone of forest and meadow around the city to building
speculation under him.[13]

[12] Adolf Hitler, *Mein Kampf* (New York, 1939), 125–30, 140.
[13] Hayes, *op. cit.*, 211–12.

The Christian Socialist party used antisemitism very skillfully to aid it in acquiring a political predominance in Vienna and in Austria which it maintained from 1895 until 1938. It was a party opposed to two of von Schoenerer's most fundamental aims, the weakening of the Catholic Church and the destruction of Austria so the Pan-German movement might be furthered. Lueger showed great ability in organizing a nationalist party which was conservative, and at the same time he offered a social reform program sufficiently dynamic to attract at least the lower middle class. He used antisemitism to bind this party together and particularly to strengthen it against attacks from Pan-Germanists such as von Schoenerer. His exceptional skill in this technique was rewarded by his being elected to the mayoralty in Vienna, in spite of the opposition of the Archbishop of Vienna and of the Emperor himself.

It was in Lueger's Vienna that Hitler became acquainted with what he called "the Jewish problem." The Christian Socialist newspaper, the *Volksblatt*, was the source of many of Hitler's beliefs. As a young man, Hitler sold this newspaper and distributed party pamphlets on the streets of Vienna. Hitler has paid great tribute to Lueger and acknowledged learning two great political lessons from him: first, the wisdom of appealing for support to classes which are threatened and will therefore fight vigorously, instead of to established and cautious classes, and, second, the determination to use existing instruments and institutions, such as the Church, or the Army, or the bureaucracy, for whatever political power they might provide.[14]

One student of antisemitism has pointed out that one cannot rightly attempt to distinguish between degrees of antisemitism. A man who distributes an antisemitic newspaper is as vicious as one who burns a synagogue or clubs a Jew in the street. Nevertheless, there are kinds of antisemitism, and the variety which appeared in eastern Europe was certainly more immediately damaging and dangerous in character than that even of Austria and Germany. Hungary, for example, was infected in somewhat the

[14] Hitler, *op. cit.*, 72–78, 88, 124–30; Konrad Heiden, *Der Fuehrer* (Boston, 1944), 62–66.

same fashion as Austria, with the antisemites in this case being largely Protestant.

When a young Christian girl, Esther Solymosy, disappeared on April 1, 1882, from the farm near Tisza Eszlar on which she worked, Hungarian antisemites, led by two legislators, fanned the charge that there had been a ritual murder. A Jew, Joseph Scharf, was accused, and his two sons, one only five years old and the other a thirteen-year-old half-wit, confessed they had witnessed the murder. Resentment against the Jews throughout Hungary was intensified on the basis of this atrocious charge, as the government stood quietly by. The body was not found—it is likely the girl ran away or drowned herself—and a trial demonstrated the complete nullity of the charges so that Scharf was acquitted. The incident shows, first, the astonishing longevity of such a medieval legend, and second, the fragility of the position of the Jews in Hungary and in eastern Europe in general because of the backwardness of the entire population.[15]

In Roumania and Poland, antisemitism provided even greater physical hazard to the Jewish community than in Hungary. The revival of feeling against the Jews there fits into the modern pattern, although Roumania has a particularly interesting complexity. When Roumania declared itself independent from Turkey in 1877, the powers at the Congress of Berlin agreed to recognize and support that independence only if the new state should grant equality of citizenship to all inhabitants, regardless of race or religious belief. Roumania finally agreed to this condition, which was resented in Roumania as a restriction upon her sovereign independence, but proved unwilling ever to put Article 44 of the Treaty of Berlin into effect. The Roumanian government declared all resident Jews aliens and provided that each one of Roumania's approximately two hundred thousand Jews could become a citizen only by a special act of the legislature. By 1911, only two thousand Jews had acquired citizenship. All of the Jews, citizens or not, suffered from the good intentions of the great

[15] Charles Morel, *Les Juifs et la Hongrie devant l'Europe* (Paris, 1883), 5–12, 38–63.

powers which the powers could not enforce. The most clear demonstration of the Jews' position was a tremendous peasant uprising in 1907, which was directed in large part against the Jews and which required a hundred thousand soldiers to quell.[16]

Antisemitism in Poland was similar to that in Roumania. It had been sponsored there in the Middle Ages by the Catholic Church, which then feared Judaism as a rival religion and which in backward Poland saw in all Jews descendants of those responsible for the death of Jesus. The Jews served there as bankers, merchants, and craftsmen for the nobles in the sixteenth and seventeenth centuries, rousing the contempt and hatred of the Polish bourgeoisie as a consequence. This middle-class antisemitism was very strong by the late eighteenth century, and it was increased by the ridicule stimulated on the other end of the economic scale by the great poverty of the great majority of the Jews.

After the division of Poland, the dissatisfied and nationalistic Poles turned their hatred more than ever towards the Jews. As the nineteenth-century changes impoverished the Polish peasant, the intensity of the feeling increased. When the Russians emancipated the serfs in Poland after the abortive 1863 revolt, the stricken nobles poured into the cities, especially Warsaw, there to compete with the Jews in commerce and the bureaucracy. The backwardness, religious fanaticism, frustrated nationalism, and economic insecurity, affecting the old nobility, the peasantry, and the petty bourgeoisie alike, all combined in Poland to make antisemitism there a common bond. The National Democratic Party was the Polish instrument for the fusion of these hatreds, and it was this party which sponsored the 1912 boycott of Jewish business in Poland and which laid the foundations for the virulent antisemitism in Poland between the two world wars, especially after 1935.[17]

In the general resurrection of antisemitism which began

[16] Salo Baron, *A Social and Religious History of the Jews* (New York, 1937), II, 244–45; Parkes, *The Jewish Problem in the Modern World*, 52–53.

[17] Raphael Mahler, "Antisemitism in Poland," in Koppel Pinson (editor), *Essays on Antisemitism* (New York, 1946), 145–72.

about 1880, the most spectacular, as well as the most brutal and tragic, outbreaks against the Jews occurred in Russia. There has been a constant thread of feeling and action against the Jews throughout Russian history. Even Catherine the Great, the enlightened despot, proved that she was "a bundle of contradictions" by granting the Jews equal rights and self-government early in her reign and later, in 1791, the year of emancipation in France, establishing the notorious Jewish Pale. The policy of the Russian government during the first two reigns in the nineteenth century was to force the Jews to become Russians, particularly to join the Russian Orthodox Church.

Many of the pressures applied to the Jews by Nicholas I in particular were adopted also towards other national minorities, under the Uvarov formula of Nationalism, Orthodoxy, and Autocracy. In 1827, Nicholas I issued a ukase providing that Jewish males spend twenty-five years in the Russian army, in which hitherto Jews had not had to serve. Every effort was made by the Russian government to force these young Jews in the army to desert their faith. There is hardly a scene in nineteenth-century fiction more heartrending than the description by Alexander Herzen of his actual encounter in the middle of a wintry forest with a group of poor Jewish youngsters being herded to service in the most brutal and backward army modern times has seen.[18]

After a brief respite from persecution by the government and by their neighbors, the Russian Jews suffered the most merciless pogroms Europe had seen before Hitler broke loose. With the assassination in 1881 of Alexander II and the accession of his son, Alexander III, a directed fury struck the Jews. The attacks began in Elizabethgrad in April, spread to Kiev and Odessa in May, and then raced all through the Ukraine. During 1881, there were more than two hundred pogroms in Russia, and in almost every case the police and the troops did not interfere, unless it were to aid the antisemites, until the assault had spent its force. The government, including the Emperor, accused the revolu-

---

[18] Marc Vishniak, "Antisemitism in Russia," in Pinson, *Essays on Antisemitism*, 121–27; Alexander Herzen, *Memoirs* (London, 1924–1927), I, 254–72.

tionaries of the riots but declared that the Jews were guilty any-
way because of their exploitation of the peasants. There was another wave of pogroms in 1882, but in that year and in the ensuing
decade the government substituted the "dry pogrom" for the
armed attacks.

This official, "legal" antisemitism began with the famous May
Laws of 1882. This long series of decrees forbade the Jews to
live in the countryside, even in the Pale, prohibited moving, forced
all Jews who were educated, guild merchants, or craftsmen to return to the Pale, and closed the legal profession to all Jews. The
school laws restricted education to Jews in secondary schools to
10 percent of the Christian population inside the Pale and 5 percent outside of the Pale, except in Moscow and St. Petersburg,
where the Jews were held to 3 percent.

There were few pogroms for almost two decades after 1883,
but a new wave broke out during the tension just preceding the
Russo-Japanese War in 1904. The most serious of these took
place in Kishenev, the capital of Bessarabia, in 1903. This was
planned by the lieutenant-governor of the province and was aided
by the police and the garrison. During two days, forty-five Jews
were murdered and approximately fifteen hundred Jewish houses
demolished and looted. In 1905, the police established a secret
printing press to publish antisemitic literature, and additional
officially sponsored assaults took place immediately after the
disastrous war and the Revolution of 1905. Nicholas II in 1906
accepted the advice of an "inner voice," rather than the suggestions of his more liberal ministers that some of the restrictions
should be lifted. It has been said that the Tsar gave more than
twelve million rubles for the subsidizing of antisemitic propaganda between 1905 and 1916, and that during those years more
than fourteen million copies of antisemitic literature were distributed throughout the country. As a result, the pogroms raged
in Russia until the monarchy fell in 1917.[19]

Approximately two thousand Jews were murdered in Russia be-

[19] Vishniak, *loc. cit.*, 130–46; Simon Dubnov, *History of the Jews in Russia
and Poland* (Philadelphia, 1918), II, 243–429.

tween the accession of Alexander III in 1881 and the outbreak of the First World War. This program is one of the most significant events in modern times. It allowed the Russian government to blind the Russian people as to the real causes of their misfortunes and so made the revolutions of 1917 more drastic and violent. It led to a natural stampede of the Jews from Russia to western Europe and the United States of America, so that about one-third of the total Jewish population in the world changed countries in the thirty years before 1914. It led to strong protests against Russian policy in Britain, France, and the United States in particular. It led also, of course, to an intensification of antisemitism in western Europe, as the dissatisfied and the ambitious acquired techniques and an example from the great eastern power.[20]

The appearance and progress of antisemitism in Germany, Austria-Hungary, Roumania, Poland, and Russia after 1870 was, of course, an influence upon the rise of agitation and action in France. Probably few, if any, Frenchmen became persecutors of the Jews because of what they heard or read about antisemitism elsewhere, but the campaign in other countries did create a consciousness of the old hatred and an atmosphere in which other discontents could fan the feeling into blaze. The antisemitic leaders also used the history of antisemitism elsewhere as a demonstration of the values and virtues of their cause.

One of the first evidences of antisemitism under the Third Republic was an article on antisemitism in Germany by Hermann Kuhn, the German correspondent of the important Catholic newspaper, the *Monde*, in the influential *Revue du monde catholique* late in 1881. Catholic journals in particular opened their columns to sympathetic comment upon foreign antisemitism, sometimes by the foreign antisemitic leaders themselves. Lueger's Christian Socialist party had substantial publicity in the more social-minded French Catholic journals six or seven years before he was elected mayor of Vienna. During the height of the Dreyfus Affair, two

---

[20] Baron, *op. cit.*, II, 265, 286–87; Baron, "The Jewish Question in the Nineteenth Century," *Journal of Modern History*, X (1938), 54.

books appeared in Paris on antisemitism in Austria, one by an Austrian priest who was a supporter of Lueger and the other by a Viennese journalist.[21]

Perhaps the most striking, as well as the most disgusting, example of direct influence in France is that produced by a German Catholic priest, Father Augustus Rohling, who in 1873 brought out a vicious book, *Der Talmudjude*. This was largely a compilation from Johann A. Eisenmenger's *Entdecktes Judenthum*, which was an open attack upon Judaism, charging that the Talmud was the real foundation of Judaism and that it bound the Jews to destroy Christianity and the Christians. Rohling was transferred during the 1870's from the Rhineland to the University of Prague, where he was named professor of theology. He continued his attacks upon the Jews throughout Bohemia, embellishing his arguments with reiterated statements that the Talmud encouraged ritual murder. Rohling helped fan the passions of Hungary during the Tisza Eszlar case in 1882.

In 1889, three translations of *Der Talmudjude* were made into French. One, by Father Maximilien de Lamarque, was published in Brussels. A second was published in Paris by Victor Palmé, owner and editor of the *Revue du monde catholique* and president and manager of the *Société générale de Librairie Catholique*. The third translation was the work of a young disciple of Edouard Drumont, the French antisemitic leader, and was published by the leading producer of attacks upon the Jews, Albert Savine. Drumont in his preface to this edition saw the misfortunes of

---

[21] Hermann Kuhn, "La Question juive en Allemagne," *Revue du monde catholique*, LXXI (1881), 70-86, 147-61; Aloysius von Lichtenstein, "La Réforme sociale et le programme antisémitique," *L'Association catholique*, XXXII (1891), 164-73, 199-207; Dr. Kaempfe, "Le Mouvement antisémitique en Autriche," *La Réforme sociale*, second series, VI (1888), 567-77; F. Ollivier, "Les Juifs en Hongrie," *Le Correspondant*, CXXXIII (1883), 625-50; Pierre Douhaire, "Le Sémitisme en France," *Le Correspondant*, CXXXVIII (1885), 938-46; Cécile Vincens (Arvède Barine, *pseud.*), "La Question juive d'après des publications récentes," *Revue politique et littéraire*, third series, XXXVI (1885), 163-67. See also, Kalixt de Wolski, *La Russie juive* (Paris, 1887); Georges Meynié, *L'Algérie juive* (Paris, 1887); Meynié, *Les Juifs en Algérie* (Paris, 1888); Alphonse Kannengieser, *Juifs et catholiques en Autriche-Hongrie* (Paris, 1896); François Trocase, *L'Autriche juive* (Paris, 1900).

France as "the revenge of the Talmud upon the Gospel." The legends of the iniquitous Talmud and of the ritual murder were used constantly thereafter by the French antisemites. The vicious cycle was completed when another Catholic priest, Father Henri Desportes, accepted Father Rohling's role in France, even to promoting a ritual murder affair.[22]

2. The Jews in France

FACT AND MYTH

IT should be a truism, although it is not, that antisemitism is not caused by the Jews, or even by the presence of Jews. The Jews are more a result of antisemitism than a cause of it. The phrase, "the Jewish question," is both meaningless and misleading, and should never be used. Antisemitism is a reflection, an effect, and it rises always because of other serious ills in society and because some groups in the society, consciously or unconsciously, refuse to accept the real issues and seek a simple, direct, quick "solution." As Jean-Paul Sartre has pointed out, "If the Jew did not exist, the antisemite would invent him." [23]

Actually, then, the number and location, the professions and trades, the philosophies and politics of the Jews have very little significance in the rise and fall of antisemitism. There were 49,439 Jews in France in 1872 and approximately eighty thousand in 1900. In 1872, the Jews in France constituted 0.13 percent of the total population of the country, and France had only one-tenth of 1 percent of the Jews in Europe within her borders. In proportion to their total populations, Russia had forty-two times as many Jews as France, Austria sixteen times, Holland eight times, Germany five times, and Turkey two and one-half times. Even

[22] Achille Plista (A. Pontigny, *pseud.*), *Le Juif selon le Talmud* (Paris, 1889), preface, 1–14; Henri Desportes, *Le Mystère du sang chez juifs de tous les temps* (Paris, 1889); Desportes, *Tué par les juifs. Histoire d'un meutre rituel* (pamphlet) (Paris, 1800), 6, 13–18; Amédée Jubert, *En Israel* (Paris, 1888), 170–72; Parkes, *The Jewish Problem in the Modern World*, 48–49; Gurian, *loc. cit.*, 219–20.

[23] Jean-Paul Sartre, *Réflexions sur la question juive* (Paris, 1946), 115.

Switzerland had more Jews, proportionately, in her total population than France.[24]

However, in antisemitism, fiction is almost always of greater importance than fact. Edouard Drumont in *La France juive* in 1886 declared that there were more than five hundred thousand Jews in France, and his disciple, Jacques de Biez, later in the same year raised the figure to six hundred thousand. By the early 1890's, the usual figures ranged from a hundred thousand to a hundred fifty thousand, though there were some antisemites who reduced their estimates to less than eighty thousand and tried to rouse France to an awareness of the danger which these very few, hidden, well-organized microbes were doing to the society. The estimates on the size of the Jewish group in France therefore obviously rested upon whether the propagandist wished to prove alien Jews were overrunning France or that a small group under Rothschild or the Socialists were trying to undermine the country.[25]

The figures given by the antisemites on the wealth and political position of the Jews were just as elastic as their population statistics. For example, Arthur Meyer, a celebrated antisemitic Jewish newspaper editor, wrote that there were six or seven Jewish prefects in France. Father Isidore Bertrand raised that figure to forty-two (perhaps by multiplying six by seven), while the *Anti-Juif*, an Algerian newspaper with much of its staff from continental France, declared there were forty-eight. The conservative and sheltered naturalist novelist, Edmond de Goncourt, wrote in his journal that sixty-eight of the less than two hundred prefects and sub-prefects in France were Jewish! Estimates of the Rothschilds' wealth, and of the total wealth of all the Jews, varied even more widely.

The royalist newspaper, the *Gazette de France*, on July 19, 1894,

[24] Isaac Levaillant, "La Genèse de l'antisémitisme sous la Troisième République," *Revue des études juives*, LII (1906–1907), 77–79; Maurice Bloch, *La Société juive en France depuis la Révolution* (Paris, 1904), 18.

[25] Edouard Drumont, *La France juive* (Paris, 1886), I, 98–104; Jacques de Biez, *La Question juive* (Paris, 1886), 5–9; Emile Cazanove, *La Révolution antijuive* (pamphlet) (Paris, 1904), 85–91; Georges Thiébaud, *Le Parti protestant* (pamphlet) (Paris, 1895), 12.

provided a succinct illustration of all of these false statistics. Very careful only to hint at Jewish wealth because of the possessions accumulated by some of its own readers, it declared first that France had three hundred thousand or four hundred thousand Jews. It then demonstrated that, proportionately, only three Jews should be admitted annually to the *Ecole polytechnique* and six to Saint-Cyr, while only one Jew should be admitted every fourth year to the *Ecole normale supérieure*. The opportunities which the Jews "deserved" were, of course, being grossly exploited, for the *Gazette de France* claimed that each year fifty or sixty Jews were entering both the *Ecole polytechnique* and Saint-Cyr and five or six the *Ecole normale supérieure*. All of these were gross exaggerations, but they served their purpose.[26]

Whether the various statements about Jewish numbers, wealth, and influence were correct or not is really of not very great importance, for the actual number and the concentration of the Jews were such that all exaggerations were believed by those already inclined towards antisemitism. The Jews are "the most urbanized people in the world," both in numbers and in terms of the duration of time during which they have been city dwellers. Deprived by law and custom for centuries of the right to live on the land, the Jews have consequently congregated in cities. In 1808, 92.3 percent of the Jews who lived in the Ile de France lived in the city of Paris. In 1872, 82.8 percent of the Jews in the department of Alpes-Maritimes lived in the city of Nice, although only 26.6 percent of the general population of that department was congregated in that city. In 1900, 82.3 percent of all the Jews in the department of Bouches du Rhône lived in the city of Marseille.[27]

The Jewish population in France was not only much more heavily concentrated in the cities than the remainder of the population, but it was also very highly concentrated within a few

[26] Isidore Bertrand, *La Synagogue et les élections de mai 1898* (Paris, 1898), 10; Edmond and Jules Goncourt, *Journal des Goncourt. Mémoires de la vie littéraire* (Paris, 1888–1896), VIII, 91–92; Salomon Reinach (L'Archiviste, pseud.), *Drumont et Dreyfus. Etudes sur la Libre Parole de 1894 à 1895* (Paris, 1898), 20.

[27] Baron, *op. cit.*, III, 153; Zosa Szajkowski, "The Decline and Fall of Provençal Jewry," *Jewish Social Studies*, VI (1944), 37, 43.

cities. Thus, in 1872 in France, excluding Alsace-Lorraine, 97 percent of the Jews lived in large administrative centers, or *chefs lieux d'arrondissement*. In that year, in France, including Alsace-Lorraine, 63.2 percent of all the Jews lived in those centers, compared to only 18.2 percent of the total French population. In 1851, nine cities had 5 percent of the total French population and 30.2 percent of the Jewish population. In 1872, five cities, Paris, Bordeaux, Lyon, Marseille, and Nancy, contained 7.5 percent of the country's total population and 63.6 percent of the Jews. Paris alone in 1872 had 23,424 Jews, or 47.3 percent of all the Jews in France. The number of Jews in Paris in 1872 was more than double what it had been in 1851 and eight times greater than the total in 1808.

The tremendous urbanization of the French Jews continued to increase after 1872. It has been said that the number of Jews in Paris tripled in the decade after 1870, but this is a very great exaggeration. Nevertheless, thousands of Jews from Alsace and Lorraine in particular moved to established centers of Jews, such as Paris, Marseille, and Lyon, after the Franco-Prussian War. The emigration was part of a movement which had developed in the nineteenth century because of the great poverty among the Jews in the eastern provinces, and the addition of the patriotic stimulus when the territories became German increased the drive.

Many families and individuals celebrated in later French history left Alsace-Lorraine in 1871–1872 to escape German rule. Captain Dreyfus and Léon Blum, for example, were both sons of families which sold their property and moved from the lost provinces. From 1871 through 1910, the population of German Alsace-Lorraine increased by 324,276, or 21 percent, but the Jewish population there declined by more than ten thousand, or by more than 25 percent. As one of the antisemites pointed out during the Dreyfus Affair, most of the Jews then in Lyon were "foreigners," which meant really that they had opted for France in 1871 and moved to Lyon. Lille and its suburbs, which had almost no Jews before 1870, likewise became centers for these refugees from

German rule, and the presence of these new, "foreign," German-accented Jews was a spark for antisemitism in that area.[28]

This very heavy concentration of the Jewish population in the cities, especially in Paris, made all the theories concerning the number of Jews in France and their power more plausible. The mysterious power of Paris was evoked successfully in those areas where there were no Jews. Thus, Montdidier in 1881 had one of the very first French antisemitic newspapers when Father E. A. Chabauty edited *Anti-Juif*, although the city had not a single Jew. André Siegfried pointed out in 1913 that there were no Jews in the rural districts in western France and very few in the cities, but that section nonetheless was one of the most antisemitic areas in the entire country.

On the other hand, the thousands of provincials who did come to Paris during the first decades of the Third Republic were struck by the presence of what they considered a foreign element which they were seeing for the first time. The magnetic power of Paris during these years was at its height, and the increase in population of Paris from 1870 through 1900 constituted 45 percent of the increase in population of all of France. Charles Maurras, who was struck first of all on his arrival in Paris on December 2, 1885, by the number of Jews, was only one of the hundreds of young intellectuals encountering an "alien race" and what they considered intolerable competition.[29]

Students of the problem have had great difficulty in determining the Jewish population in France during the nineteenth century. The lack of complete and certified data on such a basic issue emphasizes the even greater difficulty of determining the professions, the relative wealth, the political and social attitudes, and the religious beliefs of the Jews. There are no statistics on these issues, and there is no satisfactory way of obtaining this important infor-

[28] Zosa Szajkowski, "The Growth of the Jewish Population of France," *Jewish Social Studies*, VIII (1946), 300–15; Earle Stanley Randall, *The Jewish Character in the French Novel, 1870–1914* (Menasha, Wisconsin, 1941), 64; Geoffrey Fraser, *Léon Blum. Man and Statesman* (Philadelphia, 1938), 24–26.

[29] André Siegfried, *Tableau politique de la France de l'ouest sous la troisième République* (Paris, 1913), 391; Charles Maurras, *Au Signe de flore* (Paris, 1931), 31; Szajkowski, *loc. cit.*, 298.

mation with the little material now available. However, three conclusions may be stated which are definite and of consequence. First, as has been already pointed out, the Jews in France were highly concentrated in the cities and therefore in urban industry. Second, in spite of this fact and of the advantage which it might have been expected to give these urban dwellers in a society which was constantly becoming more urban and industrial, the French Jews were generally very poor. One of the myths most success-fully spread by the antisemites had led to the general belief that Jews are wealthy, or at least, prosperous. However, in Paris in the nineteenth century before 1870 "over 60 percent of the Jews who died were paupers."

Thirdly, in spite of this general poverty, the Jews were re-markably successful in a few fields. In the theater, in literature and in literary criticism, in the press, in scholarship, in law and medicine, and in Republican politics, this was a glorious and golden age for French Jewry, which produced a number of leaders in these particular fields out of proportion to the relative number of Jews in France. The remark in Proust's great novel about a dramatic producer who changed his name to Samuel so that he might be more successful was not an antisemitic gibe, but a bow to the prominence of the Jews in the theater.[30]

THE ATTITUDE OF THE JEWS TOWARD ANTISEMITISM

The relative success of the Jews in France in some fields of interest was not a primary cause of antisemitism in France, although the antisemites always acted as though it were. It was only a sec-ondary cause, and was hardly of more consequence than another attribute of the Jews which did not irritate the antisemites but which, nevertheless, aided the progress of antisemitism in France. This was the attitude taken by most Jews towards the movement directed against them.

French Jews were placed in a very uncomfortable position by

[30] Isidore Loeb, *Réflexions sur les juifs* (Paris, 1894), 79-81; Szajkowski, *loc. cit.*, 314; Bloch, *op. cit.*, 30-31.

the appearance of antisemitism there. Their legal emancipation was only a century old, and their acquisition of political and social security had progressed very gradually throughout the century. The members of the Jewish group who were prominent and prosperous feared to jeopardize this advance and their personal positions by open assault upon the antisemites. Generally, they believed it the wisest policy to ignore the antisemites and to continue working for greater assimilation and increased understanding of democratic life on all sides, in the hope that the threat would disintegrate. They were strengthened in their decision by Jewish history and by the attitudes and responses forced on the Jews in the past by persecution. It should be remembered, too, that this policy was one which had succeeded on numerous occasions in the past. The squall of antisemitic feeling in France in the 1840's, for example, had blown away without active opposition on the part of the Jews.

It is very clear that most French Jews, as most other Frenchmen, accepted the original sentencing of Captain Dreyfus as just, and that they sought not to become involved in the revisionist campaign. The reluctance of most French Jews to support even men like Zadoc Kahn and then to take issue in one of the most important personal rights cases in all history is due in large part to conservatism and fear. However, there were other elements involved as well. One was the decline of Judaism in the last third of the nineteenth century. This was a part of the general drift away from all organized religion which was a very important thread of that period and which was undermining Catholicism and Protestantism as well. Many of the leading French Jews had abandoned their religious beliefs, some, like Bernard Lazare, to become militant but tolerant atheists, others, like Alfred Naquet, to become vehement free-thinkers and anticlericals, and others, like Léon Blum, to make culture, politics, and socialism a substitute for religion. In the 1890's, most pupils at the *Ecole rabbinique* were foreign, because the sons of French Jews showed little interest in becoming rabbis.

Probably even more important than this was the general at-

mosphere of confidence so prominent throughout Europe in the
last years of "the century of hope." In an age of material and
intellectual progress, most people assumed that further progress
was inevitable and that the near future would witness the elimi-
nation of all misery, ignorance, and prejudice, whether it be racial
or religious. The French Jews, who had more to hope for from
progress than their fellow countrymen, were more inclined to
entrust their confidence to it. One of the paradoxes in the history
of Zionism is that Theodore Herzl, the man commonly regarded
as the founder of modern Zionism, was influenced most by the
antisemitism he saw in Paris when he came there as an Austrian
newspaperman to describe the Dreyfus Affair for Vienna. Yet
Zionism had almost no appeal for French Jews. Bernard Lazare
became a Zionist in 1897 and helped establish a Zionist newspaper
in 1898. However, by March, 1899, even he, "the only important
French Jew who had been a Zionist," had left Herzl's movement,
seeing the solution to French antisemitism in France itself.[31]

It is easy for us today to criticize this policy of ignoring and
appeasing antisemitism, particularly because that policy generally
encouraged, or at least did not discourage, the drive of the antisemites. However, there were numbers of Jews who fought antisemitism from its very appearance and who sought to overcome the
passivity of their fellows. Thus, the appearance of Drumont's *La
France juive* in 1886 and the flood of antisemitic writings which
the success of this publication released led to a number of defenses
of democratic principles and to assaults upon antisemitism. Some
of the most able and effective of these early efforts were by Jews.
For example, Alexander Weill, the celebrated Jewish poet who
was a great admirer of Robespierre and a fervent believer that the
French Revolution should be carried forward, wrote three very
effective pamphlets denouncing Drumont's ideas within four
years after Drumont's first tirade appeared.[32]

---

[31] Bernard Lazare, *Le Nationalisme juif* (pamphlet) (Paris, 1898); Alfred
Berl, *Le Mouvement sioniste et l'antisémitisme* (pamphlet), 2–16; Baruch
Hagani, *Bernard Lazare* (Paris, 1919), 30–42.

[32] Alexander Weill, *Blasphèmes* (Paris, 1878); Weill, *Cri d'alarme* (Paris,
1889); Weill, *Epitres cinglantes à M. Drumont* (Paris, 1888); Weill, *La France*

The problem as to the stand the Jews should take became more pressing in 1890, when the French National Antisemitic League was formed. This league soon collapsed, but it was replaced in 1892 by a successful antisemitic daily newspaper in Paris, the *Libre Parole*. These developments, and several alarming incidents which occurred during those years, forced all French Jews to reconsider their policy. Here again, most Jews decided to ignore the danger and to hope it would evaporate. Those few Jews who were convinced that the threat had to be challenged and demolished before the Jews, democracy in France, and the possibilities for progress should be secure received extremely little aid and support from their fellows.

As a matter of fact, some of the antisemites had more respect for the Jews who fought for democratic principles and their security than their fellow Jews did. Alfred Naquet was the only Jew who rose in antisemitic meetings to attack the proposals of the antisemites. Many Jews were very distressed at Naquet's vigorous defense of his race and his principles, as well as of the religion which he himself had abandoned. They disliked his vigor and resourcefulness even more than they regretted the fact that their defender was so generally unpopular in France. Known as "the dirty chemist" because he was a doctor and a chemist with a reputation for slovenliness, Naquet was known above all as the sponsor of the divorce law passed in 1884. This and the suspicion that he had urged General Boulanger to flee from France in 1889, thus discrediting the Boulangist movement, made all Catholics and conservatives hate him. Many influential Jewish leaders made it quite clear that they preferred to risk an increase in antisemitic agitation and action against them rather than to be defended by Naquet.[33]

---

catholique et athée (Paris, 1886). Other attacks by Jews upon Drumont's ideas in these early years include Raoul Hirschler, *A Monsieur Drumont, auteur de "La France juive"* (Toulouse, 1888); Eliézer Lambert, *Les Juifs, la société moderne et l'antisémitisme* (Paris, 1887), and Heber Marini, *Le Fin Mot de la question juive* (Paris, 1886). All of these were pamphlets.

[33] Julien Mauvrac, *Sous les Tentes de Japhet* (Paris, 1890), 109, 180–88; Robert Launay, *Figures juives* (Paris, 1921), 121–40.

The most distinguished Jewish defender of the French Jews and of the threatened democratic principles was the grand rabbi of France, Zadoc Kahn, a very wise, able, and excellent man. Rabbi Kahn became the grand rabbi of France in 1889, after having been grand rabbi of Paris since 1868. Energetic and intelligent, Kahn appreciated the danger potential in Drumont's crusade from the beginning. He wanted to sue the leading antisemites but was deterred by more conservative friends. Nevertheless, he did direct a spirited and shrewd attack upon antisemitism. He always reflected confidence in his moves, and he was skillful enough never to give antisemitism more power or publicity than the movement deserved.

Kahn not only fought antisemitism by denouncing it in sermons, in public addresses, and in letters to newspapers, but he also sought to demonstrate to all the French that French Jews had been assimilated and were as French as their Catholic, Protestant, and free-thinking neighbors. Moreover, born in Alsace and educated in Lorraine, Kahn was a French nationalist. He reiterated to the French Jews and to all France that French Jews shared a common future with all other Frenchmen. In November, 1892, he told the Jewish seminarians who were leaving for army service that none of them could "isolate his interests from those of his country, nor his destiny, nor that of his family, from that of the great family of the state. Each must grieve at its failures, rejoice at its triumphs, and try with all his abilities to increase the happiness of his fellow citizens."

The efforts of Kahn were particularly effective in the years just prior to the arrest of Captain Alfred Dreyfus in 1894. When a Jewish army officer, Captain Armand Mayer, was killed in 1892 by the Marquis de Morès in a duel which was caused by a series of articles in the *Libre Parole* denouncing the number of Jewish army officers, Rabbi Kahn denounced race and religious hatred so eloquently at the funeral that the antisemitic movement appeared to have suffered a serious blow. His campaign at this time led to attacks upon antisemitism in the Paris Municipal Council and in the Chamber of Deputies. The declaration in the Chamber of

Deputies by Minister of War Freycinet that "the army does not distinguish between Jews, Protestants, and Catholics" was applauded by the entire Chamber, and his assertion that it was a crime against the nation to sow division in the army was voted a unanimous order of the day.

In 1893, Kahn demonstrated the close connection between French Judaism and nationalism with an address at the celebration of the anniversary of the founding of the *Ecole polytechnique*. A funeral oration delivered that same year at the services for two Jewish army officers killed in the Dahomey campaign also effectively underlined the thesis the grand rabbi had sought to establish. When he had funeral services celebrated throughout France and Algeria for the assassinated President Carnot in July, 1894, he was again following the advice he gave the seminarians on uniting their hopes and efforts with those of all of France.[34]

The efforts of Zadoc Kahn are at once an indication of the strength and of the timidity of the campaign of the Jews to defend themselves. He was not given the support by his fellows which he sought, and at the same time he was extremely cool towards attempts to fight antisemitism by any other methods than his emphasizing the Jews' being loyal Frenchmen. Moreover, after the arrest of Captain Dreyfus and with the development of the Dreyfus Affair, Kahn's vigor lessened, apparently because he believed Jewish leadership in defense of the rights of Captain Dreyfus would only increase antisemitism.[35]

Conservative French Jews were more committed to a belief in future improvement and therefore more likely to adopt a policy of ignoring antisemitism than were more radical Jews. Zadoc Kahn was probably the most effective Jewish opponent of antisemitism,

[34] Julien Weill, *Zadoc Kahn* (Paris, 1912), 120–53; C. E. Curinier (editor), *Dictionnaire national des contemporains* (Paris, 1899–1905), III, 137–38; Zadoc Kahn, *Religion et patrie* (Paris, 1892–?); Kahn, *Discours d'installation* (pamphlet) (Paris, 1890); D. Kimon, *La Guerre antijuive* (Paris, 1898), 168.
[35] Joseph Aron, *Questions juives en 1896* (pamphlet) (Paris, 1896), 8–12; Jacques Bahar, *Restons! Réponse au projet d'exode des juifs* (pamphlet) (Paris, 1897), 15–19; Léon Blum, *Souvenirs sur l'Affaire* (Paris, 1935), 25–28; John Grand-Carteret, *L'Affaire Dreyfus et l'image* (Paris, 1898), 15; Juda Tchernoff, *Dans le Creuset des civilisations* (Paris, 1937), III, 31–34.

but there were a number of younger, more vigorous Jews who sought to crush the crusade. Isidore Singer was among the first of these to appear. He began to publish a biweekly newspaper, *Vraie Parole*, on March 29, 1893, as a reply to Drumont's *Libre Parole*. Kahn helped Singer acquire funds for this paper from Edmond de Rothschild, but no other Jewish banker would help finance the venture. Most Jews who knew of the paper were alarmed at its general criticisms of accumulated wealth. Moreover, the great virtue the grand rabbi saw in it, its scholarly approach, was its most serious defect. Long articles on the history of antisemitism did not prove an effective means either of combatting the *Libre Parole* or maintaining the *Vraie Parole*, which failed within less than a year.[36]

The only other attempts of any significance by Jews to oppose antisemitism openly were the efforts of Joseph Aron and Bernard Lazare. Aron was an American citizen who sought desperately in 1895 and 1896, particularly through Zadoc Kahn, to obtain funds to start a newspaper to attack Drumont and his work. He did found a paper, *Or et l'Argent*, in 1895, but it quickly failed. Infuriated by the fact that most Jews assailed by Drumont even refused to give him information so he might defend them properly, Aron fought on in 1896 by establishing a little bookstore and publishing a series of ten-centime pamphlets, which had a very brief success. After failing in this second venture, Aron disappeared from the scene as an active fighter for democracy.[37]

Bernard Lazare was the most courageous of the Jewish defenders against the assault led by Drumont. Twenty-five years old in 1890, this native of southern France became a literary anarchist and flirted with political anarchism. Convinced by a brief study of the history of antisemitism that the Jews themselves were to a great extent responsible for antisemitism, Lazare was

[36] Isidore Singer, *Anarchie et antisémitisme* (pamphlet) (Paris, 1894), 1–16; *Vraie Parole*, March 29, 1893–June 6, 1893; Henri Avenel, *Annuaire de la presse française*, XIV (1893), 156.

[37] Joseph Aron, *Les Mensonges de Drumont* (pamphlet) (Paris, 1896), 3–9; Aron, *Mon Pauvre Drumont* (pamphlet) (Paris, 1896), 3–4; Aron, *Questions juives en 1896*, 8–26; Anonymous, *Drumont et son oeuvre* (pamphlet) (Paris, 1898), 3–4.

"almost too impartial." He accepted many of the antisemites' charges. In a series of articles he wrote for the *Echo de Paris* and the *Revue de l'époque* in December, 1894, and January, 1895 — after the trial of Captain Dreyfus but before the public ceremony of degradation — Lazare described Drumont as "a man endowed with a violent and excellent instinctive sense of hate. He is animated by an eager thirst for justice and by a Jewish horror of wealth."

In 1896, Lazare served on a board selected by Drumont to select the best proposal made in a contest for the solution to the "Jewish question." This venture served to add an element to his education which Lazare had somehow missed during the decade. From that time forward, he was a vigorous and able opponent of antisemitism and of all injustice. His role in the Dreyfus Affair was one of the most noble, and his death in 1903 was a tragedy for France, for he was one of the few who were steadfast to their principles after the Dreyfusards had acquired political power.[38]

THE JEW IN FRENCH LITERATURE

The background of feeling against the Jew in French literature and legend was one of the most decisive factors in the creation of antisemitism in that country. The tradition of the French stage for over two centuries had been that the Jew be an odious and grotesque person. This literary habit, with its source in Shakespeare's Shylock, made the Jew on stage represent all of the sins of Israel. Even the Romantics, including Hugo and George Sand, had been led by the blind force of custom to continue the caricature. Three of the most interesting and controversial plays produced in France in the decade before the First World War pivoted upon antisemitism. One of them, *Israël*, by Henri Bernstein, was an excellent satire on the antisemites, for it culminated in the suicide of the leading royalist antisemitic agitator, Thibault, when he dis-

[38] André Fontainas, "L'Antisémitisme et Bernard Lazare," *Mercure de France*, CCXLV (1933), 51–63; Alfred de Tarde and Henri Massis (Agathon, *pseud.*), "Les Vraies Causes de l'antisémitisme," *Revue Encyclopédique* (1895), 31–33; Bernard Lazare, *L'Antisémitisme, son histoire et ses causes* (Paris, 1898); Lazare, *Les Juifs en Roumanie* (Paris, 1902); Hagani, *op. cit.*, 10–22.

covered that the principal target of his campaign, Gutlieb, was really his own father.

The other plays, however, were a part of the literary pattern in which the Jews were ridiculed and denounced. Maurice Donnay's *Le Retour de Jérusalem* in 1903 aroused a tremendous controversy. Although Donnay eliminated part of the final scene before the play gave its first public performance, it remained and was rightly considered openly antisemitic. Many French papers accused Donnay of trying to foster feeling against the Jews, even though his rapid rise as a dramatist was due in part to aid given him by various Jewish friends. His heroine, Judith de Chouzé, possessed characteristics which many antisemites agreed were common to all Jews. She was completely selfish, showed no consideration for anyone, even her lover, except her co-religionaires, and helped and praised only Jews and the work of Jews. Albert Guinon's *Décadence*, in 1904, described the rise in French society of the Strohmann family, united and interested only in money and the social advantages money could bring, and the decline of a French family, the Barfleurs, titled, lazy, and so avid of the luxuries the Strohmanns could provide that they quickly yielded to them.[39]

There were a number of novelists whose Jewish characters were more than inherited clichés and who sought, for one reason or another, to produce openly antisemitic tales. A brief survey of a few of the great number of the novels produced by some of these writers will demonstrate. Two of the first open assaults in novel form appeared in 1886, the same year in which Edouard Drumont's *La France juive* unleashed the antisemitic flood. One of these, *Baron Jéhovah*, by Sydney Vigneaux, found the source of Jewish financial power in a planned program for world rule through the establishment of a "central gold council." That same year, a

[39] Henri Bernstein, *Israël* (Paris, 1908); Maurice Donnay, *Le Retour de Jérusalem* (Paris, 1904), preface, 3–33; Maurice Donnay, *Ailleurs!* (Paris, 1908); Albert Guinon, *Décadence* (Paris, 1904); Abraham Dreyfus, "Le Juif au théâtre," *Revue des études juives*, I (1886), 49–71; Moses Debré, *Der Jude in der französischen Literatur von 1800 bis zur Gegenwart* (Ansbach, 1909), 3–8, 71–73.

translation of Adolphe van Cleemputte's *L'Agonie d'une race*, developed a theme which was very frequently used by antisemitic novelists, for it demonstrated how a Jewish banker in Poland took advantage of the love of luxury and the patriotic sacrifices of a great Polish family to succeed to the power and position of the old Christian warriors.

Another good example of the promotion of antisemitism through the novel was Georges Ohnet's *Nemrod et Cie*. Ohnet was a tremendously prolific and popular writer in the 1880's and 1890's, appealing to approximately the same level of maturity as Fanny Hurst or Zane Grey. Ohnet in this novel used one of the great antisemitic legends, for the story revolved around the noble-hearted Marquis de Port-Croix, who had invested his fortune in the great Catholic banking enterprise, the *Union générale*. The failure of this concern in 1882 was ascribed by the antisemites to the Jews, and Ohnet has a Jewish banker who had profited from this crash use some of his "ill-gotten gain" to acquire the marquis' chateau.

Probably the best of these didactic novels was Eugène-Melchior de Vogüé's *Les Morts qui parlent*, which came out at the height of the Dreyfus Affair in 1899. This novel, which Drumont praised repeatedly, described the decline of France under parliamentary government. The Jews were not the direct cause of the decline, but appeared as parasites as the nation went down and hastened its final death.[40]

The most important and influential antisemitic novelist writing during these years was Countess Sibylle Martel de Janville, who used Gyp as a pseudonym. Descended from a royalist family and the daughter of an officer of the papal Zouaves, Gyp had a thorough and intimate knowledge of conservative and aristocratic society. A master of light and satirical prose and poetry, she won

[40] Jules Verne, *Hector Servadec* (Paris, 1877); Sydney Vigneaux, *Baron Jéhovah* (Paris, 1886); Adolphe van Cleemputte (Charles Simond, *pseud.*), *L'Agonie d'une race* (Paris, 1886); Georges Ohnet, *Nemrod et Cie* (Paris, 1892); Eugéne-Melchior de Vogüé, *Les Morts qui parlent* (Paris, 1899); Biez, *op. cit.*, 9; Edouard Drumont, *Sur le Chemin de la vie. Souvenirs* (Paris, 1914), 118; *Bibliographie catholique*, LXXIV (1886), 238.

renown as a novelist, playwright, and journalist. From 1897 through 1902, she was so aroused by the Dreyfus Affair that she wrote daily articles for the antisemitic press and also contributed a half dozen extremely amusing and effective attacks upon the Jews in novel form. Her novels were a perfect counterweight to the more brutal and heavy attacks of Léon Daudet, and she was at least as skilled as Daudet in giving grotesque German names to her Jewish characters, such as Baron Sinai, Ubel de Saint-Abbas, Schlemmer, Klébrig, and Judasfruss. Gyp always wrote about "high society" and the infiltration there of the coarse, ugly, avaricious Jews, particularly through financial pressure and inter-marriage. The subject as well as the manner in which she managed it both contributed to her enormous popularity and influence, and French publishers during those years fought to obtain the right to publish her novels.[41]

It has been pointed out by scholars that the Jewish banker on the whole received better treatment from the French realist novel-ists than the Christian one, for he at least was given family af-fection, while his rivals were completely heartless and incapable of love. Nevertheless, custom provided that the Jew in the French novel be foreign, capitalist, and anticlerical. Novels or plays by antisemites with the avowed purpose of spreading hatred of the Jews usually influenced only a restricted group of readers, but the legend of the foreign, capitalist, and anticlerical Jew when carried by the greatest and most widely read novelists of the day was of tremendous consequence.[42]

Thus, at least four of Paul Adam's novels studied the power and influence of the Jews in France. Each described the Jewish char-acters in such a way as to create antipathy and to demonstrate the

---

[41] Countess Sibylle Martel de Janville (Gyp, *pseud.*), *Le Baron Sinai* (Paris, 1897); *Chansons anti-juives* (Paris, 1898); *Le Chapons* (Paris, 1902); *Les Femmes du Colonel* (Paris, 1899); *Le Friquet* (Paris, 1901); *Israël* (Paris, 1898); *Journal d'un grinchu* (Paris, 1898); Michel Missoffe, *Gyp et ses amis* (Paris, 1932), 19, 87–176; *Libre Parole Illustrée*, February 24, 1894.

[42] Marius Leblond, *La Société française d'après les romanciers* (Paris, 1905), 109–36; Miriam Beard, "Anti-Semitism—Product of Economic Myths," in Isacque Graeber and Stuart Britt, *Jews in a Gentile World* (New York, 1942), 368.

baleful effects Jewish influence was exerting upon the country. The subtitle of his 1890 novel, *L'Essence du soleil*, was *Roman social sur l'or des juifs*, and the novel described the growth of Jewish financial power in France. *Le Mystère des foules* in 1895 showed the idealistic Frenchmen trying to help the people, while the Jews sought power and pleasure. In this novel, the desire of one Jew for another's wife caused war to break out between France and Germany, while in a later one, *Le Troupeau de Clarisse* in 1904, the schemes of a Jewish banker and his mistress led to war in North Africa.[43]

Paul Bourget, perhaps the most important French novelist of the two decades before the First World War, in 1893 published *Cosmopolis*, which examined the moral decline in France and urged a quick return to the old traditions. One of the chief characters in this novel was Baron Justus Hafner, "half Protestant and half Jew." Baron Hafner was remarked because he always managed to save his wealth when his financial schemes failed, although the poor Frenchmen or Austrians who trusted him did not. Moreover, Hafner forced his reluctant daughter upon Prince Ardea, thereby gaining access to the old nobility, through direct financial pressure. Guy de Maupassant's *Mont-Oriol* developed somewhat the same situation, for the novelist here contrasted vividly the parvenu Jewish banker, Andermott, with the French noble, Marquis de Ravenel, whose daughter Christiane was forced to marry Andermott.[44]

The power of the tradition of treating the Jew in the French novel and its influence can be demonstrated most clearly perhaps by examining briefly the attitude of the three great masters of the naturalist novel, Zola, Alphonse Daudet, and Edmond de Goncourt. Zola, who became the symbol for Truth and Justice during the Dreyfus Affair, based *L'Argent* in 1891 largely on the *Union*

---

[43] Paul Adam, *L'Essence du soleil* (Paris, 1890); Adam, *Le Mystère des foules* (Paris, 1895); Adam, *Le Troupeau de Clarisse* (Paris, 1904); Earle Stanley Randall, *The Jewish Character in the French Novel, 1870–1914* (Menasha, Wisconsin, 1941), 64; Mauvrac, *op. cit.*, 175–78.

[44] Paul Bourget, *Cosmopolis* (Paris, 1893); Guy de Maupassant, *Mont-Oriol* (Paris, 1887); Randall, *op. cit.*, 46–53, 172–78.

générale crash, which was a favorite antisemitic legend. His Gundermann has a close resemblance to Rothschild, while Saccard seems to be the unfortunate Catholic banker, Bontoux. Gundermann is the typical Jewish figure, the successful banker with close family ties and a German name, and Zola even uses the term "Jewish High Finance" frequently.

Edmond de Goncourt has no obvious antisemitism in his novels or biographies or in the works on which he collaborated with his brother Jules before the latter's death in 1870. However, the nine-volume *Journal des Goncourt*, which was published between 1888 and 1896, was very widely read. It has a very large number of antisemitic jokes, stories, and remarks, and it reveals that Goncourt was a close friend and admirer of Drumont, although the leader of the antisemites had once denounced him for helping to corrupt France.[45]

The influence of the third great naturalist novelist, Alphonse Daudet, was even greater, for the book which unleashed the antisemitic storm, Edouard Drumont's *La France juive*, might never have been published but for Alphonse Daudet. It was Daudet who introduced Drumont and his book to the relatively new publishing firm of Marpon and Flammarion and who persuaded the hesitant publishers to accept the risk and produce the two volumes. Then, just at the moment when Marpon and Flammarion were deciding that it would be wise quietly to withdraw the volumes, which had attracted almost no attention for ten days or two weeks, Alphonse Daudet again rescued Drumont by persuading his friend Francis Magnard to insert a review into *Figaro* criticizing the book. This review started the press controversy which helped to make Drumont's attack upon the Jews a tremendous success.[46]

[45] Emile Zola, *L'Argent* (Paris, 1891); Edmond and Jules Goncourt, *Journal des Goncourt* (Paris, 1888–1896), VI, 108, 123; VII, 7–8, 34–35, 88, 238, 252, 281–82, 299–300; VIII, 12, 56, 76–78, 91–92, 164, 282–83; IX, 108, 125–26, 163–68, 316, 376.

[46] Madame Alphonse Daudet, *Souvenirs autour d'un group littéraire* (Paris, 1910), 67–69, 109–10, 133; Léon Daudet, *Les Oeuvres dans les hommes* (Paris, 1922), 145–56; Léon Daudet, *Quand vivait mon père* (Paris, 1940), 148, 164–71, 259–60; Drumont, *Souvenirs*, 3–11, 26–31, 76, 120–42; Alfred Gendrot (Jean Drault, *pseud.*), *Drumont, La France juive et la Libre Parole* (Paris, 1935), 5–9; Léon Fauriette, *Drumont* (Paris, 1902), 43–46.

The accepted attitudes towards the Jewess and the rabbi were important exceptions to the traditional and customary treatment of the Jew in French literature and legend. Tradition, since Shakespeare's Rebecca, has ascribed beauty and virtue to the Jewess, and custom has granted the rabbi a heritage of patriotism and bravery. Thus, Fanny Hafner in *Cosmopolis* deserted her unscrupulous father to become a Catholic, while Maupassant's Rachel in *Mademoiselle Fifi* killed the Prussian insulter of French womanhood and was saved by a priest.[47]

3. Antisemitism in France before Drumont

IN 1880, as in 1870, there was apparently very little antisemitism in France. Emancipated nearly a century earlier, the Jews had been assimilated to a great degree and were protected by the French tradition of tolerance. The racial doctrines of Count de Gobineau had been unnoticed in France, while the attempts of Fustel de Coulanges in the 1870's to elevate racial differences to the height of principles to be used in assessing civilizations had been ridiculed and ignored. Moreover, it was a Frenchman, Waddington, who sponsored the emancipation of the Danubian Jews at the Congress of Berlin in 1878.[48]

The French reaction to the Russian pogroms in the early 1880's was severe criticism in the newspapers and in numerous public addresses, and the French were particularly generous in providing financial aid to the persecuted Russian Jews through committees actively led by men such as Renan and Hugo. Cardinal Archbishop Guibert of Paris in June, 1882, gave one thousand francs for aid

[47] Guy de Maupassant, *Mademoiselle Fifi* (Paris, 1883); Maurice Bloch, "La Femme juive dans le roman et au théâtre," *Revue des études juives*, XXIII (1891), 28–49; Kuno Lehrmann's *Das Humanitätsideal der sozialistisch-romantischen Epoche Frankreichs und seine Beziehung zur Judenfrage* (dissertation) (Würzburg, 1932), 40–54 especially, has a fine discussion of this entire issue.

[48] Dr. A. Jellinek, *Franzosen über Juden* (Vienna, 1880), 1–38; Finot, *op. cit.*, 16–17. Richard Andrée, in *Zur Volkskunde der Juden* (Leipzig, 1881), considered the Jewish question in France of such little significance that he omitted a discussion of it.

to the Russian Jews, reproving Russian policy and declaring that he was "only following Church tradition" in aiding the Jews. The French press of all opinions gave very complete information on the infamous ritual murder trial in Hungary in June and July, 1883, and there was general bitter criticism not only of the Hungarian antisemites but also of the supposedly Liberal Hungarian government for not unmasking and thwarting them. Press criticism of the antisemitism of the Algerian Radicals, particularly during the June, 1884, outbreak, was similarly caustic.[49]

Although France was the first European country to emancipate its Jews and although the appearance of antisemitism in France appeared to come with the suddenness of an explosion with the publication of Drumont's *La France juive* in 1886, there had been a considerable amount of writing and some organized feeling directed against the Jews earlier in the nineteenth century. Antisemitism has ordinarily been based on traditional and conservative opposition to the Jews as foreigners, intruders, and innovators. There is no doubt but that this foundation existed in France throughout the nineteenth century, but it was not exploited, with but two or three exceptions, until the appearance of Drumont's book. This was not because the French conservatives were more enlightened than their fellow conservatives elsewhere on the continent. Probably the principal reason antisemitism did not flourish was that no Jews had played a significant role in the Enlightenment in France or in the French Revolution. The French conservatives had a "minority" of Freemasons, freethinkers, and Jacobins upon whom to vent their wrath, so the Jews in France escaped criticism from that quarter until Drumont.

[49] Georges Weill, *L'Europe du dix-neuvième siècle et l'idée du nationalité* (Paris, 1938), 100–104, 300–13, 432–33; Gabriel Jogand-Pagès (Léo Taxil, pseud.), *Monsieur Drumont. Etude psychologique* (Paris, 1890), 14–15; Claude Martin, *Les Israélites algériens de 1830 à 1902* (Paris, 1936), 215–16; Henri Dagan, *L'Oppression des juifs dans l'Europe orientale* (Paris, 1903), 16; Cécile Vincens (Arvède Barine, pseud.), "La Question antisémitique. Le Juif russe peint par lui-même," *Revue politique et littéraire*, third series, XXIX (1882), 716–21; Charles Morel, *Les Juifs et la Hongrie devant l'Europe* (Paris, 1883), 16–37, 59–62.

GOBINEAU AND GOUGENOT DES MOUSSEAUX

The two most striking exceptions to this general conservative attitude, Gobineau and Gougenot des Mousseaux, were not particularly important in France, but the ideas expressed by both of
these men are illustrative. The first of these was Count Joseph
Arthur de Gobineau, whose four-volume *Essai sur l'inégalité des
races humaines* was published between 1853 and 1855. The son of
an officer in Louis XVIII's army, Gobineau was educated in
Switzerland and became deeply interested in ethnology and in
Celtic customs. A poet and a playwright, he became private secretary to Tocqueville in 1844. The great writer and politician
took his aristocratic young aide with him in 1849 when Tocqueville became Minister of Foreign Affairs in the Second Republic.
Tocqueville's career in the ministry was very brief, but Gobineau
remained after his chief left, entering the diplomatic service in the
Second Empire and serving in many European capitals. He was
retired in 1877 without having achieved his great ambition, to
be the French Ambassador at Constantinople, and he died in 1882
in Italy.

Gobineau was a morbid, lonely, pessimistic, and frustrated man.
Extremely conscious of his aristocratic origins and very interested
in the past, he had a great hatred and contempt for the nineteenth
century. He was throughout his life a Catholic, but during the last
decade of his life he became deeply interested in the cult of Odin.
His opinion of human nature was similar to that of Hobbes, and
he thought that man was "evil and weak and degenerating." He
had a very natural hatred for democracy, and he wrote that "all
civilizations that assume democratic forms are speedily ruined."
His *Essai* not only reflects all of these views, but is also one of the
great source books for modern racial theory. His belief was, simply, that there are races clearly distinguishable from each other
and that these races have a hierarchy of merit. Civilizations of
value develop from the white races, and even then only when the
Aryan branches dominate.

Gobineau's book attracted very little attention and interest in

France when it was published. The comments which it drew were almost entirely critical of his principal theme, which was to explain the superiority of the French aristocracy over the mass of Frenchmen by demonstrating that that aristocracy represented pure Aryan stock while the great mass of Frenchmen were "degenerate products of racial intermixture." The criticism was led by Tocqueville, then at the height of his influence, and was buttressed later by Ernest Renan, the greatest Semitic scholar France has produced. A second edition of the book was published in 1884, profiting at that time from the bitterness of the aristocracy at the establishment and policies of the Third Republic, but even then its influence was by no means considerable. A third ripple of interest in Gobineau developed during the Dreyfus Affair, particularly in 1899, but generally very few people in France read him or were influenced by him.

This was not the case, however, in Germany, where after 1871 national consciousness and pride were perverted by some into a glorification of the Aryan race, particularly of its Teutonic branch. Richard Wagner read and admired Gobineau, and they became close friends in 1876. Nietzsche was very much influenced by Gobineau, and German thought in general in the final third of the nineteenth century was widely affected by this French aristocrat. A Gobineau Museum was opened in Strasburg, and a Gobineau Society was founded at Freiburg in 1894. Wagner, Nietzsche, and particularly Houston Stewart Chamberlain carried Gobineau's influence straight through to Rosenberg, Hitler, and the Nazis.[50]

Probably more influential in France, though not in Europe, was a book by Henri Gougenot des Mousseaux, *Le Juif, le judaïsme et le judaïsation des peuples chrétiens*, produced by one of the leading

[50] Robert Dreyfus, *La Vie et les prophéties du comte de Gobineau* (Paris, 1905), 3–10, 84–85, 93–106, 320–322; Alfred Gendrot (Jean Drault, *pseud.*), *Histoire de l'antisémitisme* (Paris, 1942), 93–98; Rohan Butler, *The Roots of National Socialism* (New York, 1942), 135–40; Rudolf Streidl, *Gobineau in der französischen Kritik* (Würzburg, 1935), 33–34; Andrée Combrès, *La Philosophie des races du comte de Gobineau et sa portée actuelle* (Paris, 1938), 163–80; Carlton J. H. Hayes, *A Generation of Materialism, 1871–1900* (New York, 1941), 259–60; Jean Finot, *Le Préjugé des races* (Paris, 1906), 16–24, 107–15.

French publishers, Henri Plon, on the eve of the Vatican Council in 1870. Written by a Catholic aristocrat who was a daily communicant and who called himself "a soldier of Christ," this book had a hearty preface by Father Voisin, head of the Paris Foreign Mission Seminary. Pius IX blessed the author for his courage, while Catholic reviewers, although finding Gougenot des Mousseaux "somewhat exaggerated," were delighted to note his discovery that the perverse Jews were leading the campaign against the Catholic Church.[51]

Gougenot des Mousseaux's book was particularly important because it presented the theme that the Jews were utilizing eighteenth-century liberal ideas and the secret force of Freemasonry to overthrow Christianity and to obtain rule over the entire world. Much of its five hundred and fifty-four pages was a "study" of the Talmud, which supposedly had replaced the Mosaic Law among the Jews and which taught them the most pernicious morality. Roumania, where "the most tolerant and gentle of men" had been forced into antisemitism by the Jews' savage extortion and political domination, was examined as a model, while the defeat of Catholic Austria by Protestant Prussia in 1866 was explained as a Jewish maneuver. This book did receive favorable reviews. Editions of it appeared in Austria and Roumania in 1876, but it did not go beyond a single edition in France until 1886, when Drumont's success led Gougenot des Mousseaux's family to finance another edition. It is important, however, in foreshadowing later French antisemitism and in helping lay the foundation for feeling against the Jews among the Catholics.[52]

THE SOCIALISTS

It was curious but true that most antisemitism in France before 1880 or 1885 came from the Left, not the Right, and that the

[51] Henri Gougenot des Mousseaux, *Le Juif, le judaïsme et le judaïsation des peuples chrétiens* (Paris, 1869), introduction, XXVII; *Polybiblion, Revue bibliographie universelle,* V (1870), 186–88; *Bibliographie catholique,* XLIII (1870), 211–15.
[52] Gougenot des Mousseaux, *op. cit.,* 21–25, 76–241, 333, 349, 357–82, 414–99; Albert Monniot, *Crime rituel chez les juifs* (Paris, 1914), 35, 131–32, 317–24; *Libre Parole,* April 19, 1899.

French Socialists, who claimed to be working for a new society free from all exploitation and discrimination, contributed most to the strengthening and deepening of the antisemitic prejudice in France. This was not because the Socialists in France were impostors or charlatans, but generally because they suffered from two confusions. Many of them, particularly those who believed that Christianity was a profiteer from and a defender of bourgeois society, attacked Judaism and, on occasion, the Jews, because they saw Judaism as the forerunner, parent religion, and spiritual source of Christianity. Another group made the natural but tragic error of selecting Rothschild as the symbol for financial capitalism. When this great banking family name became the symbol for all of the evils of international capitalism, Jews everywhere suffered, for "Rothschild" served also as a symbol of Jewry and Jewish power.

The prominence and significance of confusions such as these are apparent even in the works of the founder of "scientific socialism," Karl Marx, who was himself Jewish, although his father became a convert to Lutheranism and Marx himself was baptized when he was a very young boy. There has been a great deal of speculation on the significance of this part of Marx's background and of the vehemence with which he rejected it. Most historians have neglected this phase of Marx's life, and until recently there has been little study of antisemitism among Jews and antisemitism among the Socialists. However, it is perfectly clear that the collected works and the letters of Marx contain many more invidious and derogatory remarks directed against Judaism, the Jews, and individual Jews than do those of Metternich, Bismarck, or even Mussolini. Moreover, Marx used the word "Jewish" as an epithet to a degree which was not common even among many leaders of the antisemitic parties.[53]

An understanding of the reasons for which the greatest socialist

[53] Otto Rühle, *Karl Marx. His Life and Work* (New York, 1929), 371–97; Leopold Schwarzchild, *The Red Prussian* (New York, 1947), 267–88; Camillo Berneri, *Le Juif antisémite* (Paris, 1935), 8–36, 62–78; Solomon F. Bloom, "Karl Marx and the Jews," *Jewish Social Studies*, IV (1942), 11–12. 15–16.

philosopher, himself a Jew, should have written clearly antisemitic literature will illuminate the entire problem of antisemitism among the nineteenth-century Socialists, as well as illustrate many of the complexities involved in the entire movement. Marx's most significant contribution to this literature was his essay, *Zur Judenfrage*, which he wrote as a book review in 1844 when he was only twenty-six years old. An analysis of this and of his later comments reveals that his opinions and the reasons for them varied somewhat, but substantially Marx's criticism of the Jews and of Judaism can be summarized and explained in the following manner.

Marx wrote *Zur Judenfrage* and became a Socialist in the 1840's, a decade in which Metternich and the conservatives dominated Europe. It was an age in which bankers were assuming great importance in financing the flowering industrialism of many European countries, as well as one in which the same bankers were supporting the Metternich system. Since many of these bankers were Jews and since the Rothschilds at that particular time had tremendous power in England, France, and Austria, a radical, particularly a Socialist, rather naturally became critical of the Jews in being critical of the conservatives and of financiers. Marx did not escape this confusion.

A second reason was that Marx had been deeply influenced by the ideas of the eighteenth century. Many of the great leaders of the Enlightenment, especially Voltaire and Diderot, were sharply antisemitic. Marx not only imbibed this prejudice from them, but he also inherited and developed further their attack upon organized Christianity, which was under prolonged assault from the philosophers in the 1840's. Marx declared that "the emancipation of the Jew is, in its final significance, the emancipation of Mankind from Judaism." He declared that "Christianity sprang out of Judaism. It has again withdrawn into Judaism. The Christian from the outset was the theorizing Jew; the Jew is therefore the practical Christian and the practical Christian has again become a Jew. Christianity has only seemed to overcome real Judaism . . . Christianity is the sublime idea of Judaism. Judaism is the common application of Christianity." His conclusion was that "the political emancipation of the Jew, the Christian, of the religious man in general, means the emancipation of the State from Judaism, Christianity, and from religion generally." [54]

A third factor entering into Marx's attitude towards the Jews derives from Marx's ideas on the process of history and the role of commercial capitalism. He demonstrated that commercial enterprise had a progressive and even revolutionary role when it served to facilitate exchange between two non-capitalistic societies. However, when production had become capitalistic, commercial capitalism lost its revolutionary role and opposed the development of the historical process. Marx as a consequence was extremely critical of commercial and financial enterprise and of those peoples and nations which were commonly associated with commerce and finance. As a consequence, since the Jews had been forced in history to be traders and since it appeared in the nineteenth century that Jews played a very prominent role in finance capital, Marx, and many other Socialists then and later, broadened their criticism into what may fairly be termed antisemitism. This attitude was unfortunately strengthened by the tendency common among most Socialists, especially Marx and his followers, to exalt production to the neglect of distribution. As a result, those associated with distribution were again open to very severe criticism.

The significance of Marx's attitude towards the Jews is difficult to determine. He was probably the most important philosopher and economist of the nineteenth century, and his ideas of course have tremendous currency throughout the world. It is certainly significant, however, that the French Socialist journal, *Humanité nouvelle*, lamenting the public's ignorance of Marx's attitude towards the Jews, should have published a translation of *Zur Judenfrage* in 1898. There could have been no error by the journal on the probable consequences of this act, for in the same year it printed a number of other openly antisemitic articles. One of these articles was particularly clear: "The people are instinctively marching with the antisemites, seeing in them liberators, the heirs of the revolutionary tradition, the real defenders of the

[54] Quoted in Bloom, *loc. cit.*, 8, 12.

Rights of Man and of the citizen. . . ." This was during the height of the Dreyfus Affair, when the French Socialists were debating whether or not they should enter the struggle to save a Jewish army captain, the Third Republic, and the principle of the supremacy of the individual and of justice in society.[55]

The influence of Marx on French socialism was ultimately greater than that of any other Socialist philosopher or organizer, but Charles Fourier and his followers, notably Alphonse Toussenel, were more important than Marx in infecting French socialism with antisemitism. Fourier, who died in 1837, seven years before Marx published *Zur Judenfrage*, was an extreme antisemite, and his attacks upon the Jews contain the full catalogue of charges leveled at them in modern times: usury, avarice, parasitism, deceit, betrayal, intolerance, hostility to assimilation, etc. The reasons for which Fourier betrayed the ideals generally associated with socialism are as obvious as his accusations.

To begin with, Fourier was irritated and incensed by the popularity and the practical success of a rival Socialist group based on the "new Christianity" of Saint-Simon. The Saint-Simonians were few in number, but their influence in the July Monarchy, particularly in reorganizing French industry and promoting railroad development, was very considerable. The leading Saint-Simonians, Rodrigues, Léon Halévy, the Pereires, and Baron Gustave d'Eichthal, were all Jews. Although most of the Jews associated with Saint-Simonianism abandoned Judaism for the "new Christianity" and although there was considerable criticism of this school of socialism from Jewish circles, the Fourierists considered it a rival Jewish movement and sought to discredit it and destroy it.

Fourier, of course, did not reach that conclusion without prior influence. As a child, he had wished to be a military engineer, but his family, which was a wealthy merchant family, succeeded in making him a merchant. Ruined by the fortunes of war in 1793,

[55] Karl Marx, "La Question juive," *Humanité nouvelle*, III (1898), 580–85; Vicomte de Colleville, "L'Antisémitisme et les Droits de l'homme," *Humanité nouvelle*, III (1898), 344–48; Albert Fua, "Paganisme juif," *Humanité nouvelle*, III (1898), 25–32, 296–315; Bloom, *loc. cit.*, 8–16.

when presumably military engineers could have looked forward only to careers of glory and power, Fourier spent much of the rest of his life as a clerk, salesman, and bureaucrat. Both his socialism and his antisemitism are the product of this life. Commerce he considered the source of all iniquities, and Jews he declared were the incarnation of commerce. It is difficult with the information now available to know for certain why Fourrier should have assumed that the Jews were responsible to such a high degree for the sins of commerce, but apparently his career, particularly in Lyon and Marseille, happened to bring him into contact with grasping and unpleasant Jews, as well as with articulate antisemites.[56]

The most literate and influential of the followers of this believer in the utopia of phalansteries was Alphonse Toussenel, whose two-volume *Les Juifs rois de l'époque* was the most significant and effective attack upon the Jews published in France before Drumont's *La France juive*. Toussenel's eruption was published first in 1845, just a year after Marx's essay had appeared and a year before a flurry of pamphlets attacking Rothschild as a banker and railroad promoter appeared in France. A more virulent second edition of this assault upon the new "financial feudalism" was published in 1847, and the volumes were reprinted in 1886 and 1887, immediately following Drumont's initial success. Toussenel influenced Drumont to some degree, and he also helped to found a conservative "landed antisemitism" which was popular and influential in the *Action Française*.

Toussenel's life is interesting as well as informative for understanding his socialism and his antisemitism. He was born in Anjou in 1803 and spent his childhood in rural Lorraine. As a journalist, he was employed on newspapers in Paris, Lille, Toulouse, and Orléans, and he spent three years in Algeria in the early 1840's as a civilian commissioner working with the French army. In other words, by the time he was forty years old, Toussenel

[56] Hubert Bourgin, *Fourier* (Paris, 1905), 31–38; Edmund Silberner, "Charles Fourier on the Jewish Question," *Jewish Social Studies*, VIII (1946), 245–59; Zosa Szajkowski, "The Jewish Saint-Simonians and Socialist Antisemites in France," *Jewish Social Studies*, IX (1947), 33–47.

had seen a great deal of rural and urban France and had also witnessed French imperialism in Algeria.

As a Socialist, Toussenel helped found and edit the Fourierist
newspaper, *Démocratie pacifique*, which criticized the bourgeois
monarchy of Louis Philippe and its imperialism. After the February Revolution in 1848, he was a member of Louis Blanc's
Commission of the Luxembourg, and in 1848 he also helped to
establish a new Socialist newspaper, *Travail Affranchi*. The failure
of the revolution of 1848 apparently disillusioned Toussenel in
socialism, and he spent the last thirty-five years of his long life in
the country, enjoying his hobby, hunting, and writing the books
on ornithology and animal life which earned him the title, "the
Balzac of the animal world." His two-volume *Le Monde des
oiseaux* sold three editions within five years, a remarkable ac-
complishment for a study of bird life, and a volume in 1863 on
hunting was almost as successful.

Toussenel's antisemitism is similar to that of the founder of
the school to which he belonged, Fourier, but it also has some
important differences. Toussenel, as a lover of the woods and
forests and of the animals which lived in them, had the same scorn
for commerce and for merchants which Fourier and Marx had
demonstrated. Moreover, he was also bitter because "Rothschild's railroads" were destroying the hunting preserves. Like
Fourier, he declared that the Jews were the chief sinners in commerce, although he said that for him "Jew, usurer, and merchant"
were synonymous. He developed an additional charge, however,
which is rare among nineteenth-century Socialists in France and
which helps to explain Toussenel's popularity among later conservatives. When most Socialists attacked the Jews as members
of a faith which was the parent of Christianity, Toussenel criticized them because they were anti-Christian. He was probably
influenced in this by his friendship with the great Catholic journalist, Louis Veuillot, with whom he worked on the conservative
paper, *La Paix*, for some time during the 1830's. In any case, this
Socialist asserted that Christians and Jews could not live together

or cooperate, and he cited as proof the "fact" that "most distinguished Jews" were abjuring Judaism.

Toussenel added one other new element to his antisemitism when he declared, "Who says Jew says Protestant." Pointing out that the Old Testament was full of adultery, incest, rape, fraud, treason, murder, and war, he declared that that was the favored book of both the Jews and the Protestants, while the New Testament was preferred by the Catholics. The Protestant nations in Europe, the English, the Dutch, and the Swiss in particular, were "merchants and birds of prey," like the Jews. It is easy to see why the anti-Dreyfusards resurrected the antisemitic, antiforeign, anti-Protestant Toussenel. A monument was erected to this follower of Fourier in his birthplace in 1898, the same year in which antisemitic Socialists reprinted Marx's *Zur Judenfrage*.[57]

Pierre Joseph Proudhon, who was of the same generation as Toussenel and Marx, was another influential antisemitic Socialist who had a great deal of influence later in French history. Proudhon, a very controversial figure whom Professor Schapiro has analyzed as a "harbinger of Fascism," wrote his first and most sensational book in 1840. This volume, *Qu'est-ce que la propriété?*, and Proudhon's answer, "Property is theft," helped establish a reputation for Proudhon in the France of the 1840's, a country deeply and widely discontented and eager for literature critical of the July Monarchy. Proudhon's startling definition has had the same unfortunate consequences as the opening words of Rousseau's *Contrat social* had for the eighteenth-century philosopher, for the misunderstanding and confusion prevalent even today concerning the ideas of both these men, particularly Rousseau, derive in part from the dazzling effect their sensational statements had. Both Proudhon and Rousseau were, in addition, confused thinkers

[57] Alphonse Toussenel, *Les Juifs rois de l'époque* (Paris, 1847 edition), preface, I–XVII; Toussenel, *Le Monde des oiseaux. Ornithologie passionelle* (Paris, 1853–1855); Toussenel, *Tristia, Histoire des misères et des fléaux de la chasse de France* (Paris, 1863), preface, VII–VIII; Louis Thomas, *Alphonse Toussenel. Socialiste national antisémite, 1803–1885* (Paris, 1941), 24–91, 96–129, 161–84; Szajkowski, *loc. cit.*, 47–55; *Polybiblion*, XLVIII (1886), 343; *Libre Parole*, August 12–August 15, 1898.

who were frequently vague and who often revised the meaning of phrases fundamental to their philosophies. Both of them were prophets who looked far ahead of their own generations, and both were "inharmonious genii" and "the great misunderstood" of their generations.

Proudhon was a severe critic of capitalism, particularly finance capitalism, as he saw it develop in France in the middle of the nineteenth century. He was also hostile to the Old Regime, and he was almost as critical of the monarchy, the old landed aristocracy, and the Church as he was of the "new feudality." On all of these issues, and on some others, Proudhon was in essential agreement with most of the contemporary Socialists. However, there are many essential questions on which this frustrated intellectual was in direct opposition to the principal socialist trends, and there are many reasons for which it might be denied that Proudhon should properly be called a Socialist.

Proudhon spoke for the lower middle class, of which he was a member. These "worker-owners," these small tradesmen, artisans, and bureaucrats, found themselves faced by two overwhelming forces, the development of big business and an ambitious new monied aristocracy on one hand and a growing and conscious workers' group on the other. The large business interests, with great influence in the French government between 1830 and 1870, sought to destroy the small merchant and craftsman, while the workers sought higher wages, better working conditions, and greater economic and political power. Proudhon became the spokesman for this threatened lower middle class, and his socialism is largely an attack upon both of the forces grinding against it.

It was rather natural that Proudhon and the lower middle class in the middle of the nineteenth century should see finance capitalism, and not industrial capitalism, as the monster menacing them. Proudhon therefore assaulted banking and the bankers. In his attempt to attack the heavy concentration of property and power while at the same time not destroying the principle of private property, which was vital to the aims of Proudhon and the petty bourgeoisie, Proudhon sought to distinguish property from possession. The latter term he defined as "the private ownership of the instruments of production without the unearned property income received by the functionless stockholder." "Aristocratic property" was to be replaced by "popular possession" through a peaceful revolution carried through simply by the establishment of free credit from a People's Bank, which was to replace the Bank of France. Free credit would enable the middle class then to establish a new order of economic equality.

Proudhon developed this idea during the 1840's. His books and his activity as a radical led to his election to the National Assembly from Paris after the Revolution of 1848. There he introduced a bill to establish this system of free credit, but it was smashed to defeat. In July, 1848, he did succeed in having a fund of three million francs established from which loans could be made, at a rate of 5 percent, to producers' cooperatives. Most of the associations which took advantage of this opportunity failed within a few years, while Proudhon himself was given a three-year jail sentence in 1849 for being excessively critical of the President of the Second Republic, Louis Napoleon.

After 1852, the overtones in Proudhon's thought which made him more antisemitic, more influential among the later antisemites, and, in addition, more clearly a "harbinger of Fascism," became more obvious. He praised the coup d'état of Louis Napoleon in 1851 and urged the dictator to carry through the Proudhon social revolution. As Louis Napoleon ignored his pleas, Proudhon became increasingly bitter. He had never been a democrat, and he had even voted against the constitution establishing the democratic Second Republic. He denounced trade unions, he ridiculed universal suffrage, he glorified war, and he even defended slavery and supported the South in the Civil War. He was also an antisemite.

Proudhon's antisemitism stems from his contempt for the common man and his general antidemocratic attitude. It should be noted, however, that it derives in part also from his aversion to finance capitalism and his belief that the Jews, led by Rothschild, were the masters of French finance, both convictions which were common to many critics of the social system in the 1840's. He "identified capitalists with bankers, and bankers with Jews," and he declared on many occasions that the Jews controlled all power in France.[58]

None of Proudhon's books was as significant in the development of antisemitism as Toussenel's, but the influence of this original thinker was in general far superior to that of any of the other of Drumont's predecessors. The Nazis and the followers of Vichy alike were quick to recognize him as a forerunner of Fascism. His assault upon political democracy, finance capitalism, the Socialists, and the Jews were appreciated after 1933 more than they had been at any time during the nineteenth century.

Even so, Proudhon's ideas had authority in the second half of the nineteenth century. One of his friends published three books attacking the Jews within the first four years after Proudhon's death in 1865. Drumont was strongly influenced by Proudhon, and the Marquis de Morès, "the first national socialist," very clearly derived his free credit scheme from Proudhon. At Proudhon's centennial in 1909, he was lauded by people as diverse as Barrès, Mistral, and Urbain Gohier. Bourget called Proudhon "the first of the nationalists." The eminent Belgian Socialist, Edmond Picard, saluted Proudhon rather than Marx as the founder of international socialism and asserted that Marx had "conquered" Proudhon only through Jewish aid.

Proudhon's influence in France before the First World War was most clear in the extreme Rightist royalist group, the *Action Française*. Maurras joined Barrès and Bourget in praising Proudhon's attack on democracy and his promotion of nationalism. Louis Dimier, another founder of this movement, in his volume, *Les Maîtres de la contre-révolution*, omitted Drumont but declared that Proudhon was second only to Le Play as a counterrevolu-

[58] J. Salwyn Schapiro, "Pierre Joseph Proudhon, Harbinger of Fascism," *American Historical Review*, L (1945), 714-37; Shephard B. Clough, *France. A History of National Economics, 1789-1939* (New York, 1939), 170; Robert C. Binkley, *Realism and Nationalism, 1852-1871* (New York, 1935), 113-19; Szajkowski, *loc. cit.*, 55-56. Most of this material on Proudhon comes from Professor Schapiro's excellent analysis.

tionary social scientist. The bond was acknowledged and made secure when the editors installed a picture of Proudhon in the offices of the movement's newspaper.[59]

Hatred of the Jews was strong among French Socialists during the last years of the Second Empire, but the disaster of 1870 and the Commune in 1871 effectively uprooted and scattered the socialist strength. It was not until just before 1880 that the movement began to revive. One of the effects of the decade had been to reveal new enemies to the Socialists and to sharpen their knowledge of industrial capitalism. As a consequence, antisemitism among them was far weaker in 1880 than it had been during the years from 1840 through 1870.

THE RIGHT

The main current of antisemitism just prior to the explosion of Drumont's book in 1886 was distinctly conservative and Catholic. Many Catholics had been angered by the *Union générale* crash and were strongly provoked by the anticlerical legislation of the Opportunists. However, there was an even more primary source of rancor for many French Catholics and for most French conservatives, the French Revolution itself and the fundamental ideas embodied in the democracy of the Third Republic. One has only to remember that Taine's very influential six-volume *Les Origines de la France contemporaine* appeared between 1871 and 1893 and that this magnificent attack upon the Revolution and its eighteenth-century intellectual roots was but the most able of the numerous books denouncing the overthrow of the old regime. The six years

[59] Willibald Schulze, "War Proudhon Anarchist?" *Deutschlands Erneuerung,* XXIII (1939), 14–21; Georges Duchêne, *La Spéculation devant les tribunaux* (Paris, 1866); Duchêne, *Études sur la féodalité financière* (Paris, 1867); Duchêne, *L'Empire industriel* (Paris, 1869); Edouard Drumont, *Les Tréteaux du succès. Les Héros et les pitres* (Paris, 1900), 267–273; Henri Grégoire and M. C. Poinsot, "Le Centenaire de Proudhon," *Grande Revue,* LIII (1909), 132–143; Louis Dimier, *Les Maîtres de la contre-révolution* (Paris, 1906), 238–251; Charles Maurras, *Dictionnaire politique et critique* (Paris, 1932–1933), IV, 220–223.

of Opportunist rule only intensified conservative and Catholic feeling and widened the gap between *les deux France*.[60]

These conservatives, moreover, had been increasingly inclined since 1865 to ascribe the Revolution, and indeed all adverse ideas and events, to stealthy, occult forces. The prominent role of French Freemasonry in the anticlerical campaign of the Opportunists gave foundation to an attack upon that fellowship, but the new philosophy of history was gradually applied to all of French history. One has only to examine briefly the *Bibliographie catholique* and *Polybiblion*, both Catholic bibliographical journals, or any Catholic periodical, such as the *Revue du monde catholique*, to note this growing inclination.

The legend ascribing the French Revolution, especially its excesses, to Freemasonry was not new to these three decades of the Third Republic. The Jesuit Barruel had begun it while an *émigré* in the 1790's, and Burke's great work also contributed to the conservative myth. The theory acquired solidity gradually through the nineteenth century. Louis Blanc even accepted the legend of Masonic impetus in his *Histoire de la Révolution française*, thus allowing the conservatives to proclaim that their enemies had confessed.[61]

It is this thesis of a secret, organized revolutionary minority which we find expressed in a trickle of books by Catholics, usually priests or bishops, after 1863. By 1886, this trickle had grown into a steady stream, due to the "infamous laws" and to Leo XIII's encyclical of April 20, 1884, which denounced Freemasonry, especially that of France, for its anti-Christian doctrines and legislative influence. Moreover, the Pope divided the human race into "two diverse and adverse classes: the kingdom of God on earth,

[60] Hayes, *op. cit.*, 12–13, 245. Waldemar Gurian's *Die politischen und sozialen Ideen des franzözische Katholizimus, 1789–1914* (Munich, 1928), 266–74, has the finest brief discussion of *les deux France* and the reasons for Catholic anti-Republican feeling.

[61] Albert Lantoine, *La Franc-Maçonnerie dans l'état* (Paris, 1935), 85–91, 97–105, 111–93. Lantoine has an excellent discussion of the theme of Masonic responsibility for the Revolution. By the latter part of the nineteenth century, the Masons themselves adopted the myth and, as good anticlerical Republicans, rejoiced in their triumph. Their books thus furnished new proof for their adversaries.

namely, the true Church of Jesus Christ," and "the realm of Satan." On August 20, 1884, Leo XIII issued a decree of the Inquisition listing the Odd Fellows, the Sons of Temperance, and the Knights of Pythias as "synagogues of Satan." [62]

Thus, from 1872 through 1879, six anti-Masonic books were published, with no more than two in any one year. During the same period, eighteen pamphlets attributing the Revolution and sundry other evils to the Masons appeared. However, from 1880 through 1885, twenty-four anti-Masonic books and twenty-three anti-Masonic pamphlets were produced, revealing a sharp growth in conservative discontent. Of the twenty-seven books written from 1872 through 1885 which were signed, fourteen were by Catholic priests and five by bishops. The remainder were all clearly written by Catholics. The statistics on the pamphlets demonstrate the same conclusion, indicating that this campaign was not only conservative, but clearly Catholic. [63]

The books and articles ascribing all of the misfortunes of France, or of specific groups or interests within France, to secret Masonic influences had several important intellectual characteristics. There was a growing tendency throughout these years to trace the origin of Masonry beyond early eighteenth-century England to various sixteenth-century heresies and even to the Templars or Manicheans, blackening the secret order with every heresy and grievance and attempting to convince by sheer weight and volume. The stricken Catholics added a final touch to the "plot theory" of their misfortunes by describing the enemy fra-

[62] *Actes de Léon XIII* (Paris, 1925–1928), I, 242–77; E. P. Evans, "A Survival of Medieval Credulity," *Popular Science Monthly*, LVI (1900), 577.

[63] Some of these books were tremendously influential, for thousands of copies of some were sold. *La Franc-Maçonnerie et les projets Ferry* (Paris, 1879), by a Jesuit, Frédéric Rouvier, reached its twenty-second edition its first year, while Nicolas Deschamps' three-volume *Les Sociétés secrètes et la société* (Paris, Avignon, 1873–1876) was revised four times. This book had very great influence, especially as revised by Claudio Jannet. A pamphlet by Bishop Louis Besson, *La Franc-Maçonnerie. Instruction pastorale* (Paris, 1878), had enormous diffusion throughout France. [*Bibliographie catholique*, LX (1879), 306–307; LXIII (1881), 173; LXVI (1882), 497–501; LXIX (1884), 58–63; Paul Fesch, Joseph Denais, and René Lay, *Bibliographie de la franc-maçonnerie et des sociétés secrètes* (Paris, 1912–1913), II, 147.]

ternity as an instrument of Satan in his struggle against Christ and
the forces of good. This enabled them to draw a clear line of
distinction between all Christians and the powers of evil and to
call upon all Catholics, whatever their political beliefs, to combat
the Prince of Darkness and his works.[64]

This rationalization of French history not only indicates the
dangerous state of mind or "climate of opinion" of many Catholics
during these years, but it also helped to prepare the way for the
antisemitic movement. The Catholic journals which were anti-
Masonic were the first to publish antisemitic articles and reviews.
The first books attacking the Jews were written by men who had
earlier denounced the Masons; the complaints and charges made
concerning both groups were similar; and, finally, there was a
growing trace of antisemitism in the literature against the Masons
until the two movements had completely joined forces.

A brief examination of a few of these books and their authors
will demonstrate the relation between the "plot theory" and antisemitism. Father Chabauty, a Poitevin country priest who dabbled extensively in prophecy and interpretation of the Apocalypse,
in 1881 published a heavy volume with one six-hundred-page
chapter devoted to Freemasonry. This Catholic priest here declared that Satan was in control of the fraternity and was manipulating it to prepare for the rule of Anti-Christ by destroying the
Christian religion, returning the Jews to Palestine, and establishing
Jewish domination over the world. Catholic reviewers at this time
doubted the "ingenious hypothesis" of assigning the leadership of

[64] The literature on this subject is, of course, tremendous. A few of the most
important books, pamphlets, and articles are: François Gautrelet, *La Franc-
Maçonnerie et la Révolution* (Paris, 1872); Lecamu, "Sociétés secrètes. Franc-
Maçonnerie, charbonnerie, illuminisme, rose-croix," *Revue du monde catholique*, XXXI (1871), 238–57, 599–616; Auguste Onclair, *La Franc-Maçonnerie
dans ses origines* (Paris, Bar-le-Duc, 1874); Edouard Haus, *Le Gnosticisme et
la franc-maçonnerie* (Brussels, 1876); Alexandre de Saint-Albin, "Du Caractère
satanique de la franc-maçonnerie," *Revue du monde catholique*, IX (1877),
319–32; Isidore Bertrand, *La Franc-Maçonnerie. Révélations d'un rose-croix*
(pamphlet) (Paris, Bar-le-Duc, 1877); Bertrand, *Le Pontificat de Pie VI et
l'athéisme révolutionnaire* (Paris, Bar-le-Duc, 1879); Vincent Davin, *Bossuet,
Port Royal et la franc-maçonnerie* (pamphlet) (Paris, 1882); Charles Auber,
Du Démon et de son rôle contre le christianisme (pamphlet) (Paris, 1884);
Guillaume Canet, *La Libre Pensée contemporaine* (Paris, 1885).

Masonry and all of the Masonic scandals to the Jews, although they did agree that the Jews were still the leading enemies of the Church.

A second book published a year later was more openly anti-semitic, even to its title, *Les Juifs, nos maîtres!* Chabauty's theme here was that secret Jewish chiefs led the Jewish nation and all secret societies against Christianity and the Christian nations with the aim of obtaining rule of the world for the Jews. The Catholic reviews in this case were more indulgent, greeting the book as "the best description of the Jews' position today" and as a warning to Catholics of the real war being led against Christian capital. It is both interesting and important to note here that the thesis developed by Chabauty has the rough outlines of the most famous antisemitic hoax of the twentieth century, the Protocols of Zion.[65]

Another important Catholic antisemitic book prior to Drumont illustrates yet more clearly the connection between the older movement against Masonry and rising antisemitism. Father Nicolas Deschamps' original three-volume work on secret societies when published between 1873 and 1876 was a massive blow at pantheistic Masonry, but later editions, as the work was revised by Claudio Jannet, Professor of Political Economy at the Catholic Institute in Paris, show more antisemitism in each succeeding issue. The edition published between 1881 and 1884, for example, quotes Gougenot des Mousseaux and Chabauty with relish and even claims, with no justification, that the original edition had revealed the power of the Jews in Masonry. An abridged volume of Deschamps produced in 1884 with the title, *La Franc-Maçonnerie et la Révolution*, has an even more pronounced

[65] E. A. Chabauty, *Lettres sur les prophètes modernes* (Poitiers, 1872); Chabauty, (Count C. de Saint-André, *pseud.*), *Les Franc-Maçons et les juifs. Sixième Age de l'Eglise d'après l'Apocalypse* (Paris, 1881); Chabauty, *Les Juifs, nos maîtres! Documents et développements nouveaux sur la question juive* (Paris, 1882); Fesch, *op. cit.*, II, 277; John H. Curtiss, *An Appraisal of the Protocols of Zion* (New York, 1942), 62; *Bibliographie catholique*, LXIV (1882), 198–201; LXVII (1883), 398–401; *Polybiblion*, XXXVII (1883), 140–41. Some of Chabauty's books on prophecy were put on the Index. [*Catalogue général des livres imprimés de la Bibliothèque Nationale* (Paris, 1897–1950), XXV, 1047].

strain of feeling against the Jews, showing very clearly the trend.[66]

This Catholic thread of antisemitism in France derived a considerable amount of propulsion from a bank failure in 1882 which created a great mass of disgruntled Catholic investors as well as a myth of omnipotent Jewish financial power which was to be of great service during the coming years. This financial disaster was contemporary with the rigorous campaign of the anticlericals against the Church, and it strengthened the belief of thousands of thrifty Frenchmen that Jewish power was harmful and dangerous in France.

The *Union générale* bank was organized and directed by Eugène Bontoux, who had left the employ of Rothschild in 1878 because of his taste for more hazardous financial practice. Bontoux within a few short years developed this enterprise into a financial power capitalized at one and one-half billion francs and with very strong and profitable railroad interests in central and eastern Europe, particularly Austria. A fervent Catholic, a frequent contributor to the great Catholic journal, *Le Correspondant*, and a close friend of Chambord, Bontoux was considered the legitimists' banker. He had successfully resisted the attempt of many of his aides to name the enterprise the *Banque catholique*, but in 1881 he was preparing a fund, the *Trésor de Saint-Pierre*, to finance a great Catholic propaganda campaign against the anticlericals. Moreover, the *Union générale* board of directors was composed of leading monarchists and Catholics, including the Prince de Broglie, Eugène Veuillot, the editor of the Catholic paper *Univers*, and Viscount de Mayol de Luppé, editor of the legitimist *Union*.[67]

Bontoux not only disturbed political interests with his Catholic bank, but he also made it the avowed opponent of the alleged financial monopoly of the Jews and Protestants. His supporters

[66] Nicolas Deschamps, *Les Sociétés secrètes et la société* (Paris, 1881–1884 edition), II, 415–17; III, 22–27; Claudio Jannet and Louis d'Estampes, *La Franc-Maçonnerie et la Révolution* (Paris, Avignon, 1884).

[67] Eugène Bontoux, *Union générale. Sa Vie, sa mort, son programme* (Paris, 1888), 242–46; Marcel Marion, *Histoire financière de la France depuis 1715* (Paris, 1914–1931), VI, 38–39; Gabriel Terrail (Mermeix, *pseud.*), *Les Antisémites en France* (Paris, 1892), 30–34; Emile Mermet, *Annuaire de la presse française*, I (1880), 691; *Catalogue général*, XVI, 83.

were Catholics of all types, from Paris aristocrats who wanted to be members of the new Catholic plutocracy to conservative bourgeoisie and country priests, all dazzled by the hope of profits in a real Catholic enterprise. Bontoux had four successful years, and by January 5, 1882, the stock had risen from its par value of 500 francs to a peak of 2,500 francs. The Catholic banker was "the Napoleon of the hour, with even Gambetta second to him." Within less than a month, however, the bank had collapsed and all of its eager clients had discovered that they were merely participants in "a second edition of Law's Mississippi failure." [68]

The consequences of the *Union générale* failure were tremendous. Bontoux in newspaper interviews given before he fled to Spain blamed the Jews for the crash, and his supporters, people largely ignorant of financial affairs and prey at such a time to extravagancies, reiterated this view. "Merchants, workers, clerks, janitors" gathered outside the firm's doors in their anxiety over their investments. Viscount de Vogüe, the French ambassador in St. Petersburg who had followed the bank's career closely, wrote in his diary even before the actual declaration of bankruptcy that the firm had been "killed by the Jews." Catholic newspapers and journals, such as *Univers* and the *Revue du monde Catholique*, immediately sprang to the defense of Bontoux and his collaborators. They blamed the disaster upon Jewish machinations but quietly forgot the affair when a judicial investigation in December, 1882, revealed that the bank had caused its own downfall by its wild speculation and the squandering of its reserve in a futile attempt to oppose the general trend downward of the entire stock exchange.[69]

The crash of the *Union générale* not only fostered antisemitism

[68] Terrail, *op. cit.*, 21, 38–39; Arthur Meyer, *Ce que mes yeux ont vu* (Paris, 1911), 335–36; Félix de Vogüé (ed.), *Journal du Vicomte Eugène-Marie-Melchior de Vogüé* (Paris, 1932), 280; Bontoux, *op. cit.*, 144.

[69] Alexandre Zévaès, *Ombres et silhouettes. Notes, mémoires et souvenirs* (Paris, 1928), 12–14; Charles Buet, "Causerie économique," *Revue du monde catholique*, LXIX (1882), 467–68; Marion, *op. cit.*, VI, 38–39; Terrail, *op. cit.*, 38–39; Vogüé, *op. cit.*, 269–70, 280–91; *Univers*, February 4, 1882. Albert Haus in his "Chronique rurale et financière" in the *Revue du monde catholique*, LXVII (1879), 772–73, had urged his readers to support such Catholic enterprises as the *Union générale*.

among those directly affected by it but also became a very important part of the French antisemitic legend. Bontoux returned from Spain in 1888 to publish his account of the disaster. Though this book certainly presented no proof of Jewish responsibility, its sale reached eight editions, the highest for any of the attacks upon the Jews except those of Drumont. There are frequent references to the disaster in antisemitic books and newspapers, and Drumont's first three books in particular very skillfully utilized this fable in the campaign against the Jews.[70]

Happily, the *Union générale* myth is one which can now be completely exposed. The antisemitic leaders and propagandists themselves had so little faith in their version of the disaster that their frequent references to it were usually very vague, while Drumont continually sought to buttress the charge of Jewish machinations. His original account of the bank's failure was highly critical of Bontoux and his associates for not revealing more detailed evidence of the responsibility of "Rothschild and his gang." The Catholic banker's brief statement in *Figaro* on October 22, 1886, also disappointed the antisemitic leader, while Bontoux's book in 1888 evaded the issue by declaring that it was "useless to name those responsible." In two important editorials devoted to the incident in 1899 during the height of the Dreyfus crisis, Drumont confessed that he had not yet obtained clear proof of the partiality of the courts or of the responsibility of Rothschild. Twenty years after the bank had failed, Drumont and the aged Bontoux were still bickering in the press because of the latter's refusal to publish "the vital documents." [71]

[70] Drumont, *La France juive*, II, 101–104; Drumont, *La France juive devant l'opinion* (Paris, 1886), 72–95; Drumont, *La Fin d'un monde* (Paris, 1888), 44–46; Mermet, *Annuaire de la presse française*, I (1880), 691; II (1881), 1155; III (1882), 55; IV (1883), 1098–1106. See also, Auguste Chirac, *Les Rois de la République* (Paris, 1886), 123–24; Emile Cazanove, *La Révolution antijuive de demain* (pamphlet) (Paris, 1904), 49–62.

[71] The *Libre Parole* editorials of January 4 and 5, 1899, are reprinted in Paul Marin's *Quesnay de Beaurepaire?* (Paris, 1899), 77–84, 90–96, while the *Libre Parole* articles of August 17, 1902, and October 17, 1902, are reprinted in Cazanove, *op. cit.*, 52–55, and the *Almanach Agenda de la Libre Parole, 1903* (Paris, 1903), 247–49.

The reasons for the failure of the *Union générale* are rather numerous and complex. The crash of the bank represents in part the economic crisis which had affected France as well as the rest of Europe since 1877. It reflects more closely still the immediate economic situation in France, for 1881 was distinguished by a depression in French agriculture, the ravaging of the vineyards by phylloxera, an unstable national budget, and by a rage of speculation in a disorganized stock market. Moreover, the public works program begun in 1878 was heavily curtailed in 1881, when the economy most needed it. It was apparent late in 1881 to many government and business leaders, including Bontoux, that a crash in the stock market could be anticipated, but the government was powerless. Bontoux had sufficient shrewdness to sell most of his own stock two months before the crash, but the policy he adopted for the bank itself precipitated its destruction.

Bontoux was a great authority on trade and railroad transportation in eastern Europe. A skilled and successful engineer and promoter, he had written several volumes and numbers of articles on eastern European railroads and their future. He had very close contacts with important individuals in the governments of Austria, Serbia, Roumania, and Turkey, and his successes by 1878 made him the Lesseps of railroad construction outside of France. He was one of the board of directors of the *Union générale* when the company was formed in June, 1878, and in August, 1878, he became the president. The firm had been capitalized originally at twenty-five million francs, but that figure had risen to one hundred and fifty million francs by the fall of 1881, with a new issue of fifty million francs to be added on February 3, 1881.

Making use of the engineering studies he had made and of his personal acquaintances scattered throughout eastern European governments, Bontoux made the *Union générale* a very profitable venture. Almost all of the firm's investments were successful, so handsomely profitable that other French banking concerns were attracted to the same area. When the *Banque de Lyon et de Loire* threatened the *Union générale* by attracting funds from Lyon

Catholics and by developing a keen interest in Austrian railroad construction, the *Union générale* crushed the rival with a three-week bear campaign in December, 1881.

This operation occurred at the very time that French business interests, alarmed by Gambetta's government, were supporting his parliamentary enemies and causing a fall in the *rentes*. Then, early in January, 1882, Lebaudy and other speculators turned the bear movement, which the *Union générale* had begun, against Suez Company stock, beginning a general decline. Here Bontoux and his associates made their great error. Instead of drifting with the current, as such a powerful corporation could easily have done, they used the bank's reserve funds to support the market price of the stock, hoping to maintain its high level for the new issue which was to appear in February. This attempt to resist the trend of the market naturally resulted in the concentration of all of the bears against the lone weak and willful concern.[72]

It was at this juncture that the political situation became decisive. The *Union générale* was to hold a regular stockholders' meeting on February 3, and it is possible that the shareholders would have bolstered the tottering enterprise with sufficient funds. However, the Gambetta ministry fell on January 26 and was replaced on January 30 by one headed by Freycinet. A single investor protested when he could not withdraw his funds from the stricken bank, and an ambitious radical deputy then prepared an interpellation of the ministry. Fearing the attack of the extreme anticlericals if it allowed such a clearly Catholic corporation to recover, the Freycinet government intervened one day after the bank "voluntarily suspended payments" and two days before the meeting. Bontoux was arrested, and ten days later the bank was in receivership.

The suddenness with which the proud enterprise had collapsed and the apparently high-handed conduct of the ministry in cutting

[72] Claudio Jannet, *Le Capital, la speculation et la finance au dix-neuvième siècle* (Paris, 1892), 160, 179, 346, 395, 570; Auguste Chirac, "L'Agiotage de 1870 à 1884," *Revue Socialiste*, I (1887), 150–58; Terrail, *op. cit.*, 23–29; Marion, *op. cit.*, VI, 38–39. Chirac and Jannet were both antisemitic, one a Socialist and the other a Catholic professor, so their views here are particularly important.

off its hopes of recovery thus gave further impetus to the fable of the Christian firm ruined by the omnipotent Rothschild and his lackeys in the stock exchange and the government. Although there were no Jews involved in this disaster and although Bontoux's reckless policy was responsible for the bank's collapse, the Jews and "their" government were held responsible in the antisemitic myth.[73]

Although the campaign against Masonry had obtained a considerable hold upon the mind of the Catholic population in France, and although the legend of the *Union générale* failure had caused a lasting impression, it is quite evident that antisemitism in 1885 was still weak and ineffectual. None of the recent Socialist attacks upon the Jews was read except by friends of the authors, while Chabauty's books did not circulate widely. As a result of the weakness of the libel clauses in the 1881 press law, there were three attempts between 1882 and 1884 to found antisemitic papers in Paris, and Chabauty sought to establish one in Montdidier. None of them succeeded. The *Anti-Juif* produced only three issues in December, 1881, while the *Antisémitique* in 1883 lasted only ten weeks, and its 1884 successor, the *Péril Social*, disappeared even more quickly.[74]

Yet thoughtful observers agreed that France should hesitate before she ridiculed other countries for their relapse into the old hatred. At least one observer on the eve of the publication of Drumont's book predicted that the wave of antisemitism would soon sweep through France. The anticlerical and anti-Masonic

[73] Joseph Reinach, *Le Ministère Gambetta. Histoire et doctrine, 14 novembre 1881–26 janvier 1882* (Paris, 1884), 221–37; André Lajeune-Vilar, *La Bande opportuniste. Moeurs et tripotages du monde politique* (Paris, 1896), 12–17; Léonce Reynaud, *Les Juifs français devant l'opinion* (Paris, 1887), 149–66; Bontoux, *op. cit.*, 11–195; Terrail, *op. cit.*, 29–30, 33–38; Jannet, *op. cit.*, 395; *Univers*, February 4, February 12, 1882.

[74] Salomon Reinach, *Cultes, mythes et réligions* (Paris, 1923), V, 436; Gustave Rouanet, *Les Complicités du Panama* (Paris, 1893), 193; Joseph Jacobs, *The Jewish Question. 1875–1884. A Bibliographical Handlist* (London, 1884), 57; Julien Weill, *Zadoc Kahn* (Paris, 1912), 110; Drumont, *La France juive*, I, 135; II, 223; Mermet, *Annuaire de la presse française*, III (1882), 64; V (1884), XX–XXI, LX; Raymond Felix, "L'Infamie," *Revue Socialiste*, I (1889), 630–31; Benoît Malon, "La France juive," *Revue Socialiste*, I (1886), 506.

campaign, the *Union générale* crash and the Déroulède League, the confusion so evident among many Socialists, and the general discontent which led to Boulangism as well as to antisemitism all provided the perfect setting for the explosion which *La France juive* was to provide in 1886.[75]

[75] Cécile Vincens (Arvède Barine, *pseud.*), "La Question antisémitique en Galicie," *Revue politique et littéraire,* third series, XXVIII (1881), 811–14; Pierre Douhaire, "Le Sémitisme en France," *Le Correspondant,* CXXXVIII (1885), 938–46.

III

THE STORM BREAKS: DRUMONT AND

"LA FRANCE JUIVE"

ANTISEMITISM really burst into prominence in the Third Republic with the publication of Edouard Drumont's two-volume, twelve-hundred-page *La France juive* on April 14, 1886, just three months after Boulanger became Minister of War and three months before Boulanger's great triumph at the July 14 review. The sudden and simultaneous success of both men derives from many of the same causes, and there is a great parallel and even a close connection between Boulangism and the early years of Drumont's antisemitism. It is also very evident that Drumont's violent assault upon the Jews was perfectly timed. A year earlier discontent had not yet reached sufficient depth or clarity, and there was still hope among all parties that the approaching elections would be a decisive victory. A year later France had entrusted her hopes far too lavishly to the handsome general to favor a second suitor.

1. The Theme of *La France Juive*

DRUMONT'S theme was that the Jew throughout French history had been the primary cause of the misfortunes of France, especially those since 1870. He placed his antisemitism frankly on the racial basis of the idealistic, chivalric, Christian Aryan versus the materialistic, sordid, corrupt, Talmudic Jew. Shakespeare for him was thus "the Aryan par excellence who throws himself into the blue, the dream," while Dumas *fils*, half Jewish, could not but have a materialistic conception of life.[1]

The first one hundred and forty pages of this important work were devoted to proving that the Aryan race alone possessed the "notion of justice, the sentiment of good, and the idea of liberty," while the Semites, who had never produced a man of genius or a work of art, were distinguished from their handsome rivals by the hooked nose, the eager fingers, and the unpleasant odor. The Jews, moreover, were by nature spies, traitors, criminals, and carriers of disease, thriving because of the careless, happy tolerance of the Christian Aryans. Later antisemites have added little to Drumont's racial lore but a pseudoscientific basis, which Drumont tried to supply with a racial interpretation of the art and literature by and about Jews.[2]

Following his opening chapter on the two races, Drumont launched into a long antisemitic version of French history. This not only allowed him to strengthen his thesis in terms of sheer volume, but it also enabled him to burden the Jews with the onus for the Albigensian heresy, the depravity of the Templars, and the mediaeval epidemics, and to glorify such beneficent episodes as the Spanish Inquisition and the expulsion of the Jews from France in 1394. After asserting that every Protestant was half-Jew and that Protestantism was only a Jewish device for re-entering Christian society, he disclosed the sly hand of the Jews and Freemasons in the ejection of the Jesuits, the execution of Louis XVI, and the victorious coalition against Napoleon. Saint-Simonianism was a Jewish artifice to lift the Jews from their moral ghetto, while the War of 1870 was the most successful financial speculation ever manipulated, contrived by German Jews to obtain French gold to support the new German paper currency.

[1] Edouard Drumont, *La France juive* (Paris, 1886), I, 225–28.
[2] *Ibid.*, I, 3–143, especially 5–12, 27–53, 70–98; II, 434.

Such was the history of France according to the new prophet of antisemitism.[3]

Almost half of the second volume of *La France juive* is a beautifully executed diatribe on *Paris juive* and French society. Blending the righteous indignation and denunciation of an Amos with the "thorough" knowledge of that society's conduct now typical of the American columnist, Drumont here produced two hundred and forty pages of magnificent invective on the servility and immorality of the luxury-loving upper classes of Paris. This was not wholly a blind attack upon Drumont's natural supporters, but an essential part of his thesis, for the Jews, naturally, had corrupted these French Christians in order that they might more easily rule France.[4]

The purpose behind *La France juive* was plainly to denounce the Third Republic and its Jews for the "infamous laws." The final third of the first volume and the final half of the second volume are smashing attacks upon anticlericalism. The new history of France since 1871 depicted the Republicans being led by an Italian Jew, Gambetta, against the stupid monarchists and doddering Celt, MacMahon. Carefully including every scandal or adventure which blemished the Republic's record, Drumont lashed out in wild rage at the originator of the famous slogan of the anticlericals. Nor were the Jews alone in being assailed as enemies of the Church, for the Masons and Protestants each received separate attention as allies of the Semites in their perpetual war against God.[5]

An illustrated edition of Drumont's work published in 1887 offers striking proof of the clerical bait he was offering to the discontented Catholics. The advertisements for this portrayed Drumont as a second Charles Martel, clad in shining armor and attacking the nineteenth-century Saracens of the bank and stock exchange, while the cover of this edition showed Drumont, carrying

[3] *Ibid.*, I, 143–384, especially 155–62, 173–89, 194–99, 265–83, 332–34, 351–58, 374–84.
[4] *Ibid.*, II, 73–317.
[5] *Ibid.*, I, 430–35, 451–54, 468–518, 533–58; II, 315–577. Gambetta, incidentally, was not a Jew.

a cross, stomping upon an old man who was holding the tables of Sinai. Published by Gautier, one of the leading Catholic publishing houses, this edition had three illustrations of ritual murder, one of Huguenot atrocities, and three of Jewish and Masonic responsibility for anticlericalism. The closing illustration depicted the pious Drumont, prayer beads in his hand, saying a devout Our Father and Hail Mary for France.[6]

2. Edouard Drumont

A STUDY of the life and writings prior to 1886 of the French antisemitic leader reveals a great deal about his book and about French antisemitism. Born in Paris in 1844, Drumont was the son of a poor City Hall copy clerk. His mother was a niece of Alexander Buchon, the celebrated authority on the crusades and the French chroniclers, while his father had once been a student at the *Ecole des Chartes*, where apparently he did not demonstrate adequate ability. His father became the secretary of Buchon, who obtained for him the City Hall position when he married Buchon's niece. Drumont's paternal grandfather had been a handworker in Lille, while his maternal grandfather had deserted his family of fifteen and fled to California. He himself confesses that he never saw his harried parents waste a sou, and his mother and father, both Republicans under the Second Empire, worried constantly lest his father's reading aloud of Hugo be heard in the next flat and cost him his little job. Drumont never lost his fear of poverty, and he always kept his money hidden in crannies around his home so he could reach it easily.[7]

The antisemitic leader had a fair education, for his father and

[6] Edouard Drumont, *La France juive* (Paris, 1887), III, 721, 745, 769, 777, 784–85, 817, 857, 889; J. de Penboch, *Demain, Réponse à La Fin d'un monde de M. Edouard Drumont* (Paris, 1889), preface, XIII; Alfred Gendrot (Jean Drault, *pseud.*), *Drumont, La France juive et la Libre Parole* (Paris, 1935), 15; *Anti-Juif* (Algiers), March 20, 1890.

[7] Edouard Drumont, *La Dernière Bataille* (Paris, 1890), 222–32; Georges Bernanos, *La Grande Peur des bien-pensants. Edouard Drumont* (Paris, 1931), 16–17, 34–44, 523; Léon Daudet, *Les Oeuvres dans les hommes* (Paris, 1922), 184; Raphaël Viau, *Vingt Ans d'antisémitisme, 1889–1909* (Paris, 1910), 224. Drumont was always considered a poor spender by his friends.

mother were well read and his father was able to obtain a few years of free schooling for him at the *Lycée Charlemagne*, where he was a classmate of Lavisse. He was not able to acquire a university education, however, and although he posed as a scholar and was very proud of his ability to read Latin with ease, he had a deep fear that he would be a failure as his father had been. His father died in 1861, and the young man of seventeen had then to accept a hated clerical position in the City Hall. After six months of lazy torture, he left this dull work and entered his true vocation, journalism. After the *Moniteur du Bâtiment* and the *Presse Théâtrale* had proved unable to provide for his ambitions, he became a traveling salesman. Following his dismal failure as a salesman, he returned to journalism, writing for a number of newspapers and journals, including *Le Diable à quatre* and the *Inflexible*, where it is apparent that Drumont served as a police agent or government spy late in the Second Empire.[8]

Drumont in 1898 told a young reporter who was interviewing him that in his twenties he had been extremely unhappy. He was convinced that he had talent, that he should one day write a great work, and that he should exercise great influence on French opinion, but his progress seemed slow. His first real opportunity came in May, 1869, when he was twenty-five, for the young art and literary critic "found happiness for the first time" when he became a member of the staff of Emile de Girardin's famous paper, *Liberté*, after he had heaped lavish praise upon Girardin in the *Chronique Illustrée*. He remained with this paper until the outbreak of war in 1870 and then again from 1872 until December 28, 1885, though most of that time it was owned by the Pereires.[9]

The answer to the query why this French journalist, writing for

---

[8] Drumont, *La Dernière Bataille*, 210–52, 270–99; Henri d'Alméras, *Avant la gloire. Leurs Débuts* (Paris, 1903), 110–25; Stéphane Arnoulin, *M. Edouard Drumont et les Jésuites* (Paris, 1902), 28–69. Arnoulin quotes Drumont's articles in these short-lived papers as well as contemporary comment on his responsibility for them made by *Gaulois, Figaro*, and *Univers*.

[9] Édouard Drumont, *La France juive devant l'opinion* (Paris, 1886), 176–81; Drumont, *Sur le Chemin de la vie. Souvenirs* (Paris, 1914), 51–56; Drumont, *La Dernière Bataille*, 299; Arnoulin, *op. cit.*, 73–78, 89–92; *Libre Parole*, August 30, 1898.

a left-center, Saint-Simonian newspaper owned by a great Jewish family, the Pereires, should become an antisemite and publish *La France juive* in 1886 is in miniature an explanation of the anti-semitic movement. Journalism between 1860 and 1885 was a difficult trade, for the success of each newspaper ordinarily rested upon the talent and fame of one famed writer, who naturally reaped most of the reward. Modern journalism, with its greater variety of information and services, its more specialized staff, and its large circulation, was just beginning, so that the struggle for recognition by a young journalist was a very trying one. Drumont, for example, never had a respectable position until he became es-tablished on the *Liberté*. Even though important critics thought that he produced remarkable articles there, his salary was so little that he had to write for other newspapers and journals to maintain himself. He was never successful in his desire to become art and literary critic for *Univers* or *Figaro*. His only publication previous to 1886 which produced any income was a one-act play, written in collaboration with Aimé Dollfuss, the city editor of a paper for which Drumont wrote, the *Bien Public*. The two men together received 250 francs for this play, which, one should note, was produced through the intercession of Dumas *fils*, whom Drumont later denounced for being half-Jewish, and which was published by Calmann-Lévy. In other words, when *La France juive* was published in 1886, Drumont was a hard-working, re-spectable, ambitious, but frustrated journalist who believed that his great talents had been blunted and ignored because of forces beyond his control.[10]

The intellectual development revealed by his early writings is a very essential aid to the understanding of Drumont. Perhaps the most obvious attitude in all of his work, particularly before *La France juive*, when antisemitism became an obsession, is the great love he demonstrated for the past of France. It is quite clear that this love for the ancient charms of France and of Paris in particu-

[10] Edouard Drumont and Aimé Dollfuss, *Je déjeune à midi* (Paris, 1875); Drumont, *La France juive devant l'opinion*, 66; Drumont, *Les Trétaux du succès. Les Héros et les pitres* (Paris, 1900), 110; Drumont, *Souvenirs*, 9-11; Bernanos, *op. cit.*, 100; Emile Mermet, *Annuaire de la presse française*, III (1882), 790.

lar, as well as the vicious nationalism which later derived from it, were strengthened and increased by the fact that Drumont was a lone and lonely man. He was an only child, his parents both died when he was still a very young man, he married when he was thirty-eight only to have his wife die three years later, and he had no children, no close relatives, and no close friends, even at the height of his popularity and power.

The first newspaper article by Drumont available is one written in 1865, when he was twenty-one, describing affectionately a very poor glove-making section in mediaeval Paris. Many of his *Liberté* articles during the 1870's described the old city, and these formed the basis for an important book he published in 1878, *Mon Vieux Paris*. This volume, which is a delightful picture of the architectural and historical charms of Paris, is the only one of Drumont's early books which attracted attention. The very next year Drumont produced a loving picture of the enthusiastic, fraternal French people at their varied celebrations, while in 1880 he had printed an unpublished journal of Louis XIV's time and some unpublished papers of the Duke de Saint-Simon. When he produced a second collection of articles on mediaeval Paris in 1897, the antisemitic leader himself remarked that these early writings represented just "a dreamy and artistic stage of my life," succeeded by a militant one.[11]

Drumont's love for "old France" and especially for "old Paris" is marked by another significant personal trait, sentimentality, which in its anti-intellectual aspects is also typical of the entire antisemitic movement. His only novel, *Le Dernier des Tremolin*, which was published in 1878, has a strong tinge of this sentimentalism, which later became one of his most valuable techniques as a propagandist. In this novel, Drumont's hero, after gambling away his mother's fortune, escaped execution for murdering his rapacious, free-thinking uncle only at the last moment when the real murderer confessed. He then gallantly gave his

[11] Edouard Drumont, *Mon Vieux Paris* (Paris, 1878); Drumont, *Les Fêtes nationales à Paris* (Paris, 1879); Drumont, *La Mort de Louis XIV. Journal des Anthoine, publié pour la première fois* (Paris, 1880); Drumont, *Mon Vieux Paris*, second series (Paris, 1897), preface, II; Drumont, *Souvenirs*, 47–50; Gabriel Hanotaux, *Mon Temps* (Paris, 1935–1938), II, 18–19.

newly inherited fortune to his mother and marched off to war against the Prussians, falling before Paris the same day his mother died.

The rage Drumont demonstrated towards the Eiffel Tower for dominating his Paris and replacing the old charms of Paris as the city's trademark was marked from the construction of the tower until Drumont's death by a sentimental fury. Almost invariably, when he denounced Jewish bankers, industrialists, or social leaders, he introduced stories about the tragedies of poverty. In a denunciation of Rothschild, he would introduce a tearful tale concerning a poverty-stricken, desperate mother who had thrown herself into the Seine with her baby because they were both starving. In denouncing the courts for failing to convict a Jewish banker, he would describe the suicide of an old woman who, having been imprisoned for stealing food for cats she befriended, killed herself when she returned to her dark room from prison to find that the cats had eaten each other.[12]

It seems evident that just as the Catholics were prepared for antisemitism by their growing inclination to accept the Satanic "plot theory" of their misfortunes, so were Drumont and the movement he led influenced and characterized by his remarkable superstitions. An amateur palmist, Drumont in 1881 wrote an article on the lines of Gambetta's right hand, predicting a catastrophe from them. In 1890 he crowned his denunciation of Boulanger by declaring that the lines of the general's hands lacked any signs by which one recognized a superior person. It became a custom of his to read the palms of his friends just before any hazardous venture, such as a duel, and slack *Libre Parole* reporters often had their critical editor-in-chief discover signs of laziness in their Mount Jupiter or Saturnian.[13]

[12] Edouard Drumont, *Le Dernier des Tremolin* (Paris, 1878); Drumont, "Le Mouvement littéraire," *Le Livre*, V (1884), 1-5.

[13] Drumont, *La Dernière Bataille*, 159-62, 264, 512-13, 516-17; Drumont, *Les Tréteaux du succès. Figures de bronze ou statues de neige* (Paris, 1900), 335-36; Viau, *op. cit.*, 60, 363-66. See also, Drumont, *Souvenirs*, preface, VIII; Edmond and Jules Goncourt, *Journal des Goncourt. Mémoires de la vie littéraire* (Paris, 1888-1896), VII, 127-28; Léon Fauriette, *Drumont* (Paris, 1902), 29; Jules Guérin, *Les Trafiquants de l'antisémitisme* (Paris, 1906), 13.

Drumont not only carried a mandrake root and believed seers and prophets, but he also had the leader of the French spiritualists as one of his closest friends and the city editor of his newspaper during most of its existence. Gaston Méry had been drawn into the war against the Jews by Jacques de Biez, Drumont's first convert, and during the early 1890's he had wanted to rouse a Holy War of the Celts against the Latins. Leaving palmistry to Drumont, he was a graphologist and the leading publicist of the prophetesses who appeared in France during these years. One of his discoveries, a Mlle Couédon, who was considered a descendant of the Man in the Iron Mask, interrupted her predictions of dire catastrophes and the return of the monarchy to inform a disturbed Drumont in 1896 that he would be President of the Third Republic within a decade. His seers and his books about them became so popular that in 1897 Méry and another member of the staff of Drumont's newspaper, Eugène Cravoisier, founded a journal devoted entirely to sorcery, *L'Echo du merveilleux*.[14]

Not only did the new spiritualist monthly receive free advertising in Drumont's newspaper, but Drumont also aided his collaborators in their venture by contributing articles to the journal and by writing a fervent preface to Méry's book about his first protégées. Sensible Frenchmen must have been much amused by some of Méry's antics, especially by his duel for the honor of Mlle Couédon, and by one of his most famous discoveries, a Father Schnoebelin. This unfrocked priest was the great specialist in removing ghosts from haunted houses and in exorcising "the Mexican devil" from children by means of his magic sword.[15]

The love for the past of France and for the hearty French people found in Drumont's early books is a harbinger of nationalism, and the extreme credulity revealed by these extraordinary beliefs and practices is typical of the anti-intellectualism so characteristic of the antisemitic movement. However, another component, one

[14] Gendrot, *op. cit.*, 84–85, 221, 297; Guérin, *op. cit.*, 402–406, 431–32; Henri Avenel, *Annuaire de la presse française*, XVIII (1897), IX.
[15] Gaston Méry, *La Voyante de la rue de Paradis* (Paris, 1897), I, 8–64, 91–97, 103–104, 180–92; II, 67–128, 182–92; Viau, *op. cit.*, 73, 109–11, 146–53, 282; *Libre Parole Illustrée*, January 23, March 13, 1897.

connected with the ringing assault upon the Jews as the leaders of anticlericalism, had to be added before Drumont became an antisemite.

Drumont had been born a Catholic, but like so many other French Catholics, he had fallen away from the Church after his first communion and confirmation. Between 1865 and 1867, he had been a literary critic for the *Revue du monde catholique* and for Henri Lasserre de Monzie's *Revue contemporaine*, both great Catholic journals. The reviews and articles which the young Drumont wrote for these journals demonstrate a lively appreciation for the role which the Catholic Church had played in French history and attack such critics of the Church and its creed as Voltaire and Renan. The great editor of the *Revue contemporaine* almost brought Drumont back to an active profession of Catholicism, but it was more than a decade before he returned to the devout practice of his religion.[16]

It is significant that between 1879 and 1885, the period of Opportunist rule, Drumont both rejoined the Catholic Church and became an antisemite. Although his novel, published in 1878, is a very Catholic one and was highly praised by Catholic journals, in that year he had neither been converted yet nor become aware of what he later called "the Jewish problem." Catholic journals, which ceased to publish his articles in 1867, published a number of essays and reviews by Drumont during the 1880's, the first article appearing in *Le Correspondant* late in 1880.

It should be clearly stated that Drumont in the truest sense never really became a Catholic, for he had no thorough understanding of his creed — and no true Catholic can become an antisemite. His friends described him as "an historical Catholic," and Drumont late in his life admitted that this was so and that throughout his life he had known only one Catholic who had submitted his faith to a rational test before accepting it definitively. By 1882, however, Drumont had become such a fervent Catholic, at least emo-

---

[16] Drumont, *La Dernière Bataille*, 266–89; Drumont, *Souvenirs*, 14, 20–25; Bernanos, *op. cit.*, 127–33, 226; Arnoulin, *op. cit.*, 19–22; Fauriette, *op. cit.*, 26–37; *Revue du monde catholique*, XII (1865), 547–50; XVII (1866–1867), 147–68, 828–48; XVIII (1867), 176–82.

tionally and politically, that in February of that year he dueled Charles Laurent of the *Paris* for the latter's articles denouncing the defenceless Benedictines and urging their expulsion from France. Later in that same year he married his mistress in a religious ceremony.

Drumont himself has asserted that he became an antisemite when the Catholic monks were ousted in 1881, making the connection in his case between anticlericalism and antisemitism perfectly clear. It is apparent from his articles describing the services of the *Bibliothèque Nationale* and from the friends whose memoirs mention seeing him in that great library constantly after 1880 that the planning and research for *La France juive* must surely have been begun in 1880 or 1881. During the summer of 1884, the busy journalist traveled to Canterbury to submit the major part of this tremendous twelve-hundred-page work to his wealthy Jesuit friend, Father du Lac, who examined the manuscript to make certain that no theological errors had slipped in.[17]

Drumont's first published attacks upon the Jews appeared in 1884 in his literary column in the scholarly journal, *Le Livre*. It is significant that the first assault declared that the Jews "have destroyed the foundations of Christian society, if not of Christianity," and that the second accused them of destroying honest journalism and impoverishing native French journalists. During the early 1880's, all of Drumont's values were being reversed. He became a staunch defender of Louis XIV and Pius IX, whom earlier he had accused of ruining the French monarchy and the Catholic Church, respectively. His old literary idols, Hugo and Flaubert, began to feel his wrath, and contemporary science was declared to be an empty fraud. Napoleon III, whom he had earlier denounced, was portrayed sympathetically, and the history of France since 1870 was declared "purely destructive and negative."

[17] Drumont, *Souvenirs*, 26–31, 76, 120–42; Drumont, *La France juive*, II, 276, 460–61; Drumont, *La Dernière Bataille*, 321; Drumont, "Le Premier Architecte des Tuileries," *Le Correspondant*, CXXI (1880), 946–64; Drumont, "Le Mouvement littéraire," *Le Livre*, V (1884), 609–15; VI (1885), 260–62; Bernanos, *op. cit.*, 128–30; Jules Soury, *Campagne nationaliste, 1899–1901* (Paris, 1902), 120–22; Maurice Talmeyr, "Souvenirs de la comédie humaine," *Le Correspondant*, CCCIX (1927), 684–86.

An 1885 article in the *Revue de la Révolution,* which had been founded in 1883 "to disabuse readers of the false principles of the Revolution and its deplorable consequences," was Drumont's first major attack upon the Jews. This claimed that the crown jewels stolen shortly before the Revolution had been taken by the Masons and Jews and used by them to bribe the Duke of Brunswick and to organize Jacobin anticlericalism. Shortly after this article had appeared in pamphlet form, Drumont, whose invalid wife died in the fall of 1885, completed the two volumes, resigned from the *Liberté,* and accepted a position with a Catholic newspaper, the *Monde.* The approaching publication was announced to his friends early in January, and *La France juive* appeared on the shelves of Marpon and Flammarion, a new publishing house, on April 14, 1886.[18]

3. The Publication of *La France Juive*

THE success of *La France juive* was tremendous, especially when one considers that the book trade as a whole then was not thriving. Several publishers had refused to handle the two-volume tract, and it was only through the intercession of Alphonse Daudet that a new firm, Marpon and Flammarion, was persuaded to publish the attack upon the Jews. This publishing house, established in 1874, had gambled in 1880 by expanding enormously. This proved a very successful risk until 1882, when a recession struck France following the collapse of the *Union générale.* The years 1884 and 1885 were very poor ones for the firm, which was seeking desperately in 1885 to acquire a great writer to ensure its survival and continued progress.

Charles Marpon, who was the senior partner, believed *La France juive* might be an enormous success, but at the same time

[18] Edouard Drumont, "Le Mouvement littéraire," *Le Livre,* V (1884), 139–44, 200–205; VI (1885), 290; Drumont, *Souvenirs,* 26–31, 83–93; Drumont, *Le Vol des diamants de la couronne au garde-meuble* (pamphlet) (Paris, 1885); Gendrot, *op. cit.,* 27; Goncourt, *op. cit.,* VII, 101; Arnoulin, *op. cit.,* 97–99. The Goncourt entry for January 5, 1886, describes the book as one "written to satisfy the sincere hatred felt by a Catholic reactionary for the full and insolent triumph of the Republican Jewry."

he feared that it might cause such an outcry that the concern would be forever discredited. He was afraid, too, that the book might lead to a series of libel suits which would bankrupt the firm. At this juncture, Alphonse Daudet, the celebrated and successful naturalist novelist, who had introduced his close friend Drumont and *La France juive* to Marpon, persuaded Marpon to accept the risk and to produce the two volumes.

Alphonse Daudet in 1885 was one of the most prominent French writers, and he hàd a great deal of influence with French publishers, all of whom were eager to obtain publishing rights to his works. He had been a friend of Drumont since the early 1870's. He had obtained a position for Drumont on the staff of a newspaper edited by his brother, Ernest Daudet. Drumont was a frequent visitor in the Daudet apartment, and it was Drumont who taught his son, Léon Daudet, later an able disciple and a founder of the *Action Française*, how to duel. Alphonse Daudet was a sentimentalist, as any reader of *Fromont jeune et Risler aîné* or of *Jack* knows, and he was also a firm believer in the significance for France of her traditions and of what he called "her racial roots." His advice to young novelists was always to return to tradition and to the soil. It seems clear that he was in full agreement with Drumont's thesis and that he acted both as a friend and as a supporter of the antisemite when he urged Marpon and Flammarion to publish *La France juive*.

It is likely that one of the principal reasons Marpon and Flammarion agreed to Daudet's request was the fact that Daudet at that same time was contracting to allow the shaken firm to add his most successful early novels to its reprint library. From 1886 until Daudet's death in 1897, Marpon and Flammarion published more of Daudet's new writings than any other publisher in France, and by 1927 the company had sold more than one million eight hundred thousand copies of his books.[19]

[19] Madame Alphonse Daudet, *Souvenirs autour d'un group littéraire* (Paris, 1910), 67-69, 109-10, 133; Léon Daudet, *Alphonse Daudet* (Paris, 1898), 48-55, 102-109; Léon Daudet, *Les Oeuvres dans les hommes* (Paris, 1922), 145-56; Léon Daudet, *Quand vivait mon père* (Paris, 1940), 59-60, 148, 164-71, 259-60; Drumont, *Souvenirs*, 3-11, 26-31, 76, 120-42; Drumont, *La France juive*, II, 276,

Marpon was very reluctant to accept the risk of publishing *La France juive*, even when urged by one of the most successful French novelists of the era. When Drumont agreed to pay all the expenses of printing the first edition of two thousand copies, to meet all litigation expenses, and to accept a very low percentage for his own royalties, Marpon finally agreed. Drumont then gave the firm eight thousand francs from his savings to finance the printing, stored twenty-five copies in a friend's home because he feared the police might seize and destroy the entire edition, and then prayed daily in his parish church as he waited for the public reaction.[20]

Only twenty-five copies of *La France juive* were sold during the first week. For ten days or two weeks, the book attracted almost no attention from book critics. Léon Daudet, a great friend of Drumont and at that time a young man of nineteen, watched the piles of copies stand untouched and unnoticed in the publishers' windows. Just at the time when Marpon was deciding that it would be wise quietly to withdraw the volumes, Alphonse Daudet again rescued Drumont by persuading Francis Magnard to insert a review in *Figaro* criticizing the book. This review termed Drumont a credulous fanatic and hinted that the Archbishop of Paris was financing him. Catholic newspapers such as *Univers, Croix,* and the *Monde* printed the Archbishop's denial and praised the efforts of "this respectful son of the Church." When *Figaro,* the *Journal des Débats, Lanterne,* and other important papers began to denounce the book, the Catholic dailies willingly accepted its de-

---

460–61; Drumont, *La Dernière Bataille,* 321; Goncourt, *op. cit.,* VII, 101; Margret Schwesinger, *Die literarischen und buchhändlerischen Erfolge des naturalistischen Roman des 19. Jahrh. im französischen Publikum* (Miltenberg-am-Main, 1935), 12–20, 36–60. Marpon's suspicions concerning possible trials were correct, for there were a number of suits, one of which cost Drumont eight thousand francs (Drumont, *La Dernière Bataille,* 405–16).

[20] Edouard Drumont, *La Fin d'un monde* (Paris, 1888), 522; Drumont, *Le Testament d'un antisémite* (Paris, 1891), 415–16; Goncourt, *op. cit.,* VII, 78–79; Georges Renard, *Les Travailleurs du livres et du journal* (Paris, 1926), II, 204; *Almanach de la Libre Parole, 1893* (Paris, 1893), 17–19; Octave Uzanne, "Vieux Airs. Jeunes Paroles," *Le Livre,* V (1884), 750.

fense, Drumont's cause naturally profiting from the exchange.[21]

Other reviews drew increasing attention to the new crusade. Ferdinand Brunetière, in his inane discussion of the book in the *Revue des Deux Mondes*, agreed that Drumont did exaggerate but asserted that he was correct in attributing the wicked materialism of French life to the Jews. Anatole France, in one of his first articles for *Temps*, ridiculed the book for its "savage words" and its return to the old solutions of exile and confiscation, but an earlier review in the same paper had declared that the solution to the Jewish question was that the "real" Frenchmen oust the Jews from their strongholds by being better merchants and bankers.[22]

The *Echo de Paris*, which was known then as "the officers' paper," *Autorité*, and *Voltaire* recommended *La France juive*, while the second of Drumont's duels over it gave it tremendous publicity. During the duel, Arthur Meyer, who had challenged Drumont because of the charges the book made against him, seized Drumont's weapon while they were *corps à corps* and wounded the handicapped antisemite. A subsequent trial evoked wide press comment, with the leading Paris papers printing long interviews with the seconds and fencing experts. Interest in the book became so great that some people mentioned in it felt compelled to issue public denials of the charges made concerning their racial ancestry.[23]

The book profited enormously from the press controversy which soon began to rage around it after Magnard's article. Once the controversy had drawn attention to the book, it swept Paris and France. The first edition melted away, and the publishers

[21] Gendrot, *op. cit.*, 5–9; Drumont, *La France juive devant l'opinion*, 13–17; Arnoulin, *op. cit.*, 155–58; *Univers*, April 21–April 24, 1886. This paper was extremely valuable because it reprinted the comments of other Paris dailies.

[22] C. Braibant, *Le Secret d'Anatole France* (Paris, 1935), 49–51; Ferdinand Brunetière, "La France juive," *Revue des Deux Mondes*, LXXIV (1886), 693–704; Benoît Malon, "La France juive," *Revue Socialiste*, I (1886), 514.

[23] Claudio Jannet, *Le Capital, la spéculation et la finance au dix-neuvième siècle* (Paris, 1892), 546–47; *Polybiblion*, XLVI (1886), 462; *Univers*, April 25–May 24, 1886.

kept eight presses busy to meet the demand. Within two months, more than seventy thousand copies had been sold, and before the end of 1886 more than a hundred thousand copies had spread the gospel of antisemitism throughout France. Idle cabmen read it while waiting for fares, and clerks read it at their counters. The *Petit Journal*, which then had the largest circulation in France, gave copies as contest prizes and published the book in installments, while some large industrialists presented free copies to all the priests in their regions. Drumont himself was so impressed by the immediate success of his two volumes that he attempted to continue the campaign with a daily newspaper, significantly entitled *La Croisade*. It should be noted too that *Le Pilori*, the most violent of the anti-Republican illustrated newspapers of that era and one which had from the beginning strong traces of antisemitism, first appeared less than two weeks after the publication of Drumont's book.[24]

Drumont brought into his antisemitic books both the racy, journalistic style and the eagerness to bluster and offend which had been characteristic of some of his earlier writings. His antics in 1886 unfortunately did not receive the careful analysis from critics that the other works had. His offensive style and attitude contributed greatly to the effect his book produced, just as he had planned. When the *Monde* editorial board was shown *La France juive* shortly before its publication, he was asked to suppress the "unjust passages and the excessive solutions suggested." His reply is surely revealing, for he informed his fellow-workers that a moderate book would have no effect and that the essential point was to strike hard.[25]

Drumont's volumes were not only skillfully written, but they

[24] Drumont, *La Fin d'un monde*, 206; Goncourt, *op. cit.*, VII, 126; Jacques de Biez, *La Question juive* (Paris, 1886), 17–19, 27; Charles Droulers, *Le Marquis de Morès, 1858–1896* (Paris, 1932), 97; Salomon Reinach (L'Archiviste, pseud.), *Drumont et Dreyfus. Etudes sur la Libre Parole* (Paris, 1899), 12; Antonin Debidour, *L'Eglise catholique et l'Etat sous la troisième République, 1870–1906* (Paris, 1906–1909), I, 377; Baron E. van Caloen, "La France juive," *Magasin littéraire et scientifique*, II (1887), 685.

[25] Quoted by Arnoulin, *op. cit.*, 155–56, from Baron Alphonse de Claye's article in the *Monde* of April 26, 1886. The *Monde* agreed that the book had been done "with French fury" and vigorous hatred.

were an expert blend of true and false. He scattered attractive anecdotes throughout his works, giving them an interesting concrete and personal element which Toussenel and other predecessors had lacked. Moreover, his books were indexed so that individuals such as Rothschild or Deutz could be easily checked. Provincial readers were attracted by his intimate descriptions of Paris society at its worst, while romantic souls enjoyed his mystical treatment of mediaeval France and of the beauties of the countryside. At the same time, Drumont's lofty pretensions to being the successor to Carlyle and Taine gave him a false halo of scholarship and learning, though he obviously accepted everything against the Jews uncritically and eagerly generalized from rare incidents.

La France juive not only became the most widely read book in France, but it also prepared the way for a whole series of books by Drumont on the same theme. *La France juive devant l'opinion*, originally planned as a pamphlet but published as a book late in the same year, sold forty thousand copies within five years, while *La Fin d'un monde*, published late in 1888, and *La Dernière Bataille*, which appeared in March, 1890, sold seventy thousand and eighty thousand copies, respectively, by 1891.

A three-volume illustrated edition of *La France juive* was published in 1887 for twelve francs, and that same year an abridged edition appeared for half the price of the original, designed by Drumont to reach the peasant and worker. He and his publishers also seized this opportunity to produce another edition of his unsuccessful novel, while translations of *La France juive* soon appeared in Germany, Spain, Italy, Poland, and the United States.[26]

Thus, during the four years following the appearance of Drumont's first book, the antisemitic seeds were carried into all corners of France. Some interesting examples illustrate the effect it produced. Alfred Gendrot's parents, who read *Figaro* and the Bonapartist *Pays*, praised Drumont's works but disliked his

[26] Edouard Drumont, *La France juive* (Paris, 1887); Drumont, *Le Dernier des Tremolin* (Paris, 1887); Drumont, *Le Testament d'un antisémite*, 417–418, page opposite title page.

reiterated attacks upon Rothschild, their rampart of social conservatism. Raphaël Viau, then twenty-five years old and a vague
Socialist, immediately became an antisemite. Two weeks after
reading the book, he founded an antisemitic paper in Nantes
which lasted over a year. Léon Daudet "saw through all democratic eye-wash" when he read it, while Monsignor d'Hulst, the
eminent vicar general of Paris and Rector of the Catholic Institute, wrote in his letters that he considered Drumont's books
honest and tolerant efforts. The Goncourts, who confessed that
they had been worried for twenty years by the Rothschilds'
growing power in France, were frightened by the picture Drumont gave of the tremendous hold the Jews had upon France,
while Louis Dimier was so excited by the book that he could not
sit still.[27]

Almost the moment that Drumont's blow struck the Jews in the
Third Republic, other antisemites rose to attack the national
enemies by speech, book, and pamphlet. Jacques de Biez, a Republican journalist, within a month after the publication of *La
France juive* lectured against the Jews in one of the largest audi-
toriums of Paris, while Auguste Chirac drew applause from even
the conservative Catholics with his philippics. Before the end of
May, three more books against the Jews had appeared. One, by
a Jew who had become a Catholic priest, presented the thesis that
the Revolution and the Rights of Man had made the breach
through which the Jews had swarmed to power, while the others,
one in novel form, were in essence merely recapitulations of
Drumont's theme.[28]

[27] Henri Dagan, *Enquête sur l'antisémitisme* (Paris, 1899), 92–95; Léon
Daudet, *Au Temps de Judas, 1880–1908* (Paris, 1920), 134; Alfred Baudrillart,
Vie de Monsignor d'Hulst (Paris, 1925), I, 346; Louis Dimier, *Souvenirs d'action
publique et d'université* (Paris, 1920), 90–91; Gendrot, *op. cit.,* 11–14; Viau, *op.
cit.,* 1–4; Goncourt, *op. cit.,* VII, 121. See also, Maurice Barrès, *Mes Cahiers*
(Paris, 1929–1936), II, 248; Charles Maurras, *Au Signe de flore. Souvenirs de
vie politique* (Paris, 1931), 31; Arthur Meyer, *Ce que je peux dire* (Paris, 1912),
245.
[28] Joseph Lémann, *L'Entrée des israélites dans la société française et les
états chrétiens* (Paris, 1886); Sydney Vigneaux, *Baron Jéhovah* (Paris, 1886);
Biez, *La Question juive,* 123–24; Auguste Chirac, "Lettre à Drumont," *Revue
Socialiste,* I (1887), 84–85.

In 1885, Chirac's *Les Rois de la République* and novels by Charnacé and d'Orcet had been the only books preaching hatred of the Jews, but before the end of 1889 Drumont had released a flood of thirty-five books and twenty-three pamphlets. A third of these books may be discounted as hasty novels or unimportant digests of interest only to rabid antisemites or collectors of anti-semitica. However, after forty years of neglect, Alphonse Tous-senel's *Les Juifs rois de l'époque* was successfully revived in 1886, selling three more editions. Gougenot des Mousseaux's family, which believed that the Jews had purchased all of the original edition and then poisoned the author in 1876, also published a new edition of his volume immediately after Drumont's success.[29]

Perhaps a few statistics will best show how solidly Drumont's campaign in a few short years had established the Jews as the lead-ing French scapegoat. Literature attacking the Jews rose from an annual average of less than one publication from 1879 through 1885 to fifteen in 1886, fourteen in 1887, nine in 1888, and twenty in 1889. Attacks upon the Masons, on the other hand, fell from an annual average of nine from 1879 through 1886 to six in 1887, five in 1888, and one in 1889. Drumont had thus contributed greatly to the clarification of the antithesis between Catholic, conserva-tive, and monarchical France and radical and Republican France. Moreover, the introduction of this serious antisemitic movement into the French political and social scene had much influence on the increase in animosity in French politics in the 1890's, con-tributing as a consequence to the great strain on the democratic processes in France which made the Dreyfus Affair possible.

[29] Alphonse Toussenel, *Les Juifs rois de l'époque* (Paris, 1886); Henri Gougenot des Mousseaux, *Le Juif, le judaïsme et la judaïsation des peuples chrétiens* (Paris, 1886), preface; *Bibliographie catholique*, LXXIV (1886), 213–17; *Polybiblion*, XLVIII (1886), 343. Toussenel, incidentally, died only in May, 1886. [Avenel, *op. cit.*, VII (1886), 773–74.]

IV

"THE REVOLUTIONARY WORKER"

D RUMONT in *La France juive* stated that the regime he attacked weighed most upon "the revolutionary worker and the conservative Christian." From 1886 on, he sought to develop an economic and social program which was both radical and conservative, so as to keep the major wings of the movement united. Some antisemites stumbled vaguely towards a national socialism, which might have provided them a sure foundation, but no one succeeded in developing a binding program. As a consequence, most French Socialists by 1891 or 1892 had forsaken the movement, although the Dreyfus Affair was to call many back until the spring of 1898. In addition, many French Catholics by 1892 had discovered that any "radical" movement, even one directed against "the enemies of the Church" might be dangerous for all Catholics. Those Catholics still antisemitic in 1894 were confused and embittered by the maneuvers of Drumont, who became violently anticlerical as his Catholic supporters deserted him.

1. The Socialist Strand of Antisemitism: *Revue Socialiste*

THE main strand of French feeling against the Jews during the 1880's and 1890's was Catholic, but there was also a clear socialist thread. This was due in part to the heritage of socialist anti-semitism described earlier, and in part to the confusion then apparent in the minds of many Socialists between Jewish bankers and capitalism. The antireligious thought so typical of continental socialism in the nineteenth century was another cause, for this led them to hate Judaism, the forerunner of what many Socialists considered the great bulwark of capitalism, Christianity. Thus, one of the most important books against the Jews in the few years previous to Drumont was a posthumous publication written by an atheistic communard, Gustave Tridon, who attacked "the parasitic, intolerant Semitic people" and ridiculed their "idolatrous religion." He asserted that the pernicious Semitic spirit, as illustrated by both Judaism and Christianity, was the cause of capitalism and its evils.[1]

When the independent and scholarly *Revue Socialiste* began to appear in 1885, it featured studies of speculation and banking by editor Benoît Malon and by Auguste Chirac, who called himself an Independent Socialist. Dealing with financial history since 1815, they emphasized the dominance of Jews in French capitalism. Chirac in particular stressed the Jewish character of French banking, indicating that since 1815 the Protestant and Catholic financiers had been conquered by the Jews.

The second strain of antisemitism prominent in this journal was of the antireligious nature. Malon and Albert Regnard compared the spiritual bankruptcy of Christianity and Judaism with "the pure morals of Aryan philosophy." It was this dual heritage and the crushing impact of *La France juive* upon French society which caused the journal's equivocal attitude towards Drumont's antisemitism until early in 1890.[2]

Each of Drumont's first three books received two long reviews.

[1] Gustave Tridon, *Du Molochisme juif* (Brussels, 1884), especially 5-32, 155-212.

[2] *Revue Socialiste*: Benoît Malon, "Les Progrès de l'agiotage," I (1885), 101-23; Auguste Chirac, "La Haute Banque dans la politique," II (1885), 693-704; Chirac, "L'Agiotage de 1870 à 1884," (October, 1885-January, 1887); Albert Regnard's review of Tridon's *Du Molochisme juif*, II (1885), 637; Malon, "Les Morales religieuses: Judaïsme, Christianisme," I (1886), 1-18, 108-28; Albert Regnard, "Aryens et Sémites. Le Bilan de Christianisme et du Judaïsme," (June, 1887-February, 1889).

Though the criticism of his clericalism and of his distinction between capitalism and Jewish capitalism was clearly expressed,
Malon and Gustave Rouanet showed increasing responsiveness
to Drumont's attitude towards socialism and his vehement attacks upon the Jewish "financial feudality." After the publication
and success of Drumont's first book, Chirac's articles on speculation became noticeably more antisemitic. His *Les Rois de la
République*, published originally in 1885, was twice revised, each
time becoming a more vigorous attack upon the Jews, receiving
better reviews, and also selling more copies. By 1888, Drumont,
Malon, and Chirac had become close friends. Drumont often
discussed his coming books with them and attended their Socialist
meetings.[3]

Though one of the three public addresses made against Drumont's antisemitism in 1886 was given by a Socialist, other
Socialists were led by Drumont's denunciation of the evils of
finance capitalism and French imperialism into manifestations of
feeling against the Jews. On June 3, 1886, Jules Guesde, Susini,
and Paul Lafargue in a Socialist meeting at Chateau d'Eau declared that "the real Republic will not exist until the day that
Rothschild is at Mazas [a prison in Paris] or before the firing
squad." The Socialist *Cri du peuple* asserted that liquidation of the
Jews' fortunes would be just recuperation, not pillage. This newspaper, which was founded in October, 1883, by Jules Vallès as a
"revolutionary socialist tribunal" and to which Guesde was a
frequent contributor, had declared even before Drumont's book
appeared that "the social question is the Jewish question." It
became one of the most significant vehicles for injecting antisemitism into the French socialist movement.[4]

[3] Edouard Drumont, *La Fin d'un monde* (Paris, 1888), 122–25; Drumont, *Les
Tréteaux du succès. Figures de bronze ou statues de neige* (Paris, 1900), 356;
Auguste Chirac, *Les Rois de la République* (Paris, 1886), 15, 27, 193, 236, 242–
46, 275, 297–347, 396–400; *Revue Socialiste*, I (1886), 480, 505–14; II (1887),
481–87; II (1888), 560, 661–66.
[4] Jules Guesde, *Etat politique et morale de classe* (Paris, 1901), 400–405, 438–
44; Compère-Morel, *Jules Guesde* (Paris, 1937), 276–301; Edouard Drumont,
La France juive devant l'opinion (Paris, 1886), 149–61; *Alliance Anti-Israélite
Universelle* (pamphlet) (Paris, 1887), 1–22.

2. The Development of Drumont's Ideas

A DESCRIPTION of the predominant attitudes and ideas of Drumont as they developed from 1886 through 1890 will help demonstrate why some of the French Socialists were charmed temporarily by antisemitism. Probably because of the influence his Republican parents had exercised upon him, Drumont did not discover the heart of the Jewish question in the principles of the Revolution, which were the foundation of the Third Republic, but in the misuse of the Republic by the Jews and Opportunists. In a pamphlet he wrote in 1869 on Richard Wagner, Drumont noted with some satisfaction that Wagner, "as all intelligent people," had been a Republican in 1848. Drumont's 1879 volume on French national celebrations had praised the Revolution's early burst of fraternity and then had only mildly criticized the violence of 1793. At that time, the Third Republic itself was immune from criticism, and he appeared to hope that the French people would obtain the ideal Republic his father had wanted.[5]

The account of French history since 1870 in *La France juive* assigned major responsibility for the failure to re-establish the monarchy to Chambord. Though Drumont declares he wept during Chambord's illness, he ridiculed the pretender for his timidity and the Count of Paris for his American materialism. Moreover, a good share of the second volume was devoted to a blistering impeachment of the immorality and stupidity of the decadent French nobility and upper bourgeoisie, and the very important preface to the entire work was a vigorous denunciation of these natural supporters of monarchy as "a finished generation."[6]

Since Drumont believed that the failure of the royalists during the first decade of the Republic and the death of Chambord in 1883 had destroyed the possibility of the restoration of the monarchy, he had of necessity to accept the Republic or to advocate

[5] Edouard Drumont, *Richard Wagner, l'homme et le musicien* (pamphlet) (Paris, 1869), 7; Drumont, *Les Fêtes nationales à Paris* (Paris, 1879), unpaged.
[6] Edouard Drumont, *La France juive* (Paris, 1886), preface, d–s; I, 265–304, 440–49; II, 72–85, 90–93, 107–108, 155–86, 283–88.

some new type of polity. However, one of the most remarkable facts concerning the political theory of the French antisemites was their failure to suggest serious constitutional reforms for the Republican system or to endorse another form of government. In his most precise statement, Drumont left the ultimate decision to the revolutionary workers' government, which was to select "the régime most fitting for all." Throughout his career, he flirted with the royalists, especially during crises when the Republic was shaken. However, his general position was that action be taken against the Jews within the framework of a Republican form of government and that a modified type of that form of government be retained after his "revision of the Revolution." [7]

The electoral programs of the antisemites were always remarkably vague concerning political principles, and even the Dreyfus Affair failed to unite them behind a common political policy. The antisemitic clubs and leagues all urged adoption of practical methods for weakening the Jews' financial power and for obtaining control of France through parliamentary processes, but they were never clear what political course their revolution then was to take. Perhaps the finest illustration of the indeterminate nature of their views was the decision late in 1896 to form a federation of all organizations campaigning against the Jews. This "federation of free and independent clubs" endorsed no specific political principles, allowed each organization its particular beliefs, and postponed the decision concerning the form of government until after the antisemites had conquered.[8]

Until the Dreyfus Affair roused most French Socialists to the defense of the Republic, Drumont's antisemitic movement masqueraded as a kind of socialism. This position was a very clever disguise, for it won to antisemitism many Christians who could not accept orthodox continental socialism and who sought some party of opposition for voicing their discontent with the con-

[7] Drumont, *La Fin d'un monde*, 181–84.

[8] Charles Spiard, *Les Coulisses du Fort Chabrol* (Paris, 1902), 39–140; *Congrès nationale de la démocratie Chrétienne* (pamphlet) (Lyon, 1896); *Libre Parole Illustrée*, December 5, 1896.

temporary social system or their rank in that system. The disguise was so clever and Drumont's ranting about social injustices and the necessity for drastic changes was so constant that even some genuine Socialists were deceived for a few years. As a brief study of the "socialism" of antisemitism during these years indicates, there was considerable justification for several contemporary observers' believing that socialism and antisemitism were identical, or at least subversively connected.[9]

Thus, Drumont's second book, written hastily and published late in 1886, made an important advance towards the sentimental socialism which soon became typical of him and the movement. In the chapter devoted to an attack upon Rothschild, Drumont attempted to establish a distinction between Capitalism, which was Jewish and was based upon usury, and Property. Moreover, he warned the conservatives that the workers would not forever tolerate the contemporary social system and that revolution and liquidation of their wealth and position would surely come if the workers' grievances were not soon redressed.[10]

Believing that the "conservative Christian" had been converted to antisemitism, Drumont in 1888 made several other attempts to persuade the "revolutionary worker" to join his crusade. Early in that year an abridged edition of *La France juive* was published at half the original price, designed especially for the worker and peasant. This publication, which sold ten editions within two years, was followed by a hearty Drumont preface to a pamphlet which insisted in vague terms upon the dignity of labor and the respect and rights due the workers from their employers. The author of this brochure, Father Paul Fesch, became one of the leaders of the French Christian Socialist movement. His admira-

[9] Hermann Bahr, *Der Antisemitismus. Ein internationales Interview* (Berlin, 1894), 11-112, 117-18, 134-36; Anatole Leroy-Beaulieu, *L'Antisémitisme* (pamphlet) (Paris, 1897), 39-43, 58-61; Alexandre Zévaès, *Jules Guesde, 1845-1922* (Paris, 1929), 69; Alfred Gendrot (Jean Drault, *pseud.*), *Drumont, La France juive et la Libre Parole* (Paris, 1935), 5-7.

[10] Drumont, *La France juive*, I, 321-22; Drumont, *La France juive devant l'opinion*, 121-74. Drumont probably obtained the idea concerning the distinction between Capital and Property from Proudhon.

tion for "The Master" aided in the penetration of feeling against the Jews into the French parallel of the Lueger campaign in Austria.[11]

The antisemitic leader spent most of 1888 in his small country cottage writing *La Fin d'un monde*, which resembles *La France juive* more closely than any other of his works. Paris society received another severe scourging for its decadence and for the opportunities its materialism gave the ambitious Jews. Even more important, however, was Drumont's declaration that he had lost all hope of reform from either the Right or the Left, equally corrupt and equally heedless of the general welfare. His criticism of the Count of Paris and of the royalists was even more stinging than that of the Opportunists and Radicals. Asserting frankly that the return of the monarchy would bring no changes, he devoted the major part of this book to a discussion of nineteenth-century French socialism.[12]

Drumont not only described socialism as simply the natural reaction to the flagrant injustices of the contemporary social system, but he also interpreted modern history in a frightening manner for his conservative readers. The Revolution, for example, was described as a conservative bourgeois maneuver to overthrow the monarchy *against* the will of the People. After the bourgeoisie alone had profited from this great upheaval, they had simply distorted history to ensure their position. Thus, they had endorsed the legend that the Revolution had been made by the People in order to make their privileged status defensible. Then they had tried to enshrine Property, which Drumont described this time as merely another way of organizing society for the benefit of a privileged few.

Socialism represented the invincible uprising of the people against bourgeois exploitation. Drumont declared that what he

[11] Paul Fesch, *De l'ouvrier et du respect* (pamphlet) (Paris, 1888); Fesch, *Les Souvenirs d'un abbé journaliste* (Paris, 1898), 29–34; Edmond and Jules Goncourt, *Journal des Goncourt* (Paris, 1888–1896), VII, 281–82; *Revue du monde catholique*, XCIV (1888), 508–21; *Bibliographie catholique*, LXXVIII (1888), 152; *Catalogue général des livres imprimés de la Bibliothèque Nationale* (Paris, 1897–1950), XLII, 219.

[12] Drumont, *La Fin d'un monde*, 263–66, 298–304, 379–417.

termed "the revision of the Revolution" was near because the line between the enemy forces was becoming increasingly clear as the petty bourgeoisie lost their grip and joined the proletariat. The Commune, according to Drumont, had been an attempt by sagacious and ruthless conservatives to forestall this revision by destroying a whole generation of workers for crimes which they had never committed. Collectivism then received a most idealistic description, and Drumont even lashed Brousse for leaving Guesde's militant movement in 1881.[13]

Socialism as it was known then, however, was not the remedy for society because it lacked capable leaders and was so divided into squabbling groups. Neither were the Catholic Workers' Clubs of Count Albert de Mun and the Marquis de La Tour du Pin, because the workers had irrevocably left the Church earlier in the century when it had failed to show any interest in their vital problems. Moreover, Drumont declared that no movement accepting the contemporary social system could provide a solution, even though it did try to sweeten that method of organizing society with the balm of charity. Salvation lay, of course, with the antisemites, for Drumont proposed "the confiscation of all wealth won in the Jewish system" and a collectivist "revision of the Revolution" by a workers' chamber. This proposal was defined not as an attack upon Property, but only as an attack upon wealth gained through speculation.[14]

From the conservative point of view, *La Fin d'un monde* advanced an extremely dangerous program. However, there is far more evidence than this single book to explain why careful observers confused the movement against the Jews with socialism and why many conservatives became wary of antisemitism. In his next book, for instance, Drumont denounced the conservatives for supporting the Jews because of their blind fear of socialism. The bourgeoisie in this volume shared with the Jews and Masons the responsibility for the Republic and its many faults, and Drumont gravely asserted in an interview that he was "dropping the

[13] *Ibid.*, 1–40, 80–85, 98–180.
[14] *Ibid.*, 158–63, 181–84, 187–236.

Jew to attack the bourgeois world." Moreover, he ran for the
Paris Municipal Council in the spring of 1890 as "a real Socialist
in every sense of the word" and campaigned for a seat in the
Chamber of Deputies in 1893 as a Socialist.[15]

The declaration that the antisemites were Socialists became an
important part of their propaganda after 1888. Thus, Jacques de
Biez, Drumont's first disciple and the vice-president of the French
National Antisemitic League, told a reporter late in 1889; "We
are Socialists, for we demand an accounting with the financial
feudality. We are National Socialists, because we attack international finance so that we may have France for the French. We
are for the workers against the exploiters." The League's first
meeting was held on January 18, 1890, to support the candidacy of
Francis Laur, a member just a few years earlier of Guesde's *Parti
Ouvrier Français*, for the Chamber of Deputies. This meeting
voted a resolution endorsing "the citizen Laur, the enemy of
Rothschild, the Republican, and the Socialist." [16]

It is extremely difficult to analyze and summarize the program
or views of Drumont, the other leading antisemites, and the
antisemitic newspapers and organizations. Drumont's ideas were
clearly not based on a secure foundation and were constantly
shifting, except for his hatred of the Jews. There were all shades
of political and social views expressed by the other antisemites
and they were usually deliberately camouflaged, so that it is almost impossible to ascertain the program upon which they were
all agreed, except that they were all clearly antisemitic. As Léon
Daudet remarked in explaining Drumont's failure, his antisemitism
became only "a rendez-vous for people of all opinions." [17]

An analysis of the ideas and attitudes which are typical of
Drumont throughout his active life is, however, particularly re-
warding, because it illustrates to some degree the character of the

[15] Edouard Drumont, *La Dernière Bataille* (Paris, 1890), 53, 66–83; Drumont,
Le Testament d'un antisémite (Paris, 1891), 382, 436–37; *Anti-Juif* (Algiers),
March 13, 1890; April 17, 1890; *Libre Parole Illustrée*, August 19, 1893.
[16] François Bournand (Jean de Ligneau, *pseud.*), *Juifs et anti-sémites en
Europe* (Paris, 1892), 88–101; Compère-Morel, *op. cit.*, 232.
[17] Léon Daudet, *Les Oeuvres dans les hommes* (Paris, 1922), 170, 192.

movement as well as some of the reasons for its successes and failures. To begin with, although Drumont posed as a Socialist during much of his active political life, he was actually a romantic and melancholy conservative. He even described himself as "a private or sergeant in the conservative party." He was more than a conservative, however, for he was a disillusioned Tory, a decadent. Like so many nineteenth-century conservatives, such as Metternich and Pobedonostsev, Drumont believed that the established institutions and classes were doomed, that nothing but a miracle could save them. This is particularly clear in *La Dernière Bataille*, which appeared in 1890. In this book, Drumont declared that five hundred determined antisemites could easily seize Paris and could become masters of all of France within a year. But he ruefully admitted, however, that France no longer produced the kind of men necessary for such action, that the great days of France had passed, that peoples and countries evolve, and that the future belonged to the United States. The title of his next book in itself is significant, *Le Testament d'un antisémite*, as is the fact that Drumont spent so much of his time looking backward to "the good old days." [18]

The task of Socialists in modern times has been to ensure that the industrial system operate for the benefit of the workers. Drumont, however, did not approve of modern industry and even disliked electric lighting. It is clear that he knew nothing of the French industrial system or of the problems of modern economics. He loved old France and wrote constantly about it, and he spent most of his life after 1887 alone in his tiny country house. In all of his writing, there is not a single description of the interior of a factory, a mine, or of any industrial installation.

Although, as a Socialist, he should have been most interested in the conditions of the workers, he wrote and acted for the workers only when there was a strike or a disaster on a railroad or in a mine or factory owned or controlled by Jews. The class in which he was most interested was the lower middle class, to which his

[18] Drumont, *La Dernière Bataille*, 469-501, 545-51; Drumont, *Sur le Chemin de la vie. Souvenirs* (Paris, 1914), 329.

parents had belonged and out of which he himself never really grew. The only "worker" he really admired was the one "who increases the intellectual patrimony of his country."

Drumont's antisemitic movement was a lower-middle-class movement. Although Drumont spoke and wrote frequently about a reform and revolutionary movement springing from the bottom, it is clear throughout all of his writings that he remained ever a Christian conservative, and that he hoped and planned for a "Christian prince" or "an aristocratic Socialist" to lead and control the movement. He was plainly an infuriated Catholic who believed that an antisemitic program launched in defense of the Church could attract a spark of leadership from the old conservatives and win sufficient urban support to restore his "old France."

Drumont declared himself a Socialist because he was disgusted with the conservative upper classes, as his denunciations of society life clearly indicate, and because he had deep scorn for the idle, for those who lived and lived well on the work of others. This "absolute lack of respect for the idle," his natural vehemence in attack, his sentimentality, particularly about the poor, and his contempt for the conservatives who had allowed power to slip from their hands were the foundations of what Drumont described as his socialism. His program might best be labeled "sentimental socialism," except that even that phrase overestimates the element of socialism involved in his views. He had many of the characteristics of the Utopian Socialists of the first half of the nineteenth century, some of whom were also antisemites. He was romantic and emotional, as they were. He was on some occasions as foolishly confident as the Utopian Socialists had been that even the natural opponents of his program would be converted to his views once they read his books, and that "conversion" alone would solve all problems, few of which he even foresaw.

This simple-minded, Utopian view is clear throughout Drumont's works. Perhaps the finest illustration of his naïveté and of his lack of understanding of the economic forces at play lies in the solution he offered in *La France juive* and which he repeated in somewhat altered form in *La Dernière Bataille* in 1890. He proposed here that the workers seize Paris and entrust power to the Catholic bourgeoisie, who would select a "Christian prince." This leader was then to confiscate all Jewish property, bestow ownership of all French industry upon the workers, and reimburse the Catholic industrialists with the Jewish capital seized. The scheme in itself is ridiculous, but Drumont's explanation of why it might not work is even more ludicrous. The principal obstacles against it he declared were that the workers were not educated and the Jews controlled the newspapers they read, their workers' organizations, and all political parties! [19]

3. The Socialist Dupes of Drumont

IT is difficult even today to analyze Drumont's thought. The democrats and Socialists of France in the 1880's and 1890's lacked our understanding of the forces at play, did not see clearly the inevitable conflict between antisemitism and democracy, and were also hindered and blinded by the antisemitic thread which had run through French socialist tradition. As a consequence, the Socialists themselves made a significant contribution towards confusing the relationship between antisemitism and socialism.

Some French Socialists, but only a few, while realizing some of the dangers involved in the antisemitic movement, believed that eventually it would strengthen the Socialists. One of these was Clovis Hugues, the celebrated Socialist poet and deputy. He supported Drumont openly, declaring, "Drumont and his followers are rendering a great service to the cause of the social revolution because in creating antisemites, they have created Socialists in religious circles where any other propaganda would certainly fail." Paul Lafargue, Marx's son-in-law and a fervent member of Guesde's militant Socialist organization, sought to utilize Drumont in the same way. When French troops killed ten and

[19] Drumont, *La France juive*, I, 521–30; II, 576–77. Although it is based only on a study of Drumont's principal works, the best brief analysis of Drumont's political and social views is the work of a fellow antisemite and pseudo-Socialist, Walter Frank, *Nationalismus und Democratie in Frankreich der dritten Republik* (Hamburg, 1933), 316–36.

wounded thirty-five by firing into a May Day demonstration in
Fourmies in northern France in 1891, Lafargue visited the city,
attended religious services, and addressed crowds of workers with
Drumont. This approach was adopted by Socialists in other countries also. Victor Adler, a baptized Jew and the leader of the
Austrian Socialist Party, argued at the Brussels Conference of the
Second International in 1891 that antisemitism helped the Socialists. The Conference, however, roundly denounced antisemitism
and demonstrated that it was a natural enemy of social progress.

Several other prominent antisemites were sufficiently tainted by
Socialist connections to contribute heavily to the belief that the
campaign against the Jews was a part of the Socialist current.
Madame Caroline Guebhard, a prominent French journalist more
commonly known as Séverine, had been a prominent member of
Jules Vallès' *Cri du Peuple* for a brief time before Boulangism
claimed her interest in August, 1888. By early 1890, however, she
had discontinued all formal relationships with Socialist groups and
newspapers. Nevertheless, she continued to claim to be a Socialist
as well as an antisemite, although she admitted she did not understand socialism. Many of the articles she wrote in the 1890's for
such conservative newspapers as *Gaulois* and *Figaro* supported
justifiable strikes, led to collections of money for needy families,
and generally demonstrated the lively sympathy she felt for the
poor, but this hardly qualified her as a Socialist, though some conservatives may have thought so.[20]

The individual who, next to Drumont, contributed most to the
confusion concerning the relationship between the Socialist movement in France and antisemitism was Auguste Chirac, who called
himself an Independent Socialist and who was on the contributing

[20] Madame Caroline Guebhard (Séverine, *pseud.*), *Notes d'un frondeuse. De
la Boulangisme au Panama* (Paris, 1894), *passim;* Guebhard, *Vers la Lumière.
Impressions véçues* (Paris, 1900), 68; Bernard Lecache, *Séverine* (Paris, 1930),
34–48, 65–71; Gendrot, *op. cit.,* 116, 215, 223–24; Albert Cazes, "Une Princesse
du journalisme: Séverine, 1855–1929," *Grande Revue,* CXXXII (1930), 567–85;
CXXXIII (1930), 112; Henri Avenel, *Annuaire de la presse française,* V (1884),
XXIX. It is interesting to note that this feeling of pity and her sense of revolt
against the established system did lead her in old age to join the Communist
Party and to write for *Humanité* for a short time after the First World War.

staff of the *Revue Socialiste*. It is likely that Chirac never joined any of the numerous French Socialist parties of this period. He was more influenced by Proudhon than by any other Socialist, but he did address workers' groups with Jules Guesde and Auguste Vaillant, the most militant French Marxian Socialists, during the early 1880's, and he did contribute to *Egalité*, which Guesde had revived, in 1890 and 1891.

The life of Chirac has a number of resemblances to that of Drumont, and the path by which he arrived at antisemitism was very similar to that of Drumont. Born six years earlier than Drumont, Chirac came to Paris from Marseille early in the 1860's to seek his fortune as a playwright. While busy turning out plays which were never produced, although a few were published, he became a very successful publicist for the Society of Applied Industrial Arts. In 1864, the influence which the legitimist views of his parents and relatives had upon him was still so strong that he refused the Cross of the Legion of Honor from Napoleon III, whom he considered an upstart. The Catholic beliefs of his family and of his Jesuit educators failed to retain their influence, however, and during the 1870's he became a convinced and dogmatic atheist.

In 1866, when he lost his position as a publicist, Chirac became a member of the staff of Jules Mirès' *La Presse*, where he was soon put in charge of the financial page. His disappointment in his complete failure as a playwright was one of the reasons for which he became a Socialist in 1876 with a strong taint even then of antisemitism, but his experiences on *La Presse* were almost as important. Mirès, who was a financier relegated to the second rank by the Pereires and other favorites of Napoleon III, was a great influence upon Chirac, who admitted that he was completely ignorant of financial affairs then. The revelations Chirac received concerning both the real and the imagined financial practices of the large banks and of the speculators in the Second Empire and during the years immediately following the Franco-Prussian War, turned him towards Proudhon and towards the conviction that financial speculation was the cause of all economic evils. These beliefs were buttressed and applied to the international scene when Chirac worked for a short time in the Ministry of Foreign Affairs early in the 1870's. As a result, in 1876, at the age of thirty-eight, he published the first of a series of books which during the next twenty years promoted a kind of Proudhonian socialism and an ever-increasing vaguely socialist antisemitism.[21]

Chirac's ideas were revised considerably between 1876, when he first published attacks upon capitalism and upon the Jews, and 1899, when his public role in French life ceased. The strains of thought which are apparent throughout all of his work are his hatred of the Jews, especially of Jewish financiers, and his suspicion and distrust of all foreigners, particularly the English. In addition to these two elements, there are other consistent attitudes and approaches. Perhaps the most significant of these is his interest in the land and in land ownership. In his first books, he attacked speculators and financiers for ousting the old French from lands their families had owned and farmed for generations. In 1886, he proposed that all land be the property of the nation, with a kind of title to go to those actually using the land. In 1896, he continued his attacks on absentee ownership and declared that all of the revolutions in French history had been generally successful attempts by the bourgeoisie, led by the Jews and Protestants, to gain control of French soil from those who by inheritance and use had real claim to it. More than he himself probably realized, Chirac, the Independent Socialist, was really a conservative defending a status quo which he professed to despise.

This conservatism is clear, too, in his extreme attacks on speculation, which led him ultimately to denounce all credit institutions, paper money, government loans, and the national debt. It is most apparent, perhaps, in his ever-growing interest in taxes, which he insisted must be lowered and must be stabilized for at least twenty-five years, so that the farmer, the merchant, and the manufacturer

---

[21] Auguste Chirac, *Le Droit de vivre, analyse socialiste* (Paris, 1896), t–x, XVI; Chirac, *La Haute Banque et les révolutions* (Paris, 1876), 222; Hugo Thième, *Bibliographie de la littérature français de 1800 à 1930* (Paris, 1933), I, 439; Albert Savine, "Auguste Chirac," *Revue d'art dramatique*, XVIII (1903), 334–43, 348–49; *Libre Parole*, April 29, 1898.

could make proper investment plans. In 1886, he became a disciple
of Malthus, and from that time forward he bewailed the growth of
the French population and insisted something be done about "the
passionate parasites." [22]

There was, however, some reason for which Chirac might call
himself and be considered a Socialist. He was a vehement opponent of finance capitalism and proposed consistently that all
speculation be abolished by the government and that the government assume control of all credit facilities and currency issue. He
proposed in 1876 that all railroads be made state property, and in
1886 he suggested state ownership of all public utilities in France.
In 1876, he suggested that part of the workers' pay be in stock so
that they might become partners and, ultimately, the owners of
all industrial enterprise, and ten years later he urged nationaliza-
tion of the land and, vaguely, collectivization and mechanization
of agriculture.

Chirac's socialism, however, grew more and more diluted after
1886. His last book, published in 1896, offered no concrete program. Chirac urged that capitalism, which he did not define, be
abolished, but he suggested that the new society just be allowed
to "grow" and that Socialists cease to waste their time planning a
society which would be beset by problems which none could
foresee. His fundamental thesis was that in the new society each
individual should be given "the right to live," which for him
meant the right to develop one's talents freely and the right to
receive from society "according to one's needs." By 1899, all
Socialist journals and newspapers were closed to his writings.[23]

Chirac's socialism was weakened and undermined by his essential conservatism and by his canalizing his opposition to capitalism into attacks upon financial speculators, particularly English and
Jewish speculators. Antisemitism is clear in his writings as early

[22] Auguste Chirac, *Les Mystères du crédit* (Paris, 1876), 6–40, 71–101; Chirac,
La Haute Banque, 5–40, 67–77, 167–74, 233–38, 263–91; Chirac, *La Prochaine
Révolution* (Paris, 1886), 7–73, 107–10, 122–36; Chirac, *L'Agiotage sous la
Troisième République* (Paris, 1888 edition), I, 16–38; Chirac, *Où est l'argent?*
(Paris, 1891), 1–207; Chirac, *Le Droit de vivre*, 233–36.

[23] Chirac, *La Haute Banque*, 5–40, 279–91; Chirac, *La Prochaine Révolution*,
107–47; Chirac, *Le Droit de vivre*, V–XVI, 313–23; *Libre Parole*, May 9, 1899.

as 1876, and in 1883 Chirac founded and edited one of the first antisemitic papers to appear in Paris. His attacks upon the English increased as the years passed, and his references to the English as Protestant likewise became more frequent. At the same time, he dramatized the dangers inherent in French participation in international trade and began to campaign for national self-sufficiency. In his last book, he attacked all international Socialists and urged a national socialist revolution, which would make France again the strongest nation on the continent. During the Dreyfus Affair, quite logically, he spoke frequently for the antisemites.

This shift can be traced also in Chirac's attitude towards the Catholic Church. A vehement atheist, in 1886 he proposed that the government should cease to pay the clergy and should use those funds instead for medicine. As he became an acquaintance and then a close friend of Drumont, however, his eagerness to attack religion and the Catholic Church dissolved. In 1892, Chirac wrote a public letter to Monsignor d'Hulst, the vicar-general of Paris, urging that the Church "cease to shelter monopoly and wealth" and that it "ally Catholic conscience with Socialist science." In his last book, in 1896, he agreed that the influence of the Catholic Church had been of some benefit to France, and that the "economic clergy, the priests of laissez-faire capitalism," were a greater evil and danger than the religious clergy.[24]

One of the most fascinating individuals involved in the antisemitic movement, and one who also contributed seriously to the misunderstanding concerning the alliance between antisemitism and socialism was Edmond Picard. Although Picard was a Belgian of great influence in the political, social, and intellectual history of Belgium from 1865 through 1920, he also played a significant role in the development of antisemitism in France. His principal antisemitic book and most of his antisemitic articles

[24] Chirac, *La Haute Banque*, 9–24, 33–40, 79–117, 243–61; Chirac, *La Prochaine Révolution*, 39–79, 122–36; Chirac, *L'Agiotage*, I, 1–14; Chirac, *Où est l'argent?*, 207–76; Chirac, *Le Droit de vivre*, e, 41–53, 151–52, 185–219, 223–36, 253–57, 307–11; Savine, *loc. cit.*, 355; *Libre Parole*, April 25, 1892; February 16, 1898; April 29, 1898; May 9, 1899.

were published in France by Albert Savine, the leading French publisher of antisemitica, and it is evident from the writings and speeches of the leading French antisemites that his ideas had considerable influence there.

Picard was born into a wealthy, conservative, Catholic family in Flanders in 1830. Two of his sisters became nuns, but he became an atheist during the 1850's while convalescing from typhus on Staten Island. He had run away from college in 1850 to become a merchant seaman, but he returned to Brussels in 1854 to become a lawyer so he might aid the poor and the oppressed. He became a member of the First International in 1866, and he remained one of the most prominent Belgian Socialist leaders until 1906, when he left the party he had done so much to establish and develop. During these forty years, he worked with such men as Jules Destrée and Emile Vandervelde to promote socialism in Belgium. He defended workers in hundreds of cases before the Belgian courts, he fought for factory legislation, he was imprisoned for struggling for universal suffrage, and he was the first Socialist senator elected in Belgium.

Edmond Picard was unquestionably one of the very great lawyers of his generation. He edited the *Pandectes Belges*, called "one of the greatest law collections of the nineteenth century." He earned a large fortune in his profession, and he used his wealth to help develop Belgian art, literature, and education. Himself a playwright, poet, novelist, and historian, he helped found the influential journal, *Art Moderne*, in 1881, and he was one of its editors until it was crushed under the German invasion in 1914. He used this journal to promote his belief in "art for society's sake" and to help develop a national Belgian art and literature. He was known as the Maecenas of all young Belgian artists and writers, whom he entertained and financed freely, while in the Senate he sought to have the Belgian government help the talented youth of the country. In 1893, he abandoned his lavish home and transformed it into the *Maison de l'Art*, and later he was one of the principal founders of and professors in the *Université Nouvelle* in Brussels, established largely by the Socialists to carry higher education to the workers.[25]

It was as senseless for a Socialist such as Picard to become an active antisemite as it was for a Catholic. Those Catholics who erred in attacking the Jews were driven into that folly and disaster as a consequence of the political and intellectual crisis which derived from the eighteenth century and from the French Revolution, and as a consequence of the political developments of the first years of the Third Republic. Picard betrayed his democratic and socialist principles because he was deluded by Gobineau and other antisemites who claimed that it could be scientifically demonstrated that there was a hierarchy of races and that the Jews were by nature distinct from and inferior to the Aryans. Picard was the only important disciple Gobineau had in France or Belgium. Vandervelde succeeded in preventing him from having any influence as an antisemite in the Belgian Socialist movement, but he was able to influence Drumont's campaign in France.

The pseudoscientific racialist views of Picard were strengthened by a trip he made to Morocco late in the 1880's as a member of a commission sent by the great imperialist, King Leopold II, to increase Belgian economic influence there. This brief visit apparently strengthened greatly his views concerning the abilities of the Semites, and from that time forward Picard was an avowed opponent of the Jews. He tried to prove that Christ was an Aryan and that the Jews were an Asiatic people who by nature were "parasitic exploiters" who could not accept or adopt European civilization. In 1892, he appealed to Benoît Malon, editor of the *Revue Socialiste*, to assume leadership of a scientific crusade against the Jews. Four years later, by an analysis of the Sermon on the Mount he tried to demonstrate that Christ was "the Aryan par excellence" and that His views coincided exactly with those of

[25] Edmond Picard, *Pro Arte* (Brussels, 1886), 101–46; Andrew Mathews, *La Wallonie, 1886–1892. The Symbolist Movement in Belgium* (New York, 1947), 16–18, 94; Jules Destrée and Emile Vandervelde, *Le Socialisme en Belgique* (Paris, 1903), 97, 112–13, 149, 159, 171–72, 184–85, 217, 246, 373–83, 396–405; Count H. Carton de Wiart, "Souvenirs sur Edmond Picard," *Revue générale* (Brussels), CXXXVII (1937), 68–74; Maria Biermé, "Edmond Picard et ses oeuvres," *Belgique artistique et littéraire*, XII (1908), 74–79.

Picard. He was a vehement anti-Dreyfusard, declaring that "we Aryans should not support a Jew, even if justice is on his side."

One of Picard's most attractive and, in some ways, most admirable qualities, was a great stimulant to his antisemitism. This was his extreme individualism, his persistent desire to remain different, to oppose the general current of opinion, and to distinguish himself as a rebel. He revolted against all conformity and discipline, and he was called "the minority incarnate." His motto was, "I Disturb," and his letterhead bore that inscription and the figure of a porcupine prepared to discharge quills in all directions. It is generally agreed that this characteristic prevented him from becoming and remaining during a long period of years Belgium's leading statesman.

Being the lone distinguished antisemite in Belgium apparently satisfied Picard's craving to be intransigent, just as this characteristic helps to explain his becoming a Socialist, his daring as a lawyer, and his leaving the Socialists when the party had begun to acquire some political power. In 1901, he established an annual prize for the young lawyer who produced "the finest original work" in belles lettres or the arts. In 1919, at the age of eighty-nine, he was the only lawyer in Belgium willing to undertake the defense of those charged with treason during the First World War. At his death in 1921, he had established the *Fondation Edmond Picard* to grant an annual prize to the Belgian "who distinguished himself most in law, literature, sociology, or fine arts by his original and novel attitudes." It was a tragedy for Picard, for socialism, for Belgium, for France, for the Jews, and for all who believe in democracy that this paradoxical man should have been an antisemite and an evil influence.[26]

---

[26] Edmond Picard, "L'Art et la révolution," *Société nouvelle*, II (1886), 208–31; Picard, "La Bible et le Coran," *Société nouvelle*, I (1889), 133–64; Picard, *Synthèse de l'antisémitisme* (Paris, 1892), 11–44, 116–23; Picard, "La littérature et l'antisémitisme," *Société nouvelle*, II (1894), 240–50; Picard, *Le Sermon sur la montagne et le socialisme contemporaine* (Brussels, 1896), 1–5, 27–88; Picard, *L'Aryano-Sémitisme* (Brussels, 1899), 95–96; Achille Segard, *Edmond Picard* (Paris, 1898), 12–78; Henri Dagan, *Enquête sur l'antisémitisme* (Paris, 1899), 1–7; Bahr, *op. cit.*, 206–208; Maurice Dullaert, "L'Antisémitisme de M. Edmond Picard," *Magasin littéraire et scientifique*, IX (1892), 357–71; Paul Colin, "Ed-

4. The Awakening of the Socialists

IT took only the emergence of antisemitism as an organized movement to enlighten most genuine Socialists upon the real intentions
of the campaign against the Jews. The *Revue Socialiste*, which had
been antisemitic before 1886 and which had become increasingly
so after Drumont's success, never followed the antisemitic leader
blindly. As its editors saw the dangers in a campaign including
clerical and anti-Republican elements, they became increasingly
cautious and circumspect. Henri Tubiana, for example, demonstrated how mistaken and foolish the Algerian Radical Republicans were in being antisemitic. Rouanet's book reviews began to
suggest that antisemitism would be turned against the Republic,
and his review of Drumont's long discussion of socialism warned
all sincere Republicans to beware the use the monarchists would
make of the book. Still another article condemned the *Union
générale's* Serbian policy and urged Drumont to remember its wild
speculation before denouncing the Jews for its failure.[27]

The first organized meeting of the French National Antisemitic
League resulted in the journal's adopting a clearly hostile attitude
towards antisemitism. Arranged by the Marquis de Morès to support the candidacy of the Boulangist, Francis Laur, and to form a
united movement of workers and members of the aristocratic
clubs, this meeting led Rouanet to write a brilliant and conclusive
article in the February, 1890, issue. Declaring no ethnic line could
be drawn between groups of capitalists, Rouanet urged all Socialists to remain aloof from antisemitism, which this assembly
had revealed allied to the Right in an attack upon the Republic.
Questioning the sincerity of any conservative attack upon capi-

───────
mond Picard," *Europe*, IV (1924), 355–57; *Libre Parole*, January 27, February 2, 1898.
   [27] *Revue Socialiste:* Henri Tubiana, "Les Croisades au dix-neuvième siècle,"
II (1886), 634–36, 959, 1131–33; Gustave Rouanet, "La Vérité sur les chemins
de fers Serbes," I (1889), 720–42; Rouanet reviews of *La Fin d'un monde*, II
(1886), 530, 662–64.

talism, Rouanet asserted there could be no compromise between socialism, which sought racial equality and the suppression of economic inequality, and the contrary aims of antisemitism.[28]

After the Rouanet definition, the *Revue Socialiste* betrayed no trace of antisemitism. Regnard, the author of a long series of articles on the dangerous Semitic religious spirit, immediately resigned in protest. The studies of credit and banking by Chirac and Malon differed completely from their earlier ones, Chirac soon ceased to write for the journal, and Malon's new statement of policy, published in December, 1891, emphasized the need for tolerance within the Republic. A series of articles by Adrian Veber in 1892 revealed that anticlericalism had replaced antisemitism, which was denounced categorically as "a born enemy of socialist progress." Moreover, the journal's attitude during the Panama scandal was a strong defense of the Republic, explaining that corruption existed under every form of government and that Drumont's Jewish microbe was no more deadly than the others.[29]

The most effective and conclusive attacks made upon this doctrine of hate in France were delivered by Guesde and Lafargue in a public debate with the Marquis de Morès and Jules Guérin in July, 1892. The two principal lieutenants of Drumont revealed their lack of a clear program when they devoted the major part of their addresses to autobiography. Their Socialist rivals then riddled the puerile plan of Morès for five thousand francs of credit for every worker and Guérin's proposal of financial decentralization as a panacea for the French economic system. Guesde demonstrated that many leading French bankers and industrialists were Catholics and declared that "in spite of its Socialist mask" antisemitism was "an economic and social reaction." French socialism in general by 1892 had rather clearly and completely

[28] Gustave Rouanet, "La Question juive et la question sociale," *Revue Socialiste*, I (1890), 219–34.

[29] *Revue Socialiste:* I (1890), 348–49; II (1891), 641–45; Adrian Veber, "L'Action catholique," I (1892), 230–47; Veber, "La Crise politique," I (1892), 351–52; Veber, "Le Convent maçonnique," II (1892), 478–80; Pierre Boz, "Revue de la presse étrangère," I (1893), 623; Gustave Rouanet, "La Vérité sur le Panama," II (1892), 646–58.

broken away from antisemitism, although the Dreyfus Affair and the eruptions it caused in French political affairs introduced the problem again temporarily in 1897 and 1898.[30]

[30] Edouard Drumont, *Le Secret de Fourmies* (Paris, 1892); Charles Droulers, *Le Marquis de Morès, 1858–1896* (Paris, 1932), 102–104, 132–33; Alexandre Zévaès, *Jules Guesde, 1845–1922* (Paris, 1929), 109–11; Zévaès, *Ombres et silhouettes. Notes, mémoires et souvenirs* (Paris, 1928), 216–29; Zévaès, *La Fusillade de Fourmies* (pamphlet) (Paris, 1936), 11–46; Salo Baron, *A Social and Religious History of the Jews* (New York, 1937), III, 313; Compère-Morel, *op. cit.*, 375–79; *Libre Parole*, May 3, 1892.

V

"THE CONSERVATIVE CHRISTIAN"

THERE is no subject in the history of France since the French Revolution which is more confusing or more explosive than the relations which have existed between the French Catholics and the French government. This is particularly true of the period from 1879 through 1906 when a government for the first time was firmly established on the foundation of the principles enunciated during the Revolution. Moreover, in this period of the Third Republic's history, the tides of opinion and of political tactics shifted so swiftly and frequently that it is often extremely difficult, if not impossible, to assess cause, effect, and responsibility properly. This problem has been made more difficult still by the mass of evidence and of historical studies available, both usually more partisan and prejudiced than the evidence and the scholarship dealing with any sections of American history except, perhaps, the Civil War and the New Deal.

The French Catholics were divided into just as many factions or parties as the French Socialists, and acceptance or rejection of antisemitism was an important issue for each of the various groupings. The conservative and moderate Catholic groups both were divided on antisemitism and on the attitude towards the democratic Third Republic which its acceptance or rejection implied. Antisemitism not only intensified hatred of the Republic among those conservative and moderate Catholics who followed Drumont, but it also contributed to the development of a third Catholic party, the Christian Socialists or Christian Democrats. The political and social views of this group seriously alarmed both of the other combinations and increased their suspicion of democracy. As a result, Drumont's antisemitism was an important factor in the growing disagreement among French Catholic groups during the last decade of the nineteenth century and in the eventual unfortunate failure of *ralliement*. But for Drumont, Leo XIII's wise policy would have won far more general acceptance among French Catholics and the tragedy of the perpetuation of *les deux France* might have been avoided. In other words, the antisemitic movement helped to destroy the finest opportunity the French people had to unite freely from 1815 until 1944.

Pius XI and many other Popes have pointed out, "We are all spiritual descendants of Abraham. It is not possible for Christians to have any part in antisemitism. We are spiritually Semites." Leo XIII, surely one of the greatest of all Popes, was as emphatic in his denunciation of Drumont's antisemitism as any modern democrat has been of racial or religious hatred anywhere. French clergymen and French Catholic laymen from all walks of life denounced antisemitism in Russia both before and after the publication of Drumont's book, and French Catholics were among the most generous in contributing aid to the oppressed Russian Jews. Moreover, although it has never been generally recognized, many of the most early and ardent Dreyfusards were French Catholics, and many of those who fought most valiantly throughout the entire Dreyfus Affair for the defense of the Third Republic, democracy, and the rights of the individual were Catholics.

Nevertheless, the evidence from all sides is overwhelming that Catholics were the strength of French antisemitism during these years. Catholics manned the press and journals which spread Drumont's teachings throughout France, and Catholic writers, especially priests, provided much of the ammunition in the antisemitic barrage laid down after 1886. Country priests, whose background and poor education had overemphasized piety to the detriment of a scholarly intellectual foundation and whose reading of the *Croix* and little else had prepared them, were Drumont's most avid readers.

1. The Catholic Reception of *La France Juive*

ONE has only to study the reception given *La France juive* by the press to see how enthusiastically most Catholics received the new bludgeon against anticlericalism. The *Journal des Débats*, *Paix*, *Figaro*, and *Temps* led the defense of the Jews and of democratic ideas, while almost all Catholic papers, particularly those in the provinces, leaped into the antisemitic campaign. When the Archbishop of Paris denied *Figaro's* charge that he had helped finance the publication of *La France juive*, he did not advance beyond this denial to condemn the merciless assault upon the Jews. Only one French bishop declared publicly that no Christian had any right to speak without respect concerning the Jews. Priests such as Father Frémont and Father Le Nordez, who declared Drumont's doctrines were "contrary to the moral beliefs of the Catholic religion," were unfortunately rare.[1]

The *Croix*, published by the Assumptionist Fathers, printed an enthusiastic review of Drumont's book by Father Georges de Pascal on the very day it was published. Eugène Veuillot's tremendously influential *Univers* not only praised the "instructive and courageous book," but reprinted Drumont's last page on Holy Saturday in 1886 as a reminder to all Catholic Frenchmen that as

[1] Edouard Drumont, *La France juive devant l'opinion* (Paris, 1886), 13; Drumont, *Le Testament d'un antisémite* (Paris, 1891), 343–44; Claudio Jannet, *Le Capital, la speculation et la finance* (Paris, 1892), 547; Léonce Reynaud, *La France n'est pas juive* (Paris, 1886), 7–11; Georges Weill, *Histoire du catholicisme libéral en France, 1828–1908* (Paris, 1909), 151–52; Raïssa Maritain, *Les Grandes Amitiés. Souvenirs* (New York, 1941), I, 176; Cécile Vincens (Arvède Barine, *pseud.*), "La Question antisémitique. Le Juif russe peint par lui-même," *Revue politique et littéraire*, third series, XXIX (1882), 716–21; *Univers*, April 21–April 26, 1886; *Vraie Parole*, May 20, 1893.

Christ had risen after Jewish deicide, so should Christian France rise from Jewish domination. Drumont during the first half of 1886 was a member of the staff of the *Monde*, which was considered the semi-official organ of the Archbishop of Paris. This Catholic paper in its first reviews had praised the fundamental thought of Drumont while criticizing his "false and unrestrained statements and excessive conclusions," but within two weeks an editor was commending "this good soldier of Jesus" without restraint and publishing a pamphlet ridiculing the Jews. Moreover, Drumont remained on the staff of the *Monde* for several weeks after the publication of *La France juive* and was forced to resign not because of the book but because he had taken part in a duel.[2]

The welcome given to Drumont by the leading Catholic journals was similar to that given by the Catholic press. The *Revue du monde catholique*, to which Drumont was a contributor, defended *La France juive* at length to keep its readers "from heeding the cry of indignation raised against it." Drumont was chided for his censure of the French conservatives, especially the nobility, and his radical solution was slighted, but the book as a whole was praised as a "brave, tolerant assault upon the Jewish bandits." Another important Catholic journal, *Le Correspondant*, paid especial attention to the racial basis for antisemitism and urged the Jewish parasites and persecutors to accept the volumes as a timely warning.[3]

2. French Catholic Groupings

THE aim of most French Catholics was to obtain a government in France which should give to the Catholic Church heavily in-

[2] Georges de Pascal, *La Juiverie* (Paris, 1887), preface, V–VIII; Oscar Havard, *M. Edouard Drumont et La France juive* (pamphlet) (Paris, 1886). The *Monde* reviews given *La France juive* on April 26 and May 6, 1886, are quoted in Stéphane Arnoulin, *M. Edouard Drumont et les Jésuites* (Paris, 1902), 155–57.

[3] *Revue du monde catholique*: Edouard Drumont, "Louis Veuillot, le publiciste," LXXIV (1883), 196–202; Drumont, "M. Ernest Hello," LXXXIII (1885), 340–45; Arsène Guérin, "La France juive," LXXXVI (1886), 405–19; *Le Correspondant*: Pierre Douhaire, "L'Invasion juive," CXLIII (1886), 930–36; Victor Fournel, "Les Oeuvres et les hommes," CXLIII (1886), 923–29.

creased influence and power within the French educational system and ultimately, therefore, over French public opinion. In their efforts, of course, they were acting as French citizens. They were not representatives of Catholicism as such, and in many cases their philosophies and policies were clearly not based on fundamental Catholic teaching. These French Catholics differed widely as to what form of government France should have, how it should be obtained, and what kind of political and social program it should have once established. The differences between the various political groupings which were formed among French Catholics are extremely difficult to establish, in spite of the fury with which they sometimes fought each other. It is only with the very greatest care that rough distinctions can be made between the frequently shifting groups, and even these classifications sometimes collapse during crises. The most convenient, clear, and accurate classification is one made according to social and economic views.

Thus, the extreme conservative Catholics were devoted to a laissez-faire social philosophy, tempered by old-fashioned benevolent paternalism. They resented the industrialization of France and the concomitant rise of another layer of the middle class. They were generally also monarchists, although after 1883 monarchism was more a pious hope than a practical program. Politically, they were vehemently opposed to all those whom they considered enemies of the Catholic Church, although their views and actions in political affairs generally betrayed little real Christian feeling or understanding.

The Social Catholics did not differ greatly from the Tory Catholics in political views, for their leaders until the early 1890's were convinced monarchists and those Social Catholics who did adopt the Republic then were generally "reluctant Republicans." The Social Catholics, however, did believe in the necessity for and the efficacy of practical social legislation to mend the social system and to keep the workers contented. They recognized the industrialization of France as an established fact which could perhaps be directed and controlled by the old ruling classes, but which could certainly not be resisted. They were almost as paternalistic as the Tory Catholics, but they were also more realistic. Much of the very essence of conservatism at its best can be found in the policies of this group.

On the other hand, the Christian Democrats or Christian Socialists were not socialists so much as they were democrats, resolved that the privileged position of special classes, which both of the other groups wanted to preserve, should not be permanent and that the Church should break its alliance with privilege and return to the people and the Republic. This group began to appear and grow in France only during the 1890's, generally a little later than similar developments in other Catholic countries. The Christian Democrats became resolute supporters and critics of the Third Republic. With a program which respected the dignity and rights of the worker, which sought the end of monopolistic abuse and financial corruption, and which hoped to eliminate poverty and misery in France, they were determined to win mass support for their program. Their aim, then, was to give France a government which was Catholic but which was also interested in the rights and welfare of all Frenchmen.

Unfortunately, some of the impetus which propelled the Christian Democratic movement was provided by Drumont. The Christian Democrats suffered heavily from the political and intellectual tradition common to almost all French Catholics in the nineteenth century, as well as from the contemporary confusion between Jewish bankers and merchants and the evils of capitalism, which also plagued the orthodox Socialists. Many French Catholics, shocked by the successful campaign of the anticlericals in reducing the power of the Church over education in particular, were convinced that the drive against the Church had been led by Freemasons and Jews. The clear evidence of Masonic participation in the attack and the number of Jews occupying seats in the government during the 1879–1884 drive, influenced many Catholics to follow Drumont in his crusade.[4]

[4] Georges Weill, *Histoire du mouvement social en France, 1852–1914* (Paris, 1924), 409–24, has probably the clearest brief account of the ramifications of Catholic social views.

Leo XIII by 1890 "had contemplated, like a new Ezekiel, the valley of dry bones of French Royalist politics and had decided that (barring a political miracle) the cause of the Most Christian King was as dead as that of the Most Serene Republic of Venice." He therefore re-instituted the policy of *ralliement*, which simply recognized that the great majority of the French people had freely accepted the Republican form of government and that the Catholic Church should follow its traditional principle of adapting itself to the government in power. This policy would free the Church and French Catholics from the dead body of monarchism in France and would allow the Catholics to exert far more influence upon the government than the hostile attitude thus far followed had permitted. This policy would, if successful, also soften ultimately the very strong anticlericalism of the French Radicals and Socialists and would lead to the establishment of a more firm foundation for the Third Republic. Leo XIII proposed, but the French themselves, alas, disposed. *Ralliement* was crippled throughout the 1890's by the refusal or grumbling reluctance of many Catholic leaders to accept Leo XIII's suggestion. The antisemitic movement played a major role in this tortuous development, as well as in the Dreyfus Affair, which destroyed completely the wise Pope's excellent program.[5]

THE EXTREME CONSERVATIVES

In a sense, the extreme conservative Catholics were natural followers of Drumont because of their monarchism, their resentment of the new France, and their violent dislike of a generally anticlerical Republic. The early antisemitism of the conservative Catholics was particularly well presented by two priests, Father Joseph Lémann and Father Georges de Pascal. The first book upon this subject by Lémann, who was a convert from Judaism, ap-

[5] Dominique Cardinal Ferrata, *Mémoires. Ma Nonciature en France* (Paris, 1922), *passim*, especially 11-31, 66-67, 77-148, 204-55; Antonin Debidour, *L'Eglise catholique et l'Etat sous la Troisième République, 1870-1906* (Paris, 1906-1909), II, 1-78; Waldemar Gurian, *Die politischen und sozialen Ideen des französischen Katholizimus, 1789-1914* (Munich, 1928), 239-94; Denis W. Brogan, *The Development of Modern France* (London, 1940), 257-67.

peared only a few weeks after *La France juive* in 1886 and sold six editions. As a convert and a Catholic priest, Lémann naturally expressed the hope that the Jews themselves would solve the dilemma by joining the Catholic Church. He assailed them for their wealth and anticlericalism, but the heart of his book lay in a direct assault upon the Rights of Man, the breach through which the Jews had swarmed to power.

The pendant to this volume was a study of the manner in which the Jews had obtained their emancipation in 1791. Lémann asserted that this "dangerous equality" had been granted because of the national apostasy of the Catholics, the influence of the Freemasons, and the pressure of Jewish gold. The problem was thus placed purely on a religious and political basis, and the conclusion one must draw from Lémann is that if the Jews failed to join the Catholic Church they should lose all political rights.

Pascal's book was a collection of articles he wrote for *Croix* and *Univers* in 1886 and 1887, and it was published with a warm preface by Drumont. This Paris priest reproved violence, of course, and he laid the foundation for any lasting remedy in a return to the Christian way of life. Then the press and political organizations of the Jews were to be smashed, while the Freemasons and Jews were to lose all political rights. The essential features of the economic program were the restriction of land ownership to Christian Frenchmen and closer control by the government of all corporations.[6]

An examination of a few other of the most important extreme conservative antisemites and of their shallow ideas will demonstrate to some degree the elements of political and economic reaction, nationalism, religious fanaticism, and futile rage which composed their programs. It is interesting to note that the great majority of the spokesmen for the Tory conservatives were Cath-

---

[6] Joseph Lémann, *L'Entrée des israélites dans la société française et les états chrétiens* (Paris, 1886), 155–97, 234–52, 474–92; Lémann, *La Prépondérance juive. Ses Origines, 1789–1791 d'après des documents nouveaux* (Paris, 1889), 15–270; *Catalogue général des livres imprimés de la Bibliothèque Nationale* (Paris, 1897–1950), XCIV, 117; Pascal, *op. cit.*, 87–121. For good conservative reviews of Pascal's book, see *Revue du monde catholique*, XCIV (1888), 124–25; *Bibliographie catholique*, LXXVI (1887), 19–22.

olic priests and, moreover, that these priests in almost every instance lived in the provinces. The open political leaders of this group were members of the aristocracy, the wealthy old bourgeoisie, and the high clergy, a great many of whom lived in Paris or were frequently in the city, where, if contemporary novels and memoirs are accurate sources, they spent some of their time in the company of Jews. The principal strength of this movement lay, however, in the provinces, untouched by the cosmopolitan and intellectual developments of the capital.

The life and ideas of Father Isidore Bertrand, who spent most of his active life as a priest in the Dauphiné in southeastern France, illustrate many of the important characteristics of the extreme conservative movement. Bertrand, who was born in 1829, became convinced during the 1860's that the unification of the Kingdom of Italy and the consequent loss of temporal power suffered by the Papacy were due to the secret societies organized and led in Italy by Jews, Protestants, and Masons. This trio was soon to assume responsibility in his mind for all of the disasters and defeats which the Catholic Church and conservative France suffered from that time until 1906, with the subversive influence of the Jews increasing gradually after 1877. In 1879, Bertrand published a two-volume study of the pontificate of Pius VI, the Roman pontiff during the last quarter of the eighteenth century. This assigned responsibility for the French Revolution to the *philosophes* and to the Freemasons, who organized and directed them.

Fortified by his study of eighteenth-century anticlericalism, Bertrand launched himself into contemporary politics after the conservative defeat at the polls in 1877. Shocked by the disastrous results of the *Seize Mai* crisis, Bertrand published a "documented" pamphlet which attempted to demonstrate that Freemasonry was subversive of religion and society and had such a strong, mysterious power that it had forced a conservative government to wage a disastrously weak electoral campaign. This pamphlet was an enormous success, as the conservatives, astounded by the sudden reversal of their fortunes, began to realize that the magnificent opportunity they had possessed since 1871 was fast dissolving.

The fifty thousand copies of this pamphlet which were sold not only launched Bertrand as a militant crusader, but they also encouraged the "plot mentality" of the stricken conservatives.[7]

Bertrand's career as a publicist during the last thirty years of his life betrays many of the failings so common among the conservative Catholics. He maintained his attack upon "the trinity from down below," he fought the French Revolution as though he were living in the eighteenth century, and he showed no knowledge of or interest in social problems. In 1891, in a book entitled *Un Monde fin-de-siècle*, he traced contemporary French decadence from the contemporary Jews and Freemasons back through most of the heresies and schisms which had affected the Catholic Church since the birth of Christ. He was a violent anti-Dreyfusard, seeing the influence of the synagogue and the Syndicate behind the "plot against France," and in his last books he sought to demonstrate that Freemasonry was a Jewish sect.[8]

Perhaps the most unpleasant and even vicious of the extreme conservative antisemites was Father Henri Desportes, who apparently spent his priesthood in the area bounded by Rouen, Amiens, and Lille in northern France. Desportes devoted a large volume and two pamphlets in 1889 and 1890 to the practices of human sacrifice and of the Easter ritual murder among the Jews. Although several important and responsible journals swallowed the ritual murder legend, these writings of Desportes were so vile that they roused a strong reaction. Cardinal Manning of England, at the request of Rabbi Adler, protested both openly and in a letter to the Pope. Cardinal Thomas of Rouen, one of the few

[7] Isidore Bertrand, *La Franc-Maçonnerie. Révélations d'un rose-croix à propos des élections générales de 1877* (pamphlet) (Bar-le-Duc, 1877); Bertrand, *Le Pontificat de Pie VI et l'athéisme révolutionnaire* (Paris, Bar-le-Duc, 1879); Bertrand, *La Trinité d'en bas* (Paris, 1905), 143–48; Paul Fesch, Joseph Denais, and René Lay, *Bibliographie de la franc-maçonnerie et des sociétés secrètes* (Paris, 1912–1913), I, 144; *Catalogue générale*, XII, 423.

[8] Isidore Bertrand, *La Franc-Maçonnerie. Histoire authentique des sociétés secrètes* (Paris, 1883); Bertrand, *Un Monde fin-de-siècle* (Paris, 1891); Bertrand, *La Synagogue et les élections de mai 1898* (pamphlet) (Paris, 1898), 3–10; Bertrand, *L'Occultisme ancien et moderne* (Paris, 1899); Bertrand, *La Franc-Maçonnerie, secte juive* (Paris, 1903).

democrats among the higher French clergy, forced Desportes to resign his instructorship in a seminary.

Desportes, as a consequence, turned his efforts into less dangerous channels. In a novel in 1891, he appealed to the French nobility to end their personal and business connections with Jews and Freemasons. Two years later, he published a book on the glories of Merovingian France and an attack upon Ernest Renan, the most celebrated critic of Christianity and the Catholic Church which France produced in the second half of the nineteenth century. From that time forward, Desportes fought through a newspaper he established and edited in Amiens, *La Terre de France.* The program of this newspaper is in many ways representative of the remarkable policy the extreme conservatives had to offer France:

"1. A small plot of land for everyone, regardless of the effect on industry and on scientific agriculture.

2. The extermination of Jewish and Masonic power." [9]

One of the most prolific authors of this era in French history was Monsignor Justin Fèvre, who in the course of a long life which began in 1829 wrote almost fifty books and about half as many pamphlets. So far as is known, Fèvre lived a quiet, scholarly, religious life until 1879, when the attacks of the Opportunist government upon the Church roused him, as it had stimulated so many other French Catholics. Fèvre was an extreme conservative, but he succumbed to the frantic rage which led others to develop the "plot mentality" only during the late 1880's. Thus, in 1881 he ridiculed Chabauty's assertion that the Jews were responsible for the horrors of Freemasonry and declared that the only Jews who

[9] Henri Desportes, *Le Mystère du sang* (Paris, 1899), 262–367; Desportes, *Menées juives* (pamphlet) (Paris, 1890), 6–12; Desportes, *Tué par les juifs* (pamphlet) (Paris, 1890), 20–58; Desportes, *Le Juif franc-maçon* (Paris, 1891); Desportes and François Bournand, *Ernest Renan. Sa Vie et son oeuvre* (Paris, 1893); Desportes, *Mort et vivant. Récit des temps mérovingiens* (Paris, 1893); Paul Lagarde, "Revue des Revues," *Revue Socialiste,* I (1894), 485; *Revue du monde catholique,* CV (1892), 510–11; *Polybiblion,* LXIV (1892), 301; LXV (1892), 76.

were "nihilistic and Masonic" were Jews who had left their religion. Eight years later, however, in a review in the same journal, he proclaimed that Desportes' book on ritual murder was "almost a perfect book" and prayed that thousands of copies would be sold.

Fèvre's policies and actions throughout the remainder of his life were tainted clearly by antisemitism and a vehement hatred for the principles of democracy. In several books and in many speeches, he asserted that French anticlericalism since 1880 was due solely to Freemasonry and Judaism. He denounced "rationalism, Socialism, and Liberalism" as the cause of the conflicts in France. During the Dreyfus Affair, he wrote: "Under penalty of treason, we ought all to be antisemitic, Catholic, and French. We ought to have only one flag, only one battle cry, 'Down with the Jews!'" He declared that the Third Republic's government had corrupted and ruined the Catholic clergy, through a policy of maintaining the priests in poverty and promoting to bishoprics only those priests who were willing to aid the government in its program. Many contemporary bishops were attacked viciously, and this disgusted conservative at the end of his life saw a solution only in the country priests and in the doctrines of Proudhon, "the Titan of Socialism." Everywhere he looked, he saw desolation and abomination, and the Dreyfus Affair he defined as the Revolution's returning to the scene of its crime.[10]

In the battle within the Third Republic for men's minds and votes, the extreme conservative Catholics wielded a number of weapons which were generally far more effective than the ideas which they used as ammunition. One of the most valuable instruments in their possession consisted of the conservative publishing

[10] Justin Fèvre, *La Séparation de l'église et de l'état* (Paris, 1892), preface, 13–19, 179–81; Fèvre, *La Résistance à la persécution* (pamphlet) (Paris, Lyon, 1894), 5–7, 29–33; Fèvre, *La Défense de l'église en France sous Léon XIII* (Paris, 1894), 76–117; Fèvre, *L'Abomination dans le lieu saint* (Paris, 1902), 4–76, 105–59, 179–237; Fèvre, *La Désolation dans le sanctuaire* (Paris, 1902), 1–20, 44–201; Fèvre, "Franc-Maçons et juifs," *Bibliographie catholique*, LXIV (1881), 198–201; LXXX (1889), 377–79; L. Vial, *La Trahison du Grand Rabbin de France* (Paris, 1904), rear cover; *Catalogue générale*, LI, 594–604; *Libre Parole*, May 6, 1898.

houses, which spread their ideas throughout the country. Most
clearly Catholic publishers became engaged in the warfare against
the Jews, primarily because antisemitism in the publishing trade
became the successor to the campaign against the Masons, because
so many Catholic intellectuals joined the attack, and because the
Catholic publishers themselves were sincerely convinced of the
presence of a Jewish "menace." Bloud and Barrel, the *Maison de
la Bonne Presse* of the Assumptionist Fathers, Chamuel, Delhomme
and Briguet, Téqui, and Tolra, were among the most important
because of their established rank in the Catholic publishing field.
Catholic firms in the provinces, such as Séguin in Avignon, Vallier
in Grenoble, Vitte and Perousel in Lyon, and Desclée and
Brouwer in Lille, also contributed by printing and selling the
writings of local authors and spreading antisemitism among their
clientele in those localities.

The most influential Catholic publisher engaged in the campaign against the Jews was Victor Palmé, who founded his concern in 1858 to organize the great French Catholic writers in the
defense of the Catholic Church. In 1859, he established the *Revue
du monde catholique* to canalize Catholic opposition to the Italian
war. His house became the publisher of some of the great Catholic
journals and collections, such as the *Acta Sanctorum, Vie des
Saintes, Bollandistes, Analecta juris pontificii, Gallia christiana, Ami
du clergé, Enseignement catholique,* and *Le Très Saint-Sacrement.*

When Ernest Renan's 1862 lectures at the *Collège de France*
aroused the Catholics and when Renan's *Vie de Jésus* sold more
than sixty thousand copies in less than six months in 1863, Palmé
led the Catholic counterattack by publishing the works of Henri
Lasserre de Monzie. These attacks on Renan and the famous publications on Lourdes raised Palmé to great heights in the industry,
for tens of thousands of copies of these inspirational books were
sold.

Palmé was such a success by 1875 that he decided to strengthen
his publishing house as a leader in the fight against the Opportunists by transforming it into a joint-stock company, the *Société
générale de Librairie catholique.* This new company was capitalized

at four million francs, half of which was contributed by Palmé and his family. Supported by twenty-two bishops, the company advertised its stock in Catholic publications. After 1875, it became one of the leading publishers of books denouncing the anticlericals, particularly the Masons. This proved very profitable, for the concern paid a 10 percent dividend in 1877, after it had given 10 percent of its net profit to help finance the construction of the basilica of the Sacred Heart on Montmartre.[11]

The transition from publishing books and articles attacking Freemasonry to printing attacks upon the Jews was a very easy one for Palmé. His concern published Chabauty's foul and ridiculous books in 1881 and 1882, among the first assaults made upon the Jews in France during this period. It was the Palmé concern which in 1888 brought out the inexpensive edition of *La France juive*. Moreover, in 1889, Palmé published an abridged edition of the translation of Rohling's *Der Talmudjude*, which was an open vicious attack upon Judaism.[12]

The *Revue du monde catholique*, which Palmé founded and published, serves as a good index to a segment of conservative Catholic opinion concerning antisemitism. This influential journal, which had a circulation at this time of seven thousand, was among the great disseminators of antisemitism. It had shown infrequent but violent traces of a Catholic and pseudonational antisemitism before 1886, and the reception it accorded Drumont was extremely enthusiastic. Prior to 1890, the only criticisms it ever directed against antisemitic books were on grounds of style, organization, or originality. Numerous articles, invariably vicious, called attention to Jewish predominance in finance and the press and showed

[11] Henri Lasserre de Monzie, *Les Saints évangiles. Traduction nouvelle* (Paris, 1887), New York Public Library author card; Henri Avenel, *Annuaire de la presse française*, VI (1885), 116, 119; IX (1888), 657–64; *Catalogue générale*, LXXXIX, 742–54; *Revue du monde catholique*, XLIII (1875), 817–24; LIII (1878), 297; *L'Art et l'Idée*, I (1892), 253.

[12] E. A. Chabauty (Count C. de Saint-André, *pseud.*), *Les Franc-Maçons et les Juifs* (Paris, 1881); Chabauty, *Les Juifs, nos maîtres* (Paris, 1882); Edouard Drumont, *La France juive* (Paris, 1888 edition); Auguste Rohling, *Le Juif-Talmudiste* (Paris, 1889); *Polybiblion*, LXI (1890), 87; *Bibliographie catholique*, LXXVIII (1888), 78, 152; *Catalogue générale*, XLII, 219.

that Judaism, not clericalism, was the real danger to France.[13]

The French antisemitic publishing houses were the heavy artillery of the conservative Catholic campaign against the Jews, while the daily and weekly newspapers were the light weapons. The most important single weapon in the antisemitic arsenal was the *Libre Parole*, founded by Drumont in April, 1892. With the exception of a few short-lived newspapers and of the *Lillois* and *France libre*, the *Libre Parole* was the only French daily newspaper before 1898 whose main program was to strip the Jews of their property and power. However, the *Libre Parole* received substantial assistance from other established newspapers which were anti-Republican or extremely critical of the parties in power in the Republic and which adopted antisemitism as one of the tenets of their programs.

Until 1890, most of the Catholic press in Paris and all of the provincial Catholic newspapers were conservative and monarchist. The political, economic, and social views of these papers and the beliefs then prevalent in most Catholic intellectual circles fostered an antidemocratic and antisemitic tone. The royalist *Gazette de France*, for example, made frequent use of antisemitism as one of its bludgeons against the Republic, particularly after the arrest of Captain Dreyfus. *Autorité*, founded in 1886 by Paul de Cassagnac to denounce the Republic and the Republicans, also promoted feeling against the Jews by occasional quips and stories criticizing Jews in France and abroad. Cassagnac was a strange and contradictory man. Always a Catholic and always on the Right, he was now a Bonapartist, now a Boulangist, and now a legitimist. He opposed the manner in which the original Dreyfus trial was conducted, although he confessed himself an antisemite. He hailed the revisionist campaign in 1897, but he continued from time to

[13] *Revue du monde catholique:* Hermann Kuhn, "La Question juive en Allemagne," LXXI (1881), 70–86; Auguste Geoffroy, "La Situation en Algérie," LXXXIII (1885), 289–301, 414–25; Arsène Guérin, "La France juive," LXXXVI (1886), 405–19; Paul Bellet, "L'Invasion juive," LXXXIX (1887), 5–36; Dom Benoît, "La Révolution français à propos du centenaire de 1889," XCVIII (1889), 225–51; Avenel, *Annuaire de la presse française*, XV (1894), 171; XVII (1896), 185.

time to write antisemitic articles, perhaps to prevent his readers from transferring their loyalties to other newspapers.[14]

THE CROIX

The most important associate of the *Libre Parole* in the newspaper campaign against the Jews was the *Croix*, published by the Assumptionist Fathers. The political policy of this newspaper and of all of the other publications produced by the *Maison de la Bonne Presse*, the publishing company operated by the Assumptionists, was generally vague until late in 1891. However, when Cardinal Lavigerie and Pope Leo XIII launched the *ralliement* program, the *Croix* combined a formal acceptance of this policy, "fighting the battles of the Church but not the Republic as such," with a most bitter attack against the Republic, the Republicans, and Republican institutions and laws. Catholic and anticlerical historians are both in agreement with Dominique Cardinal Ferrata, the papal nuncio in Paris at that time, that the *Croix* did more than any other newspaper, with the possible exception of Drumont's *Libre Parole*, to prevent the success of the Pope's policy. Its social program was very similar to that of most of the other extreme conservative Catholic papers, for it failed generally to recognize that there were any serious social problems in France.[15]

The *Croix* and the chain of newspapers it established throughout France represent one of the great journalistic accomplishments of modern times. Father Vincent de Paul Bailly must surely be ranked with Joseph Pulitzer, William Randolph Hearst, and the Harmsworths as one of the great organizers and promoters of early popular journalism. Bailly, who had been Napoleon III's confidential telegrapher, entered his novitiate in 1860 when he was

[14] Isidore Loeb, *Réflexions sur les juifs* (Paris, 1894), 52; Frederick Conybeare, *The Dreyfus Case* (London, 1898), 8; Hippolyte Gayraud, *L'Antisémitisme de St. Thomas d'Aquin* (Paris, 1896), 30-31; Léonce Reynaud, *Les Juifs français devant l'opinion* (Paris, 1887), XI-XII, 397, 426; Edouard Lecanuet, *Les Signes avant-coureurs de la séparation, 1894-1910* (Paris, 1930), 179; Paul Marin, *Dreyfus?* (Paris, 1898), 103-27, 350-53, 470-73, 531-35; Ferrata, *op. cit.,* 286; *Anti-Juif* (Algiers), September 7, 1890; *Vraie Parole,* April 1, 1893.

[15] Paul Naudet, *Pourquoi les catholiques ont perdu la bataille* (Paris, 1904), 103-106; Ferrata, *op. cit.,* 548-60; Debidour, *op. cit.,* II, 141-42, 372-75; Lecanuet, *Les Signes avant-coureurs,* 7, 29-70, 274-76; Brogan, *op. cit.,* 260.

thirty years old. After serving as a chaplain first in the Papal army and then in the army of France, in 1877 he was named editor of a little religious monthly, *Le Pèlerin*. Within two years, this remarkably able journalist had raised the circulation of this journal from only a few hundred to eighty thousand. In January, 1880, he decided to establish a companion journal, the *Croix Revue*, specifically to oppose Freemasonry. The success of this journal was great, due largely to Bailly's provocative style and to the fact that it appealed openly to the Catholic masses, which were generally neglected by both the Catholic newspapers and journals.

While he was in Bethlehem in March, 1883, on one of the twenty-eight pilgrimages he was to make to the Holy Land during his lifetime, Bailly decided to transform the *Croix Revue* into a daily newspaper selling for only five centimes. Almost from its first appearance on June 16, 1883, this newspaper was a tremendous success. Within a year, its circulation reached thirty thousand daily. It was short, well edited, simple, and well illustrated. It was disdained by Catholic intellectuals but was very popular with priests and with devout lay Catholics, upon whom it grew to have enormous influence. By 1889, it was a very securely established newspaper with a circulation of sixty thousand.

During the decade after 1888, the *Maison de la Bonne Presse* and the various *Croix* publications reached national significance in France. The editors used the very latest equipment throughout the printing plant, and the *Maison de la Bonne Presse* was noted for its pension plan, cooperative restaurant, and sickness and accident insurance. In 1888, the editors lowered the price to one centime, sent representatives touring through France on circulation drives, and persuaded country priests not only to subscribe but to become salesmen. Working most intensively during the winter and during retreats and missions, the *Croix* developed to a very high degree many of the techniques familiar in newspaper promotion much later.

As a consequence of this capable promotion, the *Croix* became an organ of tremendous influence among the sincere Catholic masses of France. The daily circulation rose to 110,000 in 1889, to 140,000 in 1890, and to 180,000 in 1893. Although the daily circulation of the *Croix* in 1894 was only a fraction of that of the *Petit Journal* or of that of the *Petit Parisien*, the Paris versions of the new papers designed for the masses, it was more than double that of *Figaro* or of *Le Rappel*, "the most widely read Radical Republican daily." According to a Catholic priest who opposed its views, it was "the most widely read Catholic newspaper and that read by most Catholic priests."

The *Maison de la Bonne Presse* not only developed a tremendous circulation for the daily *Croix*, but it also spawned a popular Sunday edition and numerous provincial editions. The *Croix du dimanche* was founded in 1885 and in 1890 had a circulation of 200,000, which rose to 365,000 in 1894 and to 525,000 in 1899. The first two weekly provincial supplements were published in Reims and Limoges in 1889, but in 1890 there were eighteen, in 1891 thirty, in 1892 forty-four, in 1893 seventy-one, and in 1894 one hundred and four provincial supplements. During 1894, more than two million copies of various *Croix* publications were being printed each week.[16]

From its founding in 1883, the *Croix* was pointedly critical of Republicans and Republican institutions. It was the first newspaper to review *La France juive* in 1886, and it praised Drumont enthusiastically. Its antisemitism was not strong during the 1880's while the paper and the *Bonne Presse* organization were gradually rising to prominence. However, the early 1890's produced a slight weakening of radical strength in France, as well as a similar in-

---

[16] Paul Soleilhac, *Le Grand Levrier* (Paris, 1906), 55–62; Louis Bethleem, *La Presse. Son Influence et sa puissance* (Paris, 1926), 331–66; Paul Fesch, *Les Souvenirs d'un abbé journaliste* (Paris, 1898), 298–303; *Congrès national du livre. Comité d'organisation. Société des gens de lettres. Cercle de la librairie. Comité du livre. Rapports et résolutions* (Paris, 1917–1922), I, 237–40; E. Kennedy O'Byrne, "The Making of a Great Catholic Newspaper," *Irish Monthly*, VL (1917), 552–63; Virginia M. Crawford, "*La Croix* and Its Founder, 1832–1932," *Studies*, XXII (1933), 233–40; Lecanuet, *Les Signes avant-coureurs*, 221–29; Avenel, *Annuaire de la presse française*, VI (1885), 119; VIII (1887), 124; X (1889), 132; XI (1890), 136; XII (1891), 122; XIII (1892), 129–30; XIV (1893), 136–37, 164, 1062; XV (1894), 142, 143, 154, 157, 170; XVI (1895), 145, 149, 174; XVII (1896), 144, 1044; XVIII (1897), 142, 161; XIX (1898), 154; XX (1899), 1034; XXI (1900), 182, 186.

crease in conservative strength, so that the attitude of the firmly established *Croix* towards the issue of *ralliement* and towards the Republic became more caustic. Only the *Libre Parole* was more open and vociferous in its denunciations of the Jews, and the *Croix* and its national organization helped make the Protestants in France a more important target for the antisemites.

After the arrest of Captain Dreyfus in 1894, the *Croix* became even more intemperate in its antisemitism and anti-Republicanism. During 1895, it aroused bitter opposition to the tax on the property of religious orders, in spite of the plea of the papal nuncio. In 1896, Father Adéodat Debauve of the Assumptionists and the *Croix* established a Catholic electoral committee, the *Comité Justice-Egalité*, to support all electoral candidates who would oppose the Masons and Jews and who would struggle against legislation designed to restrict or control the Catholic Church. Managed with the usual efficiency of the Assumptionists, this organization established a nation-wide network, published its own weekly newspaper, and took a prominent part in the elections of 1898 and 1899 in particular.

As the power and prestige of the *Croix* grew and as the crisis of the Dreyfus Affair deepened in France, the newspaper became more violent and aggressive. Many Catholics were horrified by its excesses, which drew increasing wrath upon the Catholic Church and upon its witless "political priests." The *Croix* responded to all complaints with the open threat of denunciation and insult against those Catholic lay and ecclesiastic leaders who were reluctant to follow its lead. Thus, when Bishop Fuzet of Rouen in 1895 opposed the *Croix* policy on the tax on religious orders, it accused the eminent cleric of seeking the Archbishopric of Paris "before it was vacant."

After Dreyfus had been condemned, the *Croix* reported that his wife was going to divorce him and that his family was abandoning him. When antisemitic riots in Algiers in February, 1898, led to the ransacking of Jewish shops, the *Croix* claimed Christ had protected the Christian ones. It praised the subscription begun by the *Libre Parole* for Colonel Henry, who committed suicide after his forgeries were discovered, declaring that "this manifestation of respect and sympathy" was "a great, comforting, and consoling spectacle." The *Croix de l'Aveyron* cried that "Henry was murdered by assassins who were probably in the pay of the Jews." Many of the provincial *Croix* boasted proudly that they refused to accept advertisements or subscriptions from Jews and Masons.[17]

The Vatican in 1897 refused the request of the French government that it advise the *Croix* to cease its "organized propaganda campaign" against the Republic. The attempts by French lay and ecclesiastical leaders to induce the editors to moderate their policy also failed. As a consequence, when the tide turned against the anti-Dreyfusards late in 1899, the religious orders and, ultimately, the Catholic Church itself in France, paid a heavy penalty. The Assumptionist congregation was dissolved in France in January, 1900, and the entire publishing organization was turned over to a lay Catholic, Paul Féron-Vrau, who possessed few of the abilities the founders of the *Croix* organization had had in such abundance.[18]

THE AWAKENING OF THE CONSERVATIVE CATHOLICS

The reception given to antisemitism by the conservative Catholics during the first few years after 1886 was very warm, and in their delight with this new bludgeon against the Republic they

[17] Joseph Brugerette, *Le Prêtre français et la société contemporaine* (Paris, 1935), II, 442; Joseph Reinach, *Histoire de l'Affaire Dreyfus* (Paris, 1901-1911), I, 490; III, 537; Léon Chaine, *Les Catholiques français et leurs difficultés actuelles devant l'opinion* (Lyon, 1908), 172-73; Ferdinand Momméja, "*Il n'y a pas d'Affaire Dreyfus*" (Paris, 1908), 157; L. Vial, *Le Juif roi. Comment le détrôner* (Paris, 1897), 6, 35-36, 57-63, 91-93, 107-108; *Le Procès des douze. En Appel. Interrogatoire et plaidories. Audiences des 25 et 26 février, 5 et 6 mars 1900* (Paris, 1900), 29-30; Lecanuet, *Les Signes avant-coureurs*, 45, 170, 207; Debidour, *op. cit.*, II, 190-98; Gayraud, *op. cit.*, 8-10, 35, 44-45, 205-206.

[18] Georges Lachapelle, *Le Ministère Méline. Deux Années de politique intérieure et extérieure, 1896-1898* (Paris, 1928), 179-81; Lecanuet, *Les Signes avant-coureurs*, 209-18; *Le Procès des douze*, 5-238; Debidour, *op. cit.*, II, 261-67; Crawford, *loc. cit.*, 241-44. With a discredited cause and with much less efficient and inspired leadership, the *Maison de la Bonne Presse* was on the verge of bankruptcy in 1908. A hasty campaign for funds raised three and a half million francs, and the *Croix* thereupon was able to return to its religious mission with a vigor which political campaigns had led astray.

failed to analyze the programs which many other antisemites with different political, religious, and social attitudes were suggesting. It was only in 1889 and 1890 that signs of the impending rift among the antisemites began to appear. Conservative reviewers first carefully noted the "undeserved scorn for the upper bourgeoisie and the nobility" and the indulgence shown for the Socialists by many of the antisemites. Two "altruistic Socialists" were condemned for "attributing all vices and wrongs to the rich, just as Drumont does," while another enthusiastic admirer of Drumont was lauded for not repeating his model "in attacking respectable people."

Perhaps an analysis of the transformation and definition of the ideas of Professor Claudio Jannet of the Catholic Institute in Paris will demonstrate clearly how many conservatives began to realize that there was more than one brand of antisemitism and that some types of it might become rather frightening. Professor Jannet began his scholarly career as a French student of the United States, and his first book, a study he completed in 1876 when he was thirty-two, tended to demonstrate that the development of American institutions indicated that America was already a decadent country. He devoted the next decade or so of his life to a study of Freemasonry and its nefarious influence upon French society. The first evidence of this interest is Jannet's edition in 1881 of one of the "classics" of the nineteenth century antiliberal campaign, *Les Sociétés secrètes et la société, ou Philosophie de l'histoire contemporaine*, produced originally during the 1870's by an old Jesuit friend of Jannet, Father Nicolas Deschamps.

Jannet edited and published three editions of Deschamps' book after the death of the original author. Each later edition was considerably more antisemitic than the previous one, and Jannet by 1884, two years before the publication of Drumont's book, was clearly an antisemite. He emphasized the disastrous influence the Jews were having in France on the Catholic Church and on Catholic customs and institutions. He stated clearly in the 1883 edition of Father Deschamps' book that antisemitism was a religious question, not a social question.

Professor Jannet began to show alarm at the "socialism" apparent in the antisemitic campaign as early as 1890. He emphasized again that antisemitism was a religious question and declared that, "in spite of the true Christians," it was being controlled by "men who lead the Socialists to pillage and massacre the Jews." He urged "the great young lords who amuse themselves with antisemitism" to read some of the books which suggested expropriation as a solution. Still wrestling with the problem, late in the same year in an address to a Catholic Youth Congress he declared that, although the Jews were speculators, they should be attacked only because they were "an indelible special nationality." In 1892, he confessed that "the Jewish question" was very complex, but warned "the honest but ignorant" that the skillful Socialist leaders would try to divert it from its true religious course towards an attack upon capitalism. Frightened by the Socialist peril, just before his death in 1893 he began to abandon his strictly conservative economic position to declare that to forestall the Socialists, with all of their wily techniques, "the Christian capitalists should take a greater interest in ameliorating the fate of the masses." [19]

Victor Palmé's publishing company and his *Revue du monde catholique* also mirror conservative reluctance to continue to promote antisemitism as the "socialism" of the antisemites and the furious attacks by the disgruntled Drumont upon the conservatives began to alarm them. Palmé's *Société générale de Librairie catholique* went bankrupt in 1890. It was quickly reorganized and continued

[19] Nicolas Deschamps, *Les Sociétés secrètes et la société, ou Philosophie de l'histoire contemporaine* (Paris, 1873–1876); *Ibid.* (Paris, 1881–1883 edition), III, 22–27; Claudio Jannet, *Les Sociétés secrètes et la société* (pamphlet) (Paris, 1887); Jannet and Louis d'Estampes, *La Franc-Maçonnerie et la Révolution* (Paris, 1884), preface; Jannet, *Les Etats-Unis contemporains* (Paris, 1876); Jannet, *Les Précurseurs de la franc-maçonnerie* (Paris, 1887); Jannet, *Le Capital, la speculation et la finance* (Paris, 1892), 481–569; François Bournand (Jean de Ligneau, pseud.), *Juifs et antisémites en Europe* (Paris, 1892), 9; *Polybiblion*, XI (1874), 148–49; XVI (1876), 64–65; XX (1877), 432–33; XLI (1884), 159–60; XLIX (1887), 329–30; LVIII (1890), 320; LXV (1892), 130–31, 321–22; *Bibliographie catholique*, LXIII (1881), 173; LXIX (1884), 58–63, 541; LXXI (1885), 109–13; LXXIX (1889), 188–91; LXXX (1889), 466–69; *Revue catholique de Normandie*, III (1893), 87.

its campaign as a defender of the Catholic Church, though now not employing antisemitism, only to collapse again in 1894. Palmé sold the facilities, publishing rights, and publications to Arthur Savaète, who was never able to revive the concern very effectively, although he did turn it into an anti-Dreyfusard instrument in 1897.

An article by Urbain Guérin in the August, 1892, issue of the *Revue du monde catholique* inaugurated a new program for that conservative journal by indicating the ultimate danger behind the campaign against the Jews. Guérin feared antisemitism because it roused a revolutionary sentiment and because the war on Jewish capital would be only a prelude to that on Christian capital. He therefore urged all Catholics to abandon the campaign and suggested a program of social reform which was practically a restatement of *Rerum novarum*. The journal's attitude towards the social question from that time forward was characterized by a less strict paternalism, and the reviews of antisemitic books became increasingly critical until they were discontinued in June, 1893. During the Panama scandal, this conservative journal had only a slight tinge of antisemitism, and by the summer of 1894 all traces of feeling against the Jews had disappeared completely. As a matter of fact, just before the Dreyfus Affair revived its antisemitism, a review in this journal denounced as "only a distressing and vulgar political pamphlet" the book by a Christian Democratic priest which won a first prize in a contest staged by the *Libre Parole* for the best solution to "the Jewish question." [20]

The histories of two of the most important Catholic newspapers during these years, the *Monde* and *Univers*, supplement that of the *Revue du monde catholique* to demonstrate clearly just what happened to the conservative Catholics. The *Monde* had presented traces of antisemitism even before 1870, but the paper was reorganized in 1883 under the direction of Monsignor d'Hulst as a

[20] Henri Le Soudier, *Bibliographie française. Recueil de catalogues des editeurs français* (Paris, 1896), V. Savaète *catalogue*, 1–7; Urbain Guérin, "Juifs, capitalistes, patrons, et ouvriers," *Revue du monde catholique*, XCI (1892), 233–56; Henri d'Hessert, "A Travers les Revues," *Revue du monde catholique*, CXXX (1897), 161–66; *Polybiblion*, LXI (1890), 87.

moderate Catholic paper above political party opinion. Drumont became a member of the staff during part of 1886, and the reception granted his book as an attack upon the anticlericals was very warm. However, the campaign against the Jews was never seriously pressed there, and the newspaper's political attitude in general was so moderate and its interest in social problems so absent that few French Catholics read it. Several attempts were made to revive it, the final desperate effort being granted to Father Paul Naudet, a Christian Democrat, but finally in 1896 the *Monde* was forced to fuse with *Univers*.[21]

Univers was described in 1886 as "the most important and widely read Catholic newspaper in France." It did not pose as a defender of the Jews and democracy, but it never became wildly antisemitic and it did manage in political crises to maintain an impartial stand. The death of the extremely conservative Louis Veuillot in 1883 robbed the paper of its guiding spirit and of much of its influence, and it is clear that the board of editors after his death was sharply divided even on such critical issues as the attitude to be adopted towards the Third Republic. Thus, in spite of its generally conciliatory attitude after the death of Veuillot, one of its most recalcitrant editors, Arthur Loth, was allowed to write in the May 11, 1889 issue:

> The Jews have a right to celebrate the anniversary of the Revolution. They have been here only one hundred years and already they own half the land; soon they will own it all. They control our land, our money, our government, and our press. Rothschild and his fellows are more the masters of France than the President and his ministers. They rule the stock exchange, and that is now the real center of action and power.

The *Univers*, due in part to its ultramontane tradition and in part to its understanding of French realities, loyally accepted the policy of *ralliement*. This program led to the decisive division of

[21] Gougenot des Mousseaux, *Le Juif, le judaïsme et la judaïsation des peuples chrétiens* (Paris, 1869), 142–43, 342–43, 356, 374–82, 424–25, 452, 476–80; Alfred Baudrillart, *Vie de Monsignor d'Hulst* (Paris, 1925), II, 10–27; Edouard Lecanuet, *La Vie de l'Eglise sous Léon XIII* (Paris, 1930), 233–38; Naudet, *op. cit.*, 269–70; *Polybiblion*, XLVIII (1886), 24, 190.

the board of editors and to the loss of many subscribers and readers. In July, 1893, Loth withdrew with a part of the staff to found a new intransigent paper, *Vérité*. Financed by a group of northern industrialists, *Vérité* began a bitter campaign against the Republic and those Catholics who supported it. It treated those who accepted the Pope's encyclical *Rerum novarum* as Socialists, and no anticlerical paper exceeded *Vérité* in its attacks upon those members of the clergy who disagreed with its views. It was, of course, bitterly anti-Dreyfusard, and it led many thoughtless Catholics into the disaster of the Dreyfus Affair.[22]

The conservative Catholics, therefore, between the critical years of 1892 and 1896, divided into two groups. One group accepted the Republic but remained critical of its legislation, while the other remained irreconcilable and refused to cooperate with Leo XIII's sensible program. The Radicals naturally were suspicious of *ralliement* as an attempt by the Catholics to seize the Republic by infiltration, but the responsibility for the failure of that program lies mainly with the intransigent Catholics. All of the leaders of this group were antisemites, and most Catholic antisemites were violently opposed to the Pope's policy. The ultimate effect of antisemitism upon those conservatives who accepted it and preached it, therefore, was that their attitude towards the Republic and the issue of *ralliement* was very strongly influenced during these critical years. As a result, the Catholics not only lost a fine opportunity to construct a more satisfactory arrangement concerning the relations between the Church and the State, but they also helped to destroy the foundations of conciliation which had appeared among many Opportunists and Radicals, thus maintaining *les deux France* as the fundamental weakness of France.

THE SOCIAL CATHOLICS

The Social Catholics were not so vehemently opposed to the Republic nor so staunchly committed to the defense of the entire

[22] Lecanuet, *La Vie de l'Eglise*, 212–20; Avenel, *Annuaire de la presse française*, VIII (1887), 622–23; *Univers*, January–December, 1886; January, March–May, 1889; January–December, 1892 and 1893; *Polybiblion*, LXXXIV (1898), 80, 120, 160, 485–86; LXXXVII (1899), 40, 56; XC (1900), 320, 360.

existing social order as the Tory Catholics, for many Social Catholics believed that social change was more significant than political change and that the Republic might prove a satisfactory form of government for them. Influenced strongly by Le Play, they advocated "family wages," social insurance, factory regulations, company-controlled unions, shorter hours, and the six-day week. Antisemitism became an important part of their philosophy also. The writings of the Marquis de La Tour du Pin, who founded the Catholic Workers' Clubs with Count Albert de Mun after the Franco-Prussian War, reveal clearly the growing amount of hatred of the Jews in this group.

An article by La Tour du Pin in 1883 attacked Freemasonry as "the general staff of the Revolution," which for him was the cause of all the evils of France. In 1889, he discovered "the general staff of the gilded international, Jewish high finance." He defined antisemitism then as "the hatred ruined families have always felt for usurers." These impoverished families by 1894 had become only the Jewish leprosy's first victims in France. By 1898, La Tour du Pin had bound all of the conventional arguments about the Revolution, the Protestants and Masons, anticlericalism, and the economic power of the Jews into his thesis. One result was that he was eventually carried far beyond Social Catholicism, for his demand for an intellectual revolution and corporatism made him an important link between the older monarchists and the *Action Française*.[23]

The Social Catholic movement was crippled from the start by its close connection with monarchism. Its two leaders, Count Albert de Mun and La Tour du Pin, openly declared their preference for the monarchy to the Republic, and the former during most of these years was a leader of the monarchists in the Cham-

---

[23] Aloysius von Lichtenstein, "La Réforme sociale et le programme antisémitique," *Association catholique*, XXXII (1891), 164–73, 199–207; Dr. Kaempfe, "Le Mouvement antisémitique en Autriche," *Réforme Sociale*, second series, VI (1888), 567–77; Marquis René de la Tour du Pin, *Vers un Ordre social chrétien. Jalons de route, 1882–1907* (Paris, 1929 edition), 46, 102–104, 213–14, 224–2 240, 305–306, 327–51. The same steady growth of antisemitism can be traced arly in the three-volume work of another Social Catholic, Paul Lapeyre, *Le Socialisme catholique* (Paris, 1894–1900).

ber of Deputies. The issue of *ralliement* divided the Social Catholic movement into several groups. Most of the monarchists abandoned the movement, some led by La Tour du Pin joining the intransigents and becoming increasingly bitter against their former comrades, the Third Republic, and democratic principles. The majority, however, became Catholic moderates. Led by Count Albert de Mun, they accepted *ralliement*, swung to the support of the Republic, and generally ceased both their antisemitism and their opposition to political democracy. The liberal wing of the movement joined the Christian Socialist or Christian Democratic group. Thus, the Catholic center in France was also divided by the issue of *ralliement* and acceptance of the Republic. The virus of antisemitism not only contributed to the decision of the Social Catholic right wing to continue to oppose the Republic resolutely, but it also weakened the determination and effectiveness of those who did adopt the Pope's policy, thus helping here also to destroy the possibility of a free reunion of all Frenchmen upon a solid democratic foundation.[24]

THE CHRISTIAN DEMOCRATS

The Christian Democratic movement was largely the clever alliance of Drumont's antisemitism and "socialist" ideas with the realizations that the Third Republic was firmly established, that the workers were Republican, and that it was the duty of the Church and her priests to wean the workers from revolutionary socialism with a Catholic program of social reform. The leaders of this movement were in great part sincere young Catholic priests and journalists, strongly influenced by Drumont and his ideas and very eager to ally the Church with the people in a powerful social party. They were a great source of alarm to the conservative Catholics, for their newspapers and congresses paid little respect to privilege or propertied interests and advocated a real Catholic social democracy.

[24] Parker T. Moon, *The Labor Problem and the Social Catholic Movement in France* (New York, 1921), 85–98, 172–214; Charlotte Muret, *French Royalist Doctrines since the Revolution* (New York, 1933), 203–207; Lecanuet, *La Vie de l'Eglise*, 603–10; Debidour, *op. cit.*, II, 1–78.

When the Christian Democratic movement first began around 1890, the social and economic ideas of many of the Christian Democrats were hardly more radical than those of many of the Social Catholics. However, no Christian Democrats were monarchists, and by 1893 or 1894 the distinctions between the economic and social views of the two groups were becoming clear. The two movements were closely connected during the early 1890's, nevertheless, and there was a rather important group of Catholics who sought to unite them. Léon Harmel, a very prominent Catholic manufacturer who practiced the principles of the Social Catholics in his factories, was president of the Social Catholics' Association of Catholic Workers' Clubs at the same time that he was honorary chairman of the Christian Democratic organization. Efforts such as those of Harmel failed, however, and the Christian Democratic movement by 1895 was obviously becoming more Republican and radical, thus defining more specifically the division of the Catholic groups.[25]

The genesis of the Christian Democratic movement in France can perhaps best be described through an account of the activities and the ideas of four able young Catholic priests, all born between 1856 and 1859 and all convinced by 1890 that the Catholic Church had to accept the Republic and political democracy and to promote social reform in France, at the expense of the old ruling classes, if it were to continue to thrive. All came from different parts of France, but all were in agreement even before they met on the fundamental attitudes Catholics should have on the principal political and social problems of the day. All believed also that the newspaper was the best means of influencing the worker and the peasant and of attaining their aims. Antisemitism was an element in the philosophy of each of these young priests, in some cases a very important one. However, it is likely that but for the tremendous prestige of Drumont among those Catholics who were critical of the lack of social progress being made in France and for

[25] Georges Weill, *Histoire du mouvement social en France, 1852–1914* (Paris, 1924), 415–24; Lecanuet, *La Vie de l'Eglise*, 610–620; Moon, *op. cit.*, 175, 365–67, 445.

the unwise decision to invite Drumont and his personal followers to the first Christian Democratic congress in 1896, these Christian Democrats and the entire movement might ultimately have overcome and rejected this basically un-Christian doctrine.

The first of these talented young priests was Father Paul Fesch, born in 1858 in Clermont, about forty miles directly north of Paris. As a young priest, Fesch in his sermons and in anonymous columns he wrote for local newspapers demonstrated an understanding of the position of the workers in French society which irritated and disturbed his more conservative parishioners and readers. His first publication was a small book, *De l'Ouvrier et du respect*, which appeared in 1888 and the second edition of which had a preface by Drumont. This won praise from such diverse sources as the Catholic *Réforme Sociale* and the *Revue Socialiste*. Fesch's sermons and writings won such attention in northern France that in 1889 the *Journal de l'Oise*, a conservative paper in Beauvais, invited him to join its staff. His columns there were so successful that in 1891 Bishop Péronne of Beauvais invited him to establish a new paper to advance the social views of Pope Leo XIII and to participate in the establishment of a trade school in Beauvais. The publication of this weekly newspaper gave Fesch an opportunity to define and to promote his ideas, and it also educated him in the difficulties facing a Catholic who accepted political democracy and advanced a social reform program.

Buffeted by the conservatives on the Right as a priest who was trying to reconcile the Revolution and Christianity, and by the Republicans and Socialists on the Left as a priest in politics and a concrete example of the great danger of clericalism, Fesch was able to maintain his newspaper for only a year before it crumbled under these attacks. He joined the *Croix* organization then, but his views were too radical also for that conservative, anti-Republican newspaper system. By 1893, Fesch had advanced from a general Social Catholic position to a Christian Democratic position. He was an open advocate of Pope Leo XIII's policy of *ralliement* and a frequent speaker before workers' groups on the need for social legislation. In 1894, he came to Paris and became the editor of the old Boulangist paper, *La Cocarde*, which had then only twenty-five subscribers. He failed to revive this newspaper, just as Maurice Barrès did after him. His final attempt to promote Christian Democracy was made with Father Paul Naudet on the *Monde*, and after this ill-fated venture he abandoned his efforts in 1896 and became a traveler and bibliographer of Freemasonry, preferring to fight the enemies of Catholicism in that much easier way.[26]

Father Hippolyte Gayraud came from southwestern France, for he was born in a tiny village in Tarn-et-Garonne in 1856 and became a Dominican monk in 1877. From 1887 until 1893, Gayraud was professor of scholastic theology at the Catholic Institute of Toulouse, but in 1893, dissatisfied with life as a Dominican professor in a provincial city, he became a diocesan cleric and came to Paris. A remarkably able orator and a very capable politician, Gayraud apparently never did acquire the understanding of social problems characteristic of many of his colleagues in the Christian Democratic movement, but he did accept wholeheartedly the Third Republic and political democracy. He was one of the most avid opponents of the Catholic monarchists, and he was bitterly denounced by all conservatives as a traitor. Elected to the Chamber of Deputies from Brest in 1897 in a bitterly fought contest with a royalist, Gayraud was re-elected in 1898 and 1902 over the furious protests of such conservative organs as *Croix*, *Vérité*, and *Autorité*.

It is very apparent from Gayraud's actions in the Chamber of Deputies that he represented Catholic interests, but he spoke even in 1905 and 1906 for reconciliation between the Church and the Republic. He was suspect by all anticlericals as well as by the conservative Catholics. He was one of the leading organizers of the Christian Democratic congresses from 1896 through 1900, and he was the president of the 1898 congress. His statement at that

---

[26] Paul Fesch, *De l'Ouvrier et du respect* (Paris, 1888), 6–35, 110–37; Fesch, *Dossiers maçonnique* (Paris, 1905); Fesch, *Souvenirs*, 28–216; Eugène Ledos, *Joseph Denais, écrivain et journaliste angevin* (Angers, 1920), 167–68, 193; Lecanuet, *La Vie de l'Eglise*, 235–38; Debidour, *op. cit.*, II, 85, 151–52.

congress that the Christian Democratic party was not a purely
Catholic party, but "can, and must, include all those who call
themselves Christians, whatever be their confession or profession
of faith" was considered a clear proof by his enemies among the
Catholics of betrayal of the Catholic Church. He was generally
considered responsible for the adoption by the Christian Democrats in 1897 of the decision to unite with all Republicans of all
shades against any conservative who opposed the Republic.

Gayraud was one of the most vigorous antisemites in the Christian Democratic movement. He was an advocate of what he called
"Christian antisemitism," and he tried to distinguish this brand
of attack upon the Jews from "the fanatical commercial antisemitism of the jealous few." Declaring that "a convinced Christian
is by nature a practicing antisemite," he asserted that "the Jew
is the enemy of Christ and of Christian France." At the first
congress of the Christian Democrats in Lyon in 1896, he cried out
that the Catholic Church had always been antisemitic "on a high
moral plane" and that "all social excrement, especially the Jews,"
should be expelled from France. Gayraud's antisemitism and his
neglect of and ignorance of social issues help to explain the complete debacle of the Christian Democratic movement in France as
he rose in power in it, for the movement as a whole had a strong
social purpose and was not so deeply scarred with hatred of the
Jews as this militant priest was.[27]

Father Paul Naudet was born in Bordeaux in 1859 and became
a professor in a seminary near that city after his ordination in
1883. He became a staunch Republican and defender of Republican
institutions, although the anti-Masonic campaign of the 1880's and
Drumont's writings made him an antisemite. His attack upon the
Jews was based on their economic power in France, which he felt

[27] Julien Cordier, *Deux Ans de polémique, 1896–1897* (Nancy, 1898), 218–21,
325–29, 347–50; *Congrès nationale de la Démocratie Chrétienne, 1896* (Lyon,
1897), 68–73, 78; Henri Delassus, *La Démocratie chrétienne, parti et école* (pamphlet) (Paris, 1911), 14–16; C. E. Curinier (editor), *Dictionnaire national des
contemporains* (Paris, 1899–1905), IV, 335; Gayraud, *op. cit.*, 7–9; Lecanuet, *Les
Signes avant-coureurs*, 99–105; Debidour, *op. cit.*, II, 152, 259, 274, 284, 346, 403,
455.

excessive and dangerous. Naudet was never a rabid antisemite, however, and in the Dreyfus Affair his colleagues were disappointed by his lack of vehemence as an anti-Dreyfusard. As a matter of fact, Naudet's newspaper, *Justice Sociale*, was the first Catholic newspaper to publish letters favorable to Dreyfus, and it also became an instrument for the Catholic Committee for the Defense of Justice.

While a supporter of the Republic and an advocate of extensive social reform, Naudet was an eager opponent of socialism. A handsome man and an excellent orator, Naudet debated successfully on a number of occasions with Jules Guesde and other Socialists. His speeches were so successful that he soon received invitations to address groups of workers, largely Catholic, all over France. In July, 1893, he founded a newspaper, *Justice Sociale*, in Bordeaux to carry the message of Leo XIII's *Rerum novarum* to the workers. In this newspaper and in the addresses he delivered during the second half of 1893, he formulated clearly for the first time in France the Christian Democratic doctrine. After he had developed this program, he moved the paper to Paris in January, 1894, and rapidly became one of the most influential priests and journalists in the capital. *Justice Sociale* remained one of the principal organs of French Catholic social thought from 1893 until 1908, when it foundered during the crisis over modernism.

In October, 1894, Naudet was named editor of the *Monde*, which had then only 2,500 subscribers. His success in almost doubling the circulation within a few months, as well as the collapse of this newspaper in July, 1896, are alike tributes to his ability as a journalist and to his honesty and perseverance as a believer in the Third Republic and in the need for social change. The principal issue over which the *Monde* failed was the tax on the property of religious orders passed in March, 1895. This was fought before passage and resisted after passage by the conservative Catholics, while Naudet denounced the Right for the attitude towards the legislation of the Republic which these actions demonstrated. This stand, in addition to Naudet's advocacy of seminary reform, praise of the more democratic American Catholic laity and clergy, and promotion of social legislation, effectively destroyed the *Monde*.[28]

Father Garnier was born in Normandy in 1858. As a young priest in Caen, he organized young peoples' clubs and pilgrimages to Rome. A convinced opponent of Freemasonry, he joined the *Croix* system and became one of the great organizers who made that newspaper chain so influential in France in the 1890's. A very large and powerful man, Garnier "did not go to the people, but joined them." A good speaker as well as an excellent administrator, Garnier frequently attended meetings of the Socialists and anarchists to denounce them from the floor. Thus, Aristide Briand, then a revolutionary syndicalist, encountered Garnier before the dock workers of Saint-Nazaire on May 28, 1890, Garnier denouncing the Jews and Briand ascribing persecution of the Jews throughout history to the Catholic Church. Much of the antisemitism of the Christian Democratic movement derives from Garnier. It is apparent that he became an antisemite through the anti-Masonic campaign, which was at its height while he was in the seminary.

In 1892, this Norman priest founded the *Union Nationale*, the first popular organization established by the Catholic Republicans. This nationalistic and Catholic institution was founded "to return the masses to religion and to give France peace and happiness through a Christian regeneration." It sought complete freedom for the Catholic Church in France, protection "against usury and high finance," protection against "foreigners," and proportional representation of minorities. This organization grew slowly until 1895, but during those first three years it became more nationalistic and more interested in promoting social legislation. Thus, Garnier sponsored workers' cooperatives and advocated a vague kind of socialism. In an address delivered at the publishing company of Alfred Mame in Tours, he declared, "Socialism is the future, and we must become Socialists in order to dominate the

[28] Robert Cornilleau, *L'Abbé Naudet* (Paris, 1934), 9–63, 73–98, 144; Léon Chaine, *Les Catholiques français et leurs difficultés actuelles devant l'opinion* (Lyon, 1908), 297–298; Naudet, *op. cit.*, 269–70.

future." Since the *Croix* was alarmed by his interest in socialism, he abandoned that newspaper and in 1894 established a weekly of his own, *Le Peuple Français*, as "the journal of Christian Democracy and the organ of the *Union Nationale*." Within a year or two, Garnier was an open opponent of the conservative *Croix*, although during the Dreyfus Affair both the *Peuple Français* and *Croix* were anti-Dreyfusard.

In 1895, the *Union Nationale* was transformed into an electoral league under the banner "Religion, Family, Property, and Country." During the crisis years, it opposed all "liberal and foreign" candidates for the Chamber of Deputies. Garnier used the organization particularly as a weapon against the Jews, Freemasons, and Socialists. There were 3,100 members in Lyon in 1896, and one quarter in Paris alone then had more than 4,000 members. The organization, especially in the larger cities, provided employment offices, clinics, and savings banks for its members, and Father Garnier's hope was to transform the *Union Nationale* into a Catholic political party to follow the pattern set by Windhorst's Center Party in Germany. These political ambitions dragged the Christian Democratic movement directly into French political strife from 1898 through 1900, against the wishes of most of its founders, and the resultant confusion and failures contributed heavily to the complete collapse of Christian Democracy in France in 1900.[29]

THE LYON CONGRESS, 1896

The Christian Democratic movement in France reached its peak at its first congress, held in Lyon during the last week of November in 1896. Widely advertised, bitterly attacked by the Socialists and the conservatives alike, and a cause of much friction among the clergy, this congress attracted six thousand representatives of

[29] Georges Suarez, *Briand. Sa Vie, son oeuvre* (Paris, 1938-1941), I, 85; Salomon Reinach (L'Archiviste, *pseud.*), *Drumont et Dreyfus. Etudes sur la Libre Parole de 1894 à 1895* (Paris, 1898), 19-20; Augustin Hamon and Georges Bachot, *La France politique et sociale, 1890* (Paris, 1891), II, 4-5; *Congrès national*, 52-56, 218-47; Lecanuet, *La Vie de l'Eglise*, 239-40; Debidour, *op. cit.*, II, 152; Avenel, *Annuaire de la presse française*, XVII (1896), 165; XVIII (1897), 163; *Libre Parole Illustrée*, March 14, March 21, September 26, 1896; February 4, April 17, 1897.

antisemitic clubs, Garnier's *Union Nationale*, separate Christian Democratic groups, and associations formed by individual newspapers throughout France. It lasted a week, and it benefited enormously from the fact that so many of the members were journalists. In many ways, it represented the summit of success for all organized antisemitism as well as for the Christian Democratic movement. A study of this congress will illustrate the program of Christian Democracy in France, the qualities characteristic of the Christian Democrats and of many of the other antisemites, and some of the reasons for the failure within less than five years of the entire Christian Democratic campaign.

One of the outstanding Christian Democratic leaders was a wealthy young church organist, François Mouthon, who left law school to found a weekly newspaper in Lyon in 1890. This publication benefited from the fact that Lyon at that time had only one newspaper which conservatives and Catholics enjoyed, and after two successful years Mouthon was able to transform his newspaper into a daily. *France libre*, or the "Catholic Youths' Anti-Jewish and Anti-Masonic Newspaper," had as its standard, "France for the French; Christ and Liberty." In July of 1893, after Drumont had been defeated in his campaign for election to the Chamber of Deputies from Amiens, Mouthon staged a banquet for him in Lyon to provide publicity for the new paper. Just as he had borrowed the first half of his slogan from Drumont, so he also borrowed Drumont's antisemitism and vague ideas concerning the need for social change in France.

As a consequence, Mouthon joined the young Christian Democratic movement and soon was at its head in the Lyon area. He used *France libre*, described in 1897 by the editor of the *Annuaire de la presse française* as "one of the greatest democratic papers in France," as the core of a formidable organization which soon extended throughout southeastern France. Aided by Victor Berne, a more able organizer than he, Mouthon established a system of study clubs, youth leagues, and electoral groupings which carried the seeds of antisemitism and Christian Democracy throughout the entire area. This network was very effectively tied together by Mouthon's system of sending skilled speakers and organizers from Lyon and by arranging occasional meetings in Lyon of representatives from groups throughout the area. A congress late in 1895 attracted two thousand people and was so successful that Mouthon decided to arrange for a national congress of the Christian Democrats for November, 1896.[30]

The difficulties facing Mouthon early in 1896 are similar to those facing the historian today, for there was no national Christian Democratic organization, no clear formulation of policy or doctrine, and no simple method of determining who the Christian Socialists were. As a consequence, Mouthon decided that the congress, "although highly Catholic and Republican," should make an appeal to "all men of good will who wish to join in the common aim of national liberation." The convention was described officially as "less a fusion than a federation of movements and ideas of all those who for Christ, the People, and Liberty work for the triumph of real democracy." The congress was, therefore, really not a national congress of the Christian Democrats, for there was no agreement on policy or organization either before or after it had met. It was a collection of representatives of many groups, all Catholic and all critical of the French social system, but not in general agreement as to the political and economic policies which should be adopted to remedy the deficiencies they witnessed. In other words, like other similar movements in modern history, Christian Democracy in France was more certain of what it opposed than of what it proposed.

Thus, one day of the congress was set aside for Garnier's *Union Nationale;* another day was provided for the Catholic press, regardless of the political and economic views of the newspapers represented; a third day was devoted to a study of antisemitism, two days to "social reform," another day to Freemasonry. La

[30] François Mouthon, *Du Bluff au chantage. Les Grandes Campagnes du Matin* (Paris, 1908), preface, V; Edouard Drumont, *Nos Maîtres, la tyrannie maçonnique* (Paris, 1899), 134–36; Albert Houlin, *La Crise,* quoted by Léon Chaine, *Les Catholiques français et leurs difficultés actuelles devant l'opinion* (Lyon, 1908), 619–21; Lecanuet, *La Vie de l'Eglise,* 245; *Libre Parole Illustrée,* July 22, 1893; August 8–August 29, October 3, 1896; February 13, 1897; Avenel, *Annuaire de la presse française,* XVIII (1897), 592.

Tour du Pin, certainly not a Christian Democrat, sent a delegation and had a speech read. There were representatives from such diverse organizations as the Young Catholics' Club of Marseille, the Paris chapter of the National Students' Antisemitic League, the Poitevin Antisemitic League of Small Businessmen, and the Lille Catholic Workers' Club.

A study of the three-hundred-page report published by Mouthon two months after this first congress of the Christian Democrats reveals in detail the ideas and attitudes of the groups represented at that crucial meeting. The congress met in plenary session every morning, afternoon, and evening to hear long talks by priests, editors, journalists, and occasionally workers or industrialists. There were no clear debates, no committee meetings to define issues or policies, no attempts to decide upon a brief common program. The representatives returned to their homes after a flooded week of talk with no national organization and no established policy.

Thus, there were ten speeches on the day devoted to Freemasonry, all of which reiterated the old charges concerning the evil power and the internationalism of "the evil order." The conclusion reached at the end of all of the oration was that Freemasonry should be countered by propaganda, that this propaganda should always be documented, and that the order should be fought by electoral action "in every way possible." No organization was established, no positive concrete philosophy was defined and adopted, and nothing was added to the entire campaign which had not already been discussed at length since 1865.

The day devoted to antisemitism was as barren. In this case, there were twenty speeches, the principal one by Drumont. The old complaints concerning Jewish political and economic power were raised, and the catalogue of charges concerning the ways in which this power was used was summarized again. Gayraud asserted that "the Christian life in itself spreads an effective antisemitism," but that "some repressive laws are needed too." Drumont in a wildly applauded speech told his six thousand listeners that the French Revolution should now be revised "for

Liberty and Christ," if necessary by the same methods which the Revolution adopted towards "the glorious aristocrats." After the Jews in France had been assigned responsibility for all of the political and economic disasters in the Third Republic's history, the assembly resolved:

1. The legislation emancipating the Jews in France and in Algeria should be cancelled.
2. Jews should be prohibited from all posts in education, the civil service, and the armed forces.
3. All Catholic and patriotic newspapers should support Drumont's campaign.
4. The laws on limited stock companies and on monopolies should be revised.
5. No Jews should be allowed to supply the army.

The obvious vagueness and indecisiveness of the sessions devoted to Freemasonry and the Jews were evident also in those dealing with the Catholic press and the *Union Nationale*. One hundred journalists on the final day of the congress, when most of those attending had already left, agreed to the following program, of which not one item was ever put into effect:

1. The Catholic press should not quarrel, and a jury of Catholic journalists should be elected to resolve any disputes which might arise.
2. A permanent committee of leading Catholics should be elected to form a common antisemitic, anti-Masonic, and social program for the Catholic press.
3. An investigation should be made of the possibility of founding a Catholic News Agency.
4. A professional association of Catholic journalists should be formed.

The *Union Nationale* meetings demonstrated the most thorough preparation, because Garnier was in complete charge of that day's arrangements. However, even here there was neither dynamism nor system. Garnier proposed to unite "all men of good will"

under the slogan, "Religion, Family, Property, Country." Most
of the session was devoted to the history of the movement and to
a description of the most effective local chapters. There was a
toast to "the union of the workers and the bourgeoisie," and there
was much talk of organizing locally to defeat Freemasons in
elections. However, there was no political or social program, and
it was agreed finally that the *Union Nationale* chapters should cor-
respond and cooperate but that there should be no central organization or control.

The sessions most important for the future of the Christian
Democratic party and most revealing to the modern student were
those which dealt with "social reform." Antisemitism and Catholicism had served very effectively to draw the movement and
the congress together, but Christian Democracy needed to devise
some positive and workable political and economic policies to knit
the disparate groups together more closely and to attract other
elements of French society. This the movement did not succeed
in accomplishing. Lueger at the same time in Austria was conquering with a combination of Catholicism and "city socialism,"
and Hitler later rose with nationalism and his brand of "socialism." The French Christian Democrats borrowed the conception
of a political and social party from their Austrian and German
friends, but they did not succeed in cementing the groups they
collected even briefly with a concrete program.

Mouthon's preface to the report on this first congress declared
that the meeting proved that "the new generation of conservatives" was lively, confident, and willing to accept the Republic
and social change. He did admit that some Catholics were in clear
opposition to the movement and that the conservative press in
general had either deliberately ignored or violently denounced the
congress. However, he felt confident that the great mass of French
conservatives were enlightened to such a degree that they would
support eagerly this movement and the economic reforms it
proposed.

There was some opposition within the congress itself to
Mouthon's insistence that Christian Democracy was a party of

conservatives. Jules Delahaye on the second day devoted part of a speech to a heavy attack upon the conservatives for supporting any government which kept the country quiet and for opposing any individual or group which proposed changes which might reduce their income slightly. His attack upon conservative opportunism was followed by Xavier de Magellon's praise of antisemitism for "seizing the throats of the all-powerful millionaires" and thus allying itself with Christian Democracy. Both of these speakers justified Drumont's denunciation of the Right and declared that the Christian Democrats would have to establish a party of real social reform or that the entire movement would collapse.

However, the sessions devoted to social problems indicate that the "socialist" element in Christian Democracy in France was negligible and that the reforms proposed in this congress were very mild indeed, much more mild than many of the antisemites had been demanding during the preceding decade. Most of the speeches during these meetings were devoted to lamentations concerning the demoralizing effect of factory labor upon morals and upon the family, praise of Catholic workers' clubs, trade unions, and cooperatives, and ringing declarations that social reform was necessary.

A brief summary of the three speeches which attracted most interest in these sessions will demonstrate how vague and, perhaps, how insincere was the interest in social reform among the Christian Democrats in 1896. Thellier de Poncheville, for example, declared that the Catholics had to organize, accept the Third Republic, and develop a social program if they hoped to avoid becoming "émigrés inside France." He declared that no one should be driven out of France or deprived of his liberty, and he shouted that "only a social program will acquire votes and political power for us in this democracy." However, the "social reforms" he enumerated consisted of political and economic decentralization, universal suffrage, minority representation, and a kind of corporatism. These were to be acquired through "private initiative, association, and law."

Naudet's address, "The Right to Life" was a stirring impeachment of contemporary capitalism for the poverty, misery, and degradation it bred. He asserted that "politics is not enough" and that the Christian Democrats should cooperate in the future with the Socialists to eliminate unemployment and charity and to provide everyone in France with the right to live and the right to develop his abilities. His picture of the misfortunes of the poor and unfortunate drew praise even from the Socialists, but the only concrete suggestions Father Naudet made were for shorter hours, Sunday holidays, and an end to the employment of women.

The third of these addresses, by Father Lemire, a deputy, was even more remarkable. Lemire attacked industrialism as well as capitalism, which he declared was based upon a "pagan notion of property," and he asserted that France must return to "Small Property." "The land and the hearth" alone can preserve the country and civilization, he announced, and he defined the role of any Catholic party to be that of urging the distribution of land in France. He proposed that every family in France should have a house and a small plot of land, both tax-free, that primogeniture be established by law, that factory hours be restricted to eleven a day and sixty a week, that credit be provided for workers and peasants at 3 percent or less, that the government provide national health service, that capitalists construct low-cost housing, and that work be assured to all "if at all possible" by trade union or state intervention. He did not indicate, however, how capitalists were to be persuaded to invest in low-cost housing, how each family in France could be provided at least with a garden, or how the state or the unions could guarantee the right to work. Nevertheless, this speech by the young, intelligent priest received a tremendous ovation from a crowd of eight thousand, the largest session in the entire congress.

The social reform program approved at the close of these sessions was neither so vague nor so impractical as the suggestions made by the speakers. However, these proposals are proof that Mouthon was correct in describing the Christian Democratic party as conservative. The principal suggestions in this statement were the protection of small business, the abolition of night work and employment of women, a ten-hour day and a six-day week, the establishment under state law of insurance and pension systems, the formation of committees including both workers and employees to study labor problems, and the election of regional parliaments to represent agriculture and industry. In addition, all Catholics were urged to unite in one political party, presumably the Christian Democratic party, and representation of professional interests in Parliament was supported. The program adopted by the second congress, in 1897, added the progressive income tax, laws on "speculation and usury," the referendum, and a clearer statement concerning corporatism.[31]

The nature of the social program which the Christian Democrats developed in 1896 was, of course, one of the principal reasons the movement collapsed so quickly. The movement contained so many diverse social groups that no attainable positive platform which would attract mass support from the conservative, Republican, or Socialist parties could be or was devised. The Christian Democratic party failed because it was bound together only by Catholicism and antisemitism, both ordinarily strong cohesive forces, but even together in this instance unable to counter the effect of the centrifugal forces. The pressure which destroyed the movement came from the Right, for the extreme conservatives were shocked and terrified to see Catholics, including large numbers of priests, join a movement which accepted "the slut" and which on occasion called itself Christian Socialist, even though it was in no sense a Socialist party.

This conservative opposition was ably and vigorously—even viciously—led by *Autorité* and *Vérité* in Paris and by such provincial journals as the *Semaine religieuse de Cambrai*, edited by Father Henri Delassus, himself an antisemite but a very conservative one. Aroused by the political and social ideas of the Christian Democrats, alarmed by the tolerance shown towards other Christian religions, and seeing in priests such as Naudet and Gayraud

[31] *Congrès nationale*, 33–93, 98–247, 277–306; Cornilleau, *op. cit.*, 105–107; *Libre Parole Illustrée*, October 24–December 12, 1896; *Univers*, November 1–December 10, 1896.

another potential Lamennais, they used every means to discredit and smash the movement. They were aided in their designs by the strong participation in the movement of hundreds of Catholic priests and by the foolish decision of Berne and Mouthon to invite Drumont and some of his more rowdy comrades to the first congress.

It is evident from many sources that many Catholic priests in the 1890's were developing political and social ideas of their own and, in some cases, entering politics advocating political and economic changes for France. This had happened often before, of course, but there was a great fear lest another Lamennais appear, particularly since most of the young priests who were becoming politically minded proposed ideas which were considered radical and even revolutionary by their elders, especially those in the hierarchy. This development seemed particularly ominous in 1896, when Lemire and Father Dabry sought to organize a national federation of priests.

Lemire addressed an ecclesiastical congress of about a thousand priests in Reims in August, 1896, advancing approximately the same program he developed in Lyon in November and suggesting too that the young priests organize and hold annual congresses. Dabry, his associate, indicated he wished to free the priest politically from the hierarchy and even declared: "The altar constructed in the style of the seventeenth century is destined to follow the throne. The entire edifice must be rebuilt and put into harmony with our rising generation." About seven hundred priests attended the November Christian Democratic congress, most of them priests who had also been in Reims in August. This caused great dissatisfaction and alarm, and some bishops by the fall of 1896 were seeking a means by which they might reasonably and without criticism forbid their priests to participate in the Christian Democratic movement.

The Christian Democrats escaped trouble before the first congress by adopting a technique familiar then to all Catholic authors and administrators, that of obtaining a letter of approval from the Pope or someone close to him and securing support from other dignitaries of the Church. Thus, Mariano Cardinal Rampolla sent a brief note to Mouthon accepting the homage offered the Pope, giving the first congress his apostolic blessing, and wishing him success. Monsignor Gouthe-Soulard, Archbishop of Aix-en-Provence, Monsignor de Cabrières, Bishop of Montpellier, and Monsignor Fava, Bishop of Grenoble, all familiar with Mouthon's attacks upon Freemasonry and the Jews, also sent their blessings. As a consequence, it was difficult for critics in the hierarchy to forbid priests to attend the meetings. However, Cardinal Couillé, Archbishop of Lyon, declined the honorary presidency of the congress, and warned the sponsors tactfully by asserting, "Antisemitism is derived from a just idea and it promotes fundamentally a legitimate and even necessary crusade, but it has adopted an attitude, language, and methods which prohibit an ecclesiastic from compromising with it." After Couillé had refused, Drumont was offered the honorary presidency, and he and his closest friends and followers from Paris dominated the congress, which led to its several embarrassing episodes and contributed to the subsequent failure of the entire movement.

The difficulties of the Congress began the very first day on which a meeting was held. The *Nouvelliste de Lyon*, a conservative paper, heralded the beginning of the convention with a violent attack. When the Lyon police confiscated the convention's flag, Clovis Hugues, a close friend of Drumont from Paris and a well-known Socialist poet and deputy, led a noisy demonstration of twelve hundred to the *France libre* offices. This led to a clash with the police and the arrest of fourteen of the demonstrators, leading the conservative press to chortle gleefully at the correctness of their charges.

On the second day, Jules Delahaye, a former deputy and another close friend of Drumont, in the course of an antisemitic harangue turned to denounce the conservatives. In the course of his attack, as he sought to explain the earlier feebleness of the antisemitic movement, he attacked the Concordat, the "subservient and opportunistic" French episcopacy, and the papal nuncio, Cardinal Ferrata, the latter for his cooperation with the French hierarchy against what Delahaye declared to be the great majority of the French clergy. Jules Guérin, in 1896 Drumont's first lieutenant and the organizer during the Dreyfus Affair of primitive storm troop formations, on the fourth day irritated even the members of the congress by his brutal and rude interruption of another speaker, Thellier de Poncheville. When the latter made a plea for equal rights for all residents in France, Guérin interfered by asking whether any Jewish workers in the convention hall would help him to hang Rothschild. The assembly was stunned, and there was a flood of protests. Guérin protested feebly that he had meant his remark as a joke, but many Christian Democrats began to realize that all of these incidents revealed a side to antisemitism which they had not yet appreciated.[32]

Drumont himself contributed seriously to the approaching debacle by attacking Couillé indirectly in his opening address for refusing to accept the honorary presidency. When a Christian Democratic priest gave Mouthon for publication in *France libre* a confidential letter which the cardinal had sent to all of the clergy in the archdiocese of Lyon protesting against Delahaye's attack upon the Concordat, both Drumont and the cardinal became angry, the former at what he considered a clear case of interference on the part of the prelate and the latter because Mouthon had published a confidential letter. These incidents, plus the remarks concerning social reform, alarmed the conservative cleric so much that after the congress had disbanded he urged all of the priests in the archdiocese to abandon Christian Democracy and to cease reading *France libre*. Mouthon's subsequent violent editorials against the cardinal drove many of his subscribers away, weakening seriously the entire movement. Less than half as many priests attended the second convention in 1897. When Mouthon denounced Couillé and the episcopacy for this during 1898, the cardinal forbade the clergy to read *France libre*.

The 1897 congress was almost as well attended as the original convention, but it presented less interest because the charges made against the Jews and Freemasons were identical with those of a year earlier and no advance had been made in organization or policy. Mouthon sought desperately throughout the first eight

[32] *Congrès nationale*, 6–25, 95–97, 214–15; Lecanuet, *La Vie de l'Eglise*, 626–50; Debidour, *op. cit.*, II, 155.

months of 1898, during the Dreyfus Affair, to rouse the movement. He advocated making the 1898 congress international, but his advisers pointed out to him that that would weaken the nationalist base of the charges made against the Jews and Masons. He sought also to acquire the support of the Third Order of St. Francis, but that effort also failed. He considered then inviting all French Protestants to join the campaign, but the anti-Protestant bias of the antisemitic campaign led to the rejection of that idea as well.

As a consequence, Mouthon by the fall of 1898 was a defeated man. His fortune dissipated, his hopes destroyed, his paper now a powerless, small voice in Lyon alone, he surrendered completely. *France libre* went into bankruptcy, dragging with it the entire Christian Democratic movement in southeastern France. Mouthon, unable because of the violence with which he had expressed his views to acquire a position with a Catholic newspaper, went to Paris and joined the staff of an anticlerical journal.

Christian Democracy fell into the hands of Garnier, the *Union Nationale*, and the politicians who sought to use the movement as a means of winning election to the Chamber of Deputies. Except for Garnier, all of the leaders in the 1898 congress were men who had earlier been deputies as Bonapartists or Boulangists, or men who were to use the Christian Democratic forces and the Dreyfus Affair tension to acquire brief notoriety in the Chamber. The 1898 congress was attended by only fifteen hundred, and the movement disappeared completely after the fifth congress in Paris on July 14, 1900. Thus, even with the advantage it derived from the Dreyfus Affair, Christian Democracy in France collapsed dismally, a particularly striking commentary when compared with Lueger's simultaneous success in Austria.[33]

[33] Joseph Brugerette, *Le Prêtre français et la société contemporaine* (Paris, 1935), II, 393–94; Henri Delassus, *La Démocratie chrétienne* (pamphlet) (Paris, 1911), 14–23, 58–59; Alfred Gendrot (Jean Drault, *pseud.*), *Drumont, La France juive et la Libre Parole* (Paris, 1935), 192–93; Paul Fesch, *L'Année sociale et économique en France et à l'étranger* (Paris, 1899), 81–88; Agnes Siegfried, *L'Abbé Frémont, 1852–1912* (Paris, 1932), II, 73–74; Chaine, *Les Catholiques français et leurs difficultés actuelles devant l'opinion*, 620–21; Mouthon, *op. cit.*, preface, V; Cornilleau, *op. cit.*, 111–25; *Libre Parole*, August 29, October 6– October 24, 1898; January 31, 1899.

VI

MORÈS, "THE FIRST NATIONAL SOCIALIST"

T HE principal obstacle to the success of Drumont's campaign against the Jews in France was his inability to elaborate a program which could tie effectively "the revolutionary worker and the conservative Christian." Antisemitism served as a binding force, but Drumont was not so successful in his use of that weapon as Hitler later was in Germany. He never saw this problem clearly, as a matter of fact, and he rambled widely and carelessly in his efforts to develop an economic and social program to keep the major wings of the movement united. As has already been demonstrated, most French Socialists by 1891 or 1892 had clearly rejected antisemitism, and by 1892 many Catholics as well had become frightened by the apparent radical aims of the antisemitic campaign. Even those Catholics who were still supporters of Drumont when Captain Dreyfus was arrested in 1894 were followers of Drumont only because no other party or group could attract them.

Maurice Barrès in *Figaro* on February 22, 1890, pointed out to the antisemites that it made little difference that there were eighty thousand Jews in France, because what the antisemites really meant was, "Down with social iniquities," not "Out with the Jews." He agreed that antisemitism was an excellent device as a rallying cry, but declared that "state socialism is the indispensable remedy for the antisemites' complaint." Six years later, Barrès in an oration given at the funeral of his young "Professor of Energy," the Marquis de Morès, stated that the ruling class was still incapable of playing its role. Morès alone, he said, had been able to excite and uplift some elements of the upper classes with a new vision and new ideas capable of reviving those classes and the system. "Morès was a Socialist. . . . He was at the same time a nationalist." His union of nationalism and socialism and his desire to live an active, modern, worth-while life Barrès believed to be the remedies he offered to the conservatives. Only an active upper class, convinced that nationalism and socialism combined could save France and led by a new Richard the Lion-Hearted, could restore those classes to power and France to glory. He mourned "the first National Socialist" because no other leader was in sight.[1]

The most potentially explosive threat to the democratic system of the Third Republic which the campaign against the Jews presented during these years was offered by the Marquis de Morès, who unconsciously improved upon Drumont's formula and technique by working towards a national socialism. Morès utilized religious ties in his approach to the conservatives, but he emphasized to a higher degree an appeal to the upper classes, to the aristocrats in particular, to safeguard their economic, social, and political positions by accepting the leadership of a national and nationalistic revolution. The lower classes, the "discontented workers," were to be acquired through the expropriation of "non-Christian and foreign" wealth and through workers' credits, low-cost housing, and food subsidies. Morès never planned this carefully, and in any case he was neither a political philosopher nor a politician. Nevertheless, his approach was an important and threatening one, and the personal characteristics he possessed

---

[1] Maurice Barrès, *Scènes et doctrines du nationalisme* (Paris, 1902), 324–28; Edouard Drumont, *Les Tréteaux du succès. Les Héros et les pitres* (Paris, 1900), 4–20.

make him not only "the first National Socialist" but also "the first storm trooper."

1. The Career of Morès Before 1889

JUST as Hitler and many of the other Nazi leaders were not born in Germany or had other national strains in their ancestry, of whose Nordic purity they nevertheless boasted, Morès, one of the important links in the chain of modern French nationalism, descended from a family which had been French only since the early years of the nineteenth century. Indeed, the history of his ancestors was studded with military action against France in the service of the kings of Aragon and the dukes of Savoy. His father's most important title, Duke of Vallombrosa, was an Italian title, and both of Morès' parents came from Spanish families. Morès himself as a young man wanted to study in the Italian Naval School and serve in the Italian navy, and his father only with great difficulty finally persuaded him to remain a French citizen. A member of a family which gloried in the military careers of its ancestors, an excellent horseman, hunter, and athlete, an avid reader of the novels of Jules Verne, Morès rather naturally decided to become a soldier, or rather an officer. He followed a path which French anticlericals considered only too common, for after study in a Jesuit school in Poitiers, he attended the famous Jesuit institution on the rue des Postes in Paris, and then in 1877 went to Saint-Cyr, where he was a classmate of Pétain.

The future nationalist leader and hero resigned his commission in the French army late in 1881, and on February 15, 1882, in Cannes he married Medora Hoffman, the daughter of a wealthy New York banker. The introduction of this additional complication might have been expected to have prevented or at least to have modified nationalism in Morès, but this marriage and his subsequent career in the United States stimulated his love for France and his hatred of those "foreigners" living in his country.[2]

[2] Baron Charles de Donos, *Morès. Sa Vie, sa mort* (Paris, 1899), 13–48; Joseph Rouault, *La Vision de Drumont* (Paris, 1944), 302; Charles Droulers, "Les Débuts d'un Palladin. Morès en Amérique," *Revue Hebdomadaire*, VI (1932), 418–19; *Almanach de Gotha, 1890* (Gotha, 1890), 390–91.

Morès came to the United States with his wife in August, 1882. His career during the next five years in this country is in many ways representative of his thirst for action and of his inability to succeed in modern business enterprise, both characteristics common to many antisemites. Persuaded by a retired American army officer to spend $32,000 of his father-in-law's money for 8,000 acres of land along the Little Missouri in the Dakota Territory, Morès soon discovered the value of the land had been misrepresented. After he had unsuccessfully challenged the American to a duel, Morès spent $22,000 more to purchase 37,000 additional acres. He then set off with his energetic wife for the Wild West, purchasing 500 cattle and 3,000 sheep in Minnesota to serve as the nucleus of a ranch and of a meat-packing business.

After he had had a twenty-eight-room lumber chateau constructed and had organized a village which he named after his wife, Morès settled down to hunt and to organize a number of business enterprises, all unsuccessful. He first formed the Medora Cattle Association of North Dakota and the Northern Pacific Refrigerator Car Company to slaughter and ship the cattle of the region to the Chicago market. He employed 150 cowboys on his own ranch in 1883, and the slaughterhouse employed an additional 150 men. He had icehouses constructed every 300 or 400 miles along the railroad line to Chicago from Bismarck, and in 1883 he slaughtered and shipped 30,000 cattle and sheep from Medora. This enterprise, however, collapsed, for the Dakota winters proved far too severe for his sheep and cattle, and other packing interests discovered that it was cheaper to ship the live cattle to Chicago for slaughter. The Medora Stage and Freight Company, which he established in 1883 to connect the Black Hills mines with the Northern Pacific Railroad two hundred and fifteen miles away, also was a failure by May, 1885, as was the Bismarck Loan and Trust Company, of which he was a vice-president. Even a retail market which Morès opened in St. Paul went bankrupt. All of his enterprises were characterized by what a Bismarck friend described as "daring without experience or calm judgment," but years later, in France, the marquis discovered that his plans in every case had been foiled by the Jews.

Morès failed in his personal relations in Dakota Territory as well as in his business endeavors. An aristocrat who, although Catholic, was not Irish, an impetuous fighter, and a man who had seized and enclosed some of the important water rights in the area would in almost any case have encountered hostility in a territory as untamed as the district which so stimulated Theodore Roosevelt when he arrived there in 1885. Morès admitted later in court that he had already killed two men in duels in France, and his aggressive and offensive attitude and his friendship for men suspected of rustling finally led in 1885 to a determined effort to drive him and his family from Medora. However, ambushed by three men when he returned to his chateau from Bismarck to escort from danger an old family servant, Morès on June 26, 1885, killed one, wounded a second, captured the third, and killed the horses of all three assailants.

After twice being arrested and twice freed for lack of evidence, Morès was indicted by a grand jury in August, 1885, and brought to trial in September. The prosecution charged that his companions were "renegades of the West and outlaws from the Bad Lands" and that it was he who had ambushed the O'Connell Gang. The jury freed Morès, but his neighbors resented this decision heartily, partly because Morès had had the service of an able Eastern lawyer and partly because it was popularly believed the judge had been bribed. Less than a year later the Morès family left Dakota Territory for New York, although it retained ownership of the chateau until 1936, when the oldest son of Morès, then Duke of Vallombrosa, gave the estate to the North Dakota Historical Society.[3]

The Dakota episode in the life of Morès is significant in several ways. It represented a series of failures for the handsome young man, who had abandoned a career in the French army to marry an American heiress. It began to strain the amicable relations which had heretofore existed between Morès and his father-in-law, as well as between Morès and his own father. It gave the marquis

[3] Russell Reid, "The De Morès Historical Site," *North Dakota Historical Quarterly*, VIII (1941), 272–83; Usher Burdick, *Marquis de Morès at War in the Bad Lands* (pamphlet) (Fargo, North Dakota, 1929), 9–24; Unpublished material on Morès in the New York Public Library.

an opportunity to mingle with the unruly and to ignore the barrier that his family and his education had erected between him and the rest of society in France. It stimulated further one of his principal ambitions, to win renown as a self-made man. It also increased the desperado or ruffian element in the Morès character. This was symbolized rather effectively by the sombrero which he wore constantly thereafter. As a matter of fact, the "uniform" of the organization he founded in France, Morès and His Friends, in a way the first storm troopers, was distinguished by a sombrero and a purple cowboy shirt. Madame de Morès after his death in 1896 planned at one time to have his killers captured and punished by a group of cowboys she proposed to bring from the Bad Lands to the Sahara.

His experiences in America added one other element to the Morès attitude which became especially significant on his return to France, an earnest desire to help the workers against the large economic concerns which controlled the prices of the necessities of life. When he arrived in New York City in the early winter of 1886, the dashing marquis opened three large wholesale meat shops. Trying to compete with established concerns in the wholesale meat field was extremely difficult, for Morès was unable to sell his meats at a profit at the prices which the larger concerns could establish and he was also unable to compete with their distribution systems. As a result, Morès in 1887 developed the idea of establishing a consumers' cooperative, the National Consumers' Meat Company. When Alexander Ford, the owner and editor of the *Irish World* supported this scheme, Morès staged a meeting at Manhattan College which was attended by the mayor of New York and a number of prominent merchants and bankers. Morès outlined his program for a cooperative meat company with a hundred thousand members, each of whom would contribute ten dollars as a membership fee. With this capital, he proposed to compete successfully with the large concerns and to end the intermediaries' profit. He sought to interest "the consumers and the workers." Neither his father nor his father-in-law developed any interest in his scheme, although one New York banker did. Morès spoke on a number of occasions to crowds of office workers in the financial district, and he even attracted the sympathetic attention of Henry George. However, this enterprise collapsed as did every other endeavor of Morès, and the marquis left New York to hunt tigers in Nepal and Burma. The transition from advocating a consumers' cooperative to hunting big game with the Duke of Orléans illustrates the extremes of Morès' life, and his national socialism was an attempt to bring these extremes together into a new French unity.[4]

While returning to France from India in 1888, Morès met an adventurer who convinced him an easy fortune could be made in railroad construction from Hanoi along the Red River valley to Yunnan in Tonkin, newly added to the French Empire. Dazzled by the prospect of this enterprise and by the profit which he believed could be obtained from opening commercial relations with southern China along this railroad line, Morès quickly won financial support from several Paris friends. Convinced he was to become an empire-builder, he set out for Indo-China from Marseille in October to recoup the tremendous financial losses incurred in America. However skillful Morès might have been as a Lyautey, he came to Tonkin not as a conqueror but as a promoter and construction engineer, for which he had no training or ability. Delighted nevertheless with his initial survey of the opportunities, he made secure arrangements with the new French government authorities. When he arrived in France six months later after visiting friends and relatives in the United States and Spain, he discovered that his absence from the scene of operations and his slow travel had allowed other more enterprising and more favored individuals to usurp his position. Morès believed that the man responsible for this was Ernest Constans, who as Minister of the Interior had just driven from France another ambitious soldier who had left the French army, General Boulanger.[5]

The arrival upon the French political scene of the man whom

[4] Jules Delahaye, *Les Assassins et les vengeurs de Morès* (Paris, 1905–1907), I, 2, 10–11; Droulers, *loc. cit.*, 441–43.
[5] Pierre Frondaie, *L'Assassinat du marquis de Morès* (Paris, 1934), 14; Jean Montray, *Marquis de Morès* (pamphlet) (Paris, 1896 ?), 5–7; Alfred Gendrot (Jean Drault, *pseud.*), *Drumont, La France juive et la Libre Parole* (Paris, 1935), 53–66.

Drumont compared to "Chinese" Gordon was a very decisive event in the history of antisemitism in France. Determined to strike back at Constans, Morès immediately devoted his energy and his wealth to an unsuccessful attempt to defeat Constans' supporter, Susini, in an electoral campaign in September, 1889, in Toulouse. Shortly after this engagement, Morès read *La France juive*, which convinced him that his enterprises in America had been crushed by Jewish butchers and financiers, that a Jewish engineer had undermined his railroad dreams in Tonkin, and that a Jewish prefect in Toulouse had been responsible for his failure to weaken Constans there. These ideas and his political associations with the defeated and leaderless Boulangists led him to decide to fuse the Boulangist and antisemitic movements. As a consequence, the conservatives, made extremely nationalistic again by their escapade with "General Revenge," were exposed to a flirtation with the ideas and aims of the antisemites, many of whom at this particular time were claiming to be Socialists and were on occasion borrowing planks from the Socialists' platforms.

2. Nationalistic Conservatism and Antisemitism

BOULANGISM had begun with a strong flavor of militarism and *revanche*, and this early phase remained basic in Boulangism, although overshadowed from 1887 through the first half of 1889 by preoccupations with politics. When the Left abandoned Boulanger after the summer of 1887 and as Boulangism became increasingly anti-Parliamentarian, it became more and more an instrument for the conservatives, especially the hopeful monarchists, against the Republic. The intransigent Catholics were especially excited by the new weapon because the Socialist program for 1888 urged complete separation of Church and State and because a new law against the religious associations became a threat during the summer of that year. It was the *Croix*, which became one of the leading antisemitic newspapers, which obtained and publicized the general's declaration of August, 1888, against religious persecution, that is, anticlericalism. A good majority of the Catholic clergy supported Boulanger as a tool against the Republic of the "infamous laws," and the Catholic press helped lead the final assault of the ill-fated movement.[6]

Boulangism reached its zenith with the Paris elections of January 27, 1889, but the lack of a serious plan of government and Boulanger's failure to act at this crucial occasion led to its precipitate decline. When the wily Constans induced the general to flee France in April and when the disorganized Boulangist forces were routed in the September elections by the aroused defenders of the Republic, Boulangism as an effective power disappeared from the political scene. With the failure of this political movement during 1889, the antisemites emerged to organize a league and to appear before the Paris electorate.

In 1886, Drumont had written hopefully of a new organization, the *Alliance antisémitique universelle*, as a weapon against the Jews, and in August of that year Jacques de Biez journeyed to Bucharest to represent France at a Congress for the founding of the *Alliance anti-israélite universelle*. Biez was disappointed by the small attendance, but he joined seventeen Roumanians and Hungarians in preparing the constitution. Drumont was unanimously elected president of the new organization, and the constitution was very elaborate and detailed. However, the only measures ever undertaken by this vainglorious league were the publication of two pacifist pamphlets during the Schnaebelé crisis in 1887.[7]

After the early disappearance of this premature international federation, the antisemites did not endeavor to organize again until shortly before the important elections of September, 1889,

[6] Adrien Dansette, *Le Boulangisme, 1886–1890* (Paris, 1938), 80 *ff.*; Antonin Debidour, *L'Eglise catholique et l'Etat sous la troisième République* (Paris, 1906–1909), I, 391–97, 409–16; Gabriel Terrail (Mermeix, *pseud.*), *Les Coulisses du Boulangisme* (Paris, 1890), 148–49. Dansette has described Boulangism as "A faith for the troops, a means for his collaborators, an end for him, a doctrine for no one."

[7] Edouard Drumont, *La France juive* (Paris, 1886), I, 139–327; Drumont, *La France juive devant l'opinion* (Paris, 1886), 287–90; *Congrès de Bucarest, août-septembre 1886 pour la fondation d'une Alliance anti-israélite universelle* (pamphlet) (Bucharest, 1887), 1–14; *Pas de guerre, Le Complot juif-allemand* (Paris, 1887), 6, 13–21; Jacques de Biez, *Le Complot financier des juifs allemands* (pamphlet) (Paris, 1887); *Libre Parole Illustrée*, January 16, 1896.

when the French National Antisemitic League was founded. This League also was a great failure, collapsing in May and formally disbanding in October, 1890. However, it was through this League and under the leadership and inspiration of Morès that the antisemites formed a close, but valueless, tie between antisemitism and ebbing Boulangism. The antisemites acquired permanently a few Boulangists of authority, such as Francis Laur, Georges Thiébaut, and Jules Delahaye, but the privilege of associating with a cause already defeated was a costly one. None of the Boulangists made substantial contributions to the antisemitic campaign, although Laur especially had a fine opportunity.

Antisemitism had had little influence in Boulangism until late in 1888, primarily because Naquet and Eugène Mayer, two of the leading Boulangists, and Hirsch, a heavy contributor to the Boulangist treasury, were Jews. However, when the Left became alarmed and Mayer retired from the movement, hatred of the Jews began to infiltrate. Some Boulangists were irritated by Joseph Reinach's aid to the opposition, and a few, particularly provincial conservatives, had been both Boulangists and antisemites since 1886. Drumont himself had hailed Boulangism joyfully in 1888 as a symbol of "the universal disgust we all have for Parliamentarians," though he had refrained from visiting the general because his entourage was "unattractive." [8]

When Maurice Vergoin, a member of the Boulangist National Republican Committee and a deputy from Seine-et-Oise, attacked the Jews in an electoral address in 1888, Boulanger publicly disavowed him. Similarly, when the Algerian Boulangist League decided to admit no Jews, Naquet intervened to obtain the creation of a separate section for them. Drumont, however, managed to play an important role in the crucial elections of January 27, 1889, even though the French National Antisemitic League had not yet been formed. Interviewed shortly before the balloting, he an-

[8] Edouard Drumont, *La Fin d'un monde* (Paris, 1888), 312–19; Gabriel Terrail (Mermeix, *pseud.*), *Les Antisémites en France* (Paris, 1892), 41–42; Gustave de Fleurance, *Expulseurs et expulsés* (Paris, 1888), preface; Hermann Bahr, *Der Antisemitismus. Ein internationales Interview* (Berlin, 1894), 106; Dansette, *op. cit.*, 171–73, 320–22.

nounced he would go from mass to vote for the popular officer. This declaration not only caused a sensation in reactionary circles, but resulted in a large Jewish vote against Boulanger. The only *arrondissement* where Boulanger was defeated was that where the Jewish population was heaviest.[9]

After Boulanger failed to act during the evening of January 27, 1889, antisemitism within the declining movement grew, fostered especially by a journalist, Julien Mauvrac. This thread of feeling against the Jews demolished the opportunity for an agreement with Alphonse de Rothschild for the latter's influence with the Jewish electorate in Algeria for support of the Boulangist slate there in the September elections. This failure and Joseph Reinach's suspected instigating of Constans only helped to strengthen the trend.

It is not known when Morès became a supporter of General Boulanger, but he made his first nationalistic and antisemitic speech in Paris late in September, 1889, to a crowd of workers. This speech keynotes the approach towards the union of nationalism and socialism, of upper and lower classes, which Morès was to make. "Comrades, the hour has come! France needs all of her loyal sons. Let us fight together again, side by side, as in the time when gentlemen and plebeians mingled their blood on the battlefield to constitute the French *patrie*, which the Jew is trying to destroy."

Boulangism and antisemitism began to ally forces openly in January, 1890, when the French National Antisemitic League decided to stage its first public meeting in support of Francis Laur, an antisemitic who was a member of the National Republican Committee, in his campaign for re-election to the Chamber of Deputies. Arranged by Morès and held in Neuilly, a conservative section of northwestern Paris, the demonstration was designed both to blend the two movements and to help build a new party of young aristocrats and workers. An audience which included five deputies and several noted aristocrats heard violent anti-

[9] Terrail, *Les Antisémites*, 43–51; Léon Daudet, *Les Oeuvres dans les hommes* (Paris, 1922), 156; *Anti-Juif* (Algiers), February 20, 1890.

semitic speeches by Morès, Drumont, Laur, and Paul Déroulède, who was at that time considered the incarnation of French nationalism.[10]

This first venture into politics had disastrous results for the cause of the campaign against the Jews, although Laur was ultimately re-elected. Rabid Boulangist papers such as *Le Pilori* were vociferous in their praise, but the meeting alarmed both the conservatives and the Socialists. Several Paris dailies, including *Figaro* and *Temps*, censured the first public act of the movement, and the letter of indignation written by Grand Rabbi Zadoc Kahn was given a warm reception by all of the Republican press. Moreover, this Neuilly meeting resulted in the complete break from antisemitism of the *Revue Socialiste*, which had been an important, if critical, disseminator of antisemitic propaganda since 1885.

Laur was disavowed by the National Republican Committee, but feeling against the Jews had grown so strong within the Boulangist movement that only Naquet's threat of resignation prevented a complete alliance with the antisemites in the spring of 1890. When Morès sought Boulangist cooperation in the Paris municipal elections in April in return for his financial support, the Committee decided to leave the final decision to the general himself. Since Boulanger had swung to the extreme left as his defeats continued, it seems quite possible that an agreement could have been reached through stressing the "socialism" of Drumont and Morès and temporarily omitting any open reference to the Jews.[11]

However, in March, 1890, while this important issue was being considered, Drumont intervened by publishing *La Dernière Bataille*. This book not only denounced Boulanger as a coward

[10] François Bournand (Jean de Ligneau, *pseud.*), *Juifs et antisémites en Europe* (Paris, 1892), 88–101; Raphaël Viau, *Vingt Ans d'antisémitisme, 1889–1909* (Paris, 1910), 10–15; Isaac Levaillant, "La Genèse de l'antisémitisme sous la troisième République," *Revue des études juives*, LII (1906–1907), 92; Delahaye, *op. cit.*, I, 20–21; Terrail, *Les Antisémites*, 54–55; *Anti-Juif* (Algiers), February 20, 1890.

[11] Augustin Hamon and Georges Bachot, *La France politique et sociale, 1890* (Paris, 1891), 51–63; Dansette, *op. cit.*, 347, 355–58; Terrail, *Les Antisémites*, 55–58; Gustave Rouanet, "La Question juive et la question sociale," *Revue Socialiste*, I (1890), 223; *Univers*, January 15–January 29, 1890.

and a servile instrument of the Jews, but it also heaped ridicule upon his parents. Moreover, it paralyzed the aims of Morès because it was fulsomely dedicated to the marquis. In addition, it was supported by Drumont's statement to the press denying the antisemites had allied with the Boulangists at Neuilly or planned to in the future.

La Dernière Bataille infuriated Boulanger and led to the decision of the National Republican Committee to oppose the antisemites in the spring elections. Paul Déroulède and Gabriel Terrail thus found themselves denouncing the antisemites only a few months after they had allied with them. Both campaigned actively against Drumont and Morès, and Terrail even described Drumont as "a vile pamphleteer and wretched calumniator." The collapse of the union with the nationalistic Boulangists was, then, one of the principal reasons for the collapse of the French National Antisemitic League and for the resounding failures of the antisemitic candidates in the 1890 elections.[12]

3. National Socialism

MORÈS himself contributed heavily towards the debacle in 1890 of his version of national socialism, for both his ideas and his actions frightened his conservative supporters, even his old friends, while at the same time they did not acquire for him or for the antisemites any significant support among the middle class or the workers of Paris. The failure in 1890 epitomizes the failure of antisemitism in general throughout this period in France, for it was the inability to bind the various groups together which effectively crippled the movement. If the antisemites had not been so hypnotized by the word "socialism" and had concentrated their efforts upon gaining the support of the lower middle class, which constituted what real strength the movement did have, the threat they should have offered to democracy in the Third Republic

[12] Edouard Drumont, *La Dernière Bataille* (Paris, 1890), 137–38, 184–89; Drumont, *Le Testament d'un antisémite* (Paris, 1891), 91–92; Bournand, *op. cit.*, 104–107; Terrail, *Les Antisémites*, 58–61; Viau, *op. cit.*, 14–15; *Univers*, April 17–April 30, 1890.

would have been even more serious than the Dreyfus Affair did provide.

The conservatives in the audience at the Neuilly meeting were not frightened by the "scientific antisemitism" of Francis Laur, who was a mild, small engineer and the editor of a mining journal. When the Marquis de Morès described himself as a soldier and a Catholic and asserted that in America the Jews would have been lynched for the evils tolerated in France, they regarded his speech as that of a friend and neighbor, indeed a fellow noble, who had lived among the barbarians in the United States, India, and Indo-China and who described the reaction of those natives to abuses considered customary in France itself. Drumont himself gave an address which emphasized that the antisemites sought only justice, truth, equality before the law, and a rigorous attack upon "the financial feudality." His declaration that "none of the wealthy here in this hall would even dream of planning speculation which would harm the poor workers" seemed as harmless, and indeed as flattering, as Déroulède's inspired oration on the glories of France and how they might be restored.

However, if Neuilly did not frighten the conservatives and nationalists, the campaign of Morès during the following three months did. Early in March, 1890, he founded the *Comité de la rue Saint-Anne*, with headquarters only a block from the *Banque de France* and only a short walk from the *Bourse*. There he collected around himself a group of antisemites, anarchists, old Boulangist journalists who wanted him to finance a newspaper, and unemployed, just as in Dakota Territory he had attracted rustlers and vagrants. Morès began to outfit these men with sombreros and cowboy shirts and to lead them in minor forays designed to frighten the financiers and brokers in the vicinity. Easily flattered, Morès was persuaded by an anarchist, Lucien Pemjean, to subsidize an anarchist newspaper which appeared for two months during the spring of 1890. He gloried in his comrades and was delighted by the names they gave him, The Challenger, The Fearless Knight, The Gallant Knight, and The King of the Market. His favorite book, which he read over and over again, was Léon Gautier's

La Chevalerie, and there is much in the action of this thirty-two-year-old man in 1890 which reminds one of an imaginative boy playing with toy soldiers and dreaming of bold knights, beautiful ladies, and dreadful dragons.[13]

This was precisely what the Duke of Vallombrosa believed. He thought his son should act like a mature, conservative noble and cease his escapades with the anarchists and the "scum" of Paris. The marquis by this time, however, was convinced he had discovered the true secret of the misfortunes of France. Resenting his father's allusions, particularly to his unsuccessful ventures in the United States and Tonkin, on March 28, 1890, he refused to "abandon the dregs of society, who are more honest than many who frequent the salons." Relations between father and son were thereupon broken, with unhappy consequences later for the son.

His father was not the only conservative repelled by the new friends of the marquis. Moreover, both the duke and his class had other reasons for alarm than the entourage, for Morès became a candidate for the Paris Municipal Council in the spring of 1890 and carried on an active and energetic campaign. In a speech on April 15, he declared that there was only one way in which the misfortunes of the poor could be ended. "At the time of the Commune, 35,000 were killed. Well, this time only 200 or 300 usurers need to be killed." In his placards, he urged the people of Paris to elect only "clearly revolutionary Socialists." Declaring that only a social revolution could restore French unity and power, he asserted, "Politics divides to rule—that's its technique. Socialism will reunite us."

The French National Antisemitic League's second and last meeting, in April, 1890, was a distinct failure. A few of Morès friends from the Jockey Club, former Boulangists, a few Blanquists, and even some anarchists attended, and again Drumont, Biez, and Morès harangued the crowd, advocating their "socialism." This time, however, the meeting was broken up "by

[13] Charles Droulers, *Le Marquis de Morès, 1858–1896* (Paris, 1932), 101; Julien Mauvrac, *Sous les Tentes de Japhet* (Paris, 1890), 99–108, 139; Bournand, *op. cit.,* 88–107; Frondaie, *op. cit.,* 11; Hamon and Bachot, *op. cit.,* 230; Delahaye, *op. cit.,* I, 50–56.

Jews and anarchists," and the antisemites were forced to flee in confusion. The 1890 elections were, therefore, crushing defeats for the antisemites. Morès received 950 votes in losing to Paul Brousse, while Drumont obtained only 613 votes in a district which had had an average conservative vote of 1,500.[14]

The election defeats of April, 1890, proved to be only the prelude to a greater disaster, for Morès became even more irresponsible. He addressed an anarchist meeting with Louise Michel, the most celebrated anarchist of the period before Vaillant, and he symbolized the union of all the classes against the established system by throwing his arm affectionately around the old Communard. His speeches and placards and his statements in *Assaut* became more inflammatory as May 1 approached, and the French government, overcautious since only General Boulanger's timidity had spared it from collapse a year earlier, became seriously alarmed by the possibility of violence. When Morès on April 27 urged a "democratic and social revision of the Code and Constitution" and when he urged the workers and middle class to join the forty thousand Paris unemployed in a huge demonstration, the government's alarm increased. His statement in *Assaut* to the French soldiers that their place was beside the worker and that they should allow the officers alone to defend "the unjust law of your masters" resulted in his arrest on April 28, 1890.

It is perfectly clear now, and it should have been evident to all but the most frightened, that no violence would come from the overgrown toy soldier at that time. There is no evidence that any but his handful of paid followers would have joined his May Day demonstration, and Morès was too much an obedient soldier and a conservative to attack his own government. The Socialists themselves understood Morès and resented bitterly the suspicion and hostility which the irresponsible aristocrat was drawing upon the entire labor movement. They taunted Morès as an "amateur,

[14] Georges Bernanos, *La Grande Peur des bien-pensants. Edouard Drumont* (Paris, 1931), 226–33; Gabriel Jogand-Pagès (Léo Taxil, *pseud.*), *Monsieur Drumont. Etude psychologique* (Paris, 1890), 290–91; Drumont, *Le Testament d'un antisémite*, 91–92, 382–430; Viau, *op. cit.*, 14–15; Frondaie, *op. cit.*, 94–95; *Univers*, April 17–April 30, 1890; *Anti-Juif* (Algiers), April 10–May 15, 1890.

sportsman Socialist," and they urged him to give away his fortune if he were sincerely interested in helping the poor. The Socialists were far more familiar with the limitations Morès placed upon his schemes than the frightened police and bourgeoisie. They noted that when he declared he was a Socialist he amended this statement by announcing that he did not propose "to declare war on all of the rich." A Socialist who respected "religion, country, family, and private property" seemed to the Paris Socialists, and to the Paris workers, to be no Socialist.

The antics of Morès not only alienated the Right as well as the Left, but they also terrified even the antisemites. Drumont, aware that the government was seriously alarmed, left Paris on the arrest of Morès and issued a statement at the railroad station in which he disassociated himself from Morès and his policies. Jacques de Biez, the other musketeer of antisemitism, also fled the city. Moreover, both Drumont and Biez, as the officers of the French National Antisemitic League, from the country urged all members of the League to refrain from taking part in any May Day demonstrations.

The bitter cup was not yet full. At his trial on June 9, Morès was ridiculed by the prosecution. His companions were unmasked, he was described as "a publicity hound," and it was proved that although he was an antisemite he had borrowed five thousand francs that very spring through one of the Jews most pilloried by the antisemites, Arthur Meyer, who had wounded Drumont in the famous duel of April, 1886. Moreover, the court's study of the anomaly of this aristocrat's associations with anarchists and unemployed introduced into the trial some of the great names of France. When one of Morès' collaborators admitted that Morès had purchased two crowns late in April, the prosecution sought to demonstrate that the tiger hunting in Nepal with the Duke of Orléans had led to a plot in which Morès was to be Monk for the Duke. The denials of this issued by the Duke of Orléans and the Duke of Luynes, one of Morès' closest friends and supposedly the intermediary in this plot, were exceedingly unflattering to Morès and deeply wounded his feelings. This was not all. He received a sentence of three months in jail, and while he was in jail his father and his wife obtained a court order freeing his wife's fortune from his control.[15]

Three months in jail did not calm or mature Morès. As a matter of fact, when he met Charles Malato and another anarchist in prison, he offered to aid them in establishing an anarchist newspaper. When he left jail in November, 1890, he immediately arranged a public meeting and attacked Rothschild and the *Banque de France*. In January, 1891, he supported the strike of the Paris coachmen against the concerns which rented their carriages and horses to them. Since the French National Antisemitic League had collapsed in 1890, Morès in March, 1891, established a new organization, Morès and His Friends, which adopted cowboy dress as a uniform. The core of this group consisted of the friends who had so repelled his father and of a number of butchers from the slaughterhouses of the Villette section of northeastern Paris, where Morès had done some electioneering for a friend earlier that year.

The marquis originally won the affection of these men by his lavishness and by his ability and recklessness in dueling. He strengthened the tie in 1891 when he successfully exposed the sale of spoiled meat to the army by a Jewish firm. The Morès group became the only organization of the antisemites from March, 1891, through 1893, and its uniform of sombreros and purple shirts gave his brawny followers a group consciousness similar to that experienced by the élite guard units of a later era. A precursor in many respects of the storm troopers, the Morès group became known for its brutal street fighting, the disorders it caused during Jewish celebrations, and the manner in which it terrorized any opposition at an antisemitic meeting. This squad of "The King of the Market" was a valuable auxiliary in the campaign against the Jews, but the terror unleashed by Morès sometimes boomeranged against the antisemites.

This was particularly the case when Morès killed a Jewish

[15] Hamon and Bachot, *op. cit.*, I, 228–35, 322–26; Droulers, *op. cit.*, 98–116; Frondaie, *op. cit.*, 95–96; Delahaye, *op. cit.*, I, 23–41; Mauvrac, *op. cit.*, 122–39.

French Army officer, Captain Armand Mayer, on June 23, 1892, in one of a series of duels which resulted from the campaign Drumont's newspaper, the *Libre Parole*, had inaugurated a month earlier against Jewish officers in the French army. Morès and His Friends were the special protectors of the newspaper, and Morès himself fought a number of duels against men who felt they had been insulted by Drumont. The public reaction to this fatal duel was vigorously unfavorable to the antisemites, although Morès' butchers gave him a "sword of honor" in congratulation.[16]

In 1890, Morès called himself a "Revisionist Socialist." From 1891 through 1893, he labored as a "Socialist Antisemite." Although during these four years on numerous occasions he denied he was an anarchist and even sometimes attacked the anarchists, yet he was the companion of anarchists and advocated policies similar to theirs. Thus, early in 1893, while lecturing in Lille he denounced anarchists who interrupted him and declared that he would never betray his religion and his country as they had. He published a pamphlet in 1892 declaring that Ravachol was a tool of Rothschild and that the anarchist was also a German spy, a Jew, a murderer, and a thief.

Nevertheless, the proposals Morès offered during these years have a strong anarchist taint. In his attack upon Rothschild and Ravachol, he attacked the political system, the *Banque de France*, and classical economics. He asserted that antisemitism and syndicalism alone could save France, and he urged that syndicates, or unions of workers, be allowed credit, for the reconstruction of society on a decentralized basis, with the communes and syndicates as the effective agents, was the most sound way of strengthening France.

The negation of government so obvious in this pamphlet was

[16] Charles Malato, *De la Commune à l'anarchie* (Paris, 1894), 270; Salomon Reinach (L'Archiviste, *pseud.*), *Drumont et Dreyfus. Etudes sur la Libre Parole de 1894 à 1895* (Paris, 1898), 13–17; Ernest Cremieu-Foa, *La Campaign antisémitique. Les Duels* (Paris, 1892), 24–48; Jules Guérin, *Les Trafiquants de l'antisémitisme* (Paris, 1906), 13–19; Gendrot, *op. cit.*, 117–22; Viau, *op. cit.*, 24–26, 44–54.

evident also in a longer brochure he issued later in 1892. This little book was a severe attack upon finance capitalism, concentrated industrial and political power, England, and the Jews. Morès advocated a silver standard so that France could rally the honest agricultural nations against the gold standard and England, the great exploiter. He developed an elaborate system of workers' credit, trying to prove by evaluating the workers' military service, taxes, productive capacity, and consuming power that each worker represented a capital investment for the nation of 224,000 francs, or almost $50,000. Each worker should therefore be entitled to a loan of 5,000 francs at 5 percent from the national bank, provided he should unite in a syndicate with other workers who were also borrowing. The workers' syndicates, thus provided with the necessary capital, could smash the large corporations and restore to France a decentralized, healthy syndical credit system and economy.

There are obvious influences here of Louis Blanc and Proudhon, but the conclusions which Morès found in this system are in a sense his own. Just as Proudhon, Morès believed that a workers' credit system would not only decentralize economic and political power, but also that it would "make the workers owners and therefore more interested in their country, in which they shall have private property." He believed this system would not only "kill the proletariat, the modern slave," but that it would provide France with a "new national and social unity." Considering himself "the eyes of the new army," Morès pointed out this system would eliminate foreigners from French life and establish "France for the French." [17]

When the French Socialists, led by Guesde and Lafargue, routed Morès and his program in a number of debates held in Paris and in northern France in 1892, Morès turned more and more upon the Socialists for destroying his plan for national unity. During 1893 and 1894, he began to adopt the technique of ad-

[17] Marquis Antonio de Morès, *Rothschild, Ravachol et Compagnie* (pamphlet) (Paris, 1892), 1-21, 39-46; Morès, *Le Crédit ouvrier et la grève de l'urbaine* (Paris, 1892), 3-9, 16-20; Alexandre Zévaès, *Jules Guesde, 1845-1922* Paris, 1929), 109-11; *Libre Parole Illustrée*, May 1, July 10, 1892.

vocating socialism, while denouncing the organized Socialists as internationalists in the pay of the Germans, Jews, or English. In a series of addresses delivered before antisemitic organizations in Algeria early in the spring of 1894, he elaborated more clearly the more nationalistic socialism towards which he had been stumbling since the fall of 1889. He retained his conception of workers' credit, but relegated that idea to a minor role in his scheme.

His principal idea at this time was to destroy international Socialism and the French Radical party because both were weakening the country through allegiance to foreign powers and to anti-Christian philosophies. He indicated too that parliamentary government would have to be abolished because France needed a revolution and a strong authority "to separate and to put into their proper places the foreign elements introduced into the organism of the country." The revolution he thought would "drown France, which will be saved by the soldiers." The new society should be built upon the only elements still sound from the old one, the peasants, the workers, and the army, and the national revolution should be led by officers, managers, and "those educated in morality and science." Once this transformation had been made, Morès urged that France occupy Madagascar and ally with the Mohammedan forces of Africa versus England, which was manipulating credit and foreigners inside France to weaken and destroy the country.[18]

Morès was a powerless and ruined man in 1894, unable to promote his program effectively either in France or in Algeria. Maître Demange, who was to accept the defense of Captain Dreyfus in 1894, won Morès an acquittal after the duel fatal to Captain Mayer in 1892, but the participation of Morès with other old Boulangists, led by Déroulède, in a maneuver directed against Clemenceau in the summer of 1893 led to his downfall. The Parliamentary enemies of Clemenceau were tricked by a Negro employed at the British Embassy into purchasing forged documents supposed to prove that Clemenceau was an English agent.

[18] Marquis Antonio de Morès, *Le Secret des changes* (Marseille, 1894), introduction, 1–14, 62–76, 87–93; *Lettres au peuple*, October 30, November 1, 1894.

Morès impetuously joined the attack, campaigned against Clemenceau in the latter's race for re-election to the Chamber of Deputies, and even volunteered to testify in court that Clemenceau was a British spy.

"The Tiger" thereupon forced Morès to confess that he, a leading antisemite, had borrowed twenty thousand francs in 1891 from Cornelius Herz, whom Morès and Drumont had denounced as one of the Jews responsible for the Panama scandal and as a parasite who owed his position in France only to Clemenceau. This revelation not only held Morès up to the ridicule of Paris, but it also led Morès in defense to publish a complete account of the incident in the August 7, 1893, issue of *Figaro*. This revealed that Drumont had negotiated the loan from Herz for Morès. Drumont thereupon denounced the marquis as a false friend, and their mutual friends were able only with great difficulty to prevent a duel.[19]

4. Imperialistic Antisemitism

DEPRIVED of any further opportunity of striking at the Jews or foreigners in France by his escapades and lack of resources, Morès sought in Africa a new field for action. After three months of unsuccessful hunting, he embarked there again upon his antisemitic career, lecturing to the Socialist Anti-Jewish League in Constantine, Bone, and Algiers on the power of the Jews and on the necessity for an alliance of France with the Mohammedans of Africa to drive England out. He developed a new theory concerning the power of the Jews and England, for he now saw that the foundation of their gold was the British Empire. A successful attack upon the heart of that Empire could return the Mediterranean to French control, weaken the gold standard, and allow the "agricultural and silver powers" to regain their stature in world politics.

[19] Frondaie, *op. cit.*, 63–86; Delahaye, *op. cit.*, I, 41–45; Droulers, *op. cit.*, 156–59; Gendrot, *op. cit.*, 193–96.

During 1894 and 1895, Morès developed a number of elaborate plans by which this policy might be carried out. He spoke once of an expedition south from Algiers to add Ghadames, Ghat, and Insala, in the Sahara Desert, to the French Empire. On another occasion, he described the tremendous advantages in linking Lake Chad to Bizerte, which would become the greatest port on the southern shore of the Mediterranean as well as a great manufacturing center. A third scheme involved an expedition through Tripoli to the Libyan Desert, where Morès was to make an alliance with the Mahdi of the Senussi at Kufra for a drive against the British along the Lower Nile. The final dream, and the one which he set out to accomplish in May, 1896, was to make the enormous journey southeast from Tunis through Ghadames and Ghat across the Sahara Desert to Bahr el Ghazal, where he would be in a position on the Upper Nile to strangle British power in Egypt.

These schemes were encouraged by another romantic, anti-British adventurer, a retired, dissatisfied French army colonel, Polignac, who believed a handful of skillful Frenchmen could create an empire in northern and central Africa and quickly recoup the loss of Egypt to the British Jew, Disraeli. Polignac believed that Morès, a handsome, young, exotic former army officer, was his chosen disciple. He carefully explained that the Tuaregs, the first important tribe he would encounter, were by nature chivalric and could easily be persuaded that Catholicism and Mohammedanism were similar religions. Once their loyalty had been easily won, all of the Arabians of Africa would join the new crusade to oust the British from the Mediterranean. One had only to be firm, prudent, and lavish in order to succeed.[20]

The dreams of Morès and Polignac captivated Morès completely. After two years in Algeria, during which he studied geography, French Army reports, and travel accounts, he re-

[20] Claude Martin, *Les Israélites algériens de 1830 à 1902* (Paris, 1936), 237–39; Félicien Pascal, *L'Assassinat de Morès* (Paris, 1902), 22–34; Delahaye, *op. cit.*, I, 65–220; II, 20–21; III, 19, 650; Droulers, *op. cit.*, 165–68.

turned to France in the summer of 1895 to seek financial backing. He obtained no funds. He was unsuccessful also in February, 1896, when he thought a family celebration of his fifteenth wedding anniversary in Cannes might lead his father and wife to agree to support this patriotic venture. He returned to Algeria in March, 1896, failing there too in his campaign to raise funds to relieve a famine among the Tuaregs.

Penniless, discouraged, urged now even by Polignac not to undertake an expedition, Morès set out nevertheless. It is not clear what his final aims were, for he described different plans to different friends. In any case, after writing a long loving letter to his wife and after urging his three sons to be faithful in their religious worship, he entered the desert. Deliberately disregarding instructions from the French army authorities, he plunged south into the desert after he had left Ghadames. His tiny party of six was ambushed and overwhelmed by a force of Tuaregs, warned by the careless talk of Morès in Gabès that a weak expedition was to depart. Morès was killed by the Tuaregs on June 9, 1896, after he had killed four of those attacking his caravan.

The end of the career of this fabulous, incompetent French noble was in some senses a suicide. Morès when· he came to Algiers in November, 1893, was a completely defeated man. Although he had extravagant dreams of conquest, he did not possess the self-confidence so marked in such contemporaries as Rhodes, Lyautey, and Marchand. During the last two years of his life, he became very religious, a sharp change for a roistering young man who had killed three men in duels and one in the Dakota ambush. He told some young men and women who witnessed his departure from Algiers for France in October, 1895: "Always retain God, The Family, and the Land as guides. . . . Do not forget that a man who has no religious belief is always thinking, always analyzing fine details until he becomes meaningless and incoherent. The man who is religious knows from whence he comes, who he is, and the purpose of his life. . . . It is impossible to study any problem without involving religion. Religion is the soul of peoples and the bond of races." In his last letter, he told his wife to work and pray and he advised his sons, "Search for truth and justice, and you will always be sure of finding God."

To his friends, to whom he left the task of paying his debts, he bequeathed his newly discovered maxim, "Life is valuable only through action; so much the worse if the action is mortal." This morbid statement recalls to mind the declarations of Mussolini and Hitler concerning the value of war. It is also strikingly similar to a phrase in the Futurist Manifesto issued in Paris in 1909 by Marinetti, "Better a splendid disaster than a monotonous daily re-run." [21]

The pessimism of Morès was surely highly justified. The antisemitic campaign in France when he left the organized movement in the fall of 1893 was becoming weaker every day, and Morès discovered during his last visit to his homeland in 1895 and 1896 that the arrest and imprisonment of Captain Dreyfus had not aided it substantially. Moreover, the antisemitic drive in Algiers in 1896 was weaker than at any time since violence had flared first in 1884. Captain Marchand, who began his epic journey across Africa three months before Morès left Tunis, did arrive at Fashoda but was no more successful ultimately in ousting the English than Morès had been.

Moreover, although the body of Morès received a magnificent reception in Marseille and although representatives of the President of France, the Minister of Foreign Affairs, and the Cardinal Archbishop of Paris were present at the impressive funeral on July 15, 1896, in Notre Dame in Paris, the antisemite was forgotten soon even by those who saw in him the martyr and hero the movement needed. During the Dreyfus Affair, a statue of Morès was sculpted, but the sculptor refused to release the statue because the friends of Morès were unable to pay his fee. When the statue was finally obtained, the Paris Municipal Council refused the antisemites permission to place it even "among the people he

[21] *Congrès nationale de la Démocratie Chrétienne, 1896* (Lyon, 1897), 97; Colonel Louis Noir, *Le Massacre de l'expédition du marquis de Morès* (pamphlet) (Paris, 1896), 19; Auguste Pavy, *L'Expédition de Morès* (Paris, 1897), 8-130; Delahaye, *op. cit.*, I, 221-23; II, 1-20, 56-132; III, 8-9; Pascal, *op. cit.*, 34-158.

loved so well," at the gates of the slaughterhouses in northeastern Paris. The *Libre Parole* commented sadly on June 10, 1903, that it too would henceforth abandon Morès because the day previous his wife had entertained lavishly on the seventh anniversary of his death.[22]

[22] Delahaye, *op. cit.*, I, 68–70; III, 74–75, 679–683; Montray, *op. cit.*, 15; *Libre Parole*, April 14–April 16, 1899.

VII

THE STRENGTH OF FRENCH ANTISEMITISM

BEFORE THE DREYFUS AFFAIR

Aₗₜₕₒᵤ𝗴ₕ the power of the organized antisemitic movement in France had been declining perceptibly from early 1893 through the early fall of 1894, a considerable latent social force had been developed by the time of the arrest of Captain Dreyfus. Estimating the strength of power of this feeling is a difficult operation. Although the problem has been simplified to a very considerable extent by the availability of a great amount of source material, very few studies of the antisemitic movement within various special areas or classes have been made. Since antisemitism was adopted for varying reasons by different social and political groups in France, and since French political party organization was so much less clear and stable than the groupings in other countries, an analysis of the specific localities and of the groups or classes most strongly tainted will demonstrate again the nature of the movement and its strengths as well as its weaknesses.

The prevalence of antisemitism in such widely different locations as Radical Republican Bordeaux, radical and yet Catholic Lyon, industrial Lille, and the monarchical and clerical West reveals both the diffusion and the disparities so evident throughout the history of the movement. It reveals also that antisemitism was a national movement, although none of the antisemites was ever able to develop an effective national organization. The election in May, 1898, of antisemites as diverse in their views as the Bonapartist Lasies in Gers in the southwest, the monarchist Pontbriand in Ille-et-Vilaine in the West, the former Boulangist Millevoye in Paris, the self-styled Socialist Henri Ferrette in Meuse in the northeast, and the nationalist Pascal in Gard in Provence is another proof of the basic difficulty facing the antisemites in organizing a force which was clearly national, but which also reflected all of the complexities of French political life.

1. Geographical Areas

THE evidence from all sources shows remarkable agreement concerning the areas in which the foundations of antisemitism were laid and in which political power was developed. The birthplaces and homes of the leading propagandizers, organizers, and politicians are in general the same cities or regions in which antisemitic newspapers appeared, clubs were formed, deputies were elected, and the worst riots against the Jews occurred during the Dreyfus Affair.

Paris was the natural center of the French antisemitic campaign. The capital of its nation in a sense in which few other cities are capitals of their countries, Paris contained a high proportion of the French Jews as well as a strong concentration of the professional bourgeoisie who were so antisemitic. Within its twenty *arrondissements* there were concentrated groups representing every political view popular anywhere in France. Most of the important publishing houses, journals, and newspapers were located in Paris. Almost all of the antisemitic books were written and published in Paris, and most of the leading antisemites resided there.

The evidence concerning the prevalence of hatred of the Jews in Paris is particularly clear. Three of the first four attempts to found antisemitic newspapers were made in Paris, and the first antisemitic public addresses and electoral candidacies were Parisian. The French National Antisemitic League did not even attempt to extend its influence beyond Paris. The Students' Antisemitic League, which fostered the revival of a national antisemitic organization in 1895, had its roots very firmly in Paris, but was not very successful in spreading its influence throughout France through those members who had come to Paris from the provinces.[1]

The first openly antisemitic candidate for the Chamber of Deputies ran from Paris in 1889, and three antisemites were candidates in Paris in the 1893 elections. The Dreyfus Affair stimulated nine antisemitic candidacies in the elections of May, 1898, and one of them, Lucien Millevoye, the old Boulangist, was successful in the second *arrondissement*, where Morès had done most of his campaigning and enjoyed his greatest influence. The defeated candidates in Paris are representative of the movement, for they ranged from the extreme Right to the Left. Two of those who failed were antisemitic monarchists, and one called himself an antisemitic Revolutionary Socialist.

Paris was almost alone in France to witness antisemitic demonstrations before 1898. In June, 1895, one hundred members of the Students' Antisemitic League paraded noisily to the Strasburg statue and to Drumont's office. In 1896, this league held several public meetings, attempted to stone Rothschild's home, and broke up lectures of Jews or "philo-Semites." By late 1897, the league and its members had acquired a considerable amount of experience in early Fascist practices.

The Dreyfus Affair heightened French feeling against the Jews and increased the number of outbreaks against them. Paris, the seat of the Zola and Esterhazy trials, witnessed organized hooting and assaulting of Dreyfusards and Jews, the burning of Dreyfusard

---

[1] Joseph Jacobs, *The Jewish Question, 1875–1884. A Bibliographical Handlist* (London, 1885), 57; Raphaël Viau, *Vingt Ans d'antisémitisme, 1889–1909* (Paris, 1910), 7–14; Alfred Gendrot (Jean Drault, *pseud.*), *Drumont, La France juive et la Libre Parole* (Paris, 1935), 46–50; François Bournand (Jean de Ligneau, *pseud.*), *Juifs et antisémites en Europe* (Paris, 1892), 67–77; *Libre Parole Illustrée*, November 23, 1895; January 18, 1896.

papers, and parades and street demonstrations against the Jews.
Nowhere in France was feeling against the Jews during the
Dreyfus Affair so violent as it was in the capital.[2]

One of the first areas outside of Paris to be affected by antisemitism includes several of the leading cities of Flanders and
Picardy, where the conservative and nationalist lower middle
class resented the growth of socialism among the industrial workers and the business competition provided them by those Jews
from Alsace-Lorraine who had opted for France in 1871 and had
moved to several of these cities, Lille in particular. Lille ranks
second only to Paris as the foundation of the movement. All of
Drumont's grandparents came from Lille, and the family until
1871 owned property there. Devos, who became business manager
of the *Libre Parole* in 1895 and who was also owner of the Antisemitic Publishing Company, was a native of Lille. In the spring
of 1891, Emmanuel Gallian, a young medical student who wrote
under the name of Noël Gaulois, founded a short-lived paper, the
Anti-Youtre. This was financed by a Lille newspaper vendor,
Léon Hayard, and it was printed in Lille for sale in Paris, where
it appeared as a Paris publication.

The most successful antisemitic newspaper to appear in France
before Drumont's *Libre Parole* in 1892 was the *Lillois*. This paper
was aided by another weekly, the *Vraie France*. These Lille
newspapers were both Catholic, legitimist, and protectionist, and
they combined to spread antisemitism among the Flanders conservatives during 1890 and 1891. There were also in Lille several

[2] Charles Renaut, *L'Israélite Edouard Drumont et les sociétés secrètes actuellement* (Paris, 1896), 461; Antonin Debidour, *L'Eglise et l'Etat sous la troisième
République* (Paris, 1906-1909), II, 182, 189; Joseph Reinach, *Histoire de l'Affaire Dreyfus* (Paris, 1901-1911), III, 40-41, 216, 244, 277, 311, 315, 342-50, 462-
63, 539; Captain Paul Marin, *Drumont?* (Paris, 1899), 126-32, 146-56; Marin,
Esterhazy? (Paris, 1898), 91-95, 176-79; Marin, *Félix Faure?* (Paris, 1900), 52-
56; Marin, *Le Lieutenant-Colonel Picquart?* (Paris, 1898), 223, 330-38; Marin,
Rochefort? (Paris, 1899), 120-25, 254-57; Paul Mabille, *La Race juive* (pamphlet) (Paris, 1898), 9; Edouard Dubut, "Les Groupes antisémites," *Revue Antisémitique*, II (1897), 13; *Le Lorrain, Echo de Metz et d'Alsace-Lorraine*, June
23, 1895; *Libre Parole Illustrée*, February 15, February 29, March 21, March 28,
May 2, December 5, 1896; January 23, 1897; *Libre Parole*, April 24-May 9, 1898.

important publishing firms which turned their presses over to attacks upon the Jews and Masons, the most influential being the Catholic firm of Desclée and Brouwer. Among the books Desclée and Brouwer printed were those of Father Henri Delassus, noted antisemite and intransigent anti-Republican who edited the influential *Semaine religieuse de Cambrai* for more than twenty years.[3]

The Paris antisemites who hoped to organize a strong movement throughout France realized the potentialities of this area, for their first attempts to organize the movement outside of Paris were made in Lille and Amiens by Morès. Drumont first ran for the Chamber of Deputies in Amiens, and the antisemitic clubs of Amiens, Lille, Valenciennes, and Dunkirk were among the earliest and the most lively. There were antisemitic candidates for the Chamber of Deputies in May, 1898, from Amiens and Beauvais, and although both were defeated they did add to anti-Dreyfusard and anti-democratic feeling in those industrial cities. These northern communities also witnessed some of the most vehement demonstrations against the Jews during the Dreyfus Affair, the ostensible cause being the presence in those cities of the Jews who had moved there in 1871.[4]

The second great area outside of Paris where antisemitism flourished was the monarchical and clerical west, which had very few Jews upon whom to vent its anger but which used antisemitism as a bludgeon against the hated Third Republic. Rennes had less than a dozen Jewish families, and one antisemite from this section confessed that he did not believe there was a single

[3] Edouard Drumont, *Le Testament d'un antisémite* (Paris, 1891), 334–35; Gendrot, *op. cit.*, 67–82; Bournand, *op. cit.*, 114, 240–45, 264–65; Henri Avenel, *Annuaire de la presse française*, IV (1883), 334–35; VI (1885), 361; IX (1888), 426; XII (1891), II; XIII (1892), 493; *Anti-Juif* (Algiers), July 6, July 13, August 31, September 7, September 21, 1890.
[4] Jules Guérin, *Les Trafiquants de l'antisémitisme* (Paris, 1906), 437–38, 458–59; Charles Droulers, *Le Marquis de Morès, 1858–1896* (Paris, 1932), 122, 146–47; Gendrot, *op. cit.*, 191; Reinach, *op. cit.*, III, 276; Isaac Levaillant, "La Genèse de l'antisémitisme sous la troisième République," *Revue des études juives*, LII (1906–1907), 92; *Libre Parole Illustrée*, July 4, August 19, 1893; December 26, 1896; January 16, February 27, March 6, March 13, April 10, 1897; *Libre Parole*, April 23, May 9, June 8, November 2, 1898.

Jew in his department. Nevertheless, Normandy, Brittany, Maine, Anjou, and Poitou constituted one of the sectors most strongly influenced by this doctrine of hate.

Many of the leading antisemites came from this section of France. Georges Corneilhan, for example, published an attack upon the Jews in 1889 and began an antisemitic weekly in Poitiers in 1891. Biez and Father Chabauty, two of the early leaders, were from Poitou and Jules Delahaye from Tours, while Rennes produced Jules Ménard, Lionel Radiguet, and Eugène Cravoisier. The last of these, Cravoisier, was a member of the *Libre Parole* staff, the editor of two Rennes papers, and the founder with Gaston Méry of *L'Echo du merveilleux*. One of Drumont's first converts was Raphaël Viau, who immediately founded an antisemitic paper in Nantes which lasted until the latter part of 1887 and who received a hero's welcome when he returned to his native city from Paris for an anti-Dreyfusard lecture in December, 1898. In addition to Cravoisier and Viau, three other members of the small staff of Drumont's newspaper came from this area, for Normandy contributed Roger Lambelin, Léandre, and Boisandré. Moreover, Joseph Denais, who bought the *Libre Parole* from Drumont in 1910 and edited it until 1924, arrived in Paris from a village near Nantes on the lower Loire.[5]

At least eight antisemites were candidates from this area in 1898, two of them, Pontbriand from Chateaubriand in Britanny and Maussabré from Poitou, both on the extreme Right, being elected. The alliance between the old aristocracy and the urban

[5] André Siegfried, *Tableau politique de la France de l'ouest sous la troisième République* (Paris, 1913), 391; Georges Corneilhan, *Juifs et opportunistes. Le Judaïsme en Egypte et en Syrie* (Paris, 1889); Lionel Radiguet, *Le Ministère de la lâcheté extérieure* (Paris, 1891); Henri Desportes, *Ernest Renan, sa vie et son oeuvre* (Paris, 1893), 252–54; Edouard Drumont, *La Fin d'un monde* (Paris, 1888), 60; Jules Ménard, *Traitres et pillards. L'Opportunisme judaïque en Bretagne* (Rennes, 1895); Ménard, *Le Cultivateur ruiné par la juiverie internationale* (pamphlet) (Rennes, 1887); Ménard, *La France au pillage* (pamphlet) (Rennes, 1898); Louis Jorrand, *Lettre à un antisémite catholique* (pamphlet) (Paris, 1899), 9–10; Reinach, *op. cit.*, III, 275; IV, 426; V, 201–203; Avenel, *Annuaire de la presse française*, XIII (1892), 650; XVII (1896), 713; XIX (1898), 726; XX (1899), 458, 460; *Libre Parole Illustrée*, August 8, 1896; *Libre Parole*, December 14, 1898.

lower middle class was generally rather effective in this sector, and in Poitiers and Nantes in particular the antisemites were well organized for boycotting Jewish businesses and for intervening in municipal elections.

Aside from the lecture tours arranged in the Lyon area by *France libre*, the only attempt to send a panel of speakers through a provincial area was made by the Catholic Youth Congress, which sent four men through Poitou in January, 1897, to denounce the Jews and Masons. Poitiers and Rennes especially had strong antisemitic clubs, and the riots at Nantes, Angers, Poitiers, and Rennes were among the most serious which afflicted France during 1898. The Dreyfusard deputy, Grimaux, was driven out of Nantes on August 10, 1898, when he sought to make a speech there, and two of the younger antisemites, members of the Normandy Antisemitic Federation, planned briefly in the fall of 1899 to begin a revolution by seizing the prefecture in Caen.[6]

The third area prominent in the campaign against the Jews consisted of a section in southwestern France centering upon two cities with fairly large Jewish populations, Bordeaux and Toulouse. This area throughout the nineteenth century was a Republican stronghold, and the charts for the 1898 elections indicate that this section, especially the departments of Gironde and Landes, voted very heavily for the Radical Republicans, who were clearly antagonistic to the antisemites. Nevertheless, it was obviously one of the strongholds of antisemitism, electing to the Chamber of Deputies in 1898 five open antisemites, Chiché and Charles Bernard from Bordeaux in Gironde, Theodore Denis and General Jacquey from Landes, and Joseph Lasies from Condon in Gers. Father Paul Naudet was a native of Bordeaux, as was Father Jacquet, the head of the *Union Nationale* in Bordeaux and the editor of the *Journal de Bordeaux*, who shared first prize in the *Libre*

[6] Edouard Lecanuet, *Les Signes avant-coureurs de la séparation, 1894–1910* (Paris, 1930), 192–93; L. Vial, *Le Juif roi* (Paris, 1897), 76; Debidour, *op. cit.*, II, 189; Reinach, *op. cit.*, III, 275–76; V, 201–203; Gendrot, *op. cit.*, 270–71; *Libre Parole Illustrée*, January 25, July 18, November 14, 1896; February 13, March 6, April 3, 1897; *Libre Parole*, April 18–May 30, June 25, August 10, 1898.

Parole contest in 1896 to determine the best solution to "the Jewish question." Jacquet became an excellent lieutenant in southwestern France for Father Gayraud, who left Toulouse for Paris and national fame in 1893.

The Bordeaux and Toulouse Antisemitic Leagues were very strong and well organized. Charles Bernard, who became president of the Bordeaux league in 1897, utilized the associations and acquaintances acquired through the league to obtain nomination in 1898, and his use of the league to support his candidacy was an important factor in his success, as it was in the rise of Lasies in Toulouse. The riots in Bordeaux and Toulouse were especially numerous, and the Bordeaux nationalists and antisemites successfully broke up a Dreyfusard meeting in September, 1898, a rare feat even for these groups, although they often advocated the use of force.[7]

The deputies elected from this section to the Chamber of Deputies proved among the most important representatives and instruments of antisemitism in France. Denis in the Chamber on May 25, 1895, gave the first antisemitic speech heard there since Francis Laur had attacked Rothschild and all Jews in 1890. Describing himself as a farmer and as a member of several important agricultural organizations, Denis caused a bitter debate in the Chamber over the number of Jews in the civil service, which Denis declared far excessive and dangerous. Lasies, who was a young retired cavalry officer, was even more spectacular and became a kind of parliamentary Morès. A Bonapartist, Lasies during the Dreyfus Affair interpolated the Minister of War a great number of times. The *Libre Parole* itself admitted that Lasies "exaggerated a little" when he charged various members of the government with

---

[7] J. Jacquet, *Mémoire sur les moyens pratiques d'arriver à l'anéantissement de la puissance juive en France* (Paris, 1897); Emile Rouyer, *Exposé historique de la question judéo-maçonnique* (Paris, 1897), 37–52; Pierre Quillard, *Le Monument Henry* (Paris, 1899), 116; Paul Marin, *Le Lieutenant-Colonel du Paty de Clam?* (Paris, 1898), 60–61; Marin, *Quesnay de Beaurepaire?* (Paris, 1899), 261–73; Marin, *Félix Faure?*, 52–56; Marin, *Drumont?*, 341–68; Gendrot, *op. cit.*, 220; *Libre Parole Illustrée*, December 28, 1895–February 20, 1897; *Libre Parole*, January 16, March 29, April 5, April 27, May 17, July 6, September 9, November 9, December 12, 1898; January 18, 1899.

treason, but Lasies was, nevertheless, a shrewd politician. Both he and Bernard skillfully rode French political storms, remaining antisemites and deputies but moving from Right to Left or from Left to Right, as the occasion demanded.[8]

The Lyon-Grenoble area was a fourth section prominent in the campaign against the Jews. Organizations which spread the doctrines of antisemitism throughout the surrounding countryside were developed in both Lyon and Grenoble. Mouthon's Christian Democratic movement was particularly skillful in developing such an organization, while Bishop Fava of Grenoble, the renowned adversary of Freemasonry, made that city a great center for the movement against both the Masons and the Jews. The Grenoble publishers, led by Vallier, Vincent and Perroux, and Baratier and Dardelet, were valiant supporters of Fava and specialized in the production and sale of books denouncing the Masons. Lyon contained several important Catholic publishing houses. Two of these, Delhomme and Briguet and Vitte and Perousel, were among the most significant producers of books denouncing the Masons during the 1870's and 1880's. During the last decade of the nineteenth century, these firms turned their presses against the Jews. One of the types of antisemitic literature in which Lyon specialized consisted of directories of Jews living in various departments of France, designed to increase the effectiveness of the leagues supporting boycotts of the Jews.[9]

Most of the cities and towns in this area had antisemitic leagues or clubs. Voiron, Vienne, Chambéry, Mâcon, Bourg, and Tarare were noted for their clubs and for the vehemence of their demon-

[8] Léon Daudet, *Vers le Roi. Souvenirs* (Paris, 1921), 66–68; A. de Boisandré, *Napoléon antisémite* (Paris, 1900), 3–14; Marin, *Drumont?*, 251–66; Marin, *Quesnay de Beaurepaire?*, 180–90; Viau, *op. cit.*, 296–301; C. E. Curinier (editor), *Dictionnaire national des contemporains* (Paris, 1899–1905), II, 139; *Almanach de la Libre Parole* (Paris, 1896), 105–107; *Libre Parole*, July 27, October 11, November 20, 1898; May 9, 1899.

[9] Philippe Sapin, *L'Indicateur israélite* (Lyon, 1896); Sapin, *La Solidarité française. Noms, adresses, professions, état-civil et actes d'association de tous les juifs des départements du Nord et du Pas-de-Calais* (Lyon, 1898); Madame de Coudekerque-Lambrecht, *Léon de Montesquiou. Sa Vie politique. L'Action Française* (Paris, 1925), 51; *Libre Parole*, May 5, 1898; January 9, May 16–May 23, 1899.

strations in 1898. Father Tilloy, who shared first prize in the *Libre Parole* contest of 1896, came from Mâcon, while Meynies, one of those who won honorable mention, was a resident of Bourg.

Lyon had especial importance in the antisemitic campaign because it was the headquarters for the Christian Democratic movement. This movement in the Lyon area was adopted by several politicians such as Xavier de Magellon who clambered aboard the campaign to further their political ambitions. By 1900, however, Lyon was too clearly divided between the Dreyfusards and anti-Dreyfusards and the Christian Democratic movement was too weak to allow those politicians to capitalize politically upon a campaign against the Jews. It is interesting to note, however, that the first public meeting of the *Action Française* was held in Lyon on July 5, 1900, and that Magellon, who joined that movement after being a Christian Democrat, made the principal address.[10]

The fifth section in which antisemitism was prominent and powerful in France was the East, but the hatred felt for the Jews there must be distinguished from that which developed elsewhere in France, although the same economic and social classes were involved and although business and professional jealousy was a cause here too. The feeling in the area bounded roughly by Dijon and Besançon on the south and Bar-le-Duc and Nancy in the north was not a reaction to anticlericalism or the rule of the Opportunists, but the hatred felt towards a core of people considered foreign who were living in the midst of a French society.

Although more Jewish people lived in this area than in any other section of France, with the exception of Paris, the contribution made by this region to Drumont's brand of antisemitism was very slight until after the arrest of Captain Dreyfus. Armand Mariotte, editor-in-chief of *Le Pilori*, the violent anti-Republican and antisemitic illustrated paper founded in Paris on April 25,

[10] Edouard Lecanuet, *La Vie de l'Eglise sous Léon XIII* (Paris, 1930), 79; Rouyer, *op. cit.*, 34–38, 52; Reinach, *op. cit.*, III, 276; Debidour, *op. cit.*, I, 212, 310; II, 56, 88, 91; Vial, *op. cit.*, 74; *Libre Parole Illustrée*, November 23, 1895; March 7, June 13, September 26, November 14, 1896; January 23, March 20, 1897.

1886, was a native of Vesoul. He was also the editor of a very important conservative paper in Vesoul, but he and Willette, the very able cartoonist from Dijon, were practically the only anti-semites of any importance from that area who aided the movement in its early years.

When antisemitism began to become more organized in France after the advertising given by the arrest and deportation of Drey-fus, the East became prominent with its manifestations against the Jews. Probably the two most active antisemitic clubs outside of Paris after 1894 were those of Dijon and Langres. Almost every city and town in this part of France had riots and demonstrations against the Jews during 1898 and 1899. In Bar-le-Duc, where Henri Ferrette was elected to the Chamber of Deputies in 1898, the feeling became so strong that most of the Jews left the city. One of the seats in the Chamber from Nancy was sought by two nationalistic antisemites, Gervaize, the leader of the local anti-semitic organization, defeating Maurice Barrès in a very close election. All through the East only a spark was needed to cause serious violence.[11]

2. Social Classes

THE campaign led by Drumont against the Jews in France had not only created a number of pools of antisemitism throughout the nation, but had also created a great reservoir of dislike and dis-trust of the Jews among various classes and "estates" of French society. This dormant, ingrained sentiment of feeling against the Jews became a source for the violent explosion against the Jews in France and against the Third Republic, which sought to provide

[11] Edouard Drumont, *La France juive devant l'opinion* (Paris, 1886), 114; Isidore Bertrand, *La Synagogue de Satan et les élections de mai 1898* (Paris, 1898), 7–9, 15–16; *Derrière les masques. Résumé historique de l'Affaire Dreyfus* (pamphlet) (Nancy, 1898), 3–8; Debidour, *op. cit.*, I, 377; II, 189; Reinach, *op. cit.*, III, 275–76; Quillard, *op. cit.*, 477; Avenel, *Annuaire de la presse française*, XVII (1896), 533; XX (1899), XXVI; *Libre Parole Illustrée*, No-vember 9, November 23, 1895; January 18, February 15, March 28, April 25, June 6, June 27, September 26, 1896; March 20, 1897; *Libre Parole*, January 9, February 12–February 14, April 5, April 23, May 4, May 17, June 14, 1898; January 23–January 26, February 6–February 7, February 15, May 21, 1899; *Le Pilori*, June 23, 1895.

equal rights and opportunities for all. The antisemitic leaders of that time happily never analyzed the deposits of antisemitism so that they might make the best use of their flexible weapon and of the latent discontents abroad throughout the country. They were dazzled by their regard for the heirs of the French past into looking for leadership to the nobility and to those members of the upper middle class who had successfully invaded the old ruling class. They were fascinated too by the magic word "socialism" into believing that the workers under the leadership of the old ruling class, or if necessary by leaders generated by the antisemitic movement, should provide France with a new dynamism. Thus, they failed generally to realize where their strength lay and how it might best be organized and led.

It is evident now that despite the collapse of organized antisemitism in France by the summer of 1894, hatred of the Jews was apparent in some strength among various groups of Frenchmen. One finds traces of it, for example, among the sterile aristocracy and upper bourgeoisie, jealous of Jewish wealth gained in industry and finance and of Jewish influence in the Republican government. A second group affected included part of the professional officer class, members of a traditionally Catholic and exclusive corps. A third group affected was the professional middle class, for a great majority of the antisemitic leaders were lawyers, doctors, professional writers and journalists, and artists. A fourth group, also a part of the middle class, tinged with hatred of the Jews was the petty bourgeoisie, particularly small businessmen and bureaucrats crowded down by more successful Jewish competitors. The final class affected was the Catholic clergy, particularly the country priests, credulous, poorly educated, persecuted by the Republic, and now defended by the valiant Catholic journalist against the deicides of old.

THE UPPER CLASSES

The antisemitism of the upper classes, whose indifference to everything but luxury and pleasure so angered Drumont, was essentially social. In spite of the enjoyment they obtained from reading *La France juive*, none of them heeded Drumont's request in 1886 that they finance a daily paper. During the early days of the French National Antisemitic League, when Biez had made the league offices a museum, there was a daily line of carriages before the door as the society folk came to the Montmartre section to see the Willette posters, the portraits of Joan of Arc, and the collection of European antisemitica. Morès induced his Jockey Club friends to attend the two big antisemitic meetings of 1890, but their interest again was neither useful nor durable. With the failure of the league and the great increase in feeling against the conservatives evident in Drumont's writings after 1890, the upper classes did not return to organized antisemitism until 1898. At that time, they flocked to the antisemites' meetings held by the successor of Morès, Jules Guérin.

However, very few members of the nobility or the very wealthy middle class played an active role in French antisemitism either before or during the Dreyfus Affair. The funds which a few of them contributed to Guérin's leagues were not substantial, and most of the money was used by Guérin for his personal interests. The description of this level of society in Proust's magnificent *A la recherche du Temps Perdu* is believed substantially accurate. There was certainly antisemitism among the nobility, especially the "simple nobility," but the very success of Swann and of his daughter in being accepted intimately by the very highest circles of society is evidence that the contagion was neither deep nor strong. A society which accepted not only Swann but also the ill-bred Bloch and some of whose members, such as the Duke de Guermantes himself, became strong Dreyfusards, was surely not strongly antisemitic.[12]

ARMY OFFICERS

The conservative forces of the army and the Church had been targets for antisemitic propaganda since 1886 and had become nests of antisemitism by 1894. At Saint-Cyr, there were cliques

[12] Henri Dagan, *Enquête sur l'antisémitisme* (Paris, 1889), 94; Léon Blum, *Souvenirs sur l'Affaire* (Paris, 1935), 63; Drumont, *La Fin d'un monde*, 100–101; Bournand, *op. cit.*, 47, 68–70; Viau, *op. cit.*, 191–92; Quillard, *op. cit.*, 105-28.

of future officers who spoke to Jews only when circumstances required it. Students from Jesuit schools, which had practically a monopoly over entrance into the military schools and which resented the success of Jewish scholars, were especially bitter enemies of the Jews. The General Staff had been filled with Jesuit-trained men by General Miribel, named chief of it in 1890 by Freycinet, and was known as "La Jésuitière." The appointment of Dreyfus to the General Staff in January, 1893 had caused a strong protest in the *Libre Parole* and the *Croix*, the army's favorite newspapers. General Sandherr, who had inherited his hatred of the Jews from his father in Mulhouse, was only one of the officers who requested Miribel not to allow Dreyfus to enter. Most of the officers seriously involved in the Dreyfus Affair, including Picquart, a "Postard" or graduate of the Jesuit school on the rue des Postes, were antisemitic. Major Esterhazy, who had become acquainted with Drumont and Morès in 1892 when he served as a second for a Jewish officer who dueled Morès, sent Drumont a note of congratulation for the *Libre Parole* campaign long before the arrest and imprisonment of Captain Dreyfus became a national issue.

French army officers suffered not only from their conservative and nationalistic background and education, but also from their poor salaries and the exceedingly severe competition for promotions. It frequently required fifteen or eighteen years for a very capable officer out of Saint-Cyr to become a major. The pay for captains in the French army was particularly poor, and an officer in that rank for twelve years obtained only 5,000 francs ($1,000), only twice what he had received when first commissioned fifteen or twenty years earlier. A captain in the army of the Third Republic in the 1890's received in purchasing power only one-third as much as a captain in the army of Louis XV or Louis XVI. This, the low pensions, the very poor provisions made for widows, and the fact that the cavalry, the most romantic branch of the service and that where promotion was most rapid, was closed by cost to all but the most wealthy, made even the army officers members of "the professional proletariat" of France.

Antisemitism was strong throughout the officers' corp. The

three hundred Jewish officers in the French army faced social pressure, isolation, and discrimination. Even their friends and those officers who in 1898 openly declared their belief that Dreyfus was innocent were ostracized. Many Jewish officers were graded very severely in Army schools or failed to obtain promotion to important positions because of prejudice exercised against them by higher officers. The tactics used against Captain Dreyfus long before the arrest were those to which all Jewish officers had to become accustomed, for throughout the army antisemitic officers flaunted the *Libre Parole*, the *Croix*, and antisemitic posters and books before their Jewish fellows. More than one thousand officers, mostly anonymous but including a significant number sufficiently courageous or rash to sign their names, contributed to the fund collected by the *Libre Parole* after the suicide of the forger, Colonel Henry. Some of the comments made by officers contributing are noteworthy:

"A Versailles artillery captain, indignant not only that there are still Jewish officers in the army, but also that they are not the last to receive decorations and promotions."

"A Nancy artillery captain who never enters a Jewish store."

"A Lyon army doctor who should like to have vivisection practiced on Jews rather than on inoffensive rabbits." [13]

MERCHANTS AND BUREAUCRATS

The class which was perhaps most receptive to Drumont's inviting doctrine was the petty bourgeoisie of small merchants and

[13] Lucien Souchon, *De Sedan à Locarno* (Paris, 1931), 141; Jean France, *Autour de l'Affaire Dreyfus* (Paris, 1936), 26, 143; Frederick Conybeare, *The Dreyfus Case* (London, 1898), 5–7, 64–66; General Louis André, *Cinq Ans de ministère* (Paris, 1909), 297–304; Captain Jules Mollin, *La Vérité sur l'affaire des fiches* (Paris, 1905), 10–15, 20–22; Albert Thibaudet, *Les Idées de Charles Maurras* (Paris, 1920), 85; Salomon Reinach (L'Archiviste, *pseud.*), *Drumont et Dreyfus. Etudes sur la Libre Parole de 1894 à 1895* (Paris, 1897), 9; Henri Bérenger (editor), *Les Prolétaires intellectuels en France* (Paris, 1901), 186–91; Joseph Reinach, *Les Blès d'hiver* (Paris, 1901), 225–26, 329–33; Reinach, *Histoire de l'Affaire Dreyfus*, I, 56–74, 121–25, 146; II, 53, 67, 90–95, 208–209, 384; III, 349; IV, 248, 394, 440; VI, 67–68, 166; Marin, *Drumont?*, 34; Dagan, *op. cit.*, 91; Quillard, *op. cit.*, 7–93; Debidour, *op. cit.*, II, 35, 125–26; *Libre Parole*, September 16, 1898; March 5, 1899.

minor bureaucrats. There is no evidence, and indeed Drumont never claimed, that the French workers were at all affected by his teachings, but the lower middle class became the backbone of the organized movement. Next to the clergy, Drumont's most assiduous readers and correspondents were men who had failed to become successful and contented middle-class merchants and who were restrained by Church influence from becoming social revolutionaries. An important section of *La Fin d'un monde* is an attack upon large commercial firms for crushing the small tradesman. Drumont at that time asserted he would never found a paper because the advertising he would have to accept from the large concerns would only ruin more small merchants. Drumont himself has been described as the "sociologically typical antisemite." His paternal grandfather had been a handworker and his maternal grandfather a tradesman, while his father was a minor bureaucrat in the Paris City Hall.

Information available concerning the membership of the French National Antisemitic League provides clear proof of the participation of the lower middle class in the movement. Drumont's secretary declared that the League's strength lay among "the merchants, the bureaucrats, and the real nobility," while Julien Mauvrac described its members in 1890 as "the merchant bourgeoisie who do not forgive their commercial rivals some of their business practices, jealous bureaucrats, and some of French high society who refuse to bow to the golden calf." The secretary of the League was a jeweler named Millot who was paraded as a victim of the Jews. Called "a typical guttersnipe" by one leading antisemite, Millot designed and manufactured the League's pins and later became the prosperous printer of the *Libre Parole*.[14]

Attracted by a "safe socialism" which allowed them to denounce the rich and prosperous while at the same time it kept

[14] Miriam Beard, "Anti-Semitism—Product of Economic Myths," in Isacque Graeber and Stuart H. Britt, *Jews in a Gentile World* (New York, 1942), 393; J. E. Millot, *Aux Prolétaires de France* (pamphlet) (Asnières, 1889), 1–3; Drumont, *La France juive devant l'opinion*, 5, 147–53; Drumont, *La Fin d'un monde*, 42–44, 81–104, 133–44; Bournand, *op. cit.*, 47; Viau, *op. cit.*, 8–14, 40–41; Dagan, *op. cit.*, 39–45, 56–59, 91, 94; *Libre Parole Illustrée*, December 26, 1895; January 18, April 26, 1896; *Anti-Juif* (Algiers), November 29, 1890.

them distinct from the workers and the workers' organizations, the antisemites from the lower middle class used antisemitism against the economic and social forces which were squeezing and even crushing them. It is clear from the columns of the *Libre Parole* that many traveling salesmen became extremely antisemitic, and there were two attempts, one in Dijon and the other in Le Havre, to establish a national organization of antisemitic salesmen in 1898 "to protect their interests." Merchants' Antisemitic Leagues appeared throughout France in the 1890's in cities such as Marseille, Reims, Bordeaux, Lyon, Toulouse, Rennes, and Paris. In many cities, these organizations became the backbone of the movement against the Jews, while in other cities the merchants allied with students, bureaucrats, journalists, and priests to denounce the Jews.

Thus, Dr. Pundous formed an Antisemitic Commercial Club in Toulouse in December, 1895. In February, 1896, this group united with a students' antisemitic organization, the central committee having nine merchants and six students. This organization fostered demonstrations and supported an antisemitic candidate for the Chamber of Deputies in 1898. In Rennes, a disgruntled hay and straw merchant, Jules Ménard, became an antisemite on the publication of Drumont's *La France juive* in 1886. Ménard had inherited his father's business in 1875, and for ten years he had been successful as a supply agent for the army, the principal function of his father during the thirty-five years he had devoted to developing the business. The formation of a rival concern in 1884 which quickly drove Ménard out of business made him an antisemite, since "Jews and cosmopolitan monopolists" financed the joint-stock company which ultimately ruined him. Ménard thereupon promoted antisemitism in Rennes with every weapon at his command and had the Rennes merchants in particular alarmed about Jewish power in business long before the celebrated trial in that city.

The development of antisemitism in Poitiers followed the same pattern. The leaders in that city were a merchant named Rocheout, who claimed his prosperity had been undermined by a Jewish department store, and a gentleman farmer, Henri de Coursac. Rocheout campaigned for the Poitiers Municipal Council in 1896 as the head of the Poitevin Antisemitic League of Small Businessmen, and his associate was a candidate for the Chamber of Deputies in May, 1898 with the support of that organization. Both sought to defend small business and to exclude Jews from teaching, the civil service, and army grades. Coursac in 1898 asked for the votes of "all poor farmers, all workers hungry because of the wheat monopoly, and all merchants ruined by large Jewish shops." [15]

The programs as well as the membership of the antisemitic leagues demonstrate the strength of lower middle class participation in the campaign against the Jews. The varieties of "socialisms" introduced by Drumont, Chirac, the Christian Democrats, and Morès are an indirect proof of the class composition of the movement, although none of the leaders had a clear conception of it. The leagues advanced as early as 1890 slogans such as "Neither buy from nor sell to Jews," "Never work for nor buy from a Jew," and "Boycott Jewish shops," and proposals for "unions of French producers and consumers versus the Jewish and other monopolists" were common in all of the antisemitic literature. During the Dreyfus Affair, the Bishop of Nancy from the pulpit urged his parishioners to "buy only from Catholics for the honor and salvation of France." One critic of the campaign called it "a movement of shopkeepers," and the Socialists in 1898 saw clearly that antisemitism might successfully unite the very large French lower middle class to crush the workers and the Republic.

Perhaps the most remarkable evidence concerning participation of this class in the campaign against the Jews is an account of a three-week tour through eastern France made late in 1899 and

[15] Bernard Lazare, *Contre l'antisémitisme* (pamphlet) (Paris, 1896), 5–17; *Congrès nationale de la Démocratie Chrétienne, 1896* (Lyon, 1897), 75–77; Ménard, *Le Cultivateur ruiné par la juiverie internationale;* Ménard, *La France au pillage;* Ménard, *Traitres et pillards,* 1–108, 247–53; Quillard, *op. cit.,* 196–99; *Libre Parole Illustrée,* December 28, 1895; January 25, February 8–February 15, March 7, April 25, July 18, 1896; *Libre Parole,* January 19–January 22, February 9–February 19, March 2, March 30, April 3–April 30, May 18, 1898; March 30, 1899.

early in 1900 by Paul Marion. Travelling through the area bounded by Bar-le-Duc, Nancy, Epinal, Belfort, and Vesoul, Marion discovered that most of the antisemites were discontented petty bourgeoisie and that the leaders were petty bourgeoisie, army officers, and priests. Antisemitism in that entire area was "usually only a question of commercial rivalry," and the lower middle class was the core of the movement. In Epinal, the leaders were a tailor and a postal employee, in Bar-le-Duc and Lunéville journalists, and in Vesoul a dry-goods merchant.[16]

PROFESSIONAL MEN

The lower middle class was not the only group within "the middle class" of which many members canalized their hatred against the Jews, for the participation of large numbers of professional men, such as lawyers, journalists, and artists, in the antisemitic movement is also very obvious. The legal profession in particular was outstanding in providing young leaders, but each of these groups made a very substantial contribution to the campaign in terms of ideas and organizational leadership. Many forces influenced these groups, but the determining factor appears to have been economic. France during the 1890's had developed an "intellectual proletariat." The tremendous progress in free education under the Third Republic, the popularity of the French ideal of becoming a bureaucrat or a professional man, and the reduction in 1891 of the years of military service for the university student all led to "university over-production." Thus, less than one-half of the doctors in France in 1901 were prosperous, and engineers, lawyers, and commercial artists suffered similarly. In each of these professions, some Jews had acquired success and even prominence, and the economic burden added to the other causes described earlier led some of the "frustrated aesthetes" to become antisemites.

The pressure in these professions was especially severe upon those preparing for or just beginning their professional careers.

---

[16] Paul Marion, L'Antisémitisme dans l'Est. This manuscript is owned by Mr. Lee Max Friedman of Boston and was dated January 11, 1900, by its author. It is unpaged.

The professional schools were heavily overcrowded during the 1890's as the wave of young men profiting from the laws passed in the early 1880's reached the graduate school level. Graduate school students were very prominent in the antisemitic movement, not only in Paris but also in Lyon, Marseille, Toulouse, Bordeaux, Nantes, wherever there were universities. The competition for entrance into the professional schools and for prizes and other recognition for outstanding work was so intense that bitter feeling arose against foreigners, and also, against Jews. Thus, in 1896 more than 1,000 medical students in Paris signed a petition urging that the number of foreign students in French medical schools be restricted, that they not be eligible for prizes, and that they receive only honorary diplomas. The petition urged also that no one "not born French or a naturalized citizen or who has not fulfilled his military service" should be allowed to practice medicine in France or in the French colonies. This petition was supported by the Paris Students' Antisemitic League, and both Drumont's *Libre Parole* and Arthur Loth's *Vérité* urged that the movement be broadened to include other professions and Jews in all professions.[17]

The evidence concerning the open and active participation of professional school students in the antisemitic campaign is very clear. The only important antisemitic organization in France from August, 1893, when Morès first went to Africa, until the Dreyfus Affair inspired Jules Guérin in 1897, was the Paris Students' Antisemitic League. This organization, which was also known as the Antisemitic Youths' Club, was founded in April, 1894, by a group of law students, led by Camille Jarre and Jacques Dubuc. This organization held public meetings and distributed antisemitic literature in 1894, and as early as 1895 it staged noisy street demonstrations, broke up lectures by Jews and Socialists, and serenaded Drumont and his lieutenants on important anniversaries. When Jarre and Cailly received their law degrees, the new officers

[17] Anatole Leroy-Beaulieu, *Les Doctrines de haine* (Paris, 1902), 17–135; Leroy-Beaulieu, *l'Antisémitisme* (pamphlet) (Paris, 1897), 27–75; Hugo Valentin, *Antisemitism Historically and Critically Examined* (New York, 1936), 10–16; Bérenger, *op. cit.*, 1–48; *Libre Parole Illustrée*, March 7–March 21, 1896.

were also law students. Cailly and Jarre remained among the most intransigent antisemites, fought throughout the Dreyfus Affair, formed the National Anti-Jewish Party in 1901 to succeed the student league, and then joined the *Action Française*.

The Paris Students' Antisemitic League was important because it spread antisemitism among the young men attending all the graduate schools in Paris and because it trained a group of "intellectuals" experienced in street fighting and mob violence before the Dreyfus Affair stirred France. It also served to stimulate the formation of similar student groups in other cities in France, using the illustrated edition of the *Libre Parole* as its national journal and attempting with some vigor to form a national federation under its lead. Those members of the Paris league who lived in the provinces devoted their summer vacations to promoting antisemitism there. Thus, Renaud d'Elissagaray, a law student who came to Paris from the Basque country, organized antisemitic groups near Pau during his summer vacations. He was an unsuccessful candidate for the Chamber of Deputies in 1898, but his next candidacy was successful, owing in part to the associations and experience he had acquired during his early campaigning.[18]

Young lawyers appear throughout the antisemitic movement. François Mouthon, who at twenty-three founded the *France libre* and developed the remarkable Christian Democratic movement in the Lyon area, left law school to join the crusade. Max Régis, who at twenty-one was elected mayor of Algiers in 1898 and who became a tremendously popular figure both in Algeria and in France, also left law school to promote antisemitism. Van Elslandt of Lille, who headed the Lille organization and who founded an antisemitic club in Dunkirk, was a lawyer, as was Jean Boery, the president of the Toulouse antisemitic group. The

[18] Maurice Barrès, *Scènes et doctrines du nationalisme* (Paris, 1902), 99–103; Georges Thiébaut, *Le Parti protestant* (pamphlet) (Paris, 1895), 5; Edouard Dubut, "Les Groupes antisémites," *Revue Antisémitique*, II (1897), 13–14; Viau, *op. cit.*, 159–76, 180, 195, 220, 228, 304, 373; Gendrot, *op. cit.*, 231; *Libre Parole Illustrée*, July 13, November 9, November 23, 1895; January 18, January 25, May 2, May 9, December 12, 1896; *Libre Parole*, January 16–January 25, March 10, October 13–October 20, November 19–November 25, December 2, 1898; March 7, 1899; *La Petite République*, December 4, 1901.

heads of the organizations in Cherbourg, Nancy, Marseille, and Tours were lawyers. In Montpellier, both the president and vice-president were lawyers, and four of the members of the advisory committee were also members of the bar. Martin Saint-Léon, who in 1895 was the president of the Seine Youths' Plebiscite Union, an ally of the antisemites, and Paul Nourrisson, who became an important leader of the renewed campaign against Freemasonry, were also both young law students and then lawyers. The law students in Lille led the demonstrations in that city during the Dreyfus Affair, as they did also in Marseille, Toulouse, Dijon, and Lyon, while more than two thousand students contributed to the Henry fund established by the *Libre Parole*.

Lawyers did not confine their antisemitic activities to speeches and organizing, for some of the most important antisemitic authors were lawyers. Gustave Tridon was a lawyer, while Edmond Picard, the Belgian Socialist, was a lawyer and a professor of law. François Boisandré and Alfred Gendrot, two of the most valuable members of the *Libre Parole* staff, were law school graduates, while Gaston Méry, city editor, had failed as a lawyer and also as a teacher before he became antisemitic and joined the *Libre Parole*. One of the managing editors of Drumont's newspaper, Joseph Ménard, was a lawyer who became prominent defending anti-Dreyfusards during the aftermath of the Dreyfus Affair.

Emile de Saint-Auban, who had joined the movement with Mouthon in Lyon and who later aided Drumont in Paris, used his legal talents to help the cause, for he defended the leading anti-semites in courts all over France and Algeria. An able court lawyer, Saint-Auban injected antisemitism into his stirring appeals for those who libeled or assaulted the Jews. During the Dreyfus Affair, he defended the honor of the infamous Colonel Henry in the trial of Madame Henry against Salomon Reinach. Saint-Auban remained an extremely conservative nationalist throughout his life, and later had great admiration for Mussolini and Fascist Italy.[19]

[19] François Mouthon, *Du Bluff au chantage. Les Grandes campagnes du Matin* (Paris, 1908), preface, V; Gustave Tridon, *Le Molochisme juif* (Brussels, 1884),

WRITERS AND JOURNALISTS

Professional writers and journalists, who comprised the group most capable of spreading Drumont's teachings throughout France, were among those most seriously infected with hatred of the Jews. It must be emphasized that these men and women were not antisemites who became journalists and writers, but newspapermen and authors who became antisemites. Moreover, they did not confine their activities against the Jews to writing, for they gave speeches, organized clubs, fought duels, and sought seats in the Chamber of Deputies. Almost without exception, they remained antisemites long after the organized movement collapsed.

When *La France juive* appeared in 1886, Drumont had been a journalist for more than two decades and had published a play, a novel, and several historical studies. The life of Auguste Chirac until 1886 parallels that of Drumont in many respects. The Countess Martel de Janville, who wrote many light novels under the pseudonym of Gyp, had also been a newspaper reporter before she turned to caricaturing society and the Jews, and eight of the twelve charter members of the French National Antisemitic League were journalists.

There were a large number of important antisemites who were frustrated intellectuals. Perhaps the most interesting of those not yet described was Jacques de Biez, the scion of a poor but aristocratic Norman family and a fervent Catholic and Republican, who came to Paris late in the 1870's to be a playwright. Failure in the theater led Biez to turn to journalism, and before 1886 he had been art and music critic for a number of Paris newspapers. In an 1883 article in *Le Salon* and in a January, 1884, public lecture on

---

title page; Emile de Saint-Auban, *La Justice sous la troisième République* (Paris, 1931), 13-15, 85-86; Saint-Auban, Admiral Jean B. Degouy, and Henri de Nousanne, *Histoire contemporaine* (Paris, 1925-1927), I, 485-516; II, 369-74, 400-10, 485-503; III, 441-63; Henri Avenel, *La Presse française au vingtième siècle* (Paris, 1901), 139; *Almanach Agenda de la Libre Parole, 1903* (Paris, 1903), 10-11; Curinier, *op. cit.*, IV, 331; Quillard, *op. cit.*, 139-43, 181-95; Bournand, *op. cit.*, 139; Viau, *op. cit.*, 274; *Libre Parole Illustrée*, September 7, 1895; February 15, March 14, 1896; February 27, March 8, April 10, 1897; *Libre Parole*, February 9, February 27, July 8, August 10, December 12, December 26, 1898.

Manet, he demonstrated a lively appreciation of the art of the impressionists long before most critics were willing to grant recognition. After he left Paris in 1892, Biez wrote a novel and a widely praised study of the sculpture of Frémiet. He published a book on Italian music in 1887, and he was considered a competent authority on mediaeval art by contemporary scholars.

In spite of his antisemitism, Biez was an ardent Republican even through the Dreyfus Affair, and he became a professional journalist only when he failed in more creative literature. In 1886, he was the city editor of Gambetta's old newspaper, the *République Française*, but he lost this position when his savage attack upon the Jews was published in the summer of that year. He devoted most of his time from 1886 through the spring of 1892 to the antisemitic movement. He journeyed to Bucharest in August, 1886, to help found the *Alliance anti-israélite universelle*, and he founded the French National Antisemitic League with Drumont in 1889. He wrote three pamphlets and one book against the Jews, and for the league he collected an antisemitic "museum" of posters, pamphlets, and books from all over Europe.

Absorbed by his hobby of trying to prove that Christ was a Celt, Biez was drawn by his study of the life of Joan of Arc and of the sculpture of Frémiet into a racial blood theory very close to the modern Nazi version. Within a week after the founding of Drumont's newspaper in April, 1892, however, Biez left the movement and retired to Poitou, where he married an heiress and became a gentleman farmer and amateur scholar. He very quickly became disgusted with his extremely conservative neighbors, whom he called "forty-word farmers," but he remained a frustrated aesthete and clamored for a Holy War against the Jews throughout his life.[20]

---

[20] Jacques de Biez, "Le Premier Billet," *Saynètes et monologues*, I (1881), 111–23; Biez, *La Question juive* (Paris, 1886), 1–2, 40–43, 90, 349–75; Biez, *Un Maître imagier, E. Frémiet. La Patrie intégrale* (Paris, 1896), 133–49, 155–74; Biez, *Un coup de vent de sud au cap d'Antifer* (Paris, 1899); Biez, *Edouard Manet* (pamphlet) (Paris, 1884), 7–63; Biez, *Sur Charroux* (pamphlet) (Poitiers, 1897); Biez, *Tamburini et la musique italienne* (Paris, 1887); Biez, *Le Complot financier des juifs allemands* (pamphlet) (Paris, 1887); Biez, *Les Rothschild et le péril juif* (pamphlet) (Paris, 1891) 3–15; Biez, *Le Solécisme du bordereau*

Several other important examples can be cited to demonstrate that these individuals were writers and journalists before they became antisemites, not antisemites who turned to journalism and publishing to disseminate their ideas. Albert Monniot, for example, was seventeen when he came to Paris in 1878 and became a typographer for the *Bulletin des Halles*. He soon became editor of this market journal, and then editor of a financial sheet, *Le Messager de Paris*. In 1884, he became a member of the staff of *Le Soleil*, a monarchist daily which he left to join Drumont's *Libre Parole* when it was founded in 1892. He, too, was an unsuccessful playwright. His literary specialty was patriotic novels, one of which, *Souvenirs d'un bleu*, won a medal from the National Society for the Encouragement of Good and was immensely popular during the late 1890's. Monniot was a frequent public speaker for the antisemites, and he campaigned unsuccessfully for the Chamber of Deputies in Montdidier in 1898.[21]

Alfred Gendrot, who wrote under the pseudonym of Jean Drault and who published many very popular humorous novels during the 1890's, particularly a humorous series about a soldier named Chapuzot, was an immensely important acquisition to antisemitism. A Jesuit student and a law school graduate who rejected the family law practice in the little village of Tremblay-le-Vicomte in Eure-et-Loir to seek his fame in literature in Paris, Gendrot began his career in 1888 as music critic for a small paper, *Le Semeur*. In 1890, when his first book about Chapuzot was in its third edition, he became the Paris correspondent of the

et lettres de Dreyfus (Paris, 1898), 63–67; Biez, *Le Jardin des ciguës* (Paris, 1908), 2–24, 48–66, 72–84; Viau, *op. cit.*, 366; Gendrot, *op. cit.*, 35–45, 86–87, 179; Bournand, *op. cit.*, 45–51; Mauvrac, *op. cit.*, 56–62; *Polybiblion*, CLV (1885), 284; Avenel, *Annuaire de la presse française*, VI (1885), 111; VII (1886), 112; *Libre Parole Illustrée*, May 9, 1896.

[21] Avenel, *La Presse française au vingtième siècle*, 376; *Le Mâchoire d'âne*, October 1, 1896; *Libre Parole*, April 18–May 2, 1898. Some of Monniot's most important antisemitic writings are: *Les Gouvernants contre la nation. La Trahison du ministère Waldeck* (pamphlet) (Paris, 1900); *Que faire? Réponse d'un antisémite* (pamphlet) (Paris, 1900); *Crime rituel chez les juifs* (Paris, 1914). His other works include *Le Dernier Preux, roman de cape et d'épée* (Paris, 1895); *Souvenirs d'un bleu* (Paris, 1896); *La Religion napoléonienne* (Paris, 1902).

Algiers *Anti-Juif*. He was one of the original members of the *Libre Parole* staff, and the books, pamphlets, and articles he poured out during these years were of great value to the movement. His amusing stories in the *Libre Parole* and *Libre Parole Illustrée* served as a very effective counterweight to the heavy charges of Drumont. Gendrot served the *Libre Parole* as its parliamentary reporter from 1892 until 1900 and as its dramatic and music critic until the paper finally disappeared in 1924. The author by 1900 of about twenty volumes of humor, several antisemitic books and pamphlets, and several unproduced plays, Gendrot lived to write a history of antisemitism in 1942 and to be sentenced to jail by the Fourth Republic for his offences under the Vichy government.[22]

Another important convert to antisemitism was François Bournand, who published at least sixty books during the twenty-five years following 1885, not all of them antisemitic. Bournand's life is a further illustration of the strength of antisemitism among journalists and authors. Born in Paris in 1853 but raised in Lorraine, Bournand hoped to be a painter. Disappointed in this because he plainly lacked talent, Bournand then failed to complete his course successfully at the *Ecole pratique des Hautes Etudes*. As a consequence, he turned to journalism as a career. He spent ten years as financial correspondent for several Paris newspapers and then became an art critic, just as Biez and Drumont had done. As editor of *Dessin*, he organized and managed two exhibitions of sketches in 1885 and 1886, but he was serving also at that time as Drumont's secretary and research assistant, so apparently neither journalism nor the promotion of art was profitable for him.

Shortly after the publication of *La France juive*, Bournand's "patriotic and pious pen," as Monsignor Fèvre described it, began to become productive. Bournand called himself "a militant Catholic writer" and described Renan as "the second Judas." Most of

----

[22] Alfred Gendrot (Jean Drault, *pseud.*), *Youtres impudents!* (pamphlet) (Paris, 1890), page opposite title page; Gendrot, *Histoire de l'antisémitisme* (Paris, 1942); *La Cinquantenaire de la Libre Parole* (pamphlet) (Paris, 1942), 1; Avenel, *La Presse française au vingtième siècle*, 214; *Ceux dont en parle* (Paris, 1934), 308.

his books were histories of religious orders, biographies of famous clergymen or Catholic generals, and assaults upon the Third Republic and democratic thought. At the same time, he wrote a very widely used textbook on the history of art, was a Professor of History and Art at the *Ecole professionnelle catholique*, and was the editor of several art journals, including *Dessin, Blanc et Noir*, and *Paris-Salon*. His daily contributions to the *Libre Parole* were especially significant because they soothed and satisfied the Catholic conservative readers and those readers interested in antisemitism in art.[23]

One of the most interesting and significant intellectuals to join the crusade against the Jews was Albert Savine, who established a publishing house in Paris in 1886. Since Savine's record as an author and a publisher is so important in the history of French antisemitism and since the economic developments in publishing and journalism in the 1880's and 1890's had great influence in the genesis and development of antisemitism, a study of Savine will not only reveal the manner in which this particular frustrated intellectual turned against the Jews and the Republic, but will also serve as an introduction to a brief analysis of the tremendous changes which occurred during these years in the industries which provided writers with their financial rewards.

Savine was born in Aiguemortes in Gard, in 1859, the son of a lawyer who under the Second Empire had become manager of the department's finances. After a distinguished record in the Montpellier *lycée*, Savine went to Barcelona in 1876 for his university education, apparently because he was convinced that the Provençal literary and cultural movement then being led by Mistral, Aubanel, and Roumanille had a brilliant future and that knowledge of the Catalan language and literature would be a great aid to him.

[23] François Bournand (editor), *Catalogue illustré de l'exposition internationale de blanc et noir* (Paris, 1885), IX–XIV, 63–68; Bournand (editor), *Catalogue illustré de l'exposition internationale de blanc et noir* (Paris, 1886), 4–8; Bournand, *Le Clergé pendant la Commune* (Paris, 1892), 1–15, 249–50; Bournand, *Le Maréchal Canrobert* (Paris, 1895), 213; Bournand, *L'Alsace et la Lorraine* (Paris, 1895), XXI; Drumont, *Le Testament d'un antisémite*, 118–19; Viau, *op. cit.*, 141; *Catalogue générale des livres imprimés de la Bibliothèque Nationale* (Paris, 1897–1950), XVII, 1216–23.

He hoped on his return in 1879 to attend the great *Ecole des Chartes*, but his father urged him to become a lawyer. He therefore attended law school in Aix-en-Provence, but devoted most of his time there to work on several Provençal literary journals.

In 1882, determined to become a nationally known literary critic, Savine came to Paris, able to read and speak Catalan, Portuguese, English, and Italian, as well as French. As a young man in Paris in the early 1880's, Savine wrote critical essays for minor provincial journals, dabbled in art with some young art critics, and campaigned for the recognition of the talents of Mistral and Zola by the *Académie Française*. In 1886, he invested a small fortune his father had left him in a publishing venture. He had been convinced as early as 1883 that the French novel, with the exception of Zola, was in a great period of decline. Since it was impossible for him to obtain the works of Zola for publication and since he was very Catholic and nationalistic, he leaped with great enthusiasm into the antisemitic campaign, which Drumont's *La France juive* had just inaugurated.[24]

As the *Revue du monde catholique* remarked, "Anyone who wishes to follow Drumont can count upon the support of his valiant publisher, Albert Savine, who is very zealous in spreading antisemitism." Although, in urging in 1884 that Mistral be elected to the *Académie Française*, Savine had written, "Anyone is French who is born on French soil, speaks a language born on French soil, and expresses French ideas," he became a sincere antisemite. He wrote antisemitic books and articles himself (he believed the Boxer Rebellion had been instigated by the Freemasons), he encouraged his authors to attack the Jews, and he on occasion wrote vicious prefaces for their books. Savine was an intimate friend of

[24] Albert Savine, *Les Etapes d'un naturaliste* (Paris, 1885), IV–VI, 3–10, 27–55, 97–131, 157–164, 196–246; Savine, "L'Atlantide," *Revue des Langues Romanes*, XX (1881), 180–186; Savine, "Le Recteur de Vallfogona. Etude catalane," *Revue Lyonnaise*, VI (1883), 274–88; Savine, "Le Naturalisme en Espagne," *Revue Contemporaine*, II (1885), 235–48, 374–89; Savine, "Auguste Chirac," *Revue d'art dramatique*, 18th year (1903), 334–55; Lucien Borel du Bez, *Albert Savine, 1858–1927* (pamphlet) (Gap, 1929), 1–5; Saint-Auban, *La Justice sous la Troisième République*, 53–57; Hugo Thième, *Bibliographie de la littérature française de 1800 à 1930* (Paris, 1933), II, 742–43; *Le Livre*, V (1884), 317–18, 759; VI (1885), 178.

all the leading French antisemites. His publishing house produced more than fifty books and pamphlets against the Jews from 1886 through 1893, providing fuel for the antisemitic campaign as well as royalties and renown for his authors.

Savine attacked the Third Republic from his publishing house from many angles, fostering a sentimental view of the Old Regime and at the same time publishing many of the works of the leading contemporary anarchists. He issued many books on contemporary trials and scandals, he published volumes which demonstrated that the moral customs of France were deteriorating under the Republic, he sought to demonstrate that French literature had declined rapidly since 1885, and he attacked England as the perpetual Protestant enemy of France.

The history of Savine's publishing house and bookstore closely mirrors the history of the antisemitic movement. In spite of the fact that he published a rather wide variety of kinds of literature, promoted sensational books of all types, and used illustrations more generally and effectively than most French publishers did at that time, he went into bankruptcy late in 1893, in the heart of the publishing crisis and at a time when the campaign led by Drumont was particularly feeble. With the aid of a friend and collaborator, Léonce Grasilier, he revived his concern after the arrest of Captain Dreyfus, but by 1897 that venture also was bankrupt. The causes for his failure were his lack of publishing sense, for some of his antisemitic publications sold to no one but collectors, his zealous generosity in supporting antisemitic authors, and the extremely expensive lawsuits into which several of his publications led him. Broken, penniless, completely disillusioned about his creative talents, a thoroughly "frustrated intellectual," Savine settled down in seat 152 in the *Bibliothèque Nationale* to translate before 1914 more than one hundred novels and memoirs from English into French and to edit more than forty volumes on eighteenth-century continental history.[25]

[25] Albert Savine (editor), *L'Espagne en 1810. Souvenirs d'un prisonnier de guerre anglais* (Paris, 1909), preface, 5–6; Savine, *Mes Procès* (Paris, 1890), VII–IX, 4–23, 184–93, 338–421, 546–66; Savine, "La Question juive en 1789–1790," *Nouvelle Revue Rétrospective*, XI (1899), 145–68; Kalixt de Wolski,

FRENCH PUBLISHING AND JOURNALISM

The economic forces which helped to evoke and then to destroy Savine's publishing enterprise also helped to create the antisemitic movement. The French publishing industry enjoyed a tremendous boom from 1875 through the 1880's, but this period of expansion was followed by a sharp economic crisis throughout the industry which destroyed many important publishing houses, old and new, and from which the industry as a whole did not recover until 1910 or 1911.

The principal causes for the revolution in French publishing which began about 1875 were conditions over which neither the authors nor the publishers had any control: the tremendous improvements made in printing, communication, and transportation, and the collection of enormous masses of people in numerous and constantly growing cities. These distinctive conditions help greatly to explain why the publishing industry failed to follow the general course of the business cycle in France during the years from 1879 through 1890. The revolution within the industry which occurred in the last quarter of the nineteenth century was marked by sharp and radical changes in the form of corporate organization which generally prevailed, a tremendous increase in the number of publishing houses, the adoption and successful promotion of inexpensive reprints, and the extraordinary sale of the popular science books of Camille Flammarion, the science-and-adventure tales of Jules Verne, and the naturalist novels of Zola, Alphonse Daudet, and the Goncourts.

Some of the statistics on sales of books in France after 1875 are tremendously informative. More than fifty thousand copies of

La Russie juive (Paris, 1887), preface; Numa Gilly, *Mes Dossiers* (Paris, 1889), preface, IV–VIII, 75–76; Henryk Sienkiewicz, *Pagès d'Amérique. Récits de l'émigration* (Paris, 1901), preface, I–VI; Georges Darien, *Les Antisémites. Les Pharisiens* (Paris, 1891), *passim;* Pierre Stock, *Mémorandum d'un éditeur* (Paris, 1935–1938), I, 25–33, 78–83; Avenel, *Annuaire de la presse française*, X (1889), 139; Henri Le Soudier, *Bibliographie française* (Paris, 1896), V. Savine Catalogue, 3–32; *Catalogue générale*, CLXIV, 65–75; *Revue de monde catholique*, XCVI (1888), 488; CXIII (1893), 123–25; *Polybiblion*, LXVIII (1893), 77–78; *Le Livre*, VIII (1887), 123–26, 232–36, 345–46, 409–10, 528–36, 641–42; X (1889), 13–16, 57–58, 98, 180, 188–89, 513; *Libre Parole Illustrée*, April 24, 1894; *Libre Parole*, March 1, March 16, April 6, 1899.

Camille Flammarion's popularization of astronomy, *L'Astronomie populaire*, were sold in 1882 alone, although thirty years earlier a similar book by François Arago, one of the great astronomers of the nineteenth century, sold only two thousand copies. In the 1850's, Michel Lévy sold only eight editions of the classic of Dumas fils, *La Dame aux camélias*, although after 1870 some of the same author's less well-known works sold thirty and forty editions.[26]

The flowering of the naturalist novel began after the publication of Alphonse Daudet's *Fromont jeune et Risler ainé* in 1874, for this sentimental and tragic tale sold five hundred copies a day during the first two months after it appeared. The next year Edmond de Goncourt's *La Fille Elisa*, a story about a prostitute, sold ten thousand copies in less than two months. The publication in 1877 of Zola's *L'Assommoir*, probably his finest novel, clearly demonstrated that these publications by the house of Georges Charpentier constituted a very sharp change in French writing and publishing history. The book appeared February 24, 1877, and thirty-eight editions were sold by November of that year. An illustrated edition brought out on May 11, 1877, sold fifty thousand copies before December, 1878. By 1882, more than a hundred thousand copies of this novel had been sold, Zola had leaped to eminence and great prosperity, the naturalist novel was acquiring a dominance in French letters which symbolism in French poetry shook in vain for a decade after 1885, and the entire publishing industry had been given an extraordinary stimulus.[27]

[26] Camille Flammarion, *Mémoires biographiques et philosophiques d'un astronome* (Paris, 1911), 331–34, 356–60, 384–93, 479–83, 549; Flammarion, *Le Monde avant la création* (Paris, 1886), cover of fortieth edition; Flammarion, *Lumen* (Paris, 1888 and 1906 editions), cover page; Flammarion, *Uranie* (Paris, 1893 edition), cover page; Flammarion, *François Arago* (Paris, 1879), 1–16; Lucien Roure, "Camille Flammarion. Un Prédicant du scientisme," *Etudes*, CLXXXIV (1925), 68–73; Alexander Dumas *fils*, *Françillon* (Paris, 1888 edition), cover page; *Catalogue générale*, XLIV, LXXIV, 653–777; 142–64; B. H. Gausseron, "La Librarie française au dix-neuvième siècle," *Le Livre Moderne*, IV (1891), 222–34.

[27] Léon Deffoux, *La Publication de l'Assommoir* (Paris, 1931), 12, 67–68; Alphonse Daudet, *Trente Ans de Paris* (Paris, 1888), 196–212; Léon Daudet, *Quand vivait mon père* (Paris, 1940), 16–17; Margret Schwesinger, *Die literarischen und buchhändlerischen Erfolge des naturalistischen Romans des 19 Jahrh. im französichen Publikum* (Miltenberg-am-Main, 1935), 12–13.

The Zola sales figures alone are impressive. *Page d'amour* sold twenty-four editions in 1878 and eighty-eight by 1900. *Nana* sold ninety editions in its first year, 1880, one hundred and fifty by 1885, and one hundred and eighty-two by 1900. *Germinal* sold sixty-three editions when it appeared in 1885 and one hundred and five by 1900. *La Terre* sold eighty-eight editions from 1887 through 1890 and one hundred and twenty-nine by 1900. *La Débâcle* sold one hundred and eighty-two editions in 1892 and 1893 and two hundred and twenty-nine by 1911. *Lourdes* sold one hundred and thirty-two editions in 1894 and 1895 and one hundred and forty-nine by 1900.

The publication statistics for Alphonse Daudet demonstrate a parallel development. *Jack*, which followed *Fromont jeune et Risler aîné* in 1876, sold one hundred and four editions by 1902; *Le Nabab* appeared in 1877 and sold eighty-seven editions by 1887. *Numa Roumestan* sold almost a hundred thousand copies within two decades after its publication in 1881; eighty thousand copies of *Sapho*, his greatest success, were sold within a few weeks after its first appearance in 1884. More than two hundred thousand copies of *Tartarin de Tarascon* and of *Tartarin sur les Alpes* had been sold by 1910. Alphonse Daudet's publishing successes were so great that his son, Léon, complained of *L'Evangéliste* because it sold only forty thousand copies. Even the elder Daudet's autobiography, *Trente Ans de Paris*, sold forty-seven thousand copies.[28]

No reliable statistics on the total number of books printed in France each year were developed until 1934, and the statistics which were prepared then for the legislature covered only the preceding twenty years. It is very apparent, however, from the figures which are available that book production in France increased tremendously after 1875. Under the July Monarchy, Paris readers "consumed" about twenty-five new novels a year. During

[28] Alphonse Daudet, *op. cit.*, 157–78, 196–212; Léon Daudet, *Quand vivait mon pere*, 134–36, 164–71, 259–60; *A Catalogue of Books Represented by Library of Congress Printed Cards* (Ann Arbor, Michigan, 1942–1946), XXXV, 598–605; Schwesinger, *op. cit.*, 12–20, 60; Albert Cim, "La Vente des livres," *Revue Encyclopédique*, V (1895), 284–85; Eugène Morel, "Le Livre français et la production mondiale. Essai de statistique des imprimés," *Mercure de France*, VC (1912), 772.

the 1880's, in Paris alone twenty-five or thirty new books appeared each day, and in that decade Paris readers "consumed" about three hundred new novels a year. In 1818, in Paris 3,357 new publications (books and pamphlets) were issued, while in 1891 the total number of new books alone published in France was 14,192.[29]

The enormous stimulus provided by the technical improvements, the growth of city populations, the rise of the literacy rate, and the great financial success enjoyed by some publishing houses and authors led other enterprising Frenchmen to found publishing concerns or to come to Paris with hopes high for careers as authors and critics. Each success led another publisher to accept and sell an imitation, or to commission someone on his list or some eager young author to produce an imitation. This increase in the number of ignorant and over-eager publishers and in the output of each of them, and the "over-production of intellectuals" which the boom stimulated, led to a veritable rain of books, especially novels, after 1886. Marpon and Flammarion, and Albert Savine are only two of the publishing houses which appeared first during these years. Flammarion, after Marpon's death in 1890, developed his concern into one of the most important in all of western Europe, while Savine's enterprise was one of that large number of firms, great and small, wrecked by economic forces and conditions they could not master.

One of the greatest causes of the economic crisis in the publishing industry in France which began about 1890 was the general low level of French prosperity from 1883 through 1892 or 1893. The French economy recovered with great swiftness from the Franco-Prussian War, suffered a depression from 1873 through 1879, enjoyed three or four years of prosperity, and then sagged for about a decade. It is important to note that the great publishing boom in France began about 1875, when the French economy

[29] Octave Uzanne, "Les Ecrivains, le public et la réclame," *Le Livre*, VIII (1887), 225; Albert Cim, "Auteurs, éditeurs et libraires," *Revue politique et littéraire*, I (1894), 68–69; Marc Jaryc, "La Publicité du livre," *Courrier graphique*, I–II (1937), 21–22; Gausseron, loc. cit., 233–44; *Le Livre Moderne*, IV (1891), 186.

generally was depressed, and that the pattern of this industry does not follow the general economic curve. By 1890, however, the general economic slump had begun to affect the publishing industry. Thus, one of the basic factors causing the decline of the book trade was the growing tendency, of the middle classes in particular, to abandon the purchase of books for borrowing them and for reading instead one or more of the French representatives of the new "yellow press." [30]

The temporary expedients used to end the crisis only increased the difficulties. Many publishers resorted to more and more sensational books and to dumping entire editions hysterically into the market. Writers received smaller royalties and consequently overworked themselves to maintain their incomes at their previous levels. Critics were overwhelmed by the deluge of books and yielded to fatigue, carelessness, and corruption in their reviews. Book reviews became so numerous and vapid that newspaper and journal readers ceased to read them. Finally, by 1891 and 1892, all the newspapers ceased reviewing books.

As this situation developed, some publishers began to issue catalogues offering their new books at prices lower than those same books were obtaining in the bookstores. The bookstores then began selling three-franc fifty-centime books for three francs, then for two francs seventy-five centimes. As the price war raged, many bookstores formed trade leagues and then made price agreements with their publishers, but this technique was tardy, incomplete, and generally ineffective.

As the prices of books fell, book buyers naturally waited for prices to reach their absolute depth. The depression thus began as a general one throughout the publishing industry late in 1890, and

---

[30] Shepherd B. Clough, *France, A History of National Economics, 1789–1939* (New York, 1939), 214–19; Henri Avenel, *Histoire de la presse française depuis 1789 jusqu'à nos jours* (Paris, 1900), 796–816, 853–64; André Billy, *Les Ecrivains de combat* (Paris, 1931), 112–19; Gendrot, *op. cit.*, 67–80; Paul Pottier, "Le Prolétariat des journalistes," *Revue Mondiale*, XLVII (1903), 673–74; Albert Cim, "Auteurs, éditeurs et libraires," *Revue politique et littéraire*, I (1894), 68–69; Cim, "La Vente des livres," *Revue Encyclopédique*, V (1895), 260; Paul Gsell, "La Crise du livre en France," *Revue Mondiale*, series 4, XLVII (1903), 346–47.

then deepened in 1891. The great critic of the industry and the man who had predicted throughout the 1880's that the boom was bound to collapse, Octave Uzanne, comforted the publishers by pointing out that the recession would be a temporary one which would eliminate a few marginal publishers and thereby eliminate the cause, overproduction. To the surprise and horror of the publishers, however, 1892 became a more disastrous year than 1891 had been. 1893 revealed a new depth, for during that year two-thirds of all the books produced lost money for their publishers. Only six novelists in France in that year obtained a royalty of ten thousand francs. Most novelists considered themselves successful if their total sale in 1893 reached four thousand volumes. It was not until 1894 that a sufficient number of the weaker concerns had been eliminated and the wreckage and litter of the 1880's cleared away for the industry to recover its poise.[31]

The depression which struck the French publishing industry in 1890 left behind also a generation of "frustrated aesthetes," of men who had grown to manhood in the 1870's and 1880's with visions of following the paths of Zola, Verne, Sainte-Beuve, Taine, Renan, Flammarion, or even Georges Ohnet to fame and fortune. Their plans shattered, many of these men promoted anti-semitism with Drumont, who was one of them, and later joined the *Action Française*, making that organization into a lively force, primarily of intellectuals, operating against the entire foundation of the Third Republic. The number of these men was increased by the revolution occurring at the same time in the newspaper press. These years might well be called "the golden age of French journalism," but this golden age, like so many others, was based on the poverty and misery of a mass of under-paid workers. The

[31] Gaston Zelger, *Manuel d'édition et de librairie* (Paris, 1928), 14–16; *Congrès national du livre. Comité d'organisation. Société des gens de lettres. Cercle de la librairie. Comité du livre. Rapports et résolutions* (Paris, 1917–1922), I, 5–6; *Congrès international des éditeurs* (London, 1899), 132–35; Henri Baillière, *La Crise du livre* (Paris, 1904), 10–45; Uzanne, "Le Marché littéraire. Notes sur la crise de la librairie contemporaine," *Le Livre Moderne*, IV (1891), 63–80; Uzanne, "Le Malaise actuel de l'édition et de la librairie," *L'Art et l'Idée*, II (1892), 65–80; Albert Cim, "Auteurs, éditeurs et libraires," *Revue politique et littéraire*, I (1894), 65–73; Gsell, loc. cit., 146–66, 341–55; *Le Livre*, IX (1888), 97; *Le Livre Moderne*, III (1891), 180–82; *L'Art et l'Idée*, II (1892), 375–76.

economic change occurring in the press not only helped cause the crisis in the publishing industry during the 1890's, thus increasing the number of "intellectual proletariat" in Paris, but it also created unemployment within the newspaper industry itself, adding to the havoc among the writers and journalists.

The newspaper industry underwent several waves of change during the nineteenth century, just as the publishing industry did. In 1836, the cost of an annual subscription to a Paris newspaper was eighty francs, and in that year there were only seventy thousand subscribers in Paris. At almost the same time that Georges Charpentier caused a revolution in the publishing industry by selling books for less than four francs, Emile de Girardin, probably the greatest French journalist in the nineteenth century, transformed the newspaper business by establishing the *Presse* in July, 1836, at an annual subscription rate of only forty-eight francs. Girardin's success, based on using cheaper paper as well as on effective newspaper promotion, led to the precipitate decline of the price of all subscriptions to the annual rate of forty francs. This was one of the principal reasons for the resultant tremendous increase in newspaper circulation and in the number of newspapers. There were two hundred thousand subscriptions in Paris in 1846 and three hundred fifty thousand in 1866. The number of newspapers in Paris doubled from 1840 through 1860, and the following twenty years produced an additional increase of 60 percent.

The development and use by the newspaper industry of the various inventions which appeared during the last century promoted a second wave of great change. The railroad, the telephone, and the telegraph improved the collection of news and the distribution of the newspapers. The perfecting of the Marinoni rotary press during the 1860's made possible the printing of twenty-five thousand copies within one hour and was also an important contributing factor in the ultimate development of journalism into a big business requiring joint-stock companies and large outlays of capital. The law of July, 1881, which in effect made slander and libel in the French press unpunishable under French law, and the removal at the same time of the restrictions placed on news-paper publication by earlier regimes encouraged a tremendous flowering of the press. Paris, which in 1818 had only one hundred and fifty newspapers, in 1895 had twenty-four hundred, in 1900 twenty-eight hundred, and in 1907 thirty-four hundred.

Appearances seemed to indicate that the freedoms granted under the Third Republic and the new industrial developments had encouraged the decentralization of news collection and distribution. However, a very small group of newspapers dominated the French political scene, and none of these large papers was privately owned. The *Petit Journal* during the 1890's sold about a million copies daily, where twenty-five thousand had been a peak in 1840; after the turn of the century the *Petit Parisien* averaged 1,300,000 daily. The newspaper at that time was called "the new primary school," and many of the most influential men in France then, Clemenceau, Drumont, Rochefort, Father Bailly, and Cavaignac, were newspaper editors. It is difficult now to discover a professional novelist or dramatist, or even politician, who was not also at that time a prominent journalist. It was the end of an age, however, as well as the beginning of one. One prominent twentieth-century journalist, André Billy, lamented in 1931, "Since the death of Barrès [1923], no great artist or writer has been a journalist." [32]

Paris journalists were in an unpleasant predicament during the first four decades of the history of the Third Republic because of the newspaper situation. In Paris, a few giant newspapers dominated the political newspaper field, but two or three hundred other political papers also existed, some with a small but consistent clientele and others representing attempts to capitalize upon a contemporary political crisis, a political or journalistic personality, or the desire of some financial or political group to influence

[32] Jacques Pigelet, *Organisation intérieure de la presse périodique française* (Orléans, 1909), 23–85; Georges Maze-Sencier, *Le Rôle social et moral de la presse* (Paris, 1911), 21–23, 64–66; Carlton J. H. Hayes, *A Generation of Materialism, 1870–1900* (New York, 1941), 173–76; Emile Pierret, "La Presse en France," *Réforme sociale,* VL (1903), 357–64; Billy, *op. cit.,* 112–19; Avenel, *Histoire de la presse française,* 796–816, 853–54; *Avenel, Annuaire de la presse française,* XIX (1898), XIX; XXI (1900), XV.

opinion temporarily. Girardin's glamorous career had led to constant pressure to keep down the sales price of the newspaper. This tradition, the mechanization of news collection and of the various processes involved in the printing, cutting, and folding, and the tremendous competition established the price of an individual copy at only five centimes. Since Havas had seized almost a monopoly of newspaper advertising at the middle of the century, French newspapers failed to obtain the return from advertising which the press in other countries did. The *Petit Journal*, for example, during the 1890's sold about a million copies daily and had an annual budget of ten million francs, yet it obtained only two and one-half million francs from advertising. The *Petit Parisien* in the first decade of the twentieth century, with even greater circulation, obtained only 2,800,000 francs from advertising.

The strange lack of advertising in French newspapers had been remarked even earlier by both French and foreign observers. Newspapers in other countries acquired the major part of their income from advertising, which allowed them to improve their services and to attract more readers. A German scholar just before the First World War discovered that advertising occupied more than one-third of the space in German newspapers but only one-fourth in French newspapers. A great survey of foreign correspondents in Paris in 1902 revealed that almost unanimously the veterans of European newspaper work believed that the French inability to use advertising was the greatest single weakness of the French newspaper system and that from this shortcoming derived the other evils: lack of independence, corruption, low salaries, and extremely poor coverage of events in other countries. Even in the 1920's, a student found that French newspapers received only one-sixth or one-eighth the income from advertising which English newspapers of similar size obtained, and the League for the Rights of Man in 1933 recommended national advertising distributing agencies as one of the means of providing France an independent press.[33]

[33] Henri Loustalan, *La Publicité dans la presse française* (Paris, 1933), 18–23; Robert W. Desmond, *The Press and World Affairs* (New York, 1937), 55–58;

The consequences of the existence of a few highly capitalized, expertly managed political papers and a large number of newspapers with little capital and with the main portion of their income deriving from daily sales have been noted throughout all of the history of the Third Republic. A press which has been outstanding in expression and in scholarship, it has also been one "too poor to be independent." It has been marked by corruption, pornography, blackmail, and sensationalism. The race for subscribers has caused all of these evils and has led also to the impoverishment of the journalists, crushed by the system. A handful of extremely capable journalists, such as Girardin, Rochefort, Drumont, Léon Daudet, and Eugéne Mayer, prospered, but most, including many talented journalists who somehow did not find the correct position for their talents, were driven into hack-work. Some of these became either sincere or purchased antisemites, others became anarchists, Socialists, Communists, or members of the *Action Française*. Many retained in poverty whatever principles they may have had when they began their careers; others left Paris for the provinces, where the overproduction of journalists there also drove salaries and wages down almost 50 percent shortly after the turn of the century.

Hundreds and thousands of eager and ambitious young intellectuals were overwhelmed by these changes in the publishing and newspaper business. The lives of many of the antisemitic leaders have served already as illustrations, but others suffered the same experience. Paul Brulot, for example, came to Paris in 1888 as a twenty-two-year-old aspiring writer. He supported himself by working as a reporter for a number of newspapers, and during his spare time he worked upon a novel. In 1889, Zola granted him an interview, which he sold to *La Presse*, then a Boulangist paper

---

Joseph Reinach, "Parisian Newspapers," *Nineteenth Century*, XII (1882), 347–60; Charles Sarolea, "La Presse anglaise et la presse française," *Revue de Belgique*, series II, XXXII (1901), 289–302; Georges Boris, "The French Press," *Foreign Affairs*, XIII (1935), 319–27; Frédéric Loliée, "L'Opinion européene sur la presse française," *Revue Bleue*, XXXIX (1902), 714–21, 753–58, 790–95; Pigelet, *op. cit.*, 100–16; Pierret, *loc. cit.*, 357–60; Max Garr, *Die wirtschaftlichen Grundlagen des modernen Zeitungswesens* (Vienna, Leipzig, 1912), 44.

selling a hundred thousand copies a day during the high tide of Boulangism. The success of that interview won for Brulot a position on *La Presse* at two hundred francs per month. As Boulangism declined, however, so did the sales of *La Presse*. The collapse to a daily sale of one thousand was rapid in 1890. Then the paper began to appear only occasionally, to sell itself to financial enterprises, to fail to pay its workers. It finally went bankrupt late in 1890, and Brulot returned to his old work of writing for several papers and being paid for the number of lines accepted, until the successful publication of his novel in September, 1892, gained a position for him on the staff of the *Journal*.

The "golden age of journalism" thus crushed the journalist. Salaries for specialists declined precipitately during the 1890's. *Figaro*, which had in 1880 paid its dramatic critic three thousand francs a month, in 1903 paid only a thousand. Reporters who covered the Senate received from 350 to 500 francs a month, court reporters only 200 to 350. Short stories which had sold for 200 francs fifteen years earlier, in 1903 obtained only fifteen francs. Most newspapers at the turn of the century ceased printing articles by minor and even major literary lights. It was the unknown reporter, though, who suffered most. For a fourteen-hour day, seven days a week, he received 150 or 200 francs a month from the established papers, while many papers paid fifteen centimes for each line printed. Few journalists married, few remained in journalism as a career. The unemployed journalists, and in 1903 there were believed to be three or four unemployed for every one who was employed, wrote review articles, worked as research assistants, became publicity agents during election campaigns, edited unknown papers and journals for printers, turned to blackmail, or went to the provinces. Antisemitism, and many of the other creeds of discontent, rose from these submerged intellectuals, smashed and deprived of success by forces they could neither understand nor control.[34]

[34] Paul Brulot, *Le Reporter* (Paris, 1898); Brulot, *Lumières et grandes ombres. Souvenirs* (Paris, 1930), 68–96; Pigelet, *op. cit.*, 114–27; Pottier, *loc. cit.*, 673–97.

ANTISEMITISM IN FRENCH ART

The French antisemitic movement was very fortunate in having so many of its members journalists and writers, and it also benefited enormously from the wild antisemitism of the leading cartoonists of the age. The three outstanding caricaturists of that time, Willette, Emmanuel Poiré, and Jean Forain, were all antisemites, as were many of the less important caricaturists, such as Blass, Steinlen, Léandre, Gerbault, Huard, and others. Their cartoons were of great importance in giving antisemitism concrete expression in newspapers, books, albums, posters, and handbills. These men, moreover, did not caricature the Jews because that was a popular and profitable practice, but because they were convinced antisemites. The careers of each of the three most important are illustrative, each in its own way, of the entire movement and of the ideas and pressures which made the campaign so much one of intellectuals.

Adolphe Willette was born in 1857 in Châlons-sur-Marne and educated in Dijon, in the heart of the district in France which was the center of the most open antisemitic demonstrations outside of Paris in 1898 and 1899. His father was a colonel in the French army who served with great distinction against the Prussians in 1870. Although Willette was always savagely critical of the French army leaders who had crushed the Commune in 1871, he was "as patriotic as a drummer-boy." His parents, ashamed of him because he could not read until he was nine years old, gave him religious paintings to stir his desire to learn, and they were gratified indeed when this also stimulated Willette to become a painter.

Willette studied at the *Ecole des Beaux Arts* in Paris under the portrait painter Cabanel, but he soon left for the Latin Quarter and Montmartre. He supported himself in Paris by making sketches for illustrated newspapers, and as the salons were closed to him he soon devoted all of his time to illustration. It is quite evident that Willette was bitter throughout his life at his lack of success as an artist, and because of this he turned upon bourgeois society, the Third Republic, and "the Protestants, bourgeoisie, Jews, and England." Very much influenced by the anarchism popular in artistic circles at the time, he said he approved the Republic of 1793 but not the Republic of 1893. When Drumont fled to Belgium in the summer of 1894, Willette published a cartoon depicting Liberty, Equality, and Fraternity safely buried by the Third Republic.

The *Courrier français*, for which Willette did a great deal of illustrating in the 1880's and 1890's, predicted on January 3, 1886, four months before the publication of *La France juive*, that "Willette will someday lead a Saint Bartholomew's Massacre for all the Jews in Montmartre." He was the first Frenchman to campaign for public office in the Third Republic as an antisemite, running from the ninth *arrondissement* in Paris in September, 1889, for the Chamber of Deputies. He made his own posters for that campaign, and one of them was so remarkable that it reappeared frequently in antisemitic literature until after the Dreyfus Affair. This poster showed an old Jew fleeing as Marianne called her sons, while a hunter, a peasant, a student, and a general dug up a crowned pig's head and a Talmud. The inscription declared: "The Jews are great only because we are on our knees. 50,000 alone benefit from the constant and hopeless work of 30,000,000 French slaves. This is not a religious question. The Jew is of a different race and the enemy of our race. Judaism, that is our enemy!"

That same year, Willette exhibited a painting at the *Salon des artistes indépendants* which revealed a golden locomotive labeled Israel and Company crushing Work, Justice, Religion, Liberty, and Poetry. Antisemitism was a very strong component in *Pierrot*, an illustrated journal which he founded in February, 1889, but which went bankrupt in the summer of 1890. Throughout the 1890's, in his caricatures in the *Courrier français*, *Chat noir*, and the *Libre Parole Illustrée*, he carried on a bitter campaign against the Jews, Protestants, and English. After his marriage in 1899, at the age of forty-one, and after the birth of a daughter in 1908, he softened quite considerably and became a religious conservative. His family happiness, prosperity, and recognition led to his abandoning antisemitism and becoming a supporter of the Third Republic before the outbreak of the First World War, but the reasons for which he recovered from antisemitism are as revealing for the history of the campaign as those for which he succumbed to it.[35]

Emmaneul Poiré, known in France under his Russian pseudonym, Caran d'Ache, acquired his hatred of the Jews in Russia, where he lived until he came to France in 1878. Poiré's grandfather, an officer in Napoleon's army, lost an arm and a leg in the 1812 campaign and married the Russian girl who nursed him back to health. The grandson as a child developed a great admiration for Napoleon and came to France when he was eighteen to serve in the French army. He enjoyed his five years of service in the French army, especially because he worked in the War Ministry at his childhood hobby, drawing uniforms. When he left the army, he studied at the *Ecole des Beaux Arts* for a short time and then followed the path of Willette in becoming an illustrator. After working for some time for *La Caricature*, he sought twice to establish his own illustrated journal, but both *Arts incohérents* and *Vie militaire* failed.

Poiré was much influenced by Morès, and he developed from the marquis a deep hatred of England as well as an admiration for the Morès mustache. Although he was a professional patriot, he was very much influenced by contemporary German caricature, especially that of Wilhelm Busch. His mastery of the German techniques won him praise as "the greatest master of telling a story without words." His cartoons throughout the 1890's in

[35] Adolphe Brisson, *Nos Humoristes* (Paris, 1900), 140–58; John Grand-Carteret, *Les Moeurs et la caricature en France* (Paris, 1888), 460–464, 504–508; Ferdinand Bac, *Intimités de la troisième République* (Paris, 1935), I, 499–505; Paul Beuve, *Iconographie de A. Willette de 1861 à 1909* (Paris, 1909), 4–23, 58–70; Adolphe Willette, *Oeuvres choisies* (Paris, 1901), preface, *passim*; Edouard Fuchs, *Die Juden in der Karikatur* (Munich, 1921), 190, 208, 216, 222–233, 249, 311; Julien Mauvrac, *Sous les Tentes de Japhet* (Paris, 1890), 173–174; *Les Maîtres humoristes* (Paris, 1907–1908), series I, number 13, preface; *Qui êtes-vous?* (Paris, 1909–1910), 505–506; Curinier, *op. cit.*, supplement, 292; Bournand, *Juifs et antisemites en Europe*, 59–67; *Libre Parole Illustrée*, July 17, 1893.

Figaro were very effective in spreading a subtle antisemitism, and during the Dreyfus Affair Forain and he in *Psst!* carried caricature to great heights, although their efforts intensified feeling against the Jews and against the principles upon which the Third Republic was based. Strangely, Poiré, like Willette, recovered not only from his antisemitism but also from his hatred of England, for Edward VII of England dazzled the then wealthy French nationalist as he did so many other Frenchmen.[36]

The most celebrated and significant of the antisemitic artists and caricaturists was Jean Forain, whose career is particularly interesting because it serves to relate antisemitism rather concretely to symbolism in French literature, impressionism in French art, the contemporary vogue of spiritualism, and the nationalism generated by men such as Boulanger, Morès, Mercier, and Pétain. Forain had tremendous abilities in a number of fields, although his dislike for oil painting in an era in which oils were the chief interest of critics and collectors harmed his reputation and contributed to his extreme bitterness towards the *salons*. One critic declared that Forain was "one of the great etchers of the world," another that the religious paintings he did after his interest in politics waned were "surely the most beautiful religious works of our time," and a third that "except for Toulouse-Lautrec, Forain was unequalled as a lithographer."

There is much in the life of Forain which resembles that of Drumont, whose neighbor he was for some time. He was born in Reims in 1852, the son of a house painter in a family of thread and lace makers. Given a Catholic education and raised in a very severe Catholic family, Forain spent a great deal of time in the splendid Reims cathedral, where his love of the statuary made him resolve to become a sculptor. His artistic ambitions were discouraged by his parents, who hoped only that he would rise to the

[36] Emmanuel Poiré (Caran d'Ache, *pseud.*), *Pages d'histoire* (Paris, 1904), 11, 14, 18, 37; Gabriel Astruc, *Le Pavillon des fantômes. Souvenirs* (Paris, 1929), 52–53; H. M. Bateman, *Caran d'Ache* (London, 1933), preface, V; Robert Burnett, "Caran d'Ache, 1859–1909," *London Mercury*, XXIX (1934), 440–45; Fuchs, *op. cit.*, 221; Bac, *op. cit.*, I, 505–508; Brisson, *op. cit.*, 2–10; Grand-Carteret, *op. cit.*, 510–13.

middle class and who moved to Paris in 1864 so that he might acquire a better education. His interest in painting and sculpting infuriated his parents, who barely tolerated his brief period of study at the *Ecole des Beaux Arts* late in the Second Empire and who refused to contribute to his support when the sculptor, Carpeaux, who had been training him, ousted him from his studio. During the harsh few years which followed, he became a companion of Rimbaud and Verlaine, who were to break new paths for French poetry and who filled their "Gavroche" with a deep hatred for the smug bourgeois and the Third Republic.[37]

There is little data available on the life of Forain from 1872 until 1876, but apparently he sought training and experience in painting, using water colors in particular. He told a friend later that he was unable to finish a bouquet in 1873 because he had no colors and no money. After 1875, it is clear that he turned to making illustrations for the illustrated newspapers, his first etchings being for this purpose. *Charivari*, the most notable illustrated journal of that time, rejected his work, but he was a success with *Scapin, Cravache parisienne, Monde parisien, Chat noir,* and *Vie moderne*. During this period, he came under the influence of the impressionists, Degas in particular. He exhibited at the *Salon des artistes indépendants* in 1881 and 1882, and he stood by Degas at his salon in 1886 when the impressionist group broke up definitively.

Degas became one of the great influences in the life of Forain, who revered Huysmans, Degas, and, later, Pétain, as his masters. Forain's attitude towards Degas was "practically pious," according to one friend, and he was loyal to the bitter, cruel old man until his death. Huysmans said of the "cruel, hateful, humiliating, and pitiless" female nudes which Degas exhibited in 1886 that they "glorified hatred and disdain for the human flesh as never any artist has done since the Middle Ages." Degas imparted more than

[37] Campbell Dodgson, *Forain. Draughtsman, Lithographer, Etcher* (New York, 1936), 17–20; M. Knoedler, *Forain, Acquafortiste et lithographie, 1852–1931* (New York, 1935), 3; Enid Starkie, *Arthur Rimbaud* (New York, 1947), 165, 314; Pol Neveux, "Jean-Louis Forain," *Revue de Paris*, IV (1931), 773–79, 788; Brisson, *op. cit.*, 19–37.

this misogynism to Forain, for his bitter hatred and scorn for mankind, especially the common man, were even more influential upon the caricaturist. Degas was also a wild antisemite. He read Drumont's *Libre Parole* with great satisfaction every day, and he was an active anti-Dreyfusard, as were Rodin, Renoir, and Cézanne.

J. K. Huysmans was another great influence upon Forain, and this serves to illustrate another connection between French intellectual developments of that time and antisemitism. Huysmans was a great admirer of Forain's water colors, and his reviews of Forain in 1880 and 1881 attacked French taste very sharply for its not accepting Forain. Huysmans strengthened Forain's virulent hatred of the "satisfied and hypocritical bourgeoisie," just as Degas did his penchant for seeing and painting the ugly side of life. Huysmans was most important, however, because he interested Forain in spiritualism, giving his political and social attitudes a strong antirationalist twist for two decades.[38]

Forain's personal experiences during the 1880's completed his education for antidemocratic thought and action. He journeyed to Italy in 1882, where the art of the Middle Ages and also of Raphael made a tremendous impression upon him and where he resolved again to win recognition and fame as a painter. Persuaded by both Huysmans and Degas that he needed friends in the fashionable art circles, he deprived himself of food to buy dress clothes for the theater and dinner parties. He headed prize committees, visited the Elysée, and talked with dowagers. The view of Paris society which this gave him, and the scanty results his maneuvers won, added the final, sharp touch to the extremely ruthless and cynical caricature which his work was thenceforward to show. Convinced that a financial oligarchy and a small group of critics set all stand-

[38] Joris K. Huysmans, *L'Art Moderne* (Paris, 1883), 105–10, 246–50; Huysmans, *Certains* (Paris, 1908?), 22–27, 43–47; Hans Graber, *Edgar Degas* (Basel, 1942), 51, 105–106; Charles Kunstler, *Forain* (Paris, 1931), 7–8, 19–20; Harold J. Wright (editor), *Etchings, Lithographs, Drawings, Water Colors, and Paintings by Jean-Louis Forain* (New York, 1933), preface, VIII; John Rewald, *The History of Impressionism* (New York, 1946), 170–76, 327, 389; Elisabeth de Gramont, *Mémoires* (Paris, 1928–1935), II, 112–19; Neveux, loc. cit., 779–80, 790–93.

ards and were crushing the rest of society, he resolved to satirize this world, beginning with the theater and then as time went on including politics, finance, and foreign nations and peoples. At the same time, he developed a sympathy for "the little people among whom he grew." He posed, just as Drumont did, as a defender of the disinherited, and in his sketches he contrasted "the help-lessness of the widow and orphan or of some specimen of abandoned womankind" with the keen, rapacious lawyers and financiers.

For the two decades following 1886, Forain devoted his efforts to an unceasing satire of Paris upper middle class life. He did no etching at all for twenty-two years after 1886, and he was one of those who brought caricature directly into the arena of politics. He began with the *Courrier français* in 1887, but *Figaro*, *Echo de Paris*, *Journal*, *Gaulois*, *Comédie humaine*, and *Journal amusant* also contained his scathing attacks. He established an illustrated weekly of his own in February, 1889, and he threw *Le Fifre* into the Boulangist campaign. From Willette, he acquired an increasing obsession about the power of the Jews, and he contributed illustrations to the *Libre Parole Illustrée* and to antisemitic literature. The Dreyfus Affair brought the antisemitism of France to its pitch, and *Psst!*, to which he contributed the major part, was an enormously successful assault upon the Jews and the Dreyfusards. According to authorities upon caricature, his sketches in *Psst!* represent that art at its very best, though one cannot but lament the disgraceful use of genius in that fashion.[39]

The "violent and tender, Christian and Parisian, revolutionary and bourgeois" Forain in 1908 returned to etching, which he had abandoned in 1886. At the same time, he began to concentrate his artistic powers upon the New Testament and Lourdes, and there

[39] Jean Forain, *Doux Pays* (Paris, 1897); Forain, *La Comédie parisienne* (Paris, 1892); Forain, *J. L. Forain* (London, 1925), 1; Maurice Donnay, *Mes Débuts à Paris* (Paris, 1937), 83–84; Jacques Blanche, *Essais et portraits* (Paris, 1912), 50–77; Blanche, "Jean-Louis Forain, le champenois," *Revue hebdomadaire*, année 40, IX (1931), 396–404; Kunstler, *op. cit.*, 21–22; Bac, *op. cit.*, I, 499–502; Knoedler, *op. cit.*, 6–11; *Qui êtes-vous?* (Paris, 1908–1909), 197; Neveux *loc. cit.*, 780–787, 794–795; *Le Fifre*, February 23–June 1, 1889; *Psst!*, February 5, 1898–September 15, 1899; *Libre Parole*, February 6, 1898.

was a very strong interest in Christianity and the Christian legend during the last two decades of his life. He studied Rembrandt and was greatly influenced by him. As recognition and great prosperity came to him, like Willette he became less bitter towards the Republic and its politics. He described himself as a reactionary, and he was clearly a nationalist and a fervent anti-Socialist, but he appears to have recovered from antisemitism before 1914. As the First World War approached, he sought to become a soldier, although he was sixty years old. He had always worshiped authority and scorned intellectuals, and in the twilight of his life his attitude towards Degas, Huysmans, and Pétain became a cult, equaled in intensity only by his fear of eternal punishment after death.[40]

THE CATHOLIC CLERGY

The category of French society most afflicted with antisemitism was the Catholic clergy, particularly the country clergy. Persecuted and very poorly paid by the Third Republic, these disciples of Christ were led astray by their hatred of the anticlericals, the "plot theory" mentality, and the skillful lure Drumont offered them. It must not be forgotten that the antisemitic prophet posed as the champion of the People against the sly financiers and monopolists, and that he denounced corruption, inefficiency, cruel exploitation, and imperialism. The antithesis most common to all of Drumont's writings is that of the kindly, humble, and oppressed priest and the harsh and greedy Jew.

This contrast was most vividly developed in *Le Secret de Fourmies*, in which Durmont sought to assign responsibility for the massacre of French workers on May 1, 1891, to a Jewish subprefect. This volume, which Durmont termed "a complement to my earlier works," depicted the cowardly Jew ignoring the murdered workers while the valiant aged French priest calmly ad-

[40] Marcel Guérin (editor), *J. L. Forain, aquafortiste. Catalogue raisonné* (Paris, 1912), I, preface, V; Jean Forain, *Jean Louis Forain. Examples of His Work* (New York Public Library, 1930), *passim;* Wright, *op. cit.,* IX–XI; Blanche, *op. cit.,* 67–78, 97; Kunstler, *op. cit.,* 5–9, 35–37; Knoedler, *op. cit.,* 3; Neveux, *loc. cit.,* 787–90; Blanche, *loc. cit.,* 396–97.

ministered aid and comfort to the dying while they were still under fire.[41]

Drumont not only contrasted the priest and the Jew, but he also praised the lowly cleric while denouncing the high clergy. The Christian Democratic movement was in large part a campaign of obscure young priests against conservative ideas and interests defended by the high clergy. One of the principal reasons for the failure of this venture was the opposition to it of the French bishops, especially those who were alarmed by any use of the word "socialism." Drumont's books were fundamental in the rise of this movement, for both the leaders and the active membership were influenced by him.

The appeal to the low clergy against the hierarchy appears most clearly in *Le Testament d'un antisémite*. This book was written in 1891, after the antisemites had foundered so badly in 1890. It sought to explain the failure of Drumont's forces, and Drumont developed it into a study of the moral atmosphere of France and of the "conservative Christians," who he felt should have supported him. He assailed these conservatives who had praised his efforts as long as he attacked their enemies in writing, but who had lacked the courage to support him when his campaign became active politically. The sincerity of his feeling can be gauged by the fact that he spent several pages denouncing the servility of some of his closest friends, the Goncourts and Daudets.

The Catholic Church, particularly the high clergy, was declared responsible for the moral decadence of France, and there are many passages in *Le Testament d'un antisémite* as severe as the most violent of the anticlerical attacks. Drumont in addition assaulted the political and economic views of the high clergy and spiced his narrative with some of the more recent ecclesiastical scandals. The book was so thorough and pitiless that Monsignor d'Hulst, who had admired Drumont's earlier works, termed it "more indecent and shameful than Zola." In 1898, when Drumont ran for the Chamber of Deputies in Algiers, where it was neces-

[41] Edouard Drumont, *Le Secret de Fourmies* (Paris, 1892), 1–7, 51–82, 90–107, 116–26.

sary to pose as an anticlerical, quotations from this book were used in his program to win the Radical votes.

Drumont in *Le Testament d'un antisémite* not only attacked the high clergy but also declared himself the protector and leader of the humble priests. In 1891, he described *La France juive* as "a great act of intellectual charity for the country priests," who had been betrayed by their leaders. He considered himself "the man on horseback" who could see over the crowd and who had risen to defend the lower clergy, "the courageous but ignorant sergeants of the Catholic army." [42]

The evidence of the participation of the Catholic clergy in the antisemitic movement is overwhelming. Drumont declared in 1886 that he had been most pleased by the alacrity with which the country priests had responded to *La France juive*. He confessed later in his life that it was they who had always encouraged and supported him most. Priests from all over France wrote him letters of congratulation and visited his office when they were in Paris. Whenever Drumont was ill or in prison, gifts flowed to him from the simple country priests. Some of the *Libre Parole's* most able circulation agents were Catholic clerics. Several priests persuaded Drumont in 1886 to propagate antisemitism by lecture as well as by pen, overcoming his reluctance to speak by convincing him that the spirit of the Holy Ghost would endow him with great facility in addressing crowds.[43]

Catholic priests were not only great admirers of Drumont, but they also became leading contributors to the stream of antisemitic literature which flowed through France during these years. Almost a third of all the antisemitic books published in France from 1870 through 1894 were written by Catholic priests. In the *Libre*

[42] Alfred Baudrillart, *Vie de Monsignor d'Hulst* (Paris, 1925), II, 546; Father Des Fontenelles (*pseud.*), *Le Clergé français dans le passé et dans le présent* (Paris, 1892), preface, XX; Drumont, *Le Testament d'un antisémite*, 4–47, 170–374.

[43] Edouard Drumont, *Sur le Chemin de la vie. Souvenirs* (Paris, 1914), preface, IX–XI; Drumont, *La France juive devant l'opinion*, 7–11, 216; Edmond and Jules Goncourt, *Journal des Goncourt* (Paris, 1886–1896), VII, 184; Gendrot, *Drumont, La France juive et la Libre Parole*, 91, 180–88; Raphaël Viau, *Vingt Ans d'antisémitisme, 1889–1909* (Paris, 1910), 21, 32, 95–96; Des Fontenelles, *op. cit.*, 81–84, 94, 111–112, 168, 284.

Parole contest of 1896 for the book presenting the best solution to "the Jewish problem," the first prize was shared by two priests, another priest shared second prize with a layman, and two other priests won honorable mention. One has only to recall priests such as Chabauty, Lémann, Pascal, Charles, Gayraud, Fesch, Naudet, Garnier, Desportes, and Bailly to understand the important role Catholic priests played in the movement attacking the Jews. These priests, however, were only the most celebrated, for hundreds of priests all over France carried the seeds from *Libre Parole* and *Croix* in particular throughout their parishes.[44]

The explanation for the betrayal of their Christian mission by so many of the French Catholic clergy lies in the general Catholic reaction to anticlericalism and in the background and education of the priesthood. Ninety percent of the Catholic priests came from families of peasants or village artisans, for the aristocracy and bourgeoisie sent very few sons into holy orders. All during the nineteenth century the Church in France had had too few priests, so that both the standards and the education were poor.

The instruction at the seminaries was very inadequate, and much of the teaching was done with manuals which the students memorized. There was no training in science, law, modern controversies, or the contemporary world. "Critical history was the heresy of heresies," and the manner in which scholastic philosophy and theology were taught gave the priests a narrow, dogmatic view. Poorly paid, persecuted by the Republic, unpopular because of their spiritual interests and because of the absolutist beliefs attributed generally to them, the Catholic clergy, as even Drumont admitted, were poorly equipped for their mission.

The historical training of the French Catholic priests thus neglected all of the faults and errors of the Church, and their education and the manner in which it was acquired made them vulnerable to novelty and pious saviours. It was the emphasis upon piety rather than knowledge and discernment and the general poverty

---

[44] Father Charles, *Solution de la question juive* (Paris, 1909), 156–157; Emile Rouyer, *Exposé historique de la question judéo-maçonnique* (Paris, 1897), 4–41; J. Jacquet, *Mémoire sur les moyens pratiques* (Paris, 1897), cover.

of their intellectual foundation, especially in science and in the
scientific and critical approach to history and to all controversy,
which made the clergy so susceptible to frauds such as the "plot
theory" and antisemitism.[45]

The movement against the Jews and the uncritical assault upon
the Freemasons are only the most obvious examples of the extreme credulity and lack of critical sense shown by many of the
French clergy. Another significant and revealing example of the
absence of a rational approach and the hatred of democratic ideas
and institutions shown by some French priests was demonstrated
in their attitude to the problem of what was called "Americanism." At the World's Fair in Chicago in 1893, the American
Catholic clergy had participated in a Congress of Religions along
with representatives from all of the other religions of the world.
The next year plans were broached for a similar Congress to be
held in Paris in 1900. At this, the intransigent French Catholic
press rose to denounce any scheme placing the Catholic religion
on only an equal basis with the others and to attack the American
Catholics for their waywardness. This virulent campaign, led by
Croix, *Vérité*, and *Autorité*, was being waged when there appeared
a biography of Father Isaac Hecker, the American who founded
the Paulist Fathers and who had "recommended the Catholic
faith to the democratic American people."

The issue of Americanism in the United States and in Germany,
France, and Italy during the period from 1895 to 1900 became an
extremely confusing one, and there were really several American-
isms. The entire controversy in France became connected with
the basic issue of *ralliement*, thus relighting the old fires and
introducing into the struggle the entire history of the relationship
between Church and State. Pope Leo XIII defined and resolved
most of the theological problems in his apostolic letter, *Testem
Benevolentiae*, on January 22, 1899, but the controversy is significant in this study of antisemitism because of the intellectual char-

[45] Lecanuet, *La Vie de l'Eglise*, 288-98; Joseph Brugerette, *Le Prêtre français
et la société contemporaine* (Paris, 1935), II, 43-55, 269-83; John Bodley, *The
Church in France* (London, 1898), 97-98; Drumont, *Le Testament d'un antisémite*, 347-49; Bérenger, *op. cit.*, 101-16.

acteristics revealed during it by those French Catholic leaders who were vehemently opposed to what they called Americanism.

The assault upon Hecker and upon Americanism was typical in several ways. In the first place, Hecker and his ideas were denounced not as he himself presented them, but as they were described in a French abridgment of a hasty biography of him written by Father Walter Elliott. The French opponents of "the myth of Americanism" made no attempt to ascertain what Hecker's ideas were. "They did not appear to be familiar with anything that Hecker himself wrote. They appealed entirely to the selections of his work that Elliott's translator used and the various interpretations put upon Hecker's words by his protagonists."

Secondly, it was that section of the French Catholic clergy which refused to accept *ralliement* which was so vehemently anti-Americanist. As Monsignor Ireland noted, "Their hatred of America was only an expression of their hatred of democracy." Moreover, their attacks were marked by virulent and unreasoning hatred. James Cardinal Gibbons said of one of the principal volumes that it united "the most complete bad faith to the most violent hatred." An American priest who has studied the problem declared of the same book that it was "inaccurate, biased, vitriolic, libelous, and venomous."

The author of the book just described, *Le Père Hecker, est-il un saint?*, was Father Charles Maignen, who had been head of the Catholic Workers' Club to which Drumont had belonged in the 1880's. Maignen was an active antisemite, and he published numerous articles in the reactionary *Vérité* denouncing the Jews, Huguenots, and Freemasons. A supporter of Maignen was Monsignor Turinaz, Bishop of Nancy, who attacked *ralliement*, ridiculed intellectuals and intellectualism, and during the Dreyfus Affair declared that Dreyfusard Catholics were "only those who betrayed their faith."

A third leader in the campaign against Americanism in France was another staunch antisemite, Father Henri Delassus, who has been described as "the most implacable enemy of the program of

Leo XIII" and who in June, 1897, wrote that the Pope was neither impeccable nor infallible. Delassus was for many years the editor of the strongly antisemitic *Semaine religieuse de Cambrai*, and he wrote five strongly antisemitic volumes. On one occasion, this French priest charged Cardinal Gibbons and Monsignor Ireland with "being in collusion with the Jews and Freemasons to hasten the overthrow of the Catholic Church and the triumph of Antichrist," surely an indictment which reflects seriously upon Delassus and everyone associated with him.[46]

THE MARVELOUS CAREER OF LÉO TAXIL

An even more devastating illustration of the credulity and gullibility of many of the French Catholic clergy and of their most loyal followers can be seen in the career after 1885 of Gabriel Jogand-Pagès, more popularly known as Léo Taxil, who exploited the simplicity and lack of critical sense of the clergy to an incredible degree. The remarkable feats executed by Taxil from 1885 to 1897 are extremely significant also because they demonstrate again the connection between the entire antisemitic campaign and the general current of antirationalism manifested at that time also in symbolism, impressionism, spiritualism, and the various utopias which could be gained only through violence.

The connection between the rise of antisemitism and the vogue of spiritualism is particularly strong. Many of the antisemites,

[46] Léon Chaine, *Les Catholiques français et leurs difficultés actuelles* (Paris, 1903), 360–65; Chaine, *Les Catholiques français et leurs difficultés actuelles devant l'opinion* (Lyon, 1908), 254–69; Louis Dimier, *Souvenirs d'action publique et d'université* (Paris, 1920), 101–102; Charles Maignen, *Le Père Hecker, est-il un saint?* (Paris, 1898); Henri Delassus, *L'Américanisme et la Conjuration antichrétienne* (Lille, 1899); Delassus, *Le Problème de l'heure présente* (Lille, 1904); Delassus, *La Conjuration antichrétienne* (Lille, 1910); Delassus, *La Question juive* (Lille, 1911); Charles Denis, *Les Vrais Périls* (pamphlet) (Paris, 1902), 19–20; Michel Latty, *Le Clergé français en 1890* (Paris, 1890), 1–7, 21–58; John Ireland (J. St. Clair Etheridge, *pseud.*), "The Genesis of Americanism," *North American Review*, CLXX (1900), 681–92; Thomas T. McAvoy, "Americanism, Fact and Fiction," *Catholic Historical Review*, XXXI (1945), 133–53; Vincent F. Holden, "A Myth in 'L'Américanisme,'" *Catholic Historical Review*, XXXI (1945), 154–70; Lecanuet, *La Vie de l'Eglise*, 572–602; Lecanuet, *Les Signes avant-coureurs*, 6–7; Bournand, *Juifs et antisémites en Europe*, 115–19.

notably Gougenot des Mousseaux, Chabauty, and Drumont himself, dabbled in low magic, clairvoyance, and chiromancy. This relationship is not isolated to France. One of America's leading Fascists and antisemites, William Dudley Pelley, head of the Silver Shirts, believes he is endowed with a number of the intuitive divinatory arts. The extraordinary beliefs of the Nazis were even more extravagant and ludicrous.

Perhaps the clearest demonstration of the connection between spiritualism and the other antirationalistic developments is that offered by Stanislas de Guaita and Maurice Barrès. As students, these men were classmates in a Nancy *lycée* in 1878, and as close friends they roomed together in the summer of 1880. Guaita was interested in poetry, particularly the poetry of Baudelaire, who inflamed him with the desire to break through reality and to escape beyond this dull world. He infected Barrès with his enthusiasm, and the two read romantic poetry together. Guaita came to Paris in November, 1882, read several of the occult classics, visited Saint-Yves d'Alveydre, then the spiritualist dean, and abandoned poetry forever to become the historian of the occult sciences. Barrès came to Paris in January, 1883, and was tempted by Guaita's dream of "communing with divinity," but he was led by his poetic muse into a racial nationalism which was just as antirational as Guaita's occultism.

The last two decades of the nineteenth century were seriously affected by the spiritualist wave of which Stanislas de Guaita was only one casualty. Contemporary scholars by 1890 were beginning to be worried by the popularity occult literature was acquiring, and by the turn of the century lay leaders of the Catholic Church were expressing public alarm over the inroads occult doctrines were having among the faithful, even among the priesthood. During the period from 1885 to 1898, five publishing houses were established in Paris alone which handled only the "divinatory arts," magic, and the "metapsychical sciences." Many of the established publishing concerns during the same period added large occult collections to their lists, and the impact of this entire antirationalist wave upon rationalism and democracy has been very serious. Taxil was sufficiently clever to profit from the credulity and the prejudices of many of the people infected by occultism, and his shrewd combination of "low magic" and a vigorous attack upon anticlericalism was a source of great profit to him and a source of information about the characteristics of the antisemites to the historian.[47]

Léo Taxil is one of the most interesting characters involved in the entire antisemitic drama. Born in 1854 into the family of a very prosperous and extremely religious Marseille merchant, Taxil received a thoroughly Catholic education in a Jesuit school near Lyon and in other Catholic schools in Marseille. A very quick boy and a lad known at home and at school as a prankster, Taxil was dazzled in the summer of 1868 by the Republican opposition to the Second Empire. He secretly began to devote all of his spare time to reading newspapers criticizing the Empire and to studying Masonic symbolism and the Masonic rites. At fourteen, he decided to leave home to join his great idol, Henri Rochefort, then in exile in Brussels. After he had been apprehended by the police at Digne, he was placed by his worried father in a severe reformatory near Tours. This only made him more radical, so his father brought him home again after ten weeks and resorted to prayer.

Taxil as a youth then became a kind of senior Gavroche. He was forced to leave the *lycée* for a revolt he led against short holidays, he wrote articles damning the Empire's educational system for the Marseille Republican papers, and he delivered literature critical of the Empire even into the garrison at Marseille. As a matter of fact, he became so much the radical Republican that he was infuriated because Gambetta in a speech made a remark critical of Marat, his great hero of 1793. After September 4,

[47] Jules Bois, *Le Péril occultiste* (Paris, 1899); Maurice Barrès, *Un Rénovateur de l'occultisme, Stanislas de Guaita* (Paris, 1898), 5–32; Joanny Bricaud, *L'Abbé Boulan* (pamphlet) (Paris, 1927), 44–90; Joseph Grasset, "L'Occultisme," *Revue des Deux Mondes*, CXCVI (1906), 115–52; Simon Newcomb, "Modern Occultism," *Nineteenth Century and After*, LXV (1909), 126–39; *Polybiblion*, LXXXVI (1899), 511–12; *Le Livre*, X (1889), 470; *Annuaire de la librairie française*, XIV (1907), 334; XVIII (1911), 368; XX (1913), 55, 63, 366.

1870, Taxil became a zealous supporter of the new government, and he was one of the founders of the Young Men's Legion, which helped defend the Republican government established in Marseille. It was during the tumult of 1870 and 1871 that Taxil broke all ties with his family, changed his name, and adopted his true trade, "poison-pen, yellow journalism." From 1871 until 1876, he was the editor of a series of vitriolic anticlerical newspapers in Marseille. Whenever the courts issued a heavy fine, he changed the name of the paper and carried on. He fought many duels, mostly for defamation, and the total of the sentences imposed upon him in thirteen trials early in 1876 was so great (eight years) that he fled into exile to Geneva.

When the amnesty law was passed early in 1878, Taxil went to Montpellier, where he revived his most recent newspaper and renewed his campaign against the Catholic Church. Twenty-four years old, penniless, and the father of two young children, Taxil in November, 1878, decided to join the stream of young Republicans flowing to Paris now that the Republicans were obtaining control of the Republic. In the capital, Taxil quickly demonstrated that he had many of the journalistic talents so evident in Drumont and that he combined with them an imagination and an ability to organize reminiscent of another great contemporary journalist, Father Bailly, who at about the same time was founding the *Croix* and its network.[48]

Taxil's original program when he went to Paris was to transform the Montpellier *Frondeur* into a Paris paper. However, he soon decided instead to establish an anticlerical bookstore to take advantage of the rise of the anticlericals to political power and to use that as the core of a system of anticlerical or free-thought societies which would distribute newspapers, pamphlets, and books throughout the country. With the aid of his wife, who apparently at this time was also a sincere anticlerical, he founded the *Bibliothèque Anti-Cléricale* on March 21, 1879, published his

[48] Gabriel Jogand-Pagès (Léo Taxil, *pseud.*), *Confessions d'un ex-libre-penseur. Mémoires* (Paris, 1887), 7–184; Jogand-Pagès, *La Prostitution contemporaine* (Paris, 1883?), 3–12, 461–63.

first pamphlet, the *Almanach anti-cléricale pour 1879*, and began to write anticlerical pamphlets.

Taxil's second pamphlet, *A Bas la calotte!*, an attack upon Pius IX and several of the French higher clergy filled with several completely fictional incidents, was such a tremendous success that Taxil wrote and published six or eight eighty-page pamphlets each year for the next six years. The translated titles of a few of these will demonstrate how broad a bludgeon Taxil was wielding: *The Popes' Mistresses; The Jesuit's Son; Leo XIII, The Poisoner; The Female Pope;* and *The Crimes of the Clergy*. He published a long-volume entitled *The Secret Books of the Confessors Revealed for Fathers*, a translation of several books supposedly used in seminaries to teach young men studying for the priesthood the mysteries of sex so they might understand the sins they were to hear in the confessional. His "study" of prostitution emphasized the same pornographic appeal, while his book on Joan of Arc sought to prove that the clergy not only had been completely responsible for her death but had first violated her.

Taxil was by no means simply a crude profiteer upon the more base passions of man, for he showed great skill in his editing and in his organizing. His books, pamphlets, and newspapers were all illustrated, and illustrated in such a way as to stimulate attention and sales. He capitalized upon his friendship with Garibaldi, which he had made in Marseille in 1870, by having the aging romantic Italian hero write prefaces for several volumes. He had songs, albums, childrens' books, and even writing paper printed and sold, and he preceded even Marpon and Flammarion in his skilled promotion of illustrated *livraisons*. Moreover, he arranged with the important Republican newspapers in Paris so that he might use their distribution systems in sending his literature into the provinces. This proved an enormous boon, for it placed copies of his anticlerical writings in the hands of newspaper dealers all over the country at a time when it was both expensive and difficult for people outside of Paris and its environs to obtain books.

Taxil also organized free-thought or anticlerical societies all over France in those communities where his records indicated sales of his publications. He collected all of these clubs into the

Union de France, or French Anti-Clerical League, which he claimed had seventeen thousand active members in 1884 and which served as a sales and advertising system. He was an active participant in the General Congress of Free Thought in Paris in 1881, he fostered the establishment of anticlerical leagues to promote the sale of his publications in Spain, and in 1882 he even suggested an International Congress of Free Thought to aid his enterprises.

One of Taxil's established techniques was to insult and defame in order to attract reprisals, trials, attention, and sales. This had proved effective locally in Marseille and Montpellier, and it was to be successful nationally as well. His original attack upon Pius IX, *A Bas la Calotte!*, sold 130,000 copies, and the sales records of Taxil's newspapers, pamphlets, and books were in many ways as sensational as those being established at the very same time by the naturalist novels of Zola and Alphonse Daudet. However, Pius IX, or at least his nephew, Count de Mastaï, proved to be a rather formidable antagonist, and the Count's suit against Taxil for the latter's charges that Pius IX was a "debaucher, forger, adulterer, and assassin," cost Taxil sixty thousand francs in damages and about ten thousand francs in costs. His appeal against the decision led the court to increase the damages to eighty thousand francs. A large number of other unfavorable decisions, none of them as costly as this, led Taxil by 1883 to transfer most of his property to his wife and to decide upon "more blasphemy and less defamation." The cost of the trials, the decline of his publishing business, and the gradual conservative revival of the early 1880's, which reached its peak in the 1885 elections, led to one of the most celebrated and financially successful conversions of the entire nineteenth century, for on April 23, 1885, Léo Taxil, the *bête noire* of all French Catholics, recognized and abjured his errors and returned to the fold.[49]

The "brilliant and completely unexpected" return of Taxil to

[49] Gabriel Jogand-Pagès (Léo Taxil, *pseud.*), *Les Livres secrets des confesseurs* (Paris, 1884), 683–87; Jogand-Pagès, *Calotte et calotins. Histoire illustrée du clergé et des congrégations* (Paris, 1880–1882), I, 2; Jogand-Pagès, *Jeanne d'Arc, victime des prêtres* (Paris, 1884), page opposite title page, 111–119; Jogand-Pagès, *Confessions*, 195–342; *Almanach Anti-Clérical et Républicain Illustré pour 1881* (Paris, 1881), 16–22, 76–78; *Le Livre*, II (1881), 448, 590, 783; III (1882), 126–27, 400; IV (1883), 351–52; V (1884), 349–50; VI (1885), 493.

Catholicism, just three or four years after Drumont had rejoined the Church and just a year before the publication of *La France juive*, was very clearly a business enterprise. Taxil affirmed that his work on the documents of the trial of Joan of Arc convinced him of the errors of his ways. He declared, moreover, that his concern in January, 1885, was valued at 675,000 francs, and that his conversion destroyed the business so effectively that his wife, who separated from him temporarily, was forced to go into bankruptcy in November, 1885. His critics, however, demonstrated that the concern's business had been declining sharply since 1883. They noted too that Taxil and his wife separated only during the ten weeks during which the publishing house was being liquidated and that they were reunited in the new business venture in December, 1885.

The flood of publications which Taxil poured out during the years after his conversion are another proof that this was a business affair. During the first seventeen months, he wrote six lengthy volumes and two pamphlets denouncing Freemasonry and ascribing to that order all of the ills of France. Between the fall of 1886 and the summer of 1891, he had published at least six more volumes which broadened the attack from Masonry to the Republic and Republican politicians. At the same time, he edited a newspaper, the *Petite Catholique*, and with Father Paul Fesch, one of the early Christian Democrats, he edited a journal dedicated to his new patron saint, Joan of Arc.

Taxil's first publication, a pamphlet which appeared in September 1885, sold 38,300 copies within two months. Within two years, each of his next two volumes had sold almost twenty-five thousand copies. The sales of the others ranged from ten thousand to twenty thousand, while even a collection of documents on the Vatican's attitude towards Freemasonry sold more than four thousand copies. Between August 15, 1886, and December 1, 1889, Taxil received more than sixty thousand francs from his publisher. His earnings declined after that, because his publications depended heavily upon their early sale, but he received an additional ten thousand francs during the next year and in 1890 was offered

first forty thousand and then sixty thousand francs by his publishers to end the suit he had initiated against them for failing to
pay him his proper share of the profits.[50]

Taxil's campaign against the anticlericals of course won wide
acclaim among French Catholics. His conversion caused such a
stir that Catholic newspapers from outside of France sent reporters to interview him. The papal nuncio received him in July,
1885, and advised him not to isolate himself but to join those
fighting the enemies of the Church. He was received by the Pope
in 1887, and for one of his books he acquired letters from seventeen bishops for use in the preface. Catholic journals gave numerous enthusiastic reviews to each of his books, and by 1890
the disgruntled Drumont, who had hailed his conversion in *La
France juive*, was referring to him petulantly as "the spoiled
darling of the conservative Catholics." In the Paris municipal
council elections in 1890, Taxil campaigned against Drumont on
an "essentially Catholic program." In this election, Taxil won
the support of the Paris high clergy, and the papal nuncio heard
one of his philippics against Drumont.

Letouzey and Ané, his publishers, were, as a publishing firm,
as Catholic as Taxil. Father Bieil, director of the *Grand Séminaire
de Saint-Sulpice*, was a relative of one of the partners, and as a
result the firm became the official publisher of the great seminary.
The firm specialized in clerical trade books and in religious publications, and in 1890 it mailed copies of its catalogues to every
priest in France. In 1890, thirty-five of the seventy-five authors
on its list were priests, and the first seven sections of its 1894
catalogue dealt with sacred writings, theology, canon law, liturgy,
asceticism, preaching, and hagiography. Taxil and his publishers
were thus very clearly exploiting the Catholic reading public in
their enterprise. This is particularly important because of the
next campaigns the astute imposter was to wage in the country.[51]

[50] Gabriel Jogand-Pagès (Léo Taxil, *pseud.*), *Affaire Letouzey-et-Ané* (Paris,
1890), III–XV, 1–60, appendix, 4–143; Jogand-Pagès, *Le Procès des éditeurs de
Saint-Sulpice* (Paris, 1892), 16–232; *Le Livre*, VI (1885), 654.
[51] Gabriel Jogand-Pagès (Léo Taxil, *pseud.*), *Monsieur Drumont. Etude
psychologique* (Paris, 1890), V–XXVIII, 57–74, 184–235; Jogand-Pagès, *Affaire*

After Taxil and his publishers profited from his conversion and his revelations concerning the diabolical role of Freemasonry, Taxil's writings began to change. He abandoned the Freemasons to concentrate upon the Republic and the Republican politicians. Albert Savine, the most important antisemitic publisher, printed and sold two illustrated assaults upon "the vampire, Jules Ferry," "the drone, Henri Rochefort," and the remainder of the menagerie. Neither of these sold more than three thousand copies, so early in 1891 Taxil published a book which sought to demonstrate that the Republic had stimulated an enormous wave of immorality, just as eight years earlier he had ascribed responsibility for prostitution in France to the moral restrictions imposed by the Catholic Church, whose clergy evaded those restrictions. Some Catholic journals were mildly critical of the long descriptions of immoralities, leading Taxil to rejoin, "Let there be no false shame, gentlemen, when a voice rises to denounce vice." Even this attempt to arouse public interest failed, so in 1893 Taxil began the creation of the greatest hoax he had yet played on his gullible Catholic readers, an escapade so ridiculous as to illustrate remarkably well the credulity of those hundreds of Catholic priests and thousands of Catholic laymen who followed this valiant defender as witlessly as many of them at the same time were following their other champion, Drumont.[52]

In his next venture, Taxil set out to exploit the sincere anti-Masonic fanaticism of many French Catholics by publishing in 1893 with Dr. Charles Hacks, who wrote under the pseudonym

---

Letouzey-et-Ané, 79–80, 114–17, appendix, 81–82; Jogand-Pagès, *Confessions*, 344–402; Jogand-Pagès, *Le Procès*, 13–15; Paul Fesch, *Les Souvenirs d'un abbé journaliste* (Paris, 1898), 48–65; Drumont, *Le Testament d'un antisémite*, 405–408; Le Soudier, *op. cit.*, IV. Letouzey et Ané catalogue, 2–15; Mauvrac, *op. cit.*, 24–30; *Polybiblion*, XLIV (1885), 454; XLV (1885), 380; XLVI (1885), 237–38; XLVII (1886), 42, 537; XLIX (1887), 262–63; L (1887), 261; LIV (1888), 298; LV (1889), 35; *Bibliographie catholique*, LXXIII (1886), 518; LXXIV (1886), 513, 518; LXXV (1887), 101–105, 119–20.

[52] Gabriel Jogand-Pagès (Léo Taxil, *pseud.*), *Les Assassinats maçonniques* (Paris, 1889), preface, I–V; Jogand-Pagès, *La Ménagerie politique* (Paris, 1889); Jogand-Pagès, *La Ménagerie républicaine* (Paris, 1890), 3–8, 49–52; Jogand-Pagès, *Y-a-t-il des femmes dans le franc-maçonnerie?* (Paris, 1891), preface, II–VI; *Polybiblion*, LXV (1892), 174–75.

of Dr. Bataille, a most remarkable book entitled *Le Diable au dix-neuvième siècle*. This book was published in Paris and Lyon by one of the most respectable Catholic publishing houses, Delhomme and Briguet, and advertisements were sent to every rectory and religious community in France and to every Catholic family which was known to have purchased any of Taxil's earlier writings. The book was a two-volume, twelve-franc collection of all of the worthless legends concerning the Freemasons and all other sinister secret societies. Written supposedly by a man who had traveled all over the world as a ship's surgeon, it had a series of incredible new stories calculated to alarm the French Catholics. Lutherans were described as Luciferians, Singapore as a resort of godless criminals, and England as a state governed by Satan through scoundrels. The head of American Masonry had a telephone system invented and operated by devils which enabled him to obtain instantaneous communication with the seven major capitals of the world. He also had a magic bracelet for summoning Lucifer, and Satan had once taken him on a trip to Sirius. The most startling disclosure, perhaps, was that there were devils working busily in caves under Gibraltar, preparing epidemics with which they would engulf the Catholic world.

Hacks, who confessed his part of the new hoax late in 1896, was in 1893 a thirty-seven-year-old French army doctor who had joined Taxil in order to make a huge profit. The book was an enormous success, and Hacks, who thought of himself as "the Jules Verne of the occult," by 1896 had used his share to purchase a Paris restaurant and retire from the practice of medicine.

Not content with this triumph, Taxil proceeded to invent a Miss Diana Vaughan and to carry her through an astonishing series of adventures in Freemasonry and the higher occult spheres, with his gullible readers blithely accepting every revelation. Diana Vaughan was a descendant of the famous Rosicrucian, Thomas Vaughan, and the goddess Astarte, whom Vaughan married March 25, 1645. Diana herself was born February 29, 1874, a date which did not exist, although none of her admirers noticed it. She was educated according to Luciferian principles, became the fiancée of the god Asmodeus, who took her to purgatory and Mars on excursions, and was selected in 1879 by Albert Pike to be the high priestess of the Palladium, or the inner and Higher Order of Freemasonry. Her refusal to commit the final rites, one of which was to spit upon and stab the Holy Eucharist, led to the rise in favor of Sophia Walder, almost as glamorous a young lady as Diana. Sophia's real father was the devil Betru, who declared that she was the predestined great-great-grandmother of Antichrist, who was to be born in 1962. Her apparent father was a Protestant parson, and her mother a Rosicrucian Jewess.

Diana caused a schism because she refused to surrender her claim to be high priestess. To strengthen her position, in the spring of 1895 she organized the Independent Regenerated Luciferians and began to publish a monthly journal in Paris. Three numbers of this extremely anti-Catholic review appeared, describing the Blessed Virgin as a deserter from Lucifer and announcing that Antichrist and a Jewish Pope were to obtain control of the Catholic Church in 1995, before it was replaced on July 1, 1895, by another one, *Mlle Diana Vaughan*. With this new journal, Taxil's hoax began to reach its climax, for the *Mémoires d'une ex-Palladiste*, which it published, revealed that Diana Vaughan, like Taxil, had been converted to Catholicism by Joan of Arc. During the twenty-three months which followed her conversion in June, 1895, Diana Vaughan in these memoirs and in several other publications excelled Jules Verne at his imaginative peak, while her readers eagerly swallowed every incredible tale.[53]

The adventures retailed by Diana Vaughan were a wonderful burlesque of the entire anti-Masonic campaign. Perhaps her most remarkable feat was her attack on Crispi, for she related how the Italian Prime Minister had been poisoned fatally in 1862 but

[53] Gabriel Jogand-Pagès (Léo Taxil, *pseud.*) and Dr. Charles Hacks (Dr. Bataille, *pseud.*), *Le Diable au dix-neuvième siècle* (Paris, Lyon, 1893–1894); Louis Nemours-Godré, *Diana Vaughan et ses répondants* (pamphlet) (Paris, 1897), 16–17; E. P. Evans, "A Survival of Medieval Credulity," *Popular Science Monthly*, LVI (1900), 579–86, 706–708; Henry Charles Lea, "An Anti-Masonic Mystification," *Lippincott's Magazine*, LXVI (1900), 953–56; *France Militante*, February 20, 1897.

had been recalled to life by Mazzini, who won an agreement from the dead Crispi that he would follow blindly all Masonic orders. This was followed by a travesty on Italian history from 1862 through 1896, when Crispi was said deliberately to have caused the Italian disaster in Ethiopia. Father Mustel in the *Revue catholique de Coutances* described this as an "historical monument of the very first importance." He compared it to *La France juive*, but said that it was "more scholarly and secure on the Devil problem than Drumont on the Jewish problem." Bishop Fava wrote Diana a number of letters congratulating her and warning her to be ready for martyrdom. Father Delassus was a warm admirer, while the Marquis de Morès before his death sent her an Emmenthaler cheese with a prayer carved into the rind. Even Drumont had high praise for "the new crusader."

Taxil utilized every promotional technique for Diana which he had developed at any point in his career. Acting as her business agent, he attracted the great Catholic names for his enterprise. He acquired letters from many French bishops, obtained Leo XIII's blessing for a book of prayers, *La Neuvaine Eucharistique*, which Diana published in 1896, and won support from many Catholic newspapers, including most of those promoting anti-semitism. Diana wrote hymns and books of verse, established a new series of anti-Masonic pamphlets, denounced the Republic as "the devil in French politics," and established a new chain of leagues across France, modelled on the anticlerical *Union de France* Taxil had erected during the early 1880's but called now the *Union Anti-Maçonnique de France*. In addition to her journal, she edited another, *L'Anti-Maçon*, which was the official organ of the leagues she had organized. Late in 1896, she began a semi-monthly review, *Le Clergé contemporain*, which was designed especially for the provincial clergy and which specialized in short biographies of notable contemporary priests.[54]

The perpetuation of Taxil's profitable pranks was ultimately

[54] Paul Fesch, Joseph Denais, and René Lay, *Bibliographie de la franc-maçonnerie et des sociétés secrètes* (Paris, 1912–1913), I, 67; II, 122; Avenel, *Annuaire de la presse française*, XVII (1896), 18; XVIII (1897), XI; *Polybiblion*, LXXVIII (1896), 210; *L'Anti-Maçon*, January 1–December 17, 1896.

spoiled by the healthy scepticism finally demonstrated by some of Diana's less gullible admirers and by the professional rivalry of other authors who were profiting from the incredulity of the same group of Frenchmen. When Taxil erred in declaring on one occasion that Diana had been born in Paris in 1874 and on another that she had been born in Louisville, Kentucky, in 1864; when the devil Asmodeus continued to be her stalwart guardian a year after her conversion; and when Diana declared that Asmodeus had turned a Freemason's head backward for three weeks for vowing to kill Diana, some of her followers began to express doubts concerning the reality of her existence and of her experiences. This attitude was strengthened by tales such as the one concerning a devil who transformed himself into a young lady in order to marry a Freemason and who every evening transformed himself into a crocodile so he might play the piano with his tail.

The request made by some sceptical followers of Diana that she strengthen their belief in her by leaving her convent sanctuary in Paris and appearing before her followers for the first time was adopted by some of her rivals, especially Gaston Méry, the city editor of Drumont's *Libre Parole* and one of the great propagandists for spiritualism in France during the 1890's. Méry lamented the press triumph of Diana over one of his discoveries, a Mlle Couédon, who was very popular as a clairvoyant in 1896. Méry sold thirty-five thousand copies of his book about her, and in 1897 he founded a monthly journal devoted to sorcery, *L'Echo du merveilleux*. When Jules Doinel, a lieutenant of Taxil, wrote in *L'Anti-Maçon* that Mlle Couédon was under a supernatural influence, but that it was not Gabriel, as she claimed, but Lucifer, "and a mediocre, dull, second-rate Lucifer at that," Méry turned the *Libre Parole* upon Diana. Father Garnier followed, saying to all Catholics that the *Anti-Maçon* editors were "the worst enemies of the Church" and that Diana was really Taxil. Other newspapers entered the war, and in the summer and fall of 1896 a lively campaign of recriminations developed. When Hacks confessed in November, 1896, that the book on which he had collaborated had been a speculation upon French gullibility, the controversy increased.[55]

The rise of scepticism concerning Diana reached a peak at the International Anti-Masonic Congress held in Trente in Italy in September, 1896. Blessed by Leo XIII as "a new crusade against the den of Satan," the congress sought to strengthen the campaign being waged against Freemasonry in all Catholic countries. Taxil was one of the French representatives. On September 29, 1896, at the special session held to resolve the question of Diana's existence and veracity, he explained that the campaign against her was a Freemasonic trick, that Diana had no birth certificate because she had been born in the backward United States, and that he would tell only the Pope, or the Pope's representative, the name of the Paris priest who had baptized her. A special committee of six was named at the congress to investigate the entire problem.

Back in Paris, *Univers* took up the issue, hoping to prevent a scandal damaging to the numerous clergy involved. When Taxil finally named the Bishop of Edinburgh as the priest who had baptized Diana and when the latter denied this, *Univers* relentlessly pursued Taxil, who claimed he was only Diana's business agent, distributing all of her royalties to charities. He then claimed Hacks had been paid a hundred thousand francs by the Masons to lie. As his critics increased, he asked them to recall "whom doubt will profit." Finally, after the commission had reported that there was neither proof that she did exist nor that she did not exist, Taxil issued invitations to a conference Diana had called in the auditorium of the Geographical Society of Paris on April 19, 1897, Easter Monday.

A crowd of priests and journalists attended this celebrated

---

[55] Gaston Méry, *Un Complot maçonnique. La Vérité sur Diana Vaughan* (pamphlet) (Paris, 1896); Nemours-Godré, *op. cit.*, 16–17; Evans, *loc. cit.*, 713; *L'Anti-Maçon*, May 10, July 16, September 16, October 1, November 7, November 14, 1896; *France Militante*, February 6, February 20, 1897; *Libre Parole Illustrée*, January 23, March 13, 1897; *Libre Parole*, July 4, July 11, November 14, 1896.

meeting. After checking their canes and umbrellas at the door, they heard Taxil explain the entire incident. He revealed that Diana Vaughan was entirely his creation, ridiculed her followers as ignorant and dishonest imbeciles, taunted them for their incredible stupidity, and fled through a rear entrance when his enraged dupes rushed at him.[56]

It is extremely significant that Léo Taxil was so successful during the period from 1885 through 1897 and that he had such great influence upon French Catholic priests and laymen, for it was during this same period and over this same group that Drumont exerted his greatest influence. Many of those who were antisemites were followers of Diana Vaughan, and surely there is little distinction in believing that the French Jews caused the defeat in 1870 or the *Union générale* crash in 1882 and in believing that Diana Vaughan had visited purgatory and Mars. The uncritical acceptance and even dissemination by so many French Catholics, especially Catholic priests, of the ridiculous charges made against the Jews and the fantastic tales concerning the role of the devil in Freemasonry demonstrate that antirationalism is the foundation of French antisemitism. Some of Diana Vaughan's staunch followers, including Father Mustel and Bishop Fava, both of whom were also antisemites, refused even to believe Taxil when he confessed his hoax. They retained their faith in Diana until the end of their lives, just as they resolutely refused to budge from a stolid anti-Dreyfusard position, regardless of the facts which were introduced.

Many priests disillusioned by Taxil followed Drumont even more fervently, and some helped to found the four psychical societies which were thriving in Paris in 1898. Although these societies quarreled and disagreed on methods, they did agree in adopting the antirational attitudes which any believer in the occult must accept. Lecanuet has demonstrated that the *Croix*, one of the leading transgressors, by 1899 had not yet developed its critical

[56] J. Angot des Rotours, "La Question Diana Vaughan," *Le Correspondant*, CLXXXVI (1897), 528–35; Evans, *loc. cit.*, 708–15; *L'Anti-Maçon*, September 16–December 5, 1896; *France Militante*, February 13, 1897; *Libre Parole*, November 28, 1896.

senses, for its publishing house, the *Maison de la Bonne Presse*, in that year published a *Vie de saint Anthoine de Padua*, which a Marcel Dhanys claimed to have found in Rome. This biography, "written in an unknown language by the saint's companion," contained a preface by Father Drochon which cited its "admirable simplicity" and its "tone of naïve candor" as proof of its authenticity. The entire book was an invention by Dhanys, and it serves as a final indictment of the antisemites and of the uncritical attitude which was the basis of antisemitism.[57]

[57] Lecanuet, *Les Signes avant-coureurs*, 156; Lea, *loc. cit.*, 959; *Polybiblion*, LXXXVI (1899), 90–91; *Libre Parole*, April 11, 1898.

VIII

---

1. The Weakness of French Antisemitism

ALTHOUGH antisemitism before the arrest of Captain Dreyfus in 1894 had developed into a clearly national movement and although there were strong traces of antisemitism apparent in influential strata of the French population, the campaign against the Jews in France was by no means a powerful, aggressive one until the development of the Dreyfus Affair introduced other important issues and passions. Although in retrospect it is plain that they were adopting a dangerous policy, French Jews before the Dreyfus Affair generally showed little alarm at Drumont's campaign and were careful not to increase its fury by offering resistance.

In 1890, as in 1894, the antisemitic leaders themselves were discouraged about the movement's lack of power and its future. The French National Antisemitic League crashed ignominiously in the fall of 1890, and the electoral campaigns of 1890 had not only failed miserably but had roused such a storm of resentment among prominent Frenchmen that the antisemites openly confessed the movement's weakness and their discouragement. The total number of votes cast for all of the antisemitic candidates for the Paris

Municipal Council in the elections of April 27, 1890, was only
3,083, and Drumont himself received barely 600 in a district in
which he had lived and worked most of his life. In a letter to his
supporters after the election, Drumont declared that his defeat had
been "as complete as possible" and that antisemitism had failed
utterly to convert the people of Paris. The first book he wrote
after these reverses not only had a significant title, *Le Testament
d'un antisémite*, but it also acknowledged that antisemitism had encountered complete apathy. Hix next book early in 1892 revealed
that there had been no renaissance, for Drumont continued bitterly
to denounce French indifference to his teachings.

Alfred Gendrot, one of the leading antisemitic journalists and
authors, was one of the many collaborators of Drumont who
agreed with his pessimistic view in 1890. In a series of dispatches
which he sent from Paris to the Algiers *Anti-Juif*, Gendrot continually bewailed the lack of interest the antisemitic campaign
had roused. He admitted that there was "no Jewish question for
anyone who reads only the leading daily newspapers." Blaming
his disappointment upon the power of Jewish gold and the antisemites' lack of a newspaper and funds, he confessed that neither
Drumont's books nor the League's activities had reached the
workers and that antisemitism at the end of 1890 had a very
bleak future.[1]

Clearly the most fundamental reason for the inability of the
antisemites to develop a thriving campaign was the existence of
strong contradictions in the economic and social aims of the
various groups and classes which were antisemitic. As has been
demonstrated, the failure of the antisemites to discover clearly
for themselves and to explain to others their program was one

[1] Edouard Drumont, *Le Testament d'un antisémite* (Paris, 1891), 170–76;
Drumont, *Le Secret de Fourmes* (Paris, 1892), 150–52; Henri Desportes, *Le
Mystère du sang chez juifs de tous les temps* (Paris, 1889), 359; Augustin
Hamon and Georges Bachot, *La France politique et sociale, 1890* (Paris, 1891),
I, 51–70, 210, 269–70; II, 335–46; Gabriel Terrail (Mermeix, *pseud.*), *Les An-
tisémites en France* (Paris, 1892), 60, 68; François Bournand (Jean de Ligneau,
pseud.), *Juifs et antisémites en Europe* (Paris, 1892), 108; *Anti-Juif* (Algiers),
April 3, May 29, June 5, July 13, November 29, December 21, December 28,
1890.

which they never overcame, even during the Dreyfus Affair. The use of ambiguous principles on occasion can be a tactical advantage, but the clumsy counterfeit socialism and the failure of the antisemites to define a clear political program were in this instance disastrous. Probably the contradictions inherent in the social structure of the movement would have rendered ineffective even the most masterful and judicious exposition of the movement's aims and aspirations. At any rate, the antisemites succeeded in frightening the conservatives with their "socialism" and the workers with their clericalism.

A second serious handicap for the antisemites was their lack of effective leaders and organizers. Drumont was an extraordinary propagandizer, but he never attempted to be an organizer or dynamic leader. Moreover, unfortunately for the antisemites, his success as a writer was so enormous that he remained the sole head of the movement. Even the lieutenants whom he attracted were adventurers, not selected expert and able leaders.

A movement such as antisemitism requires a leader with a forceful personality and dramatic personal appeal. Drumont was a complete failure in these respects. He was not an affable man, and he had very few close friends. His writings reveal clearly that his most happy hours were spent by himself, walking along the quays in the morning as he thought over his next article or chapter, or riding through the countryside near Soisy-sous-Etoiles. His extraordinary liking for solitude alarmed his neighbors and close friends, the Alphonse Daudets, and Madame Daudet even noted with alarm that Drumont's country cottage had windows on only one side and that away from the road.

He was seriously hampered in his rare public speeches by his dull voice and very poor eyesight, which forced him to read his speeches slowly and haltingly. His control over the staff of his newspaper was so loose and each member had such great independence that the *Libre Parole* became a favorite of young men eager to obtain journalistic experience. Drumont later used to bridle when Barrès and Maurras told him he was not a man of action, but he always described himself as an historian, a sociologist, "a philosopher and moralist," or a prophet. He once described himself as "a simple, solitary fellow" who did not understand modern life and "should have been a librarian or a country priest." He enjoyed his three months in Sainte-Pélagie enormously, and he wrote from this prison that he was "created to live in retreat" and that he regretted leaving the pleasant life of prison for the busy world. In February, 1895, when he returned to Paris as a hero who had predicted the treason of Dreyfus, he told the cheering crowd that he had disliked leaving quiet Belgium.[2]

Drumont not only was an ineffective commander, but he attracted to his movement no one who could head his forces ably. Much was expected of Francis Laur when the antisemites decided to support him, but the small-town engineer who was twice elected to the Chamber of Deputies lacked the necessary qualities. Laur had been a close friend and follower of Gambetta and then a member of Guesde's *Parti Ouvrier Français*, but he had left socialism for Boulangism and antisemitism. His ideas possessed the correct blend of rage against social injustice and scorn for parliamentary inability to accomplish anything which was typical of the antisemites. However, Laur was a very short man with a thin, squeaky voice, and these physical handicaps combined with his lack of driving power to remove him from consideration.

The two other men who formed "The Three Musketeers of Antisemitism" with Drumont from 1889 until 1892 both had remarkable qualities, but neither was an organizer and both soon broke from Drumont. Jacques de Biez abandoned Drumont within a week after the founding of Drumont's newspaper in April, 1892, while the Marquis de Morès, who possessed the personality needed for leadership of the campaign, lacked other necessary qualities and left Drumont in August, 1893. Perhaps the only other

[2] Edouard Drumont, *La Fin d'un monde* (Paris, 1888), 509-30; Drumont, *La Dernière Bataille* (Paris, 1890), 1-16, 521, 537-43; Drumont, *Le Testament d'un antisémite*, 349-64; Madame Alphonse Daudet, *Souvenirs autour d'un group littéraire* (Paris, 1910), 67-68, 133; Léon Daudet, *Les Oeuvres dans les hommes* (Paris, 1922), 144-45; Arthur Meyer, *Ce que je peux dire* (Paris, 1912), 287; *Almanach de la Libre Parole, 1893* (Paris, 1893), 66-71; *Libre Parole*, November 3, 1893; February 5, 1895.

potential leader of the campaign against the Jews to appear in France during this period was Jules Guérin. Guérin in 1890 was a thirty-year-old oil promoter who had had ambitions as a playwright, but who had turned to journalism and business. He had been involved in several shady oil deals with both Jewish and Christian partners. After fines and failing schemes had ruined him financially in 1892, he devoted all of his energies to antisemitism. Morès had drawn him into his band in 1890, and the tall, handsome lieutenant soon became known among the Morès group as "The Arm." Throughout the lifetime of Morès, however, Guérin remained only his faithful lieutenant, and it was only with the Dreyfus Affair that Guérin rose to brief prominence in French history.[3]

2. The *Libre Parole*

THE failure of the French National Antisemitic League and of the electoral ventures of the antisemites in 1890 were so resounding that Drumont in discouragement wrote his "political will" and practically withdrew from his campaign for a year. The year 1891 proved to be only a respite, however, for on April 20, 1892, the first issue of Drumont's daily newspaper, the *Libre Parole*, appeared. Drumont had hoped to publish a newspaper in 1886 to continue the campaign inaugurated by *La France juive*, and it was only natural that as a journalist leading a movement which contained so many writers and newspaper men he should use this fine modern weapon against the Jews. The publication of the *Libre Parole* thus marked a renewal of the barrage against the Jews on a daily basis.

During the last decade of the nineteenth century, the newspaper

[3] Jules Guérin, *Les Trafiquants de l'antisémitisme* (Paris, 1906), 9–12; Marcel Barrière, *Les Princes d'Orléans* (Paris, 1933), 12; Pierre Stock, *Mémorandum d'un éditeur* (Paris, 1935–1938), III, 131–33; Compère-Morel, *Jules Guesde* (Paris, 1937), 252; Alfred Gendrot (Jean Drault, *pseud.*), *Drumont, La France juive et la Libre Parole* (Paris, 1935), 30–31; Francis Laur, *Le Coeur de Gambetta* (Paris, 1921), 9–10; Drumont, *Le Testament d'un antisémite*, 110–17, 131–38; *Revue du monde catholique*, CXVI (1893), 176; Henri Avenel, *Annuaire de la presse française*, VII (1886), 343; VIII (1887), 110, 346.

business all over the world underwent a revolution. The cheap and sensational newspapers of Pulitzer and Hearst in the United States marked the appearance of a new type of journalism as modern business instinct and practices were applied to a new field of endeavor. The new press capitalized upon the tremendous improvements made in printing and communications to flaunt a gigantic appeal to the vulgar tastes of the masses. The first edition of the *Libre Parole* thus appeared at a time when a full-scale assault upon the standards and position of the dignified and conservative older newspapers was being launched.

Drumont's was not the first important attempt to found an antisemitic newspaper in France. Several brief efforts had appeared in 1882 and 1883. Boulangism had brought into existence *Le Pilori*, a violent anti-Republican paper with strong traces of antisemitism, and in 1887 another short-lived paper had appeared in Paris. As the antisemites attempted to organize more formally and to enter politics in 1889 and 1890, a flurry of ephemeral papers appeared. Although most of these publications produced little permanent effect upon the movement, because each was the work of a small isolated group, their activity did contribute to the spreading of antisemitism. The most impressive of the Paris weeklies was *La Croisade française*, founded in 1891 "to defend Catholic and French ideas" and including among its regular contributors two viscounts, Father Vial, Quesnay de Beaurepaire, a judge who played an important role in the Panama scandal as well as in the Dreyfus Affair, and Professor Jules Soury, one of the founders of the *Action Française* and one of the few French educators to become an antisemite.[4]

Significantly, neither of the two successful predecessors of the

[4] Joseph Jacobs, *The Jewish Question, 1875–1884. A Bibliographical Handlist* (London, 1885), 57; Marius Garredi, *Catholicisme et judaïsme. Réponse à La France juive* (Paris, 1888), XII; Antonin Debidour, *L'Eglise catholique et l'Etat sous la troisième République, 1870–1906* (Paris, 1906–1909), I, 377; Drumont, *Le Testament d'un antisémite*, 405–406; Isaac Levaillant, "La Genèse de l'antisémitisme sous la troisième République," *Revue des études juives*, LII (1906–1907), 87; Avenel, *Annuaire de la presse française*, III (1882), 64; V (1884), XX–XXI, LX; VI (1885), XX; VIII (1887), LXXIX; IX (1888), CXVI; XII (1891), II, III, XXXV, 160; XIII (1892), XXIV; *Anti-Juif* (Algiers), March 20, December 21, 1890.

Libre Parole was produced in Paris. The Algiers *Anti-Juif*, which devoted more space to the Jews of France than those of Algeria, was published during most of the last decade of the nineteenth century, although there were occasional lapses. This publication displayed remarkable abilities throughout 1890, collapsing for the first time early in 1891 because of financial difficulties. In spite of its failures, it managed to provide an important medium for the ideas of Biez, Gendrot, and Laur, and it helped prepare Algeria for the electoral campaigns of Drumont and his lieutenants in 1898.

The two most important antisemitic papers to appear in France itself prior to 1892 both were produced in Lille. One of these, the *Lillois*, was an established conservative paper which was drawn into a bitter campaign against the Jews by its hatred of radicalism and of anticlericalism. Supported by the Catholic petty bourgeoisie, this publication strove to rouse Lille by a campaign of defamation against the Jewish merchants. However, the stand of the Jews was so courageous and firm that the expenses of continuous lawsuits and fines ultimately forced the newspaper into bankruptcy.

Though not so successful as either the Algiers *Anti-Juif* or the *Lillois*, the *Anti-Youtre* is probably the most interesting of the antisemitic papers which appeared during these years. Five numbers of this weekly were published in March and April of 1891, and the evidence available provides valuable information concerning the actual machinery of the movement. The *Anti-Youtre* was printed in Lille for sale in Paris the following day. It was published without the knowledge or aid of the Paris antisemites. Although Dentu, Savine, and Marpon and Flammarion, the leading antisemitic publishers, awarded the struggling weekly large advertisements, it was unable to continue publication.

The *Anti-Youtre* was the work of a twenty-five-year-old medical student, Emmanuel Gallian, whose pseudonym was Noël Gaulois, and Léon Hayard. Gallian urged Drumont to accept the indifference of the conservatives and to turn to the lower middle classes and socialism. His newspaper was a serious attempt to convert the campaign against the Jews to more direct action, the first step being the use of the daily or weekly press as a medium.

Hayard was a veteran Lille newspaper vendor who moved to Paris in 1892 and whose career is significant for the understanding of the antisemitic movement. A Republican under the Second Empire, a Communard, and a rabid Boulangist, Hayard was a large, handsome, generous, likeable man who had the same deep interest in uniforms so marked in the antisemitic caricaturist, Poiré. Hayard by 1890 was the leading newspaper agent in Lille, and in that year he began to expand his interests to include the publication of posters, pamphlets, and even periodicals. The *Anti-Youtre* was thus for him just a publishing venture, one which was less successful than most of his later ones. After he moved to Paris, Hayard established an organization of peddlers. During the Dreyfus Affair, as "Emperor of the *Camelots*," he adopted the name Napoleon and rented squads of his peddlers by the hundred to the antisemites for their demonstrations. He became a great pamphlet publisher, emphasizing pornography, crime, and antisemitism, and his influence in Paris was so considerable that he became known as "the megaphone of French antisemitism." [5]

During the decade after 1892, Drumont's *Libre Parole* was one of the most important daily newspapers in France. There were occasions during the Panama scandal and the Dreyfus Affair when the *Libre Parole* was the most widely read and influential newspaper in Paris. The primary reasons for its success were the great fame and the remarkable journalistic abilities of Drumont, who alone held the allegiance of all antisemites in France. In addition, however, the newspaper had sound financial backing and an extremely able staff.

Most of the predecessors of the *Libre Parole* had had scant hopes of lasting success because they had been the attempts of individuals or small groups without any careful preparation or pro-

[5] Raphaël Viau, *Vingt Ans d'antisémitisme, 1889-1909* (Paris, 1910), 327-330; Drumont, *Le Testament d'un antisémite*, 334-335; Bournand, *op. cit.*, 114, 240-45, 264-65; Gendrot, *op. cit.*, 67-82; Georges Dangon, "Napoléon Hayard, empereur des Camelots," *Le Courrier graphique* (1939), 3-6, 8-13; Avenel, *Annuaire de la presse française*, IX (1888), 426; XIII (1892), 493; *Anti-Juif* (Algiers), January 23, 1890-January 11, 1891.

gram. Each of them failed at its first crisis because of its weak financial foundation. Drumont, however, succeeded in founding a company with an authorized capital of 1,600,000 francs. Although perhaps not even half of this sum was ever actually paid up, the paper had ample resources to advertise its appearance fully, to publish its first numbers as a complete Paris daily, and to withstand the financial shock which delayed success might have caused.

The major contributor to the financial power of the *Libre Parole* was J. B. Gérin, the editor of the *Semaine financière*, "one of the most important economic and financial journals in France, an authority consulted by the outstanding leaders in banking and investment." Gérin contributed three hundred thousand francs towards financing the *Libre Parole*, although only a year earlier his journal had campaigned actively in defense of the French Jews, particularly the bankers. An old Boulangist and a very active nationalist, Gérin probably financed Drumont so that a printing firm which owed him a considerable amount of money might be able to sell its equipment to the *Libre Parole*. He retained financial control of the paper, wrote the paper's financial column, and named the business manager for the first three years to ensure his new investment. This arrangement was a great benefit to the antisemites, for the paper was remarkably well managed.[6]

As the new focus of the entire movement, the *Libre Parole* attracted the support of all French antisemites. Country priests traveled to Paris solely to give their blessing to their defenders, and all of the antisemitic writers, known and unknown, volunteered their services. Drumont was thus able to collect a remarkably zealous and active staff and to obtain free contributions from such talented writers as the Countess Martel de Janville, a popular novelist who wrote under the pseudonym of Gyp, and of Madame Guebhard, or Séverine.

---

[6] Edouard Drumont, *Sur le Chemin de la vie. Souvenirs* (Paris, 1914), 132; Léonce Reynaud, *Les Français israélites* (Paris, 1901), 2–5; C. E. Curinier (editor), *Dictionnaire national des contemporains* (Paris, 1899–1905), III, 70; Gendrot, *op. cit.*, 89; Guérin, *op. cit.*, 17–33, 44–46, 54–59; Viau, *op. cit.*, 22; Avenel, *Annuaire de la presse française*, VIII (1887), 50; *Libre Parole Illustrée*, September 30, 1893; February 10, 1894.

The regular staff was composed of six journalists whose average age in 1892 was thirty-one. These young men not only showed considerable skill and versatility, but they also labored for Drumont at some financial sacrifice. Talented Raphaël Viau thus spent seventeen years on the *Libre Parole* at 150 francs a month. Writing for such a newspaper required some physical courage, too, for *Libre Parole* policy demanded articles which frequently were the cause of duels. Viau, for example, fought twelve duels before 1900 and was wounded in four of them.

During its first three weeks, the *Libre Parole* caused no sensation in Paris. The informal party held in the office to celebrate the publication of the first issue was attended by members of the Jockey Club, legitimists, Bonapartists, priests, and communards. Each office had a crucifix on the wall, and the assembly listened to Drumont tell the staff to be "Catholic anarchists." A week later a reporter described the paper as one "read by priests and communards." [7]

The *Libre Parole* aimed to be as sensational and provocative as possible. Its methods did not differ from those of the earlier antisemitic papers, for it concentrated upon individuals such as Rothschild and Arton, referred constantly to all Jewish villains from Judas forward, and sought always to rouse a lawsuit or a duel by its attacks. These tactics naturally drew attention to the new publication, but the first two publicity ventures almost destroyed the infant paper. One was an anonymous series of articles denouncing the growing number and the special privileges of Jewish officers in the French army. This group resulted in three duels. In the third duel, on June 23, 1892, the Marquis de Morès, the special protector of the paper, killed a Jewish officer, Captain Armand Mayer.

The reaction to this unhappy incident was so tremendous that the *Libre Parole* was severely shaken, although its circulation did

[7] Bernard Lecache, *Séverine* (Paris, 1930), 132–61; Michel Missoffe, *Gyp et ses amis* (Paris, 1932), 147–54, 186; Drumont, *Souvenirs*, 299; Viau, *op. cit.*, 37–43, 61, 72, 112, 182–272; Gendrot, *op. cit.*, 88–96, 116, 191–92; *Almanach de la Libre Parole, 1894* (Paris, 1894), 92–103; *Libre Parole Illustrée*, February 24, 1894; *Vraie Parole*, February 28, 1893.

increase. Grand Rabbi Zadoc Kahn's vigorous denunciation of the paper and of Morès was acclaimed by almost all of the Paris press, and the Mayer funeral procession attracted thousands of sympathetic Frenchmen. Moreover, the affair led to an interpellation of the Minister of War in the Chamber of Deputies. Freycinet's declaration that "the army does not distinguish between Jews, Protestants, and Catholics" was applauded by the entire Chamber, and his assertion that it was a crime against the nation to sow division in the army was voted a unanimous order of the day. Drumont himself was so moved by the death of Captain Mayer that he wrote that it was the misfortune of France that such a courageous soldier should not have died on the battlefield fighting her enemies.[8]

The second event which brought the *Libre Parole* to the attention of Paris was a suit for libel instituted against Drumont by a well-known, popular deputy, Burdeau. On May 13, 1892, Drumont published an article denouncing the project to renew the privileges of the Bank of France and declaring that Burdeau had reported favorably on it because of a bribe he had received from Rothschild "to ensure his old age." These charges were renewed in a public address two days later, when Drumont added that Rothschild's butler had delivered the finance committee report to Burdeau, and Burdeau immediately sued.

The trial which followed revealed the flimsy foundation of Drumont's charges and presented Burdeau's attorney, Waldeck-Rousseau, a magnificent opportunity to condemn antisemitism. Drumont was forced to admit that he had only "moral proofs" of Burdeau's having been bribed, for the only evidence he could present was that ten years earlier the deputy had opposed the renewal of the Bank's privileges. Morès and Edouard Demachy testified with second- and third-hand rumors of corruption, so Drumont was declared guilty of libel. His sentence included three

[8] Ernest Cremieu-Foa, *La Campagne antisémitique. Les Duels. Les Responsibilités. Mémoire* (Paris, 1892), 24–72; Salomon Reinach (L'Archiviste, *pseud.*), *Drumont et Dreyfus. Etudes sur la Libre Parole de 1894 à 1895* (Paris, 1898), 13–19; Gendrot, *op. cit.*, 113–17; Viau, *op. cit.*, 24–26; Levaillant, *loc. cit.*, 95; *Journal officiel*, June 26, 1892.

months in prison, a fine of a thousand francs, and the expense of printing his recantation in eighty newspapers, a high price for the type of publicity the trial had given him.

The death of Captain Mayer and the Burdeau trial were the most serious tests which the *Libre Parole* had to face during its first months. There were other embarrassments and scandals, but these did not entail the publicity or the expense of the Burdeau affair. Late in June, 1892, however, Republican newspapers poured ridicule upon the *Libre Parole* when they discovered that Gaston Wiallard, an employee in the business office of the paper, was a Jew. Drumont had to endure the taunts because Wiallard was Gérin's representative. Another blow was the discovery of the anticlericals that the business manager of the paper had been the manager of a Jesuit school prior to 1892 and had a brother high in the Paris clergy.[9]

During the summer of 1892, the circulation of the newspaper managed to climb slowly, particularly in the provinces. Drumont and the staff were so dissatisfied with their progress, however, that August and September witnessed a new rash of duels. These tactics were not successful, but fall brought a great opportunity to the *Libre Parole* in the form of the Panama scandal.

The financing and construction of the Panama canal had been a matter of interest and concern to the French people for almost fifteen years, and rumors of scandal had been particularly current since the Panama Company had crashed in 1889. Drumont himself in *La Dernière Bataille* in 1890 had covered one hundred and thirty-five pages with his account of the misery, waste, and corruption involved. Drumont then declared Ferdinand de Lesseps the responsible villain and considered the entire affair crushing evidence of French degeneracy and decadence. On September 6, 1892, however, the *Libre Parole* began a series of anonymous articles on the

[9] Marcel Marion, *Histoire financière de la France depuis 1715* (Paris, 1914–1931), VI, 148–149; Walter Frank, *Nationalismus und Demokratie im Frankreich der dritten Republik, 1871–1918* (Hamburg, 1933), 303; Drumont, *Souvenirs*, 132; Guérin, *op. cit.*, 20–38; Viau, *op. cit.*, 23–25, 34–60, 96; Gendrot, *op. cit.*, 101–12, 211; *Burdeau-Rothchild contre Drumont. Le Procès de Libre Parole. Débats complets* (pamphlet) (Paris, 1892); *Libre Parole*, May 13–June 20, 1892.

canal, charging unlimited corruption in the press and Chamber of Deputies, the corrupting agents being three notorious French Jews.

It was a great error for the Republican press to allow the privilege of unveiling such a great scandal to fall to an anti-Republican paper. After a few weeks, the carefully organized series began to be effective. The circulation soared, and the campaign began to attract wide interest, particularly as no one was able to deny the charges made. Finally, Baron Jacques de Reinach, who had helped to arrange the company's last loan and to provide favorable publicity for it, yielded valuable information to Drumont in an attempt to shield himself. Others tried the same practice, with the result that the *Libre Parole* obtained incriminating evidence on the newspapers and deputies involved.

The results were staggering. "At one blow, the *Libre Parole* became the most feared and widely read paper in Paris." Early in 1893, its daily circulation surpassed two hundred thousand and there was a frantic rush for it each afternoon as anxious and interested Frenchmen sought to discover the latest revelations. It is possible that had Drumont foreseen the course of events and planned his program carefully, he might have emerged from the scandal a tremendously powerful figure in France. However, it is evident that the *Libre Parole* was simply using its classical tactics to increase its circulation and that Drumont failed to appreciate the political potential which able manipulation of this issue might have developed. At any rate, he chose November 1, 1892, to begin serving his three-month sentence for the Burdeau libel, and he spent these crucial days of the Panama scandal directing his newspaper from the prison, Sainte-Pélagie.[10]

For three or four months, Panama remained the center of the political stage in France. As the evidence was revealed, each

---

[10] Guy de la Batut, *Panama* (Paris, 1931), 51; Georges Bernanos, *La Grande Peur des bien-pensants. Edouard Drumont* (Paris, 1931), 285–93; Léon Daudet, *Panorama de la troisième République* (Paris, 1936), 127; Maurice Barrès, *Leur Figures. Le Roman de l'énergie nationale* (Paris, 1902), 25, 62–92; Drumont, *La Dernière Bataille*, 324–460; Frank, *op. cit.*, 276–80, 334; Gendrot, *op. cit.*, 144–51; Viau, *op. cit.*, 47–50, 61; *Libre Parole*, September 6–October 31, 1892.

newspaper, politician, and political group tried to wield the information as a club against its opponents. The Socialists saw it as proof of the inherent evils of capitalism, although most of them defended the Republic, particularly when they saw the scandal being used against it by its enemies. The antisemites sought to prove the wickedness of the Jews, although Herz, Arton, and Reinach had become involved long after the major damage had been done. The Right, including such papers as *Univers, Croix, Autorité*, the *Gazette de France*, and *Cocarde*, tried to besmirch the Republic and the Republicans. As the facts appeared, however, and as it became evident that almost every Paris paper had accepted bribes, each paper had to defend its own receipts with the theory of advertising costs. So many politicians of all parties became involved that France discovered that virtue was the monopoly of no one party or group.

Some politicians succeeded in repaying political grudges during Panama, but most of them were delighted when it faded from public interest. The suicide, early in the affair, of Jacques de Reinach and the successful escape of Arton, the intermediary for much of the corruption, added a touch of mystery and intrigue. The government's inability to find Herz and Arton and then to obtain their extradition gave the press an opportunity to digress from the real issues, and the distant Arton particularly was erected into a fabulous figure of tremendous knowledge and power.[11]

Panama gave the *Libre Parole* and Drumont a brief period of fortune, but from early 1893 until the arrest of Dreyfus was announced in November, 1894, the newspaper and the movement both declined perceptibly. Even Panama had become such a political football by February 1, 1893, that Drumont was greeted

[11] Auguste Lucas, *Précis historique de l'affaire du Panama* (Paris, 1893), 211–16; Jules Quesnay de Beaurepaire, *Le Panama et la République* (Paris, 1899), 118–67; Gustave Rouanet, *Les Complicités du Panama* (Paris, 1893), 161–281, 334; Camille Ducray, *Paul Déroulède, 1846–1914* (Paris, 1914), 186–90; Debidour, *op. cit.*, II, 94–99; Gendrot, *op. cit.*, 123–58, 384; de la Batut, *op. cit.*, 51–361; Levaillant, *loc. cit.*, 97–98; *Journal officiel*, November 20, 1892—March 30, 1893; *Univers*, November 1, 1892—March 30, 1893; *Libre Parole*, November 1, 1892—March 30, 1893.

only by his staff when he left prison. When he ran for the Chamber of Deputies in Amiens in May, 1893, he was decisively routed, obtaining less than four thousand votes to his successful rival's thirteen thousand. A new series of duels was instigated to rouse interest during the summer of 1893, but any advantage these tactics might have won were lost by the manner in which Morès left the movement in August of that year. The revelation that Drumont had negotiated a loan for Morès from Cornelius Herz, a notorious Jewish financier and lobbyist who had an important role in the Panama scandal, not only discredited the antisemites in the eyes of most sensible Frenchmen, but also directly weakened the party. Their mutual friends were able only with great difficulty to prevent a duel between Morès and Drumont, and the resignation of Morès led to the withdrawal of many of his followers as well.[12]

The most important political issues which faced France during the years 1892 through 1894 were *ralliement*, the growing power of the Socialists and syndicates, and the rash of anarchism. On each of these critical questions, particularly the third, Drumont was led by sentiment and temperament into a stand which cost the movement numbers of supporters. As a result, by the fall of 1894 organized antisemitism had reached its nadir in France and seemed ready to disappear completely.

Drumont originally hailed Leo XIII for his decision to ask French Catholics to accept the Republic, but by the summer of 1893 he had become the most bitter and venomous of the opponents of *ralliement*. He denounced the Pope as "the most poorly informed sovereign in Europe," a prelate who "with his Italian mentality, which is always Machiavellian, bows down before the Republic only because it is victorious." At one time, Drumont was so enraged at the program of the Pope that he prayed in an editorial for a "modern iron-fisted Nogaret for the modern Boniface VIII."

Drumont not only stormed at the policy of *ralliement*, but he

[12] Charles Droulers, *Le Marquis de Morès, 1858–1896* (Paris, 1932), 168; Viau, *op. cit.*, 57–61; Gendrot, *op. cit.*, 191–96; Curinier, *op. cit.*, I, 93.

ridiculed and insulted the Church and those Catholics who adopted it. He described the *ralliés* as "degenerate nobles and corrupt bourgeois." When the marriage of a prominent Catholic was annulled, Drumont declared that the Church always granted special privileges to the wealthy and powerful and neglected the poor and faithful. The papal nuncio, Cardinal Ferrata, and Count Albert de Mun, an old friend of Drumont, were abused by the *Libre Parole* as though they were common criminals. An old opponent of the antisemites, Bishop Fuzet of Beauvais, was accused of having stolen tapestries from the cathedral, and Cardinal Bourret a short time later was charged with having accepted a cash bribe from the government to support submission to the *loi d'abonnement*. One Catholic priest who was also an antisemite, Father Charles Renaut, was so disturbed by Drumont's attacks upon the Pope and the Church that he became convinced Drumont was a disguised Jew using antisemitism to deceive the Catholics and ridicule the Church! [13]

The antisemites always posed as defenders of the poor, but conservative followers of Drumont who had not been thoroughly alarmed earlier by his "socialism" were seriously frightened by the social and economic views which appeared in the *Libre Parole* during 1893 and 1894. After the Panama scandal had disappeared as a political issue and the antisemitic campaign had begun to slacken, Drumont in the summer of 1893 began to write of socialism and the Socialists with increasing enthusiasm. Jules Guérin, a member of the Morès band and a close friend of Briand throughout this decade, helped the militant syndicalist found his strongly revolutionary newspaper, the *Réveil social*, in July, 1893. In 1894, Briand was occasionally given space in the *Libre Parole* to advocate his League of Corporative Action. Statements concerning the Socialist views of antisemitism became increasingly

---

[13] Charles Renaut, *L'Israélite Drumont et les sociétés secrètes actuellement* (Paris, 1895), 192–306; Dominique Cardinal Ferrata, *Mémoires. Ma Nonciature en France* (Paris, 1922), 298–99; Edouard Lecanuet, *Les Signes avant-coureurs de la séparation* (Paris, 1930), 30–31, 38–46, 67–68; Lecanuet, *La Vie de l'Eglise sous Léon XIII* (Paris, 1930), 576; *Libre Parole Illustrée*, May 16, 1895; *Libre Parole*, July 12, July 17, September 8, December 5–December 20, 1893.

frequent, and one member of the editorial board even declared that the antisemites no longer recognized any distinction between Jewish and Christian capitalism.[14]

It was Drumont's stand on anarchism, however, which weakened antisemitism most. At a time when all Frenchmen were terrified by the wave of anarchist outrages which swept the country, Drumont alone defended the disciples of Bakunin and Kropotkin. He did this partly from sympathy for all poor persecuted wretches and partly from friendship for some anarchists he had met in prison, but primarily because of his disappointment at the indifference with which France had greeted his own campaign. Nothing could have aroused the French people more in 1893 and 1894 than such a defense of terrorists.

The outstanding instances of anarchist activity were Auguste Vaillant's throwing a bomb into the Chamber of Deputies in December, 1893, and the assassination of President Carnot in Lyon on June 24, 1894, by Santo Caserio. Drumont defended Vaillant first on the ground that he had not understood the teachings of anarchism and that, in any case, he had not killed or seriously injured anyone. Then he declared that society was anarchic and that the legislature itself was guilty because of the materialism it preached. Finally, he upbraided the entire bourgeois world, declaring that the anarchists were merely putting into practice principles which the bourgeoisie themselves had applied a century earlier. A cartoon published in the illustrated edition of the *Libre Parole* expressed this attitude when it commented that "many of those who exploit us today have no right to become indignant, for their fathers and grandfathers were nearly as pitiless as today's anarchists."

When Drumont organized a subscription for Vaillant's little daughter, Sidonie, and obtained a home for her, his actions in defending the anarchists were viewed somewhat less critically. However, the antisemitic leader and his newspaper failed to heed the warning that the Vaillant case had been, and continued to

[14] Georges Suarez, *Briand. Sa Vie, son oeuvre* (Paris, 1938–1941), I, 170–79, 216–18; Renaut, *op. cit.*, 490; *Libre Parole Illustrée*, June 1, 1895.

defend the anarchists in 1894. When Jean Grave was sentenced to two years in prison for his attacks on property and the family, Drumont ridiculed the decision by declaring that bourgeois property was only robbery and that the lay schools had already destroyed the respect in which the family had been held.

The assassination of President Carnot by Caserio brought what would probably have been the fatal eclipse of organized French antisemitism, but for the arrest and imprisonment of Captain Dreyfus. When all the press joined to praise and lament the dead president, the *Libre Parole* denounced France for its attitude towards the grandson of the man who had murdered so many Frenchmen in 1793. Drumont compared eminent Monsignor d'Hulst to Judas for having supported the rigid police and press laws which the anarchist actions had called forth, and during early July, 1894, his newspaper prosecuted an astonishing campaign against all those who resented the assaults of the terrorists. By the middle of July, Drumont was so alarmed by the reaction his stand had roused and so feared arrest and imprisonment that he fled to Belgium "to defend his freedom." [15]

3. The Strength of French Antisemitism in 1894

THUS, organized antisemitism during the summer and early fall of 1894 was at its lowest strength since 1886. Leading antisemites continually lamented their failure and prayed for five hundred resolute men or a battalion to rescue France from chaos. On March 24, 1894, the day on which Drumont had attacked Monsignor d'Hulst so unmercifully, Emile de Saint-Auban declared that "we antisemites are soldiers of the Idea of Democracy" and will succumb while struggling for it, "just as Jesus and Joan of Arc did." André de Boisandré wrote in the *Libre Parole*: "If we are not here to see the organization necessary for the triumph of the Idea, we shall at least have the satisfaction of knowing that

[15] Alfred Baudrillart. *Vie de Monsignor d'Hulst* (Paris, 1925), II, 405–407; Jean Forain, *Doux Pays* (Paris, 1897), 9; Gendrot, *op. cit.*, 197–98; Viau, *op. cit.*, 76–97; Bernanos, *op. cit.*, 293–94; *Libre Parole Illustrée*, November 18, 1893—July 23, 1894; *Libre Parole*, April, 1892; December 10, 1893—July 15, 1894.

our efforts made it possible and the joy of dying with the satisfaction of having accomplished our duty up to the very end." From Brussels in September, 1894, Drumont warned his followers that their common duty was to educate men for action and to help train the coming generation. "It is our solemn obligation not to become discouraged and to retain belief in the power of our ideas. I still refuse to believe that a moralist and philosopher such as I cannot accomplish more than a practical politician."

By the summer of 1894, the circulation of the *Libre Parole* had dropped to a few thousand, and both the *Libre Parole* and its illustrated weekly edition were in financial difficulty. Every newspaper trick was used to increase the circulation, with new contests and features each week. However, 1894 produced such a great dearth of news for the antisemites that the editors of the *Libre Parole* were forced to use incidents six and seven years old to fill the paper.

The *Libre Parole Illustrée* was reduced to half its original size in the fall of 1893, and in August, 1894, both it and the *Libre Parole* adopted a poorer grade of newsprint and finer, space-saving type. The 1894 dividend was only 1.5 percent, the lowest paid from 1893 through 1899. Drumont himself had lost hope, and during the summer of 1894 he made several attempts to sell the *Libre Parole* at a financial loss.

Thus, the Dreyfus arrest was injected into the political scene at a time when Drumont, still in shelter in Brussels, was trying to promote the sale of his chief weapon against the Jews. The news of the arrest of Captain Dreyfus not only checked Drumont's attempts to sell the *Libre Parole* and retire from the campaign against the Jews, but it also allowed him to proclaim the vindication of his campaign and to exploit the feelings it had aroused. When Drumont returned to France early in 1895, a noisy crowd of two thousand escorted him to the *Libre Parole* offices. The arrest of the unfortunate Jewish officer renewed the vitality of the campaign against the Jews, a campaign which within a few years had allied with other political issues to create the crisis for French democracy known as the Dreyfus Affair.[16] This great crisis, and the role which antisemitism played in it, will be the subject of volume II, which will continue the analysis of antisemitism in French history during the years between 1894 and the outbreak of World War I in 1914.

[16] Gabriel Astruc, *Le Pavillon des fantômes. Souvenirs* (Paris, 1929), 150-51; Renaut, *op. cit.*, 483, 560-65; Viau, *op. cit.*, 93-102; Gendrot, *op. cit.*, 175; Suarez, *op. cit.*, I, 160; Guérin, *op. cit.*, 86; *Almanach de la Libre Parole, 1894*, 62; *Libre Parole Illustrée*, November 11, 1894–December 7, 1895.

INDEX

341

Index